The Fai

The Faithful Librarian

*Essays on Christianity
in the Profession*

Edited by GARRETT B. TROTT

Foreword by Gregory A. Smith

McFarland & Company, Inc., Publishers
Jefferson, North Carolina

LIBRARY OF CONGRESS CATALOGUING-IN-PUBLICATION DATA

Names: Trott, Garrett B., 1973– editor. | Smith, Gregory A., 1972– writer of foreword.
Title: The faithful librarian : essays on Christianity in the profession / edited by Garrett B. Trott ; foreword by Gregory A. Smith.
Description: Jefferson, North Carolina : McFarland & Company, Inc., 2019 | Includes bibliographical references and index.
Identifiers: LCCN 2019033361 | ISBN 9781476671161 (paperback : acid free paper) ∞ | ISBN 9781476637570 (ebook)
Subjects: LCSH: Christian librarians—Religious life. | Libraries—Religious aspects—Christianity.
Classification: LCC BV4596.L52 F35 2019 | DDC 261.5—dc23
LC record available at https://lccn.loc.gov/2019033361

BRITISH LIBRARY CATALOGUING DATA ARE AVAILABLE

ISBN (print) 978-1-4766-7116-1
ISBN (ebook) 978-1-4766-3757-0

© 2019 Garrett B. Trott. All rights reserved

No part of this book may be reproduced or transmitted in any form or by any means, electronic or mechanical, including photocopying or recording, or by any information storage and retrieval system, without permission in writing from the publisher.

Front cover image: © 2019 ping198 / Shutterstock

Printed in the United States of America

McFarland & Company, Inc., Publishers
Box 611, Jefferson, North Carolina 28640
www.mcfarlandpub.com

Table of Contents

Foreword
    Gregory A. Smith   1

Introduction
    Garrett B. Trott   3

Integrative Pastoral Librarianship in a Flipped Church: Equipping Laity for Ministry with Missional Faith Learning
    Rebecca Klemme Eliceiri   9

With Quiet Diligence: How Claude Elbert Spencer Formed an Archival Tradition in the Stone-Campbell Movement
    McGarvey Ice   27

Libraries in the New Creation: Christian Librarianship as an Extension of the Christian Temple and Priesthood
    Jacob W. Gucker   45

In a Manner Worthy of God: Hospitality and the Christian Librarian
    Denise D. Nelson   66

Information Overload, Information Anxiety and Theological Ethics
    Paul A. Hartog   76

Scholarship as Conversation: Using a Shared Research Method (ALEA) to Help Students Seek Truth and Wisdom in a Post-Truth World
    Patricia R. Harris, Michelle Norquist, Dianne Zandbergen *and* Andrew Zwart   87

Knowledge, Understanding, Wisdom: A Biblical Model of Information Literacy
    Jeff Gates   103

Faith, Freedom and Information: A Christian Perspective on Intellectual Freedom
    Steve Silver   123

Communities of Scholarship, Communities of Faith: The Academic Library as Place
  NANCY FALCIANI-WHITE 138

Loving Your Co-Worker as Christ Expects: Personnel Practices Through the Eyes of Faith
  ESTHER GILLIE 154

Discerning and Following Christ's Call to Leadership
  NADINE P. ELLERO 170

Christian Faith and Its Impact on Library Interpersonal Relationships and Professionalism
  DANA M. CAUDLE 179

The Relational Interaction: A New Look at Glorifying God through a Reference Interview
  GARRETT B. TROTT 189

The Information Therapist Is In
  ROBIN R. HARTMAN 206

Holy Listening in Reference Work: A Sacred Aspect of the Christian Librarian's Calling
  CYNTHIA STRONG 223

About the Contributors 235
Index 237

Foreword

GREGORY A. SMITH

The notion of Christian librarianship is one that many members of the library profession regard as odd or even offensive. To those most devoted to the principle of neutrality, the idea of practicing library work from the vantage point of a specific ideology may seem counterproductive, as if faith commitments are irrelevant to effective professional practice. Those who are more forthcoming about their own social ideals may conclude that the pursuit of religious aims conflicts with the progressive stance that they perceive as essential to librarianship. But for those librarians who profess a definitive identity as followers of Jesus Christ, integrating religious and professional vocations is not merely a logical possibility, but a necessary and rewarding endeavor.

The contributors to *The Faithful Librarian* belong in this latter category. Their essays exude confidence in the merits of examining library practice through the lens of a Christian worldview. The book thus follows the pattern set by a collection that I edited about 20 years ago, *Christian Librarianship: Essays on the Integration of Faith and Profession*. I am thankful that McFarland has seen fit to publish this sequel—surely a testament to the conversation that has ensued since 2002.

The time is ripe for the publication of this book, and I commend the editor for having the vision to compile it. The past two decades have brought many changes, calling for fresh research and reflection on what it means to think about and practice librarianship as a Christian. The environment in which libraries (like all other organizations) operate has become increasingly globalized. The proliferation of networked data and devices has rendered geographic distance relatively insignificant. Nevertheless, the globalized society that has emerged is not a utopia. Terrorism, breaches of digital data, and conflict along racial, ethnic, and religious lines are very real threats. Additionally, the global economy, highly interconnected, is vulnerable to disruptions in the natural environment and the sociopolitical sphere.

Institutions concerned with information and learning have not been insulated from prevailing conditions. Colleges and universities face pressure to enhance quality, improve access, and lower costs, and many are in financial distress. Librarians can no longer assume that library stakeholders regard their services as valuable. Ironically, the information environment is more volatile than ever, with numerous corporate and individual actors vying for the attention of consumers and learners. Librarians sense a need to address issues like information overload, predatory publishing, and "fake news," but struggle to muster the resources needed to achieve desired impacts. Furthermore, library services are increasingly mediated by networked systems and outsourced to external entities, diminishing the professional discretion exercised by librarians at the local level.

Clearly, the milieu of librarianship is very different than it was a generation ago. Moreover, given the nature and extent of the challenges mentioned here, optimism about the prospects for liberal learning and informed citizenship may be in short supply. Christian educators and librarians, conscious that historic Christian beliefs and institutions face a hostile climate in many parts of the world, might seem particularly susceptible to despondency. But the contributors to this volume are upbeat, winsomely articulating their visions for librarianship—visions that are rooted in aspirations for the kingdom of God. Their essays are diverse, alternately emphasizing professional, academic, theological, and even devotional elements. Sacred reflection is a feature rarely found in mainstream library literature. Those who engage with the contents of *The Faithful Librarian* may find that they satisfy in a way that the standard fare cannot. As someone who has found that faith integration provides deep motivation and meaning for library work, I encourage an attentive reading of this book.

Gregory A. Smith is the associate dean for library technologies and collection services at Liberty University, Lynchburg, Virginia. His academic and professional interests include librarianship, organizational leadership and management, higher education, evangelical Christianity, and scholarly communication.

Introduction

Garrett B. Trott

What does it mean to be a Christian librarian? For the longest time, if anyone asked that question of me, I would have just given him or her an awkward glance followed by silence. My journey to begin discovery of an answer to that query began with a conviction: I understood that God desired me to give myself to Him completely. Initially, I saw a pastoral or ministerial role as the ideal (and perhaps the only) means to do so; subsequently, this was my initial vocational pursuit. Due to some wonderful counsel, I chose an alternative path: librarianship. After the newness of this career path wore off, I found myself coming back to that conviction: How can I give myself completely to God when working in a library? What made this even more challenging was the fact that an even greater question loomed my mind: Is it even possible to glorify God as a librarian?

What I found most challenging at this particular time was that I did not have an answer to these questions. I sought some counsel from good friends, I did a bit of reading, but I really could not arrive at an answer. It was about this time that I began my interviews for employment at Corban University in Salem, Oregon. Corban University is a member of the Council for Christian Colleges and Universities (CCCU). When I was offered the position at Corban University, I was convinced that now, simply because I was working at a CCCU institute, I would know what it meant to be a Christian librarian. If I work for a Christian university, would that not make me a Christian librarian? A naïve assumption, but one to which I held dearly.

After the newness of the job wore off, that same question came back to me: What does it mean to be a Christian librarian? I was surprised. I thought I knew what it meant. The simplicity of my original assumption was accompanied with a restless heart that was not at peace over the issue. Looking back, I am reminded of Romans 8:28 (ESV), "And we know that for those who love God all things work together for good, for those who are called according to his purpose." God allowed me to wrestle with this question again at this particular time because the pursuit of an answer would be incredibly beneficial.

When I finished my first year at Corban University, the provost announced that the faculty would be working through a book during the next academic year: David Claerbaut's (2004) *Faith and Learning on the Edge*. For those familiar with works related to faith and learning, you will acknowledge that Claerbaut's work is one of several resources that discuss the faith and learning dialog. Claerbaut's work provided a great introduction to the conversation.

Although it is a bit ironic, honestly, I had never heard of the faith and learning

4   Introduction

dialog prior to Claerbaut's work. I was so involved with getting my feet wet, per se, in my first year as a librarian at Corban University that I really had little time to look at the bigger picture of what my colleagues were doing in relation to faith integration. Nor did I find the time to dig into some of the resources in the CCCU that might have assisted in discovering more about the faith and learning dialog at that time. Regardless, I am thankful for Claerbaut's work and its introduction to the faith and learning dialog.

I drank from Claerbaut's work like an individual thirsting for depth and understanding. I found it refreshing, encouraging and engaging. It caused me to ask: "How could I glorify God through my day-to-day profession as a librarian?" While Claerbaut does not directly answer this question, his work did provide a path leading to one. It was through that work (and several others subsequently read) that I began to understand how I could make a difference in the world for Jesus Christ through my profession as a librarian.

After reading Claerbaut's work, I soon discovered a collection of essays edited by Gregory A. Smith (2002) entitled *Christian Librarianship*. This was another work that I savored and treasured. After reading these two works, the floodgates opened. I read whatever I could in relation to faith and learning, and I began to direct my professional development opportunities towards integrating my faith in Jesus Christ towards my profession as a librarian. Needless to say, there were several efforts that were used by God to shape and mold me, even though some did not come to full fruition. However, I have become very thankful for the opportunities to continually develop my understanding of how God can be glorified through my work as a librarian.

So what is a Christian librarian? Some in the faith and learning dialog argue that in order to truly understand what a Christian librarian is, one must look at the philosophical and theoretical components that undergird librarianship (Claerbaut, 2004, p. 125). In this case, for librarianship, a true manifestation of faith and learning would look at elements such as how a Christian perception of knowledge or information impacts information literacy. Or perhaps one would look at developing a biblical framework for relationships when developing a way that Christian librarians should look at reference interviews. While these are notable inquiries to pursue, is a quest for looking at the foundational elements of a discipline through Christian lenses the only way faith and learning can be manifested? Particularly in disciplines with a more pragmatic bent, such as librarianship?

Jacobsen and Jacobsen (2004) suggest a different twist on faith and learning. While not denying the validity of looking at the theoretical undergirding of a discipline, what is often called "the integration model," in order to integrate one's faith into a discipline, Jacobsen and Jacobsen suggest multiple ways through which faith integration can take place. Jacobsen and Jacobsen (2004) argue that while the integration model tends to align well with Reformed theology and disciplines with a more theoretical base (loc. 489), one should look for other means of integration for more pragmatic disciplines.

Historically, librarianship has a pragmatic bent (Burke, 1947), and some argue that pragmatism dominates librarianship in the 21st century as well (Cossette, 2009). Subsequently, while not dismissing the validity of the integration model (Jacobsen, 2004, loc. 481), Jacobsen and Jacobsen (2004) suggest that utilizing a variety of integration models when integrating faith into the profession of librarianship is the best way to look at how librarianship should be perceived through a Christian lens. This collection of essays does exactly this.

The Christian faith speaks to both the mind and the heart. Many aspects of faith and learning integration, however, have followed suit with academia and have primarily focused on the intellectual dynamics of integration (Smith, 2009, p. 17). James K. A. Smith (2009) convincingly argues that "the way we inhabit the world is not primarily as thinkers, or even believers, but as more affective, embodied creatures who make our way in the world by feeling our way around it" (p. 47).

Smith (2009, 2013, 2017) develops this ideology throughout three volumes in his *Cultural Liturgies* series. Many argue that the development of a Christian worldview, which Smith argues is primarily the transmission of facts and information, is a key element in Christian education (Smith, 2009, pp. 27–8). While Smith does not disagree that worldview development is an important element, he argues that if people are primarily moved by their loves, passions, and desires, should not Christian worship (which is ideally an expression of an individual's loves, passions, and desires) play a critical role in formation (Smith, 2009, p. 32)? Smith's arguments in this trilogy makes an excellent case that the goal of a Christian education should be moved from simply learning and acquiring a Christian worldview to "the same goal of Christian worship: to form radical disciples of Jesus and citizens of the baptismal city who, communally, take up the creational tasks of being God's image bearers" (Smith, 2009, p. 220).

With Jacobsen and Jacobsen's (2004) argument that a variety of venues can display the faith and learning dialog, and Smith's (2009) argument that worship should play a foundational role in Christian education (where much, though not all, of the faith and learning dialog develops), where does this leave faith and learning? I would like to suggest that it leaves faith and learning as something that can be manifested in a variety of ways with different dynamics touching different people in different but distinct ways. Different elements of a worship service often touch individuals distinctly with the intention of reaching a wide and diverse audience. In a similar manner, this collection of essays provides a variety of styles, a variety of contexts, and a variety of topics with the intention of reaching an audience of individuals interested in implementing their Christian faith through librarianship.

This work contains fifteen essays, which cover nine general areas: church librarianship, collection development/archives, general librarianship, hospitality, information literacy/instruction, intellectual freedom, library as place, management and leadership, and reference services.

Rebecca Klemme Eliceiri looks at how the knowledge of metaliteracy, theological education, and librarianship can play critical roles in equipping believers for worship. The narrative format of this essay enables Klemme Eliceiri to share her insight into how God used her training in librarianship to shape her ministry in an ecclesiastical context.

Next is a biographical essay on Claude Elbert Spencer, an archivist of the Stone-Campbell Movement, by McGarvey Ice. While one may take away a bit of Spencer's methodology related to archives and collection development, Ice shows how Spencer's Christian faith played a critical role in his drive for excellence in his archival and collection development work related to the Stone-Campbell Movement.

Jacob W. Gucker utilizes a broad stroke and paints a picture of what the practice of librarianship could look like through the biblical lens of priesthood. Gucker develops his theological background and provides examples of how a librarian can function as a priest, serving his or her community.

Hebrews 13:2 is a verse that often come to mind when thinking about hospitality: "Do not neglect to show hospitality to strangers, for thereby some have entertained angels unaware" (ESV). Denise D. Nelson provides an excellent picture of how this hospitality can be implemented in and through library services.

In today's world, patrons, and even librarians at times, are overwhelmed by the amount of information available and the relative ease of access to all of it. Paul A. Hartog offers a glimpse at how information overload and the resulting information anxiety should be looked at through a theological lens.

Librarians provide information literacy and instruction to their patrons. Patricia R. Harris, Michelle Norquist, Dianne Zandbergen, and Andrew Zwart provide an example of how library instruction is utilized at Kuyper College to empower students to find wisdom in the midst of their research pursuits. Jeff Gates establishes a theological foundation for information literacy.

Steve Silver provides a Christian perspective on intellectual freedom and touches upon several relevant issues in relation to it. In so doing, he provides insight regarding how Christian librarians should respond to these issues.

Library as place has been a popular issue in librarianship for some time. Nancy Falciani-White looks at this issue through a theological lens, arguing that the library can serve as the place where the critical elements of solitude and togetherness can both thrive. This unique context that libraries provide enables them to be a place where both scholarship and spirituality can develop, subsequently making them a critical piece of any Christian institution of higher education.

Next we consider how management and leadership can be perceived and practiced in academic libraries through a biblical lens. Esther Gillie, Nadine P. Ellero, and Dana M. Caudle all show, in a variety of ways, how faith should impact managerial and leadership practices.

Reference inquiries are a foundational element of library services. I, Robin R. Hartman, and Cynthia Strong give our takes on how inquiries can be looked at through a Christian lens. Through utilizing reference works to build relationships, acting as an information therapist, empowering the reference interview through holy listening, and equipping the librarian to combat information anxiety and information overload, we enable a Christian librarian to embed his or her faith into the foundational service of reference inquiries.

Now that almost twenty years have passed since the publication of Smith's *Christian Librarianship*, we have a fresh and new collection of essays with similar purposes. The first is to help brothers and sisters in Christ serving in the library profession integrate their faith with their vocation.

The second, according to Smith (2002), is to "provide a foundation for further discussion of library issues from a Christian perspective" (p. 6). His work accomplished its goal and this collection of essays is one (of many) results of Smith's initial work. It develops, strengthens, and extends that foundation even more.

The third, again according to Smith, is to serve as a window through which students and scholars of library science may see a manifestation of the Gospel through our work as Christian librarians.

Soli Deo Gloria.

REFERENCES

Burke, R. (1947). Philosophy of librarianship. *The Catholic Library World, 19*, 12–15.
Claerbaut, D. (2004). *Faith and learning on the edge: A bold new look at religion in higher education*. Grand Rapids: Zondervan.

Cossette, A. (2009). *Humanism and libraries: An essay on the philosophy of librarianship*. Duluth: Library Juice Press.
Jacobsen, D., & Jacobsen, R. H. (2004). *Scholarship and Christian faith: Enlarging the conversation*. New York: Oxford University Press.
Smith, G. A. (Ed.). (2002). *Christian librarianship: Essays on the integration of faith and profession*. Jefferson, NC: McFarland.
Smith, J. K. A. (2009). *Desiring the kingdom: Worship, worldview and cultural formation*. Grand Rapids: Baker.
Smith, J. K. A. (2011). *Imagining the kingdom: How worship works*. Grand Rapids: Baker.
Smith, J. K. A. (2017). *Awaiting the king: Reforming public theology*. Grand Rapids: Baker.

Integrative Pastoral Librarianship in a Flipped Church

Equipping Laity for Ministry with Missional Faith Learning

REBECCA KLEMME ELICEIRI

Abstract

The Christian Church (Disciples of Christ), a mainline and generally progressive Protestant denomination experiencing decline in membership and funding, continues engaging its many strengths in faithful 21st-century ministry. This essay considers the ways in which my library career, call to ordained ministry, and faith-based community organization leadership support the Disciples' ultimate aim to be a "movement for wholeness in a fragmented world" as an ordained Disciples minister, academic librarian, and faith-based community organization leader. I explore this theme considering the Disciples' core beliefs, especially its vision of the "priesthood of all believers," the role that metaliteracy and theological education in the church play in the realization of this vision, and the ways in which integrative teaching and librarianship in ordained pastoral ministry may equip the faithful for their ministries both in and outside of the church.

Mash-Up or Crash? Life Between the Church, the Library and the Streets

I have long loved a good mystery, whether in the form of a classic detective novel, unexplained natural phenomena, theological conundrum, or any other unanswered question. Theologically speaking, I have often wondered in the continued search for meaningful 21st-century life, why still Jesus? Why are we here? What's it all mean, anyway? And a more practical question, how are Christians to live on this one planet with so many others in light of our answers to these questions? Even as I have actively chosen Jesus, Christianity, and the church as the primary place in which I situate this quest, nothing has managed to drum the yearning out of me to understand more about humanity's origins, consciousness, and their implications.

Though not all mysteries are solvable, I have come to believe that God put wonder and curiosity into humanity, prompting us to explore this creation and our place in it. Vocationally speaking, I have spent years puzzling out the broader implications of being a librarian employed in a secular institution, an ordained minister in the Christian Church (Disciples of Christ), and a leader at Metropolitan Congregations United (MCU) who feels called toward helping the church truly live out its purpose to which Jesus called us of loving God and neighbor. Even as I have struggled with God I have found that the Christian Church (Disciples of Christ) welcomes my struggle with deep faith and life questions as it struggles with its own 21st-century church issues.

In the midst of the life abundant that Jesus and the church have given me, I have also felt God calling me to help the church rediscover its life through "flipping it right-side-up" through the concept of missional faith learning (MFL) (Klemme Eliceiri, n.d.). The "flipped church" is in many ways simply an authentic 21st-century response to the Disciples' mission: "To be and share the Good News of Jesus Christ, witnessing, loving, and serving from our doorsteps 'to the ends of the earth'—Acts 1:8." I consider the flipped church in two ways: first, a shift in lived mission from maintaining a "church machine" (those practices and structures that look inward to member comfort and building maintenance) to a focus on God's mission, people, and work in the world. Secondly, flipped churches utilize the concept of flipped learning that is student (disciple)-centered, rather than teacher or institution-centered, and educational resources (including sermons) that are available to church participants prior to church gatherings, including meetings and worship. Time spent together may then be used to discuss material, build relationships, and actively work on projects together. MFL is a religious education model that integrates faith, mission/activism, and learning using metaliteracy, a robust and inclusive model for real-world implementation of information literacy, equipping people of faith to courageously and actively live their faith in the world.

This essay explores the ways in which my library career, call to ordained ministry, and faith-based community organization leadership support the Disciples' aim to be a "movement for wholeness in a fragmented world." I explore this theme considering the Disciples' core beliefs, especially its vision of the "priesthood of all believers," the role that metaliteracy and theological education in the church play in the realization of this vision, and the ways in which missional faith learning in a flipped church may equip the faithful for a variety of ministries. It concludes with where I envision the future of MFL in the flipped church, helping Disciples to more fruitfully think and act their faith in the world.

The Disciples Into the Twenty-First Century

It is a fascinating time to be a Christian in the United States. Several modern-day prophets, including Phyllis Tickle, Brian McLaren, and George Barna, have noted for various reasons that religion, particularly Christianity, is in the midst of an incredible shift, described by Tickle as "The Great Emergence." As part of this shift, American churches have hemorrhaged members and money for some time. The Disciples, whose membership has dropped from nearly two million in the mid–1960s to just under a quarter of a million people as of 2015, are in good company as more and more people call themselves religious "nones." This hemorrhaging, while disturbing to some, is also a tremendous opportunity for greater religious authenticity: as religion is no longer compulsory, people may much more freely live out their faith or lack thereof.

Those of us who remain in congregations have the opportunity to re-envision ministry in forms that are more integral to authentic Christianity, rather than being held culturally captive by compulsory religion. Dean and DeVries (2016) celebrate this necessity:

> There is little doubt that, two or three decades from now, the church as we know it will be a very different place. With shrinking resources, most will no longer have the luxury of standing still. Most will be required to innovate or die. We think that is great news for the church, because it forces us to take a good hard look at who Christ calls us to be and navigate to that point, whether we have maps to guide us or not [p. 10].

Those of us who remain in church may find new freedom to try new things and deeply consider what the Gospel looks like in our 21st-century context. Kinnamon and Linn (2009) affirm that the Disciples are up for this challenge, as "this particular heritage has great strengths that it can give powerful witness to Christ in the twenty-first century, as it has for the past two hundred years" (p. 2).

The need for the Disciples to innovate while maintaining a steadfastly biblical faith is merely church as usual, according to Kinnamon and Linn (2009). "[C]hange has never been anything that has caused Disciples to cower or fear. Our trust is in God and not ourselves" (p. ix). The Disciples' beginnings in Barton Stone's spirited 1801 Cane Ridge Revival, Alexander Campbell's *Declaration and Address,* and subsequent splintering from our Presbyterian and Baptist predecessors were nothing if not innovative. Even as Disciples have also firmly committed to a restored New Testament church, Fife (2004) notes Alexander Campbell's affirmation that

> whenever discipleship leads to greater understanding of the will of God as set forth in Scripture, piety requires believers to conform to that new knowledge. Restoration, therefore, could never be a wooden concept or a mechanical process. It entailed dynamic engagement with, and maturing understanding of, the scriptural Word [p. 639].

Disciples champion a fierce freedom of belief and conscience, firmly holding to the maxim "no creed but Christ," "heralding the belief that faith in Jesus Christ is a personal faith" (Cummins, 2003, p. 34) with a great many interpretations of just what Christ means to the Disciples.

Stone and Campbell additionally agreed with the Reformation ideal that all Christians had the right and the responsibility to read the Bible for themselves. They believed the Bible, especially the New Testament, should be the only governing book of the church. Campbell believed that "reason and revelation went hand in hand" (Morrison, 2004, p. 293) and "that careful historical study of all biblical writings strengthened each believer's faith," while Stone believed "that God worked through the testimony of scripture and that understanding the Bible was not dependent on elaborate critical analysis" (Cummins, 2003, p. 28). Even in their difference of opinion, Stone and Campbell understood the complexities of reading and exploring the Bible for oneself, and were thus invested in equipping Disciples for responsible biblical interpretation and freedom of conscience in belief.

The other particularly important Reformation idea the Disciples took to heart was the "priesthood of all believers," a then-unprecedented empowering of laypeople. Stone and Campbell took this more seriously than most churches, perpetuating a dislike of clericalism. Kinnamon and Linn (2009) note, "Alexander Campbell believed laity could and would lead the church as long as they were equipped biblically and theologically to do so" (p. 117). Campbell's main complaints about the ordained centered mostly around the church relying too much on the ordained to be the church. He feared that "the clerical class" inhibited "people from hearing and reading the word of God" (Williams, Blowers, and Foster, 2004, p. 522), and thus embedded a robust structure for lay empowerment and congregational decision-making within the Disciples. They envisioned clergy and laity being church together in mutual respect and responsibility, a growing necessity as more churches call or hire part-time pastors with less traditional ministerial education and formation who must increasingly rely on laypeople to accomplish essential church work.

The Disciples' Identity Statement, a recent expression of common Disciples belief, states, "We are Disciples of Christ, a movement for wholeness in a fragmented world. As part of the one body of Christ we welcome all to the Lord's Table as God has welcomed us." As with any church statement, there is much to unpack. The Disciples note its inclusivity at God's table—that we are all one family of God; practice believers' baptism in order that our members may actively choose to be baptized; the ecumenism we hold so dearly is lived out in "unity, not uniformity." Rather than adhering to creedal statements and having tests of faith, we are called to faithfully and critically read and digest Scripture for ourselves; and answer God's call for justice, especially regarding creation care, women and children, poverty and hunger, and immigration. Within these stated principles of Disciples identity come a great deal of freedom of conscience in individual beliefs, as well as the responsibility of living them out covenantally in gracious Christian love.

Our heritage and bold denominational ideals call all Disciples to fully participate in God's mission. Our core practices highlight our openness and inclusivity toward all in God's widely open table, freedom of choice and conscience in belief. Our core practices also emphasize that our unity is not dependent upon all believing the same thing. I love the Disciples for these aims, and yet we have traditionally fallen short when it comes to putting our money and bodies where our mouths and spirits are. As in most churches, we have often valued worship taking place in the church and charitable acts over the long and difficult work of justice. Pastors today, including those in the Disciples, are challenged more than ever to actively make church a welcoming space in which to explore questions about God and theology, so that the church may become increasingly vibrant and truly be the gathered community of Jesus. In such exploration the church may further live, build relationships, and worship with those outside of its literal doors and walls, continually finding vibrant new ways in which to express the few timeless truths upon which faith stands. This may keep "church machine" in check so that the church can indeed live out God's mission, build God's realm, and practice God's love and justice in the world.

More and More Curious: Down the Rabbit-Hole of Ultimate Reality

My hometown United Church of Christ (UCC) that I attended from birth until I left for college, which I love to this day, never said, "don't bring your questions to church," but also never explicitly said, "your questions about God are valuable, and church is absolutely the right place to explore them!" Maybe Iowa farm girls were not supposed to ask too many questions, and so until I left my hometown for college, I simply lived with a great many unexplored mysteries about God. I believed that being a good Christian meant going to church every Sunday, otherwise being involved in church, and being a "good person." I learned implicitly that church proficiently expressed a meek and mild love to comfort the afflicted but was ultimately meaningless, powerless, and ineffectual when it came to afflicting the comfortable in dealing with the problems of this world. At the same time, God was a very real presence in church and life on my rural Iowa family's farm—so much a part of my context and the ground of my being that it never occurred to me to question whether or not God was real. While information literacy had not made its way to my rural Iowa community, the books I encountered in my public and school libraries opened possibilities and new worlds to me.

When I left for college, my pendulum of epistemology swung from childlike faith and credulity to the exploration of questions and the verification of belief by reason and critical thinking. All it took was a single question from my first college roommate for me to leave Christianity: "Why are you a Christian?" I attended church my whole life until that point, but never had to think about why I was a Christian before that moment. The very secular environment of college taught me the importance of critical thinking, and implicitly, information literacy without teaching me *how* to research, think critically, or be information literate. The secular context of collegiate life taught me the importance of social justice, but not how to be an activist or community organizer. Immediately following college, still outside of the church but with a burning desire to do "something good" in the world, I became an AmeriCorps VISTA "America Reads" initiative volunteer. As part of our training we read some of Saul Alinsky's works and we were encouraged to read more. A week of training was not sufficient to organize communities for the kind of community change envisioned by AmeriCorps VISTA.

My integration of faith, learning, and activism began with my leap of faith into a more progressive church. I was asked, "What do you want to do with your life?" by the church's pastor, shortly after I began attending services. I am uncertain why my response was "I would really like to study the Bible in depth." With that response, she came back with the question "Have you ever thought about seminary?" Actually, I had never thought about seminary—or any other graduate-level education, for that matter, having assumed that my first-generation college struggles and matching GPA automatically disqualified me from further education, though at one point post-college I had wondered if library school might take me anyway due to my visible passion for librarianship.

Yet somehow a mere year and a half after that conversation, I had been accepted to Eden Theological Seminary in St. Louis, opening the door to a most incredible adventure. Though afraid that I would not be able to handle graduate-level theological education and that I would be discovered and dismissed in shame as a heretic, I actually had an easier time in seminary than did many of my classmates who appeared to come from a more traditional Christian background. My overall response to shocking discoveries such as the possibility that Moses and other beloved biblical presences may not have been historical figures, rather than "They're taking my God and my Jesus away from me!" was instead more like "Why didn't I *know* this stuff? Why was I never taught? Why isn't this information available in congregations?" The Rev. Dr. John Bracke, one of my professors, when asked this question in class, attributed these omissions to "pastoral failure of nerve" to bring back seminary learning into their congregations.

Farley (2002) laments both this endemic lack of congregational theological exploration as well as the sequestering of the term "theology" to professional learning, observing that "theology was not just the scholar's possession, the teacher's trade, but the wisdom proper to the life of the believer" (p. 161). Theological and biblical ignorance lead to a variety of real-life consequences, including legislative decisions. Flanery and Werline (2016) observe, "On both sides of the aisle and at every level of political life, political officials, party representatives, and pundits employ biblical imagery, allusions to biblical texts, and explicit quotations from the Bible as support for public policy" (p. 18). Those unable to critically engage with the Bible's themes and stories may find themselves held hostage to irresponsible theological interpretations. As John Kutsko (2016) says, "The Bible does not give simple answers to the problem of good and evil, mercy versus justice, or friend versus foe" (p. 207), and so Christians have a particular moral imperative to understand and encourage this complexity in discussions invoking biblical grounds.

During seminary I vowed to bring theological learning into congregational life, but upon graduation instead took a break from church and continued my employment at Eden's library, a year later accepting a management position there. One of the greatest joys in my job at Eden's library was in teaching Eden students who were deeply intimidated by using the library how to unlock the theological treasures contained therein by learning about its resources and other information literacy concepts. Six months after I began working full-time, a friend and regular alumni library patron from seminary began inviting me to Liberation Christian Church, her Disciples new church start. While I was skittish of church at that time, in hearing my friend and the founding members talk about their vision of a community of people who loved Jesus but were finished with traditional church, wanting to build a thinking community who expressed their love for God and Jesus via art and hip-hop, inspired me to stay.

While I had learned about the Disciples as a denomination from seminary classmates and in my second-year Contextual Education placement in a Disciples congregation, I began truly experiencing life abundant in the Disciples within this new church start. Within this freedom in Christ I began envisioning a flipped church in which faith, love, learning, activism, and art could truly flourish. Liberation provided me with the opportunity to begin realizing my dream of embedding genuine theological education and librarianship in the church, including in our worship, as I often led a section of worship called "Scholarship Meditation" in which the congregation read and briefly discussed a scripturally relevant quotation. A year and a half after that I began library school and began developing an online congregational library to support Liberation's mission.

Vocational Awe, Awfulness and Possible Eventual Awesomeness

Librarianship is a wonderful profession, all the more so because so many passionate people believe they are truly called to it. Placing one's interests under a "sacred canopy" (Berger, 2011) is not without risk, as one may feel tempted to "lightwash" (Saad, n.d.) the very real difficulties involved in following God's call in life. Ettarh (2018) recently named and discussed this in the essay "Vocational Awe and Librarianship: The Lies We Tell Ourselves," articulating ways in which library staff are willing to endure any number of indignities and/or hardships because they are truly convinced that librarianship is a form of higher calling.

The potential for vocational awe may intensify in overtly theological environments.

Ettarh (2018) observes the common belief that libraries [and for the purposes of this essay, I would add, "churches and seminaries"] "as institutions are inherently good, sacred notions, and therefore beyond critique" (para. 3). However, even as theologians and seminaries are subject to a higher power, they are also still subject to the current world, in which seminaries face particularly steep challenges in the form of declining enrollments, decreasing donations, and diminishing denominational support. In the midst of this environment, seminary libraries, along with all academic libraries, must continually justify their value and need to exist, lest they be sold or consolidated.

I lived through this in December of 2009, when I learned that Eden's library building had been sold to the university across the street. The changes in theological education which led to this sale and the elimination of my position forced me to confront my vocational awe of theological librarianship. Eventually, I began to consider the possibility of vocational awesomeness in the changing context of theological education and the church as a whole, and the ways in which theological librarianship could be present in settings beyond that of the seminary. As churches grow smaller in membership and in budget, as their pastors and other leaders have less or different education from the traditional Master of Divinity degree, they force the church and its leadership to consider education that empowers and equips the whole church for authentic 21st-century ministry.

Out of the pain and anger of losing the library and my job I began the organization BiblioMinistry, with the goal of connecting churches and laypeople to the kinds of resources that would equip them to become better informed Christians. While there were and are several fine organizations and projects offering high-quality open access resources, getting them into the hands of laypeople continues to be a challenge, as many laypeople may not know where to look for theological resources or how to distinguish well-informed resources from those which are not. I wanted to unleash the power of theological resources hiding in seminary libraries to the people in the pews. If pastors "lose their nerve" when it comes to taking their seminary learnings into congregations it makes sense to bring them out directly into the world and congregations. With increased open access resources, theological educators of all sorts may release wisdom directly into the church and world at large, rather than waiting for dissemination through frightened clergy that may never happen.

As time and library school went on I became aware that my work went beyond encouraging churches toward vibrant library ministries and providing people with solid open access theological resources. In library school I was introduced to information literacy and an incredibly robust manifestation, metaliteracy, which provided me with an inspiring vision for the ways in which the church could believe smarter. Pastors often take only one Christian Education or Faith Formation course during their time in seminary, and though most denominations understand the office to which ministers are ordained is both pastor *and* teacher, most ordaining bodies focus more on the role of pastor, inadvertently neglecting that of teacher. Even as Disciples "took an energetic lead" in developing Christian Education as a profession (Davison, 2004, p. 295), education that considers the tools, resources, and processes of theology and its research is too often absent or lacking from what it means to Disciples to be church. At the same time, emphasis on faith as belief rather than experiential, missional learning has stripped churches of their identity and left them intellectually and missionally impoverished. In the same manner that Badke (2012) advocates getting "the teaching of research out of the library and into the academy" (p. 101), I believe that rudimentary understanding of theological research needs to move beyond not only the theological library to the seminary but also to the church at large. In realizing this I began to understand part of God's call in my life as continually equipping pastors to teach beyond the sermon and the Sunday School with their whole lives. I also saw the need to create and shift the normative theological culture into one in which reliable scholarly resources are integrated into congregational life and learning.

As I continued developing the mission and work of BiblioMinistry I became convinced that congregations needed to place greater emphasis on education without necessarily, as Kinnamon and Linn (2009) imagined, becoming "miniature theological seminaries where the primary focus is on study" (p. 118). However, I have long believed that seminaries could bring the content and processes of theological learning into the realities and rhythms of congregational life without replicating issues facing seminaries today.

Churches can be informed and relevant in the 21st century if people of faith are well-equipped to take responsibility for their faith and the faith communities that nurture them. God is with us in a variety of places—including our studies, our books, the databases, and in the relationships we form with texts when we spend time in deep study. Martin (2012) warned,

> with so many great educational resources available to us, we often see educating ourselves more and more as the "works" without which the apostle James declares our faith "dead." But I don't think God ever intended us to view the wonderful array of educational resources as anything beyond fuel to prepare us for action [p. 136].

Yet there is a beautiful balance to be had between faith, learning, and action. Metaliteracy offers people of faith a way to reflect on their beliefs and actions. As I continued experiencing life in a curious and open congregation, I came to understand that the point of Jesus' ministry and Christian faith was not merely to know or believe certain things, but to live out the Gospel of Jesus Christ in life for the purpose of being God's people, building and revealing the Empire of God on Earth.

Beyond "Thoughts and Prayers": Faith-Based Community Organizing (FBCO)

BiblioMinistry needed one more element before it could begin truly equipping the church to do the work of God: a clear vision on how to educate congregations toward and in the midst of mission and action. Jesus' mission went far beyond charitable works to a radical reordering of society in which everyone matters and has a vital role to play in the building and revealing of God's realm on earth. It took one more leap of faith for me to become a leader in a modern-day manifestation of this work, Metropolitan Congregations United (MCU), the St. Louis-area Gamaliel affiliate organization. MCU, as do other FBCO affiliates, provides people and communities of faith in the St. Louis area with an organization in which they can work together collectively to live out their dreams of God's justice in the world. While I did not know it at the time, the world of FBCO would provide me with the missing link between social justice and spirituality for which I had searched in some way ever since college. Conder and Rhodes (2017) remind us,

> Power is ultimately God's, and the church is by nature essentially a reality of this power. While there's no doubt that power is exercised corruptly, and that it is often we who distort it, we should also rec-

ognize that God's creative power is what brings the church into existence and it is our mission to continue to participate in God's ongoing act of re-creation [p. 32].

FBCO reminds us of the biblical importance of justice, that God calls us to truly care for those who are marginalized, and that Jesus was executed as an enemy of the Roman Empire.

The same pastor who led me back to church eventually led me to MCU and the world of FBCO. In spite of Liberation's yearning for justice it took the church some time to discover, understand the benefits of, and become involved with MCU. Upon hearing my pastor's call for more Liberators to help develop MCU's Break the (School-to-Prison) Pipeline campaign, rather than elation I instead felt a sense of holy obligation in responding to it. I was slightly terrified to attend my first MCU meeting, as abstractly learning about working for God's justice is far more comforting than getting out into the public sphere and actually doing justice work. This is normal and expected: as Martin (2012) reminds us, "there is no way to engage in the work of biblical justice without experiencing and confronting fear. This is true simply because there is no way to be faithful to the call of Jesus without experiencing and confronting fear" (p. 215). And yet MCU's strategic work of keeping children in school and out of prison with key structural decision-makers to create policies that better serve the needs of the people, rather than the needs of human empires, spoke to my spirit in such a way that I knew that I needed to be there and face my fear of confronting powerful people and structures.

Leadership at Metropolitan Congregations United (MCU) complements and challenges my work as a librarian, and my work as an ordained minister. On one hand, FBCO is more often about ordinary people jumping into the fray of public life, doing mundane things such as going to meetings, making phone calls, e-mailing, and keeping in touch with the group than it is about civil disobedience. On the other hand, the underlying premises of this work drive straight to the very heart of God's dream for humanity, providing people of faith with frameworks and networks by which to speak their truth to power, live out God's justice in the world, and build and reveal God's realm. Its emphasis on community organizing through relationship-building and appropriate risk-taking provides a powerful corrective to the private, individual, safe faith that characterizes too much of American Christianity.

The promise of FBCO, however, has yet to come to full fruition. While Han (2014) names organizing as the most effective model of social justice change-making, he notes it needs "extensive resources for training, coaching and reflection" (p. 9)—resources too often lacking in these organizations. Additionally, while God may call the whole church to be a part of this work, getting the whole church to hear this call and join this work presents challenges. Much in American secular and faith life encourages people to sit down and shut up, rather than stand up and speak out. While FBCO is an effective way of working toward God's justice, FBCO networks and affiliates must successfully engage with "good church people," challenge their assumptions that they are supposed to be meek and mild, and otherwise adequately equip them for public justice work. As Martin (2012) explains, "if we enter well prepared, we will be ready to handle the costs and challenges as they arise. Our ministry will be more effective and more sustainable" (pp. 130–131). FBCO would benefit from the reflective nature of metaliteracy.

A key component to preparing people for FBCO is helping them to understand its elements and how they work together for community change, particularly its emphasis on relationship-building. Gregory Galluzzo, founding director of Gamaliel, has gone so far as to say that "organizing 'is a commitment to lead an interesting life' and that 'issues are just an excuse for building relationships.' There is no interesting life without relationships" (as cited in Jacobsen, 2017, p. 15). Jacobsen (2017) affirms this commitment: "Organizing is essentially a relational process. At its best organizing is rooted in unconditional love for other persons, which seeks relationships that move toward empowerment, community, and justice. At its heart, organizing is about relationships, not issues" (p. 107). As I imagine what the church might look like if it took building relationships as seriously as does FBCO I also imagine what FBCO could look like if its leaders devoted more time to building relationships within its organizations.

Another core aspect of FBCO is self interest. Local FBCOs need to help people find ways to answer the question "Why are you here doing this work?" at the "gut" level of "values, our faith, our need for relationships, our longing for community, our thirst for justice" (Jacobsen, 2017, p. 98). FBCO requires its leaders to understand their and others' self-interest, as "self-interest honors both the 'self' and the 'other' in the relationship" (Jacobsen, 2017, p. 94). In knowing one's own and others' self-interest, it is possible to get to a place of mutual interest from which to work toward the common good.

The last key gift that FBCO has given me is its emphasis on risk-taking as a means of "losing your life to find it." Martin (2012) laments the loss of actual risk in church life and challenges, "What would happen if churches actually began to *lead* in risk taking? Taking God at [God's] Word and living as if it's true. This is just the sort of risk-taking spirit that engaging in the work of biblical justice requires of us" (p. 113). Gamaliel national leadership training, highly encouraged of all leaders, encourages participants to take risks in the safety of the training environment so they learn what that feels like before trying it out back home.

From "Believing Smarter" at BiblioMinistry to Missional Faith Learning

The life experiences as detailed above have all been a part of God's call to equip congregations and Christians to publicly live their faith in ways that take faith in Jesus, solid scholarship, and meaningful action toward God's justice equally seriously. Myers (2002) lamented the divide between these areas:

> The worlds of the seminary [and by extension, the library], the sanctuary, and the streets generally spin in very different orbits, with little conversation or accountability among them.... All three spheres are profoundly impoverished by their isolation from each other, and the holistic mission of the church languishes [pp. 9–10].

This divide is lamentable but not inevitable. As I continued my work of calling and equipping the church to a higher standard of educational ministry I increasingly saw ways in which librarianship could bring these worlds together for God's glory and the benefit of congregational life.

Seminary gave me permission to explore the mysteries of theology; theological librarianship gave me the resources and information literacy education to do so. Not only do theological libraries contain the literature of theology, they are also generally staffed with kind and helpful librarians who both formally and informally teach library users information literacy concepts. While discipline-specific educators (including theologians) are generally exceptional at conducting their own inquiry and research, as well as sharing their learning and the content of their discipline with students and other interested parties, most of the time it is the librarians who prioritize teaching students about the tools, resources, and processes that go into academic work.

Librarianship and librarians are therefore important to lifelong learning. Head (2016) observes that while information literacy education has made amazing headway into educational systems, "[f]ew [educators] have thought to ask what happens to college students once they graduate" (p. 7). Badke (2012) fears "the real failure of information literacy to this point is that it is simply not robust enough" (p. 108). Even in the midst of metaliteracy's relative obscurity compared to information literacy, its robust flexibility and devotion to lifelong learning make it a better fit for life in the church than information literacy on its own.

Ordained ministry is nothing if not equipping God's people for missional faith learning—education is at the very heart of the church and the office to which one is ordained in the Disciples is that of pastor *and* teacher. However, underwhelming religious education has become so expected by laypeople and embedded into the church that the church has by and large failed to realize its responsibility to integrate advances in learning and educational theories into its life. The failure of the church to prioritize Christian education, privileging the office of pastor and minimalizing that of teacher leads me to believe why the church faces such an intellectual deficit today.

During my ordination process I continued developing a comprehensive description of my approach to Christian education while writing about an online open religious metaliteracy course (see appendix) I taught entitled "Faith Thinking Foundations" (Klemme Eliceiri, 2015). The course provided its students with the opportunity to explore a faith topic they were curious about using metaliteracy research tools and processes, sharing their experiences and learning with the rest of the class via a self-chosen, self-directed project. Mimicking Harris' (1989) idea that learning should be implemented through "creative vision that sees all the facets of the church's life as the church curriculum" (p. 18), I have expansively termed this approach missional faith learning (MFL). The key points of MFL are distilled through BiblioMinistry into the more lay-accessible Think! Pray! Act! Website on which I post weekly updates encouraging readers to think, pray, and act on resources related to biblical and life mysteries and themes from a MFL perspective.

At its heart, MFL is a constructivist, praxis-oriented integration of thought/study, prayer/faith/worship, and activism/mission/action (Klemme Eliceiri, n.d.), permeated throughout by the principles of metaliteracy (Forte, Mackey, Jacobson, O'Keefe, & Stone, 2018). It embraces Seymour's (2014) vision of Missional Christian Education, empowering "all to true humanity and calling the wider church to partner with God in restoring 'new creation'" (p. 117), while lifting up metaliteracy's orientation toward lifelong, metacognitive learning. The goals of information stewardship, information discernment, information evangelism, and missional planning, assessment, and evaluation draw extensively from metaliteracy (Klemme Eliceiri, n.d.). While metaliteracy is as expansion of information theory, MFL addresses metaliteracy in light of the particular concerns of theology and the church.

The first goal, information stewardship, is aligned with metaliteracy's goal of finding, using, storing, and sharing information. It encourages people to do this in ethical, God-honoring ways that encourage people of faith to deeply consider the role information plays in their lives. The book *Love to Share* (World Association for Christian Communication, 2008) encourages a creative perspective on copyright, considering that "creative producers who seek to bear testimony to the resurrection of Jesus and proclaim God's good news cannot be limited by the rules of the marketplace" (p. 27).

The second goal, information discernment, aligned with metaliteracy's first goal of critically evaluating content, encourages a prayerful approach to information and knowledge, calling the church to reclaim the biblical role of wisdom. It calls the church to consider the wisdom tradition, including Lady Wisdom in the book of Proverbs, as well as the claims that Jesus was Wisdom personified.

> In much the same manner that Jesus fearlessly, lovingly, and critically engaged with the world around him, metaliteracy encourages learners to expansively and critically engage with any and all information, rather than eschewing information encountered outside of more formally vetted sources [Klemme Eliceiri, 2015, p. 8].

The third goal, information evangelism, largely follows metaliteracy's goal of responsibly sharing and creating new information, collaborating with people in a variety of environments. It considers how people of faith use information to share the Gospel, living this vision out beyond words. This goal encourages people of faith to share not just factual information, but also build relationships through sharing their lived experiences with others.

MFL's fourth goal, missional planning, calls people of faith and the church to evaluate the goals, objectives, and outcomes of educational and life endeavors. While this may sound more clinical than Christ-like, there are many faithful ways of planning and evaluating educational ministries. Rendle and Mann (2003) suggest that church planning provides opportunities to build transformative relationships. "It is not the plan that will change people and give direction to the congregation. It is the conversation of the people with one another and with God—that is a part of the planning process—that changes people" (p. 19). It matters more that congregations are intentional about planning than how they plan. People are more willing and able to be engaged with ministries and endeavors if they believe they have been heard during the planning process: it matters that churches thoughtfully plan their life, setting goals, objectives, and outcomes after having listened to those in their neighborhoods, and church members discuss their needs and concerns.

While MFL continues evolving based on new insights into metacognitive learning, it provides the church with a model of Christian education that takes seriously the particular theological concerns of the church. It provides congregations with a tool by which to consider their educational efforts in light of the ways in which 21st-century Christians encounter and interact with information, discerning through this new ways for people of faith to be God's people in the world.

Flipping the Church Right-Side-Up: 21st-Century Disciples Indeed

The upside-down church is a building one visits for an hour or so on Sunday to get "fed" by God for the rest of the week in the form of pastor-led, lay-followed worship. In flipping church right-side-up, Patterson's (1998) historical Jesus work helps churches remember its initial identity and responsibilities: "[t]o 'seek [God's] Empire' means to order life in such a way that the Empire of God becomes a reality. If one does this, or rather, if a community does this, the necessities of life will all fall into place" (p. 106). It reminds people of faith about our obligation to humanity: "Jesus' words speak about ordering human relationships in such a way that no one is expendable and all have unbrokered access to the means for life" (p. 106).

Missional Faith Learning in the flipped church offers Disciples and other courageous Christians the opportunity to remedy exclusively inward-looking faith, revitalizing the life of the community. Jacobsen (2017) rightly notes that the Holy Spirit sends the church out into the world, using its power to publicly and tangibly witness to the resurrected Christ amidst the principalities and powers.

> The church enters the "this-worldliness" of the public arena because God is encountered in the encounter with those who suffer in the world. Jesus was born not in a church but in a stable. Jesus died, not of a heart attack from too many high cholesterol church dinners, but of crucifixion as an enemy of the Roman Empire. The public arena is God's arena [Jacobsen, 2017, p. 43].

Church is not about a building or just about worship, but about being the gathered community of people who love God and Jesus. As my professor and Disciples minister, the Rev. Dr. Michael Kinnamon, often said in class, "The church doesn't have a mission; the church *is* mission. There is no church without mission; the church participates in God's mission on earth." This flies in the face of much of what I see in church life. Preparation for weekly worship and care of church buildings and other spaces often take precedence over what the church is actually here on earth to do. If the church is truly interested in being the church, in participating God's mission on earth, it will need to flip right-side-up.

The "flipped church" originated from the concept of the "flipped" or "inverted" classroom, beginning with Alison King's article (1993) "From Sage on the Stage to Guide on the Side" in which King considers implications of constructivism for education: placing students at the center of student-directed, integrative, praxis-oriented learning. Lage, Platt, and Treglia (2000) added to this concept with the idea of the "inverted classroom" for inclusive learning. They stated that "[i]nverting the classroom means that events that have traditionally taken place inside the classroom now take place outside the classroom and vice versa" (p. 32). Students gain content knowledge via lectures and PowerPoint presentations prior to class and subsequently use class time for integrative discussions of the material and collaborative, experiential learning opportunities. Jon Bergmann, Aaron Sams, and Kari Afstrom were some of the first to utilize technology to flip the classroom. They would record their lectures and expect students to watch them outside of formal classroom time. This empowered their time in the classroom to be focused on teaching instead of content, subsequently the terms "flipped classroom" or "flipped learning" developed (Noonoo, 2007).

In time, innovators began considering how flipped learning might apply to the church. Wilson (2013) imagines flipped preaching in that the congregation could listen or watch the sermon before coming to church and subsequently using the valuable time which church attenders gather to discuss the sermon, pray for each other, and plan action based on their discussion. Ward (2013) speculates that church relationships would improve and would more likely inspire real community, action, and change. Murrow (2014) believes watching sermons before church would improve our retention of them, particularly if we discussed them at church. Flipped learning improves student outcomes; there is the distinct possibility it could improve church outcomes as well. How far is the world of ministry willing to reconsider its ideas on preaching and worship in light of educational best practices that could give the church new life and help people who love Jesus to truly follow him in thought and deed?

The flipped church may also benefit church mission discernment, planning, and implementation. Baughman (2016) echoes Kinnamon's concept of mission, believing "that God is already at work in our neighborhood, that Jesus is already at work in the lives of the people who walk in our doors. Our responsibility is to see what God is doing in our neighborhood and become a part of that" (p. 20). What goes on outside the church building is a key part of what God is doing in the world, yet too often churches plan their work without understanding or engaging the needs of the people around them, thus dismissing the FBCO concept of relationship-building with those in their midst. MFL's information evangelism and missional planning give churches who need its "permission" to leave the church building to see what God is doing in their neighborhoods.

Evangelism also changes with MFL in the flipped church, logically following from a church's experiences in information evangelism and missional planning. Once a church has discovered where God is working in their neighborhood, how can Disciples be the church outside of the building? How can a church integrate itself into people's lives beyond Sunday and equip them to be a church outside of the building? What will motivate them to put themselves on the line for "the least of these," the poor and marginalized people to whom Jesus calls us to align our faith? Lived evangelism is less about the right words and more about forming authentic relationships in faith.

Flipped learning can bring new life into the church building as well. Today's church attendees are generally there voluntarily but continue having limited time and energy. In church planning it is worthwhile to consider the points and goals of a congregation's time together, making the most of it in worship, study, and missional activity. Worship—including the sermon—in the flipped church can truly support our journey in discipleship, if we are willing to make some changes. The format of most sermons—a preacher and a congregation who listens to the preacher—mimics the traditional scholarly lecture format, which is not always the optimal way for people to learn. Preachers who provide their congregations with the opportunity to watch the sermon before church and respond at church may find themselves surprised at the life-giving nature of doing church this way.

MFL in a flipped church may appeal to the Disciples' enthusiasm for innovation as well as our historical commitment to self-directed learning in community. The Disciples have an expansive vision, claiming and continuing "the saving ministry of Jesus Christ," including "all who join together in witness to God's justice and reconciliation through worship, daily work, sharing the Gospel, pastoral care, relief of human suffering, engagement in the struggle for peace and justice, and realization of the unity of the Church Universal" (Christian Church [Disciples of Christ], 2011, p. 5). Fulfilling such a vision requires the kind of serious learning and authentic relationship-building inherent to MFL.

Living Into a Future of Perpetual Missional Faith Learning

Many of the deep faith and life mysteries that are constant companions to some of us on our life journeys may only be explored, not solved, during life on earth. As for the slightly more practical question with which we begun, how are we to all live together on this one planet, MFL in a flipped church offers Christians seeking more fruitful lives as disciples of Jesus that integrate faith with serious intellectual thought and God-honoring action. Shirley Guthrie's (2008) book, *Always Being Reformed*, reminds us that the Reformation was not a one-time event; church reformation is always happening. We get a choice in whether or how we want to be a part of God's ever-changing work in the world. The issues and potential solutions discussed here, while not exhaustive, are some key trends and alleviations to current church issues that allow may the Disciples to revitalize their ministries in 21st-century ways that remain faithful to Jesus.

Even if it is impossible to solve the mystery of why we are here, the fact remains that we are here on this planet together, called by Jesus to love one another in the midst of it all. As a Christian, I am not to fear, but to love people in tangible ways. As an ordained person, I am to show leadership and equip the people in my midst to do that as well as they can. As a librarian, I am called to fling wide open the doors of the theological library's impressive array of resources, tools, and learning processes that all God's people may better understand and live the Gospel in their lives. MFL in the flipped church provides us with fruitful ways to do so in the midst of our respective life journeys. For 21st-century Disciples and the rest of the church to see and be a part of what God is doing in the world, we need to live a thoughtful, missional faith that takes us well outside the church doors. MFL in the flipped church offers the Disciples a way to truly be that church, to "pray with our feet" without losing our minds.

Appendix

Faith Thinking Foundations:
Religious (Meta)Literacy For Everyone

(Complete syllabus available at https://drive.google.com/file/d/0B8oh6QqNu3d_alFkV1ExQWpMcUk/view?usp=sharing)

Course Description:
People of faith, including those of us who love Jesus, are better equipped to discern and act on God's truth if we are also knowledgeable about encountering information in world around us. Faith Thinking Foundations covers the topics of encountering information as people of faith for lifelong learning, and learning how to learn, particularly about Christianity from an integrated spiritual/intellectual/social justice perspective. This class will help you to develop your own research framework and process with which to explore all those big, deep life questions that keep you awake at 3am, better discover and use information as a committed Christian, and think more clearly about information from a faith perspective. If you have questions about any of the material, lessons, or assignments, please contact the instructor, Rebecca Klemme Eliceiri, at *rebecca@thinkprayact.org*.

Course Goals:
Students will be able to:

1. Integrate faith, intellect, and social justice on both personal and communal levels
2. Understand and articulate the integration of faith, intellect, and activism
3. Demonstrate an awareness of this integration via reflective work (class discussion, blog, Facebook posts, art, music, etc.) and completion of an integrative project (student-chosen, instructor-approved) to be shared with the class and relevant organizations upon completion

Main Textbook:
Bernnard, Deborah, Greg Bobish, Daryl Bullis, Jenna Hecker, Irina Holden, Allison Hosier, Trudi Jacobson, and Tor Loney. *The Information Literacy User's Guide: An Open, Online Textbook*. Geneseo: SUNY Textbooks, Milne Library, 2014. http://opensuny.org/omp/index.php/SUNYOpenTextbooks/catalog/book/170.

24 The Faithful Librarian

The Bible:
We begin each week of study with a scriptural meditation passage. As someone who is interested in serious Bible study, I recommend that you obtain a study Bible if you don't already have one. There are many wonderful options in print, online, and e-book versions of the Bible.

For a basic overview of the most widely-used biblical translations, read this short article:

Society of Biblical Literature. "Versions and Translations." *Teaching the Bible: An E-Newsletter for Public School Teachers by Society of Biblical Literature*, April 2012. http://www.sbl-site.org/assets/pdfs/TBv4i2_Chancey_VersionsandTranslations.pdf.

Course Outline

Week 1: Introduction to Faith Thinking
Our biblical text for the week is part of a far greater body of Wisdom literature, and is counted within conventional biblical wisdom, which provides the groundwork for the wisdom embodied by Jesus. How does this passage speak to you about the character of wisdom today? Is wisdom unchanging, or has it changed, and if so, how?

Week 2: Introduction to Research
This week we will discuss types of research and the research process, considering the ways in which research becomes Wisdom. We will discuss taking your original big question from big question to research question, as well as beginning steps in research. Since some of what we are covering this week may be review for some of us, see if you can find any differences between what you may have been taught about library and information research and what you read in this week's reading.

Week 3: Information Stewardship
Information stewardship is not only how we store or otherwise manage information that someone else has created—it is also, from a metaliteracy standpoint, what we create or produce with the information available to us. What can we do with information that pleases God? Reflexively, the better information stewards we are, and the more we learn about information stewardship and stewardship at large, the better we may be able to view, orient, and manage our lives toward living into the baseilia (empire) of God, as Jesus imagined.

Week 4: Religious and Theological Research
"A Jesus who was simply a 'teacher of wisdom' would claim his place within the tradition of Israel's great teachers. But the Jesus who is remembered in the Synoptic tradition made a claim, both implicitly and explicitly, which transcended that of his precursors and which in the event could only find satisfactory expression in the evaluation of this Jesus as 'Wisdom incarnate'" (Dunn, p. 92).
This week we will discuss tools, techniques, and processes that are specific to the world of theological research, and how to further integrate these things with Jesus' radical wisdom.

Week 5: Information Stewardship, Part 2: Resources and Access
This week we will go further into information stewardship, discussing the ways in which information resources are available to people and who are are not able to access some types of information. We will discuss the effect that Open Access materials have on information stewardship.

Week 6: Information Discernment
"…[W]hat is 'discernment'? Illustrated by the concepts of wisdom and understanding in the Book of Proverbs, an exegesis of the scriptural texts of Proverbs 1:1–7 and Proverbs 8:1–21 help conceptualize discernment as the ability to regulate one's thinking in the acquisition and application of knowledge to make decisions that are right, fair, and just." (Hazel C. V. Trauffer, "Towards an Understanding of Discernment: A 21st-century Model of Decision-making" (ProQuest Information & Learning, 2009), p. iii) This week we will discuss the relationship between discernment and wisdom.

Week 7: Information Evangelism: Sharing the Results of Your Research
In light of what we have studied so far, what is the Gospel—the Good News? What about what you have discovered so far is good news? This week we will discuss the theological and practical implications of information evangelism—sharing what you have learned with others in fruitful ways.

Week 8: Assessment and Wrap-Up
This week we will discuss evaluation of ourselves, our projects, and the class.

REFERENCES

Badke, W. (2012). *Teaching research processes: The faculty role in the development of skilled student researchers.* Oxford: Chandos.

Baughman, M. (2016). Start a church. Bring God to the neighborhood. In *Flipping church: How successful church planters are turning conventional wisdom upside-down* (pp. 17–30). Nashville: Discipleship Resources.

Berger, P. L. (2011). *The sacred canopy: Elements of a sociological theory of religion.* New York: Open Road Media.

Christian Church (Disciples of Christ). (2011). Theological foundations and policies and criteria for the ordering of ministry of the Christian Church (Disciples of Christ). Retrieved from http://disciples.org/wp-content/uploads/2014/07/TFPCOM-Final.pdf.

Cummins, D. D. (2003). *A handbook for today's disciples in the Christian Church (Disciples of Christ).* St. Louis: Chalice Press.

Conder, T., & Rhodes, D. (2017). *Organizing church: Grassroots practices for embodying change in your congregation, your community, and our world.* St. Louis: Chalice Press.

Davison. L. W. (2004). Educational ministry: Christian Church (Disciples of Christ). In D. A. Foster, P. M. Blowers, A. L. Dunnavant, & D. N. Williams (Eds.), *The encyclopedia of the Stone-Campbell Movement* (pp. 294–295). Grand Rapids: William B. Eerdmans.

Dean, K. C., & DeVries, M. (2016). Foreword: Cartographers. In *Flipping church: How successful church planters are turning conventional wisdom upside-down* (pp. 8–10). Nashville: Discipleship Resources.

Ettarh, F. (2018). Vocational awe and librarianship: The lies we tell ourselves. *In the Library with the Lead Pipe.* Retrieved from http://www.inthelibrarywiththeleadpipe.org/2018/vocational-awe/.

Farley, E. (1985). Can church education be theological education? *Theology Today, 42*(2), 158–171. Retrieved from http://library3.webster.edu/login?url=http://search.ebscohost.com/login.aspx?direct=true&db=rfh&AN=ATLA0000948912&site=ehost-live.

Fife, R. O. (2004). "Restoration," meanings of within the movement. In D. A. Foster, P. M. Blowers, A. L. Dunnavant, & D. N. Williams (Eds.), *The encyclopedia of the Stone-Campbell Movement* (pp. 638–642). Grand Rapids: William B. Eerdmans.

Flannery, F., & Werline, R. A. (2016). *The Bible in political debate: What does it really say?* New York: Bloomsbury.

Forte, M., Jacobson, T., Mackey, T., O'Keefe, E., & Stone, K. (2018). Goals and learning objectives. Retrieved September 1, 2018, from https://metaliteracy.org/learning-objectives/.

Guthrie, S. C. (2008). *Always being reformed: Faith for a fragmented world.* Louisville: Westminster John Knox Press.

Han, H. (2014). *How organizations develop activists: Civic associations and leadership in the 21st century.* New York: Oxford University Press.

Harris, M. (1989). *Fashion me a people: Curriculum in the church.* Louisville: Westminster John Knox Press.

Head, A. (2016). Foreword. In T. E. Jacobson and T. P. Mackey (Eds.), *Metaliteracy in practice* (pp. 7–11). Chicago: ALA Neal-Schuman.

Jacobsen, D. A. (2017). *Doing justice: Congregations and community organizing, 2nd edition.* Minneapolis: Fortress Press.

King, A. (1993). From sage on the stage to guide on the side. *College Teaching, 41*(1), 30–35. Retrieved from http://www.jstor.org/stable/27558571.

Kinnamon, M. K., & Linn, J. G. (2009). *Disciples: Reclaiming our identity, reforming our practice.* St. Louis: Chalice Press.

Klemme Eliceiri, R. (2015). Faith thinking foundations: Online religious (meta)literacy education within a congregational context. *Advances in the Study of Information and Religion, 5*(1). https://doi.org/10.21038/asir.2015.0002.

Klemme Eliceiri, R. (n.d.). Missional Faith Learning (MFL) overview, elements, goals, and objectives. Retrieved September 1, 2018, from http://www.thinkprayact.org/missional-faith-learning-mfl-overview/.

Kutsko, J. F. (2016). Compromise as a biblical value. In *The Bible in political debate: What does it really say?* (pp. 197–210). New York: Bloomsbury T&T Clark.

Lage, M. J., Platt, G. J., & Treglia, M. (2000). Inverting the classroom: A gateway to creating an inclusive learning environment. *Journal of Economic Education, 31*(1), 30–43. https://doi.org/10.1080/00220480009596759.

Martin, J. (2012). *The just church: Becoming a risk-taking, justice-seeking, disciple-making congregation.* Carol Stream, IL: Tyndale House.

Morrison, J. L. (2004). Education, philosophy of. In D. A. Foster, P. M. Blowers, A. L. Dunnavant, & D. N. Williams (Eds.), *The encyclopedia of the Stone-Campbell Movement* (pp. 292–294). Grand Rapids: William B. Eerdmans.

Murrow, D. (2014, January 15). The flipped church. Retrieved August 22, 2018, from http://www.patheos.com/blogs/churchformen/2014/01/the-flipped-church/.

Myers, C. (2002). Word and World: A People's School: Alternative theological education between the seminary, the sanctuary, and the streets. *Clergy Journal, 78*(9), 8. Retrieved from http://library3.webster.edu/login?url=http://search.ebscohost.com/login.aspx?direct=true&db=a9h&AN=7290521&site=ehost-live.

Noonoo, B. S. (2012, June 20). *Flipped learning founders set the record straight*. Retrieved August 17, 2018, from https://thejournal.com/articles/2012/06/20/flipped-learning-founders-q-and-a.aspx.

Patterson, S. J. (1998). *The God of Jesus: The historical Jesus and the search for meaning*. Harrisburg: Trinity Press International.

Rendle, G., & Mann, A. (2003). *Holy conversations: Strategic planning as a spiritual practice for congregations*. Washington, D.C.: The Alban Institute.

Saad, L. (n.d.). I need to talk to spiritual white women about white supremacy (Part One). Retrieved August 17, 2018, from http://laylafsaad.com/poetry-prose/white-women-white-supremacy-1.

Seymour, J. L. (2014). *Teaching the way of Jesus: Educating Christians for faithful living*. Nashville: Abingdon Press.

Ward, K. (2013, July 7). Flip the classroom, flip the church. Retrieved August 22, 2018, from http://www.churchinacircle.com/2013/07/07/flip-the-classroom-flip-the-church/.

Williams, D. N., Blowers, P. M., & Foster, D. A. (2004). Ministry. In D. A. Foster, P. M. Blowers, A. L. Dunnavant, & D. N. Williams (Eds.), *The encyclopedia of the Stone-Campbell Movement* (pp. 521–532). Grand Rapids: William B. Eerdmans.

Wilson, C. (2013, February 13). Flipping churches. Retrieved August 17, 2018, from https://churchm.ag/flipping-churches/.

World Association for Christian Communication & World Council of Churches. (2008). *Love to share: Intellectual property rights, copyright, and Christian churches*. Toronto & Geneva: World Association for Christian Communication & World Council of Churches. Retrieved from http://www.oikoumene.org/en/programmes/unity-mission-evangelism-and-spirituality/spirituality-and-worship/love-to-share.html.

With Quiet Diligence

How Claude Elbert Spencer Formed an Archival Tradition in the Stone-Campbell Movement

MCGARVEY ICE

Abstract

As the pioneering archivist of the Restoration Movement or Stone-Campbell Movement, comprising the Christian Churches, Churches of Christ, and the Christian Church (Disciples of Christ), Claude Elbert Spencer (1898–1979) came onto the scene during the emergence and professionalization of library study and the concomitant higher expectation of library work in the academy; he possessed a native impulse and a unique vocational imperative to collect history; and finally he owned a theological subjunctive to embrace the breadth of Stone-Campbell material in a single archive. This essay narrates the contours of his life's story and work as it relates to the formation of the archive he conceived. Further, it attends to the values and virtues that compelled his collecting and guided his service. Spencer's bibliographic work was exemplary and his archival work was peerless in his denomination. The story behind this work and the values that undergird it invite contemplation by those who would serve as archivists in denominational settings.

Beginnings: From Kahoka to Canton by Way of the Libraries

Claude Elbert Spencer was born 13 March 1898 on the family farm in Johnson Township, Scotland County, Missouri, to Harvey John Spencer and Ettie May Prickett Spencer. They attended the Shiloh Church of Christ, a congregation Ettie's father, John Prickett, established. Prickett was a storekeeper and sometime postmaster who read the leading writers of the Christian Church, particularly Alexander Campbell, James A. Garfield, "Raccoon" John Smith, and Alexander Wilford Hall (Spencer, 1941a, [1965b], 1980).

Claude first attended school at age seven in a rural one-room affair with a single teacher for eight grades. A too-busy teacher and his late start caused him to struggle and he was still illiterate at the age of nine. His parents "had faith that I was not dumb," Claude remembered, "and could learn in a different school. They decided to move to Kahoka, a town of 1500 where the school was graded with a teacher for each grade …

[where] ... an entirely new phase of my life began" (Spencer, 1980, p. 4). In a week he was reading and progressed so well that he passed the seventh grade exams the summer after his sixth grade year, which caught the attention of School Superintendent Seth Mapes (Spencer, 1980).

In the summer of 1914 Mapes ordered $1500 worth of books and hired Claude to arrange them according to Dewey's *Abridged Decimal Classification*. Mapes received some training in librarianship from the University of Missouri and taught Claude to classify, number and shelve the books and institute a charging system. "I was a sophomore that year," Claude remembered,

> and for the rest of my high school life I had charge of the library. All the time I was not in class, I spent in the library. And I was paid, as nearly as I can recollect, $13.00 a semester! Although I didn't know it at the time, this was preparation for my life work [Spencer, 1980, pp. 7–8].

Three years later he would take a momentous step toward his career at Culver-Stockton College in Canton, Missouri, a small liberal arts college affiliated with the Christian Church. Byron Ingold, Professor of Mathematics at Culver-Stockton, often preached for the Christian Church in Kahoka where the Spencer's attended. He tried to recruit Claude to Canton, but finances prohibited it. About the same time, John Hepler Wood, President of Culver-Stockton sought accreditation in part by purchasing several thousand volumes for the library. He asked Seth Mapes, who by then was superintendent of the Canton schools, for recommendations concerning staff capable of supervising library services. Mapes suggested Spencer. Claude was "tending the soup bean patch" the morning Wood's long-distance call came and took the next train to Canton for an interview (Spencer, 1980, p. 9).

After introductions and a tour of the library it became clear to everyone the interview would be little more than a formality. By dinnertime Wood waived Spencer's tuition, room and board for a year in exchange for a reduced course load and the expectation he train and supervise library student workers. Spencer returned to Kahoka that evening with a college education lined up and gainful employment due to begin early the next Monday morning.

Though a student, Spencer's name also appeared in the faculty roster as librarian from 1917 to 1922, a position he assumed full-time upon graduation. His supervision of students in cataloging, shelf-reading, inventory, circulation control and light reference work, though borne of necessity for lack of trained faculty, freed him to focus on advanced reference work, collection development, and to teach a course in Library Methods (Culver-Stockton, 1918, 1919, 1920, 1921, 1923). A decade of part-time experience under the apprenticeship model served him well, first under Mapes and next with fellow students. Yet so that his training would match his newly created professional position, his administration sent him to the University of Illinois Library School (later the Graduate School of Library Science).

By the early 1920s, first Katharine Sharp and then Phineas Windsor (both trained by Dewey) burnished Illinois's reputation as a preeminent incubator of professional, highly trained, and thoroughly equipped librarians. They mated their conviction regarding the potency and efficacy of knowledge to a dogged commitment to excellent librarianship. Recognizing how the compelling force of librarianship undergirded the pursuit of knowledge by providing access to information and its concomitant cultural and societal impact, they formed a degree track that was as rooted in library economy as it was grounded in the cultural, historical and theoretical commitments of the liberal arts. The courses were equally rigorous in the classroom as they were thorough in the laboratory (Grotzinger, 1992).

Spencer took 16 hours over two summers, 1922 and 1923, the equivalent to the first year of traditional residential work which "covered the generally accepted methods and practices in library work" which was sufficient to "prepare [students] to accept positions in library service" (University of Illinois, 1922, p. 168). Spencer and the Culver-Stockton administration felt this was adequate. In the era of emerging formalized professional standards, Spencer's training was on par with many of his peers and his decade of experience, and, at the age of twenty-five, was superlative. Had he completed the remainder of the program, he would have been among the first recipients of the Illinois master's degree in library science (University of Illinois, 1923, "[List of students]," 1923). In 1934 the Missouri Library Association issued him a professional life certificate, the requirements of which called for "four years course in college or university, one full year's work in [an ALA-accredited] library school, and two years' successful experience in a responsible position" (Elliott, 1936, p. 19, 54; see certificate in Spencer Papers, DCHS, Box 1, "Mills Book Store" folder).

Inaugurating Professional Librarianship at Culver-Stockton College

In 1917, Spencer inherited a library of about 10,000 volumes. Of the 72 libraries in Missouri, Culver-Stockton ranked 29th in terms of holdings and 16th among 21 colleges. But by 1933 the collection of 22,000 volumes (Missouri Library Commission, 1932; Patterson, 1920) contributed in part to three successive accreditations: Missouri College Union, 1920; North Central Association of Colleges, 1924; and the Association of American Colleges, 1926 (Lee, 1984). Spencer was a founder and sometime President of the Canton Public Library Board of Directors and was active on campus and in civic clubs ("Culver-Stockton has new librarian," 1951). He became a campus institution, one of the core faculty who persevered through the rise of the 1920s, then into—and out of—the Depression and the War (Allen, 1972; Lee, 1984; Peters, 1941). He shepherded the library from a haphazard assortment of books and periodicals stored in basement rooms of two academic halls, the women's dormitory and still more in the attic of the gymnasium, to a competitive and respectable collection of nearly 40,000 volumes housed in a new, fully modern three-story facility, including the premier collection of Disciples of Christ historical materials (Lee, 1984).

He expected student assistants to be loyal, cooperative, patient, consistent, and accurate. That he insisted on these "virtues" indicates which values and disciplines most informed his vision of librarianship (Spencer, 1944, 1965b). In 1947, to celebrate his 25th anniversary as librarian, 85 colleagues and former students presented a book of letters that lauded his impact and repeatedly mentioned his joy, gratitude, humor, diligence, loyalty, and patience ([Book of Letters], 1947).

Claude Spencer enjoyed the respect of his peers and students on campus as well as in Canton and across Missouri libraries and historical associations. By many measures he built a successful and meaningful career. Yet his enduring contribution was just emerging in a pregnant bloom. The fruit of the decades ahead exceeded even Spencer's wildest imaginings. By 1947 Spencer engaged his archival sensibility, his collecting dream, his curatorial vision, and his theological convictions in full force to build a collection of Disciples historical materials of a scale and quality so deep, so broad and of such incontestable utility as to rank it without peer within the denomination and propel it into the company of the elite American Protestant church archives.

The Henry Barton Robison Collection and Disciples of Christ Historical Society: Two Collections with a Singular Mission

In 1924 George L. Peters, Culver-Stockton board member and minister of the Christian Church in Canton (he baptized Spencer in 1921) asked Claude if he could assemble from the college library all volumes by or about Disciples. "My reply to him was," Spencer said, "brother Peters I wouldn't know a Disciple book if one came along and hit me in the head" (Spencer, 1959a, p. 4). They identified three shelves of books yet overlooked that many more. Peters' interest may have been piqued by a rousing editorial in *Christian Standard* calling for the awareness and preservation of Disciples literature:

> The Restoration Movement is now facing the greatest opportunity of its history. There is only one thing lacking. We as a people are not as enthusiastic as should be in pushing the plea; it is because we are not sufficiently posted to appreciate our peculiar position; our lack of information is caused by our lack of study, and our lack of study is very largely accounted for by the scarcity of books in our libraries—especially books through which great minds of both the past and the present speak to us concerning the fundamentals of the Christian religion.
> Let there be a revival of interest in Restoration literature! [(Editorial), 1921, p. 2010].

Peters' nudge was sufficient to spark Spencer's interest. A "born collector," he recognized the challenge—and opportunity—of a field that "was almost totally untouched" (Spencer, 1959a, p. 5; Spencer & Pierson, 1962, p. 40) and sought printed bibliographies to develop the nascent collection. The premier bibliographical guide to American church history at the time listed merely 23 entries for Disciples, fewer books than Spencer gathered on his three shelves (Mode, 1921). In time he discovered Monser's *Literature of the Disciples of Christ* (1906), with 150 entries and Garrison's article "The Literature of the Disciples of Christ" in *Bulletin of the Disciples Divinity House* April 1923 with 500. DeGroot and Dowling's *The Literature of the Disciples of Christ* (1933) contained approximately 2,000 citations yet reflects no knowledge of the Culver-Stockton collection or Spencer's input. However, by 1933 Spencer "assembled and classified a collection of literature ... conceded to be the largest classified collection in the Disciples' colleges" (Horn, 1933, p. 386).

To accomplish this, he fused his collecting instincts to his training in cataloging and voraciously examined the literature itself for clues to the existence and contours of Disciples material. The process was slow and laborious, calling for extraordinary persistence, attention to detail, and the foresight to document and preserve any findings no matter how incomplete or seemingly inconsequential. When asked how he acquired a comprehensive grasp of the web of personalities, publications and issues that comprise the essence of Disciple history, Spencer replied,

> I acquired it the hard way. There isn't any easy way. I acquired it mostly by a study of the periodicals over the whole span of time, starting with the *Millennial Harbinger* and actually looking page by

page. This was acquired when I was working on my author catalog and my periodical check list. That was twenty years in the making [Spencer and Pierson, 1962, p. 40].

In time the three shelves doubled, then doubled again, and yet again until a separate room was required. In 1928 the college Ministerial Association named the collection in honor of Henry Barton Robison, long-time professor of Religion, and endowed it with the purpose of making it "one of the most comprehensive collections of Disciples of Christ literature in existence" ("Board of Education," 1928, p. 40). Spencer, Peters, Robison, and W. H. McDonald, Culver-Stockton President, hunted, gathered, collected, scoured, scouted and hauled back to campus a steady stream of books, periodicals, pamphlets, and archival material. Students sorted, classified and cataloged it under Spencer's watchful eye. All the while he "continued, literally, to 'burn the midnight oil,' learning about the Disciples and working with the books received. Most of my work on the Disciples," he said, "was done between 11:30 P. M. and 2:30 A. M." (Spencer, 1965a, p. 42). In a talk to the Canton Public Library Round Table Club in about 1938 he remarked how he had "for the past fourteen years ... given almost every spare moment of my time to the study of the literature produced by that religious congregation known as the Disciples of Christ" (Spencer, [ca. 1938], p. 1).

By the mid–1930s the Robison Collection held 4,000 items assembled from hundreds of donors (Spencer, 1959a, p. 6). Among his peers in Disciple colleges and seminaries, Spencer was preeminent in terms of his collection size and scope, yet almost totally unknown. While his peers developed collections to meet accreditation requirements and serve curricular needs, and though they offered instruction in church history, even Disciple history, the few who actively sought Disciple material did so independently and with great "local ambition" (Spencer, [ca. 1940], p. 3).

Spencer knew his collection could be of tremendous research value. He was keenly disappointed that few knew of it, fewer still utilized it and most of all that little was being published in the way of source-based history. All the while his experience and instincts told him much more material was in attics, shoeboxes, church closets, even chicken houses (Spencer, 1965a, p. 41–42).

To break this logjam, in 1930 he proposed a cooperative society. No one took him seriously, a few scoffed and one of them, Edgar C. Riley, Superintendent of Kentucky Female Orphan Home (which housed a sizeable library), candidly admitted the few Disciple colleges with collections would not cooperate because of the "promotional value" of their respective holdings. In other words, they leveraged nostalgia into fiscal support (Spencer, [ca. 1963]; Spencer & Pierson, 1962, p. 52).

As a librarian and archivist, and therefore as a close reader of history and its underlying sources, Spencer would have read with keen interest five notable books published just after his 1930 proposal. One, the most up-to-date history of the Disciples, and that by a trained historian, relied on mainstream periodicals, widely available debates and other massproduced published monographs, but no manuscript or archival materials (Garrison, 1931). Similarly, while a pair of biographies of Alexander Campbell (Kellems, 1930; Smith, 1930) anticipated a wider use of print materials, neither utilized archival materials because such were simply unavailable. Charles Crossfield Ware issued a monumental biography of Barton Warren Stone rooted in an array of print sources heretofore unused by earlier historians (Ware, 1932). Alonzo Willard Fortune relied heavily on manuscripts in detailing a chronicle of Disciples events in Kentucky (Fortune, 1932). These monographs suggested of great possibilities for source-based critical research. At the same time, Spencer's nagging concern was the relative scarcity and inaccessibility of primary sources that could support new breakthroughs in Disciples historical and biographical studies.

In about 1933–1934 he proposed to collectors, historians and preachers a membership-based "Historical Research Association of the Disciples of Christ" the goals of which included fostering and encouraging historical study (including its publication), the identification and exchange of source material, and the creation of a union catalog and other research aids (Spencer, 1933–1934). His proposals again fell flat. "By the middle 1930s, I was rather discouraged because, seemingly, no one was interested in any co-operative organization and no one knew anything about the Henry Barton Robison Collection at Culver-Stockton or what we were attempting to do there" (Spencer, 1959a, p. 6).

However, George L. Peters heavily utilized the Robison Collection for his history of Missouri Disciples. Spencer in turn helped Peters, the first in-depth reference assistance he provided (Spencer & Pierson, 1962). Peters' acknowledgment of the Robison Collection's value and Spencer's assistance catalyzed the visibility and legitimacy Spencer long hoped for (Peters, 1937).

Shortly thereafter, Spencer formed friendships with two well-connected scholars whose advocacy launched the Culver-Stockton collection to national prominence and prepared the way for establishment of Disciples of Christ Historical Society. In 1937 Professor George N. Mayhew recruited Culver-Stockton students for the Disciples Divinity House at the School of Religion of Vanderbilt University. After meeting Spencer and seeing the collection "he stayed an extra day to talk about it and became enthused about the organization of a society" (Spencer, 1959a, p. 7). Then, J. Edward Moseley, Assistant Editor of the pre-eminent Disciple periodical, *Christian-Evangelist*, came to Canton to prepare the seventy-fifth anniversary issue of that paper. He came for an afternoon but stayed three days (Spencer & Pierson, 1962). "We had long talks," Spencer remembered,

> concerning what would be done for the collecting and using of Disciple material. He became convinced that a society should be formed and that the proper way to do it was to work through the International Convention. Since he was traveling about 35,000 miles a year attending all kinds of Disciple meetings, he had the opportunity to talk with the entire national leadership of the Brotherhood. Largely, through his work, a resolution was passed in the 1939 International Convention at Richmond, Virginia that a historical commission should be set up to consider the best way in which the historical materials of the Brotherhood could be preserved [Spencer, 1959a, p. 7].

The president of the International Convention in 1939 was Roger T. Nooe, colleague of Mayhew at Vanderbilt and pastor of Vine Street Christian Church in Nashville, Tennessee, the home congregation of a young woman who was rapidly establishing herself as the preeminent biographer of Alexander Campbell. Eva Jean Wrather, too, by 1939 understood the value of the Robison Collection and benefited first hand from Spencer's curatorial expertise and leveraged her influence to sustain the Historical Commission. W. P. Harman was named chairman; Colby D. Hall, vice-chairman; and Eva Jean Wrather, secretary. Other founding members included J. Edward Moseley, Merl R. Eppse, A. T. DeGroot, C. C. Ware, A. W. Fortune, and Claude E. Spencer, who was present but whose name was omitted from the published program. Eva Jean Wrather wrote his name in her copy of the program indicating his presence (Program, 1941). Since an International Convention was not held in 1940, the Commission next met at the 1941 convention to form the Disciples of Christ Historical Society. They elected J. Edward Moseley as president; W. H. Hanna, vice-president; A. T. DeGroot, secretary-treasurer; and Claude E. Spencer, curator, a position he held until retirement in 1965.

Spencer supplied the Society with its foundational vision, essentially unchanged from his 1930s proposals. The only modification to emerge by 1941 was an enlarged scope and a heightened sense of urgency. As curator he liaised among collectors, colleges, seminaries, publishing houses, and other libraries. He secured goodwill, fostered cooperation, raised awareness of the Robison collection, and advocated for the need to preserve historical material. "As word got around of the organization of the Society," Spencer said, "we began to receive letters offering materials.... It would seem that many people had been waiting for just such an organization to be formed before disposing of many valuable and cherished items" (Spencer, 1959a, p. 8, see also Seale, 1991). The growth of the Society's holdings in this way was beyond what most of the founders imagined in 1941. "I think everybody except maybe two there would have said, 'You are crazy,'" Spencer remembered, "[except] Eva Jean Wrather and myself" (Spencer & Pierson, 1962, p. 53). Crazy or not, those involved knew then they launched something special. Ronald Osborn remembered,

> In the early days, when the Board was made up of penniless history buffs, the high point of our meetings was not the business sessions but Spencer's guided tour through the archives to point out new acquisitions and to encourage our professional gloating [Osborn, 1976, p. 17].

"WE WANT IT!" An Archivist's Dream

What Spencer lacked of the requisite political and personal connections to be effectual in the promotional game Edgar Riley described in 1930. Instead he collected out of his inner proclivities, by his perception that the need was great, the field was wide open, and the material available if it could be located and the owners persuaded of his competence and trustworthiness.

Beginning with Alexander Campbell himself in the 1830s, Disciples in every generation called for preservation of historic materials but none materialized because no one followed through, either out of lack of time to adequately pursue the idea to reality, the means and wherewithal to handle the material when it did trickle in, or both (Spencer, 1959a). Claude Spencer, however, was trained in the emerging theory, science, and practice of professional librarianship. Spencer's relative ignorance of Disciples literature in 1924 initiated an iterative process of discovery and rediscovery. As he read to locate materials, he acquired as much as he could, catalogued it and by virtue of this process discerned, as only a trained librarian could, the gaps in the available literature. In some cases the materials were unknown to the historians, in other cases excellent relevant material was overlooked or ignored either by carelessness or its inaccessibility, in still other cases it seems no one created literature in certain areas. By virtue of cataloging activities, Spencer noticed where the literature (and his collection) was robust, where it was lean, and where it was nonexistent.

As an archivist, he dreamed of a comprehensive collection that could fully support any kind of research inquiry. He modeled this expansive philosophy on the work of the Missouri Historical Society, of which he was a member. There, they simply sought almost anything and everything by or about Missouri and its history. Likewise, for Disciples, Spencer pled, "If there is anything that deals with the restoration movement in any manner, shape or form, not now in the collection," he wrote in 1941, "WE WANT IT" (Spencer, 1941a, p. 13, emphasis in original; see also Whitehill, 1962).

He first sought books published by or about Disciple on religious topics, then religious works published by or about the Christian Connection and Churches of Christ. He finally expanded his scope to include religious fiction and poetry by and about these groups. In every case he sought all editions, printings and binding variations. He expansively defined "published" to include "not only books and periodicals, but all kind of miscellaneous items, such as pamphlets, broadsides, posters, pictures, badges, programs, etc." (Spencer, 1941a, p. 13).

He also sought personal papers, diaries, sermons, photographs, account books, congregational, institutional, and organizational records, plus realia and artifacts. In this way his work reflects a marked shift from earlier collectors or his peers in college and seminary libraries. No one attempted to collect the types and kinds of Discipliana (a term he coined) on the scale he pursued. He viewed each item as a carrier of information that could, given excellent description, preservation and accessibility, support historical study.

The awareness Spencer's work generated for the Society was beyond his capacity to manage. Materials flooded in at a pace that made timely processing and cataloging difficult. In 1947 the Society received gifts of materials and funds "from 162 individuals in 32 states, the District of Columbia, New Zealand and South Africa. An additional 100 organizations, publishers, and institutions sent publications issued by them ... and in addition to answering many reference questions by mail, the curator was able to give advice and information to nine individuals who came to headquarters" (Yearbook, 1948, p. 124). In 1953–1954 some "588 receipts were issued to 332 different individuals, churches, organizations and institutions, as compared with 410 issued in 1952 to 244 persons.... [A total of] 9,683 pieces of material were received in 1952 as compared with 14,913 pieces in 1953 ... 279 periodicals are received regularly as exchanges" and "353 reference and public services interactions were logged, 203 of them by personal visit, mail or telephone, and 19 were instances of counseling for theses" (Yearbook, 1954, p. 50). The year Spencer retired, 1965, the Society received

> 1,169 lots of materials from 738 sources ... an all-time record for the number of contributors. Contributions came from 433 individuals, 252 churches, and 53 agencies, organizations and publishers. In addition, more than 225 general periodicals of Christian Churches and Churches of Christ, and newsletters and Sunday worship bulletins from more than 1,100 churches were received regularly ... requests for information and services by mail were slightly over 600 ... 1,030 visitors from 33 states and seven foreign countries visited the Society headquarters for research or tours [Yearbook, 1965, pp. 89–90].

"There is yet a great deal to do": A Curator's Vision

As described above, Spencer's knowledge of Disciples history grew iteratively and reciprocally with his discovery and understanding of the scope and depth of the literature. Each facet informed the other to forged expertise "the hard way"—a page at a time, a book at a time, a tract at a time. The insight gained from attentive persistence suited him exceptionally well to curate library and archival materials. Spencer's work was inherently user-focused. He self-consciously performed it for the benefit of students, faculty, research workers, graduate students involved in any phase of American church history as it related to Disciples, and interested members of Stone-Campbell congregations.

His enduring curatorial work appeared in print in 1941 when he issued the first of three aids for researchers, each a path-breaking and enduring compilation. *Theses Con-*

cerning the Disciples of Christ (Spencer, 1941d; see also 1941b, 1965c) listed all known theses by and about Disciples on religious and historical topics in just 54 leaves containing 196 entries, more than doubling the list of 80 by DeGroot and Dowling (DeGroot & Dowling, 1933). His student assistants mimeographed it and he hand-stitched and bound the limited press run of 125 copies (Lemmon, 1942; Spencer, 1941c, 1956). By 1956 he prepared 277 additional entries; his last publication while employed by the Society was a completely revised and updated edition noting 743 graduate and professional theses and dissertations by 701 authors writing at 89 institutions. Like the first edition, Spencer mimeographed and hand-bound them (Spencer, 1964). It remains an indispensable tool (compare Barrow, 1955; O'Brien, 2009 with Lollar, [ca. 1995]; Meredith, 2005).

In 1942 he issued *A List of Publications of the Standard Publishing Company, Cincinnati, Ohio*. At the time, Cincinnati-based Standard was the most prolific publisher among Disciples. Spencer understood it was incomplete, containing only the known books and pamphlets and no periodical, curricular or Sunday School materials, yet pressed forward with publication to generate interest and facilitate research. He listed the 531 entries first in chronological order by date of publication, then alphabetically by author and title. A third section, proposed but never issued, was to have listed titles alphabetically. These arrangements reveal he intended to make a large body of data easily accessible so a scholar could systematically mine Standard Publications for their yield of insight into Disciple thought. He anticipated, but never issued, a similar list for the Christian Board of Publication and its predecessor Christian Publishing Company, both of St. Louis (Spencer, 1942a, 1942b).

In 1943 he issued *Periodicals of the Disciples of Christ and Related Religious Groups* (Spencer, 1943), an original work twenty years in the making. It was "the first attempt at a comprehensive list of the periodicals of the Disciples of Christ, the Christian church, and the churches of Christ ... [comprising] every periodical designed for more than individual church circulation" (Spencer, 1943, p. iii). He included 1,100 entries in alphabetical order under the last title used, with references to earlier titles. Where known he included also "the places of publication, the inclusive volume numbers, the inclusive dates of publication, the names of the editor or editors ... previous titles with inclusive dates, and other notes tending to identify the periodicals" all of which he secured "through actual examination of the periodical, through a careful search of the news notes in hundreds of volumes of periodicals, and through lists and statements made by others working in this field" (Spencer, 1943, pp. iii-iv). In carrying out this work he consulted with colleagues and peers from across the Stone-Campbell spectrum: from the Christian Publishing Company, the Standard Publishing Company and Gospel Advocate Publishing Company, to C. C. Ware, Edgar Riley and Don Carlos Janes. Such cooperation on behalf of research aids in service to historians and authors proved to be an enduring facet of Spencer's ethos.

Periodicals was so thorough and definitive it has endured unsurpassed as a bibliography; by contrast Garrison listed just under 70 and DeGroot and Dowling listed 80 titles (see DeGroot & Dowling, 1933; Garrison, 1923; Garrison, 1943). W. T. Moore (1909) famously quipped, "The Disciples have no Diocesan Bishops, and consequently their leading religious periodicals have practically occupied that place" (p. 12). Lin D. Cartwright (1958), editor of *Christian-Evangelist*, succinctly stated in 1958 "it was within the pages of the earliest journals that the major doctrines of the Disciples were forged" (p. 7). Henry Shaw (1960) elaborated, saying that not only are periodicals the "backbone of seminary reference material" they are *the* primary source from which material is gathered for most books. Many of the important books connected with Disciples' history were first a series of articles in some religious journal. Each article in turn was based on other articles in some other periodical [p. 3, emphasis in original].

He further explained how in the periodicals "writers who would never author books have found expression for their views ... even if only in the lowly letters to the editor" (Shaw, 1960, p. 9; see also Barrow, 1955). Until Spencer produced his checklist, researchers and librarians could not comprehend the vastness, much less the texture and variety, of Disciples periodical literature. Though he never revised it, Spencer maintained his files and by 1957 discovered an additional 400 titles.

In 1946 Spencer issued his magnum opus. W. W. Greg's comment about enumerative bibliography captures the reason why no bibliography of Disciples literature appeared until Spencer's 1946 *Author Catalog*. "Before books can be studied," W. W. Greg writes, "they must be known to exist and survive, and it is therefore evident that one of the first tasks of bibliography is enumeration. Enumeration involves description, and description involves intensive study of the books described" (Greg, 1945, p. 25; see also Harlow, 1956). Claude Spencer was uniquely qualified and uniquely willing to undertake a project demanding the type of assiduous labor Greg described. Few before Spencer had the inclination to attempt archival collection and bibliographic description at all, and no one among them had the training or sensitivity to bibliographic conventions, much less the vision of the potential utility of the discovery tools, to do it well. Those who compiled checklists were either church historians with course loads and administrative duties or preachers with weekly sermon deadlines and pastoral duties. Spencer, however, had trained student assistants and administrators who freed his time with a sabbatical to make the contribution only he was uniquely suited to provide (Spencer, 1942c, 1944c, and 1945a).

An Author Catalog of Disciples of Christ and Related Religious Groups appeared in 1946 with 10,000 entries, a monumental achievement that "insofar as is known, [was] the first time that any American Protestant body has ever published such a master list of authors and titles" (Moseley, 1946, p. iii). A. T. DeGroot's review in *Christian-Evangelist* said,

> From this date forward there is no excuse, except inadequate investment of time, for the writing of incomplete history of the Disciples and the Churches of Christ. The sources are designated here, for all who will creep through its large triple-columned pages, to read [DeGroot, 1946, p. 1246].

C. E. Lemmon (1947) said "it is an important reference work for any library of church affiliation or for any scholar who would make a pretense to an understanding of Disciple history" (p. 16). Nelson Burr (1961) heralded it as "the most scholarly and extensive work in the field" of Disciple literature (p. 289; see also Prucha, 1987). In 1989 Karl Frantz of the American Theological Library Association (ATLA) Preservation Office, asked the Campbell-Stone librarians "if they would be willing to compile a monograph list of Discipliana for the [ATLA monograph preservation] project. Group opinion was that such a list is already available in Claude E. Spencer's *An Author Catalog*" (American Theological Library Association [ATLA], 1989, p. 72).

Bibliographic work was not only a constant feature of Spencer's daily routine, he repeatedly published his findings to foster additional research. His bibliographies on hymnody (Spencer, 1950), Christian unity (Spencer, 1955) and Alexander Campbell (Spencer, 1966; see also O'Brien, 2009) and his enumerative lists on such diverse topics as Disciple poets (Spencer, 1959b), Disciple West Virginia imprints (Norona, 1958) and Disciple educational institutions, some 485 of them in the revised edition (Spencer, 1965c) broke new ground as he surfaced previously unnoticed textures and variations within Disciple thought and literature.

Further, under his direction Disciples of Christ Historical Society located and published key, and yet truly scarce, primary source documents in their occasional *Footnotes to Disciples History* series. Through his curatorial work the reading public had wide access for the first time in over a century to materials like Alexander Campbell's "Lunenburg Letter," Rice Haggard's "Address … on the Christian Name" and McVay and Campbell's 1834 "Report" (Spencer 1953, 1954b, 1957).

Yet, undaunted even in late career he sailed into uncharted bibliographic waters when in 1963 he completed *The Christian-Evangelist Index*. The 12-member planning group of historians, librarians, editors, and publishers he convened in 1955 agreed the preeminent nationwide organ of news and thought among Disciples, the *Christian-Evangelist* was ripe for indexing. The team agreed to index authors and subjects of all articles and editorials, plus headline news items, book reviews, letters to the editors and obituaries. Such an index for a century's worth of periodical literature would open entirely new vistas for research at the micro and macro levels. He assembled a full run of the entire paper, then microfilmed it while his team of five indexers, plus a dozen typists, file clerks and other assistants completed some 250,000 index entries in time for the paper's centennial celebration (Spencer, 1962). Upon publication it was lauded as a key to unlock "an almost unworked gold-mine of valuable material" (Pierson, 1963, p. 166).

Claude Spencer formally retired from Disciples of Christ Historical Society on 30 June 1965 and vacationed the remainder of the summer. On 1 October he, with one assistant indexer, began an even more ambitious indexing project for *Christian Standard*. The Cincinnati–based *Christian Standard* was the other major periodical voice among Disciples. As a weekly it contained substantially more and larger pages than *Christian-Evangelist*.

By 1972 a staff of 19 produced entry cards for the authors and subjects of every article and editorial; all head line news items of individuals, churches, organizations and institutions; all obituaries, book reviews, poems, marriage notices, illustrations, and news of congregations under state headings. Spencer regretted that space and time constraints precluded indexing of personal news notes and news in general columns. In 1965 he projected the index would yield 300,000 entries. In reality, his team generated 600,000 entries not including cross-references (Spencer, 1965d, 1972).

It was a fitting capstone project for a long career devoted to the acquisition, description, and accessibility of information objects. In his foreword to the *Index*, James DeForest Murch stated it is "believed to be the largest of its kind in religious journalism" (Murch, 1972, p. ix). Fellow librarian Roscoe M. Pierson said he could find no comparable index for a weekly journal covering a century of publication. Of this "unparalleled venture," Pierson said it was "scrupulously done, little has escaped Dr. Spencer's net that would be of interest to either the scholar or the amateur" (Pierson, 1974, p. 15).

One additional aspect of Spencer's curatorial services must be mentioned. His wide reading and familiarity with the literature led him to propose several avenues of research years before anyone took them up in terms of theses, dissertations or monographs. In 1938 at a Round Table Club meeting at the Canton Public Library Spencer read a paper in which he sketched in thumbnail fashion the basic historical circumstances, issues and personalities of the Disciples with special reference to the literature. "Although so much has been done in the field of historical research," he said, "there is yet a great deal to do" (Spencer, [ca. 1938], p. 3). Not only did he recognize fertile fields of study decades ahead of other historians, he urged students to take up neglected and important topics in formal research projects.

"When Brother Peters wrote his <u>History of the Disciples in Missouri</u>," he said, "there was found to be very little material in regard to the colored church. Someone needs to spend several years hunting source material and writing about <u>The Colored Disciples</u>" (Spencer, [ca. 1938], p. 7; compare Spencer, 1946b). Lawrence Burnley describes historiographical situation and Spencer's role in encouraging a remedy.

> The problem of neglect regarding black agency within the historiography of the Christian Church in general, and its educational mission in particular, is one that has long been recognized. In November 1954, Claude E. Spencer ... wrote to Elmer Lewis saying, "There have been no theses, so far as I know, written concerning Negro education among Disciples of Christ. In fact, the whole problem of our Negro work is a much neglected field and one in which much work could be done profitably" [Burnley, 2008, pp. 5–6; see also Lewis, 1957].

Lewis's study paved the way for Lyda (1972), *The Untold Story* (1976), and Burnley (2008). Marvin D. Williams oversaw production, with Spencer's input and suggestions, in 1971 of *A Preliminary Guide to Black Materials at Disciples of Christ Historical Society. (Preliminary Guide,* 1971).

In his next comment in his Round Table speech, Spencer said,

> Today women are accepted in the church and have a voice in church affairs on an almost equal footing as men. Not so in our pioneer churches. When did the change come, and why? The Place of Women in the churches of the Disciples should be the answer [Spencer, (ca. 1938), p. 7].

Twenty-five years later he issued an article and a bibliography in *Discipliana* (Spencer, 1963b, 1963c); in time full studies by Lollis (1970) and Hull (1994) followed. Virginia Hughes describes how Spencer's enumerative list of educational institutions suggests vast untapped areas of historical inquiry when she states how Spencer noted the Christian Church operated over forty educational institutions for women prior to 1865 (Hughes, 1994).

"There must be no partiality": A Theologian's Conviction

Disciple theologian and historian Howard Short recognized the latent power of source material to shape meaning-making by virtue of how it shapes history-writing: "The direction the brotherhood takes may easily be determined by what is collected, preserved, studied and interpreted under the auspices of the Disciples of Christ Historical Society." Short also recognized two qualities in Spencer, "We have a curator whose knowledge of his task and devotion to it I do not expect to see repeated in this generation" (Short, 1961, p. 9). This paper heretofore dealt with Spencer's knowledge; in this section I shall describe and set in context a certain kind of devotion that I characterize as the theological subjunctive undergirding Spencer's work.

Claude Spencer's praxis of archival science reflects the modern turn, most notably and fundamentally his organization of the mountainous accessions into discrete units, no larger nor smaller than the seminal *fonds* of their creators. Further, his unrelenting and vocal commitment to an impartial manner of collection development and discharge public services would elicit Schellenberg's highest praise (Schellenberg, 2003). Yet, a close reading of his constant pleas in the pages of *Discipliana*, though, reveal a man who was too well-read in the polemic literature of the Christian Churches and Churches of Christ to naively think that a pure or undetached neutrality was possible. His legacies, rather, are the sleuthed materials of his heritage, their container lists, finding aids, and descriptive bibliographies. The collection he assembled and his service to the public reveal his commitments. Knowing the traditions as he did, he chose to transcend altogether the modern illusion of neutrality by practicing the Christian virtue of charity.

In the 1920s it became clear to Spencer, as it was clear to anyone reading Disciples literature, the fellowship was under considerable strain. When he launched *Discipliana* in 1941 the first editorial, penned by a student under his supervision, stated "the editors shall do their best to remain neutral and express no personal opinions on controversial subjects since controversy is not a part of the purpose of this quarterly" (Robison, 1941, p. 10). A short while later he said "as in the past our opinions will be bibliographical instead of theological. The collection and DISCIPLIANA want to serve all types of thought throughout the Brotherhood" (Spencer, 1944b, p. 11). Readers responded by sending materials. The following year receipts came from 32 states, District of Columbia, Canada and England from a donor base that was "truly representative" of "various shades of thought" among Disciples. The Society under Spencer's counsel was the "common meeting ground for all persons interested in the collection, preservation and use of the manuscript and printed materials of our movement," he said (Spencer, 1945b, p. 31).

His activity aligned with his rhetoric, as he argued in a 1954 *Discipliana* editorial.

> An historical society must be impartial in its collection of materials. The sources for the study of any one group must not be built up while those other groups are neglected. Materials for research should have no limitations.
>
> There must be no partiality toward favored groups in the use of the materials. And every research student must be allowed to form his own interpretation about what he reads.
>
> We have tried to follow in our collecting of materials and in our giving of service these principles of impartiality, and we believe that we have succeeded. We do know that members of Churches of Christ and "Independents" have used our facilities equally with "cooperatives," and our treatment of each has been the same. Everyone has been welcome [Spencer, 1954a, p. 44].

A refrain repeated in his Yearbook reports reads,

> The resources of the Society are open to all persons, regardless of race or creed, and the curator at all times is willing to advise graduate students, research workers, and all who are seeking a knowledge concerning the Disciples of Christ, Churches of Christ and the Christian Church. The Society is not an opinion-forming group [Yearbook, 1952, p. 31].

This stance proved a decisive factor in the decision to relocate the Society from Culver-Stockton to Nashville, in part because of the opportunity for greater relationships with Churches of Christ. This stance endeared the T. W. Phillips family to Spencer's vision to the extent that B. D. Phillips agreed to fully fund real estate and construction costs for a million-dollar facility, dedicated in 1958 (Murch, 1969, 1973; compare T. W. Phillips Memorial, 1958). When opened this facility was hailed as the crown jewel among American Protestant archives facilities.

The researchers who utilized the Society's collection and counted on Spencer's expert consultation were in fact often diametrically opposed to each other in their interpretations of Disciple history. David Edwin Harrell, Jr., in the course of his 1966 Reed Lecture under the Society's auspices forcefully explains than how such a situation could obtain. In it he said,

> My faith, and the traditional legalism of the members of the Churches of Christ, has nothing to offer "Christianity" in the broad sense of the term. Theologically, I have nothing in common with a modern liberal. We have two totally different religious minds. I am much closer to a Primitive Baptist, or a Seventh-Day Adventist, or a medieval Roman Catholic than I am to a liberal Disciple. As a historian, I hope that I understand his mind, but I do not share it. Reconciliation is inconceivable.
>
> The only common ground which gives meaning to this lecture series, from my point of view, is the one that this building symbolizes and that this society is a tangible expression of. We have a common interest in the contradictory figures of the past from whom, curiously enough, we all learned our lessons. It is fitting that we meet here to discuss the paradoxes of the past, the diversity of the harvest, the perplexing meaning of the Disciples heritage [Harrell, 1967, p. 44].

The Society's president, Willis Jones, shared Spencer's basic outlook. Harrell praised Jones as one "who leaves behind a heritage of understanding and appreciation of diversity which has been the key to the success of the Society as a scholarly institution … [he] convinced me that he believed that an historical society of American Disciples must provide a platform for conservative pronouncements well as liberal" (Harrell, 1970, p. 28).

This ethos on Spencer's part was born first of all in the pews of the Shiloh Church of Christ in Neeper, Missouri. There when the congregation honored John Prickett's convictions and refrained from using an organ in worship, Claude learned at an early age that conscientious students of the Bible could reach differing conclusions about some matter of doctrine or practice and still defer to each other in love. Further, he modeled this kind of charity in his professional life—in his collecting practices and public service—as a virtue he wished for his spiritual kin.

Conclusion: The Remarkable Claude Spencer

It is remarkable that a boy who learned to read at age nine would five years later become de facto librarian of his high school, and five years after that lead the library at his college in exchange for tuition, room and board. It is remarkable that a librarian who would not have known a Disciple book if it hit him in the head would compile a bibliography so authoritative it remains unsurpassed after seventy years. It is remarkable that he formed a collegial society to serve the academy and the congregation, the graduate seminary and the Sunday School roundtable. It is remarkable that he maintained an unrelenting commitment to charity and equal representation in collecting scope in the face of bitter intramural disputes over bureaucracy the very existence of which fractured the ecclesial fellowship he loved and served the entirety of his career. It is remarkable that he recognized the need for, and advocated for needed research topics that were years ahead of their time. It is remarkable that though he held no degree beyond the *ars baccalaureus* in education, no less than 84 master's theses and doctoral dissertations credit his advice, counsel, and assistance. It is remarkable that he attained expertise with minimal formal coursework and professional training, but so mastered "library economy" and was so productive in keeping up a demanding schedule, that the upon his retirement he was replaced by two and one-half full-time equivalents with graduate degrees in history, library science, and theology.

Spencer's legacy survives in the several bibliographic works he authored, in the catalog records he generated, in the finding aids he assembled, and in the indexes he compiled. His legacy survives among the holdings of Disciples of Christ Historical Society, of which he was visionary and architect. His legacy endures in the community of librarians, archivists, historians, students and independent scholars he formed. His legacy endures in the scholarship he facilitated by virtue of his quiet diligence in collecting, organizing, describing, preserving, and advocacy for print and archival materials of the Stone-Campbell heritage, consisting of the Christian Churches, the Churches of Christ, the Christian Church (Disciples of Christ) and related groups.

References

Allen, A. N. (1972). *42 years on the hill*. New York: Vantage Press.
American Theological Library Association. (1989). Proceedings from ATLA '89. *Summary of proceedings: Forty-third annual conference, June 19–22, 1989*.
Barrow, J. G. (1955). *A bibliography of bibliographies in religion*. Ann Arbor: Edwards Brothers.
Board of education and work of our colleges. (1928). *World Call, 10*(12), 40.
[Book of Letters] Presented to Claude E. Spencer, '22 at a Dinner honoring his Twenty-Five Years as Librarian of Culver-Stockton College. (1947, October 24). Claude E. Spencer Papers (AC 80-17, Box 5). Disciples of Christ Historical Society, Bethany, WV.
Burnley, L. A. (2008). *The cost of unity: African-American agency and education in the Christian Church, 1865–1914*. Macon: Mercer University Press.
Burr, N. R. (1961). *A critical bibliography of religion in America*. Princeton: Princeton University Press.
Cartwright, L. D. (1958). The influence of the religious journal upon the life and development of the Disciples of Christ, delivered at the 5th annual president's dinner, Nashville, Tennessee, September 14, 1958. [Typescript speech]. Disciples of Christ Historical Society, Nashville.
[Clipping]. Claude E. Spencer Papers (AC 80-17, Box 1, Clippings). Disciples of Christ Historical Society, Bethany, WV.
Culver-Stockton College. (1918). *Annual catalogue for the sixty-first session, 1917–1918*. Canton: Culver-Stockton College.
Culver-Stockton College. (1919). *Annual catalogue for the sixty-second session, 1918–1919*. Canton: Culver-Stockton College.
Culver-Stockton College. (1920). *The Culver-Stockton College Bulletin, 6*(4), 9, 90.
Culver-Stockton College. (1921). *The Culver-Stockton College Bulletin, 7*(5), 17–18, 11.
Culver-Stockton College. (1923). *The Culver-Stockton College Bulletin, 9*(2), 18–22, 73, 106.
Culver-Stockton has new librarian. (1951, September 21). *Herald-Whig*, Quincy, IL.
DeGroot, A. T., & Dowling, E. E. (1933). *The literature of the Disciples of Christ*. Advance, IN: Hustler Print.
DeGroot, A. T. (1946). Month's survey of books. *Christian-Evangelist*, p. 1246.
[Editorial]. (1921). Restoration literature. *Christian Standard, 56*(24), 2010.
Elliott, A. M. (1936). History of certification of librarians in Missouri. *The University of Missouri Bulletin, 37*(12), 17–19, 54.
Fortune, A. W. (1932). *The Disciples in Kentucky*. The Convention of the Christian Churches in Kentucky.
Garrison, W. E. (1923). The literature of the Disciples of Christ. *Bulletin of the Disciples Divinity House of the University of Chicago*. April 1–18.
Garrison, W. E. (1931). *Religion follows the frontier: A history of the Disciples of Christ*. New York: Harper & Brothers.
Garrison, W. E. (1943). Books received. *Christian Century, 60*(50), 1474.
Greg, W. W. (1945). Bibliography, a retrospect. *The Bibliographical Society, 1892–1942: Studies in retrospect*. London.
Grotzinger, L. (1992). Remarkable beginnings: The first half century of the Graduate School of Library and Information Science. In W. C. Allen and R. F. Delzell (Eds.), *Ideals and standards: The history of the University of Illinois Graduate School of Library and Information Science*. Urbana: Graduate School of Library and Information Science, University of Illinois.
Harlow, N. (1956). The well-tempered bibliographer. *The Papers of the Bibliographical Society of America, 50*(1), 28–39.
Harrell, D. E., Jr. (1967). Peculiar people: A rationale for modern conservative Disciples. In *Disciples and the church universal*. Nashville: Disciples of Christ Historical Society.
Harrell, D. E., Jr. (1970). Willis R. Jones from a conservative perspective. *Discipliana, 30*(2), 28.
Horn, M. H. (1933). Culver-Stockton library. *World Call, 70*(12), 386.
Hughes, V. M. (1994). *A systems approach to changes in roles and positions of women in the life of the church*. (Unpublished doctoral dissertation). Berkeley: Graduate Theological Union.
Hull, D. (1994). *Christian Church women: Shapers of a movement*. St. Louis: Chalice Press.
International Convention of Disciples of Christ. (1941). *Program of the International Convention of Disciples*

of Christ to be held in the Municipal Auditorium, May 1–7, 1941, St. Louis, Missouri. Indianapolis: International Convention of Disciples of Christ.
Kellems, J. R. (1930). *Alexander Campbell and the Disciples.* New York: Richard R. Smith.
Lee, G. R. (1984). *Culver-Stockton College, The First 130 Years.* Canton: Culver-Stockton College.
Lemmon, C. E. (1942). Book Chat. *World Call, 24*(5), 47.
Lemmon, C. E. (1947). Book chat. *World Call, 29*(1), 16.
Lewis, E. C. (1957). A history of secondary and higher education in Negro schools related to the Disciples of Christ. (Unpublished doctoral dissertation). Pittsburgh: University of Pittsburgh.
[List of students]. (1923, October). *Illinois Libraries, 5*(4), 74.
Lollar, S. (ca. 1995). *Dissertations pertaining to the American restoration movement.* N.p.
Lollis, L. (1970). *The shape of Adam's rib: A lively history of women's work in the Christian Church.* St. Louis: Bethany Press.
Lyda, H. (1972). A history of black Christian Churches (Disciples of Christ) in the United States through 1899. (Unpublished doctoral dissertation). Nashville: Vanderbilt University.
Meredith, D. (2005). Theological doctoral studies by members of Churches of Christ, 1904–2004. In W. Lewis and H. Rollmann (Eds.), *Restoring the first-century church in the twenty-first century: Essays on the Stone-Campbell restoration movement in honor of Don Haymes* (pp. 397–421). Eugene, OR: Wipf and Stock.
Missouri Library Commission (1932). *Annual Report of the Missouri Library Commission.* Jefferson City: Missouri Library Commission.
Mode, P. G. (1921). *Source book and bibliographical guide for American church history.* Menasha, WI: George Banta.
Monser, J. W. (1906). *The literature of the Disciples: A study.* St. Louis: Christian.
Moore, W. T. (1909). *A comprehensive history of the Disciples of Christ.* New York: Fleming H. Revell.
Moseley, J. E. (1946). Foreword. In Spencer, *An author catalog of Disciples of Christ and related religious groups*, p. iii. Canton, MO: Disciples of Christ Historical Society.
Murch, J. D. (1969). *B. D. Phillips: Life and letters.* Published privately.
Murch, J. D. (1972). Foreword. In *Christian Standard index: 1866–1966.* Nashville: Disciples of Christ Historical Society.
Murch, J. D. (1973). *Adventuring with Christ in changing times.* Louisville: Restoration Press.
Norona, D. (1958). *West Virginia imprints 1790–1863: A checklist of books, newspapers, periodicals and broadsides.* Moundsville: West Virginia Library Association.
O'Brien, E. J. (2009). The wilderness, the nation, and the electronic era: American Christianity and religious communication, 1620–2000: An annotated bibliography. *ATLA Bibliography Series no. 57.* Lanham, MD: Scarecrow Press.
Osborn, R. E. (1976). *Experiment in liberty: The ideal of freedom in the experience of the Disciples of Christ.* St. Louis: Bethany Press.
Patterson, H. L. (1920). *Patterson's American Educational Directory.* Chicago: American Educational Company.
Peters, G. L. (1937). *The Disciples of Christ in Missouri: Celebrating one hundred years of cooperative work.* The Centennial Commission of Missouri Convention of Disciples of Christ.
Peters, G. L. (1941). *Dreams come true: A history of Culver-Stockton College.* Canton: Culver-Stockton College.
Pierson, R. M. (1963). The Christian-Evangelist index: 1863–1958. *Register of the Kentucky Historical Society, 61*(2), 165–166.
Pierson, R. M. (1974). [Review of Christian Standard Index]. *Discipliana, 34*(1), 14–15.
Preliminary guide to black materials in the Disciples of Christ Historical Society (1971). Nashville: Disciples of Christ Historical Society.
Program of the International Convention of Disciples of Christ to be held in the Municipal Auditorium, May 1–7, 1941, St. Louis, Missouri. (1941). Indianapolis: International Convention of Disciples of Christ.
Prucha, F. P. (1987). *Handbook for research in American history: A guide to bibliographical and other reference works.* Lincoln: University of Nebraska Press.
Robinson, C. B. (1941). Editorial policy. *Discipliana, 1*(1), 10.
Schellenberg, T. R. (2003). *Modern archives, principles & techniques.* Chicago: Society of American Archivists.
Seale, J. M. (1991). *Forward from the past: The first fifty years of the Disciples of Christ Historical Society.* Nashville: Disciples of Christ Historical Society.
Shaw, H. K. (1960). Having fun with periodicals: An address delivered at the dinner meeting of the program in acceptance of the Christian Board of Publication gift of Disciples periodicals and in observance of the eighth anniversary of the move to Nashville by the Disciples of Christ Historical Society. [Typescript speech]. Disciples of Christ Historical Society, Nashville.
Short, H. E. (1961). Heritage of splendor, an address delivered at the 20th anniversary dinner of the Disciples of Christ Historical Society, October 3, 1961, during the International Convention of Christian Churches Assembly. [Typescript speech]. Disciples of Christ Historical Society, Nashville.
Smith, B. L. (1930). *Alexander Campbell.* St. Louis: Bethany Press.

Spencer, C. E. (1933–1934). Plans for the organization of an "Historical Research Association of the Disciples of Christ." [A typescript dated, in Spencer's hand, 1933 or 1934]. Claude E. Spencer Papers (AC 80–17, Box 1, Writings). Disciples of Christ Historical Society, Bethany, WV.

Spencer, C. E. (ca. 1938). [Round Table Paper on Disciples of Christ]. [A typescript speech read at the Canton Public Library]. Claude E. Spencer Papers (AC 80–17, Box 1, Writings). Disciples of Christ Historical Society, Bethany, WV.

Spencer, C. E. (ca. 1940). A National Library for the Disciples of Christ. [A typescript very likely submitted for publication in *Christian-Evangelist* yet not published]. Claude E. Spencer Papers (AC 80–17, Box 1, Writings). Disciples of Christ Historical Society, Bethany, WV.

Spencer, C. E. (1941a). Henry Barton Robison Collection—growth and scope. *Discipliana* 1(2), 13.

Spencer, C. E. (1941b). The collection at the convention. *Discipliana*, 1(2), 20.

Spencer, C. E. (1941c). Historical society publishes first book. *Discipliana*, 1(4), 41.

Spencer, C. E. (1941d). *Theses concerning the Disciples of Christ.* Canton: Disciples of Christ Historical Society.

Spencer, C. E. (1942a). Some new collection projects. *Discipliana*, 2(1), 8.

Spencer, C. E. (1942b). *A List of Publications of the Standard Publishing Company, Cincinnati, Ohio.* Canton: Disciples of Christ Historical Society.

Spencer, C. E. (1942c). The Disciples have published books! *Discipliana*, 2(3), 29.

Spencer, C. E. (1943). *Periodicals of the Disciples of Christ and related religious groups.* Canton: Disciples of Christ Historical Society.

[Spencer, C. E.]. (1944). *The Library, Culver-Stockton College, manual for student assistants.* Canton: Culver-Stockton College. [A typescript manual Spencer issued to each assistant]. Claude E. Spencer Papers (AC 80–17, Box 2, Loose items). Disciples of Christ Historical Society, Bethany, WV.

Spencer, C. E. (1944b). DCHS notes, our membership. *Discipliana*, 4(1), 11

Spencer, C. E. (1944c). 1941–1944. *Discipliana*, 4(2), 21.

Spencer, C. E. (1945a). Research in progress. *Discipliana*, 4(4), 44.

Spencer, C. E. (1945b). DCHS notes, our membership. *Discipliana*, 5(3), 31.

Spencer, C. E. (1946a). *An author catalog of Disciples of Christ and related religious groups.* Canton: Disciples of Christ Historical Society.

Spencer, C. E. (1946b). Negroes in the church. *Discipliana*, 6(1), 8.

Spencer, C. E. (1950). *The Campbell hymn book, a bibliographical study.* Canton: Disciples of Christ Historical Society.

Spencer, C. E. (1953). Introduction. In A. Campbell, The Lunenburg letter with attendant comments. *Footnotes to Disciple history number two.* Nashville: Disciples of Christ Historical Society.

Spencer, C. E. (1954a). We serve. *The Harbinger & Discipliana*, 14(4), 44.

Spencer, C. E. (1954b). Introduction. In Haggard, R. An address to the different religious societies on the sacred import of the Christian name. *Footnotes to Disciple history number four.* Nashville: Disciples of Christ Historical Society.

Spencer, C. E. (1955). Appendix VI-A bibliography of Christian unity: Books and pamphlets by Disciples of Christ. In W.E. Garrison, *Christian unity and Disciples of Christ.* St. Louis: Bethany Press.

Spencer, C. E. (1956). Academic research: theses and dissertations. *Harbinger and Discipliana*, 16(7), 75, 76, 79.

Spencer, C. E. (1957). Introduction. In J.T. M'Vay and A. Campbell, Report of the proceedings of general meeting of messengers from thirteen congregations, held in Wellsburg, VA. On Saturday, the 12th of April, 1834. *Footnotes to Disciple history number five.* Nashville: Disciples of Christ Historical Society.

Spencer, C. E. (1959a). The Disciples of Christ Historical Society, it's early years. [A typewritten paper prepared at the request of Harry M. Davis, Chairman of the DCHS Board of trustees, October 1959]. Claude E. Spencer Papers (AC 80–17, Box 1, Writings). Disciples of Christ Historical Society, Bethany, WV.

Spencer, C. E. (1959b). *Poets, hymn writers, fiction writers and story tellers of the Disciples of Christ.* Charlestown, IN: Mimeographed by Charles Willard.

Spencer, C. E. (1962). Introduction. *The Christian-Evangelist Index 1863–1958.* St. Louis: Christian Board of Publication.

Spencer, C. E. (ca. 1963). [My acquaintance with Joseph Edward Moseley]. [Manuscript authored by Spencer ca. 1963? detailing his first meeting with Moseley and the founding of DCHS]. Claude E. Spencer Papers (AC 80–17, Box 2, J. Edward Moseley). Disciples of Christ Historical Society, Bethany, WV.

Spencer, C. E. (1963b). Women have not been idle. *Discipliana*, 22(6), 83–84.

Spencer, C. E. (1963c). Basic bibliography: Disciples women and the church. *Discipliana*, 22(6), 91–95.

Spencer, C. E. (1964). *Theses concerning Disciples of Christ and related religious bodies* (2d ed.). Nashville: Disciples of Christ Historical Society.

Spencer, C. E. (1965a). From box to box: Or, the random reminiscences of a book collector. *Discipliana*, 25(3), 41–44.

Spencer, C. E. [1965b]. Spencer, Claude Elbert, 1898- (Essential and non-essential facts in his life). [A typewritten professional resume with biographical facts]. Claude E. Spencer Papers (AC 80–17, Box 1, Biographical folder). Disciples of Christ Historical Society, Bethany, WV.

Spencer, C. E. (1965c). *Educational institutions of the Disciples of Christ* (rev. ed.). Nashville: Disciples of Christ Historical Society.
Spencer, C. E. (1965d). The indexing of the Christian Standard, a challenging project. *Discipliana, 25*(4), 51.
Spencer, C. E. (1966). A comprehensive bibliography of Alexander Campbell's writings. In S.M. Eames, *The Philosophy of Alexander Campbell*. Bethany, WV: Bethany College.
Spencer, C. E. (1972). Introduction. In *Christian Standard index, 1866–1966*. Nashville: Disciples of Christ Historical Society.
Spencer, C. E. (1980). [Untitled]. (Biographical notes, undated, authored by Claude Spencer and photocopied "from ½ sheets" in 1980). Claude E. Spencer Papers (AC 80–17, Box 1, Biographical folder). Disciples of Christ Historical Society, Bethany, WV.
Spencer, C. E., & Pierson, R. M. (1962). Spencer-Pierson interview. [Typescript of an interview of Claude Spencer by Roscoe M. Pierson]. Claude E. Spencer Papers (AC 80–17, Box 1, Biographical folder). Disciples of Christ Historical Society, Bethany, WV.
T. W. Phillips memorial. (1958). *Christian Standard, 94*(38), 536.
University of Illinois. (1922). *University of Illinois Annual Register 1921–1922*. Urbana: University of Illinois.
University of Illinois. (1923). *University of Illinois Annual Register 1922–1923*. Urbana: University of Illinois.
The Untold Story, a short history of black Disciples. (1976). St. Louis: Christian Board of Publication.
Ware, C. C. (1932). *Barton Warren Stone, pathfinder of Christian union, a story of his life and times*. St. Louis: Bethany Press.
Whitehill, W. M. (1962). *Independent historical societies, an enquiry into their research and publication functions and their financial future*. Boston: Harvard University Press.
Yearbook of Christian Churches. (1952). Indianapolis: International Convention of Disciples of Christ.
Yearbook of Christian Churches (Disciples of Christ). (1965). Indianapolis: International Convention of Disciples of Christ.
Yearbook of Disciples of Christ (Christian Churches). (1954). Indianapolis: International Convention of Disciples of Christ.
Yearbook of International Convention of Disciples of Christ. (1948). Indianapolis: International Convention of Disciples of Christ.

Libraries in the New Creation

Christian Librarianship as an Extension of the Christian Temple and Priesthood

JACOB W. GUCKER

Abstract

An increasing interest in the historic liturgies of Christian worship in recent years has prompted the question of how such worship contributes to Christian formation. Moreover, philosopher James K. A. Smith has proposed that educators can apply a "liturgical anthropology" to their teaching by educating student desire through bodily practices and rituals, leading them to acquire and appropriate for themselves a vision of "the good" which includes excellence in their field. The present writer has applied Smith's ideas to information literacy instruction in the theological library, proposing a "liturgy" of theological research and shepherding students through it during library workshops. This essay will examine how priesthood in the tabernacle, temple, and church is a fitting metaphor for the librarian vocation. Moreover, it will show how service to library users is an extension of the priesthood of all believers and a recapitulation of God's hospitality through word and sacrament in God's house. This is not merely an extension of abstract Christian ideas or principles but flows from the patterns and practices of Christian life and worship. Viewing Christian librarianship this way can give librarians a vision of their vocation as participation in the Lamb's bride-city of the new creation.

Introduction

Nancy Kalikow Maxwell's 2006 book, *Sacred Stacks: The Higher Purpose of Libraries and Librarianship*, proposes that libraries function as community institutions similar to churches in a secular age. She argues that libraries promote community, uplift society, bestow immortality, preserve and transmit culture, organize chaos, and provide sacred space (Maxwell, 2006). A recent article is highly critical of this association, seeking to "dismantle the idea that librarianship is a sacred calling" because of the harm that can come to librarians as a result of their own attitudes and assumptions about the profession (Ettarh, 2018). If librarians see themselves as heeding a sacred call, it may lead them to overlook injustices against themselves and others by institutional librarianship (Ettarh,

2018). According to Ettarh, Maxwell's book was publishable because "vocational awe" has so saturated the profession (2018). This association of librarianship with the sacred is quite natural for theological librarians and for Christian librarians in non-theological contexts. Many theological librarians only entered the profession because they responded to a more general call to Christian service and found their way into librarianship while completing a theological degree.

This essay will explore the ways in which the Christian concept of priesthood serves as a metaphor for librarianship and how changes in biblical priesthood mirror the changes in librarianship over time. In greater detail, it will explore how librarianship is an extension of Hebrew and Christian priesthood and how librarians can understand their worship and work as direct participation in the great project of New Creation. This will require a discussion of the telos of Christian worship with reference to biblical texts and commentary by Bible scholars.

Priesthood as a Metaphor for Librarianship

Priesthood serves as a metaphor for librarianship because both are mediators. In general, a mediator helps two parties at variance come to terms on an issue. Priesthood is divine-human mediation, but how are librarians mediators? The role of librarians as mediators is discussed in a number of different ways in library literature. For instance, a 1992 issue of *The Reference Librarian* consists entirely of articles on this subject. Hafner and Camarigg discuss several of the ways that librarians require the skills of mediation but note that the "quintessence of librarianship as mediation" is in information retrieval and collection development (1992). People go to the library to answer questions, and librarians serve as mediators when they "relieve the tension between what is knowable and yet still unknown" (Hafner & Camarigg, 1992). Through information retrieval, they resolve the variance between people and the sum total of human knowledge, which is too vast and practically unapproachable without mediation. Through collection development, librarians represent what is known in accordance with the principles and rules of the library profession and the policies of their respective institutions. Librarians "check the influence of their personal prejudices as they discharge their duties" of selecting media which fairly represents human knowledge on a subject (Hafner & Camarigg, 1992).

How does the biblical concept of priesthood compare to the mediation task of librarians? The sum total of human knowledge is unapproachable, and yet it is best for an individual to relate to it and to know something of it. In the same way, it is best for human beings to know God even if He cannot be fully known. God and human beings are generally understood to be at variance in two ways: God is transcendent and human beings are transgressors of divine will. It is thus the role of priests to help people meet with God despite this transcendence and to make atonement for the variance due to human transgression by some divinely ordained means.

Divine-human mediation is different from mediation between human parties in that God has no need to compromise, and humans have no legal case other than to call God to remember His covenant promises. Moreover, God is omniscient and does not need to be made aware of the human position. Any liturgical action such as a prayer or sacrifice which might be considered a memorial to God concerning His covenant obligations or the state of affairs is practically unnecessary. Thus, the service of priests objectifies the variance, as well as the atonement, for the sake of the human. They do this through divinely prescribed words and actions and through the use of sacred objects such as vessels, veils, furniture, and food. Objectifications of this variance, such as a sacred space that cannot be entered without resulting in the death of the transgressor, communicates the facts even to those without the cognitive ability to understand a verbal description.

The priests themselves are not necessarily privy to the exact nature of the variance between a particular human being and God. A priest does not know how a person has transgressed unless there is a confession. In the case of Israel's priests, they would not have known how a person had become ceremonially unclean, whether they had touched a dead body or eaten a forbidden animal, etc. The transgressor would have to appear before the priest and the priest would have to examine the transgressor and objectify the variance in a ceremonial way, such as through a prescribed washing or a word of absolution. The priest had to decide, based upon the Torah or law, how to resolve the variance between the human transgressor and God. This objectification of variance between human beings and God might be compared to the reference interview, which is how librarians assess and atone for the variance between a patron and what is known.

Priests are also responsible for collecting, maintaining, and managing all of the objects necessary for successful mediation. They are responsible for managing the sacred space, partitions, vessels, consumables, etc., of divine-human interaction. Israel's Levitical priesthood was responsible for overseeing the set-up, break-down, and movement of Israel's Tabernacle and everything in it, for example. Due to the ever-present reality of Israel's Tabernacle, which defined life in Israel for a time, there was a constant objective reference for where the nation stood in relation to God. This was literally true in that each of the twelve tribes were given assigned places to camp around the Tabernacle in the wilderness. The Ten Commandments were the written word of God on stone tablets which had been brought down from Mt. Sinai after Israel's inaugural meeting with Yahweh. The priests were responsible for keeping these tablets safe in the Ark of the Covenant. No one in Israel could waltz into the Tabernacle and ask to read them, for the Tabernacle had more than closed stacks, and yet these ten words from heaven shaped their entire lives. The priests were responsible for keeping all the objects of Israel's worship in accordance with Torah. This priestly responsibility might be compared to collection development through which librarians faithfully keep and secure the objectifications of human knowledge. By keeping books, periodicals, paintings, videos, and realia representing the appropriate breadth and depth for their respective institutions, librarians help people access "ideas that span time and distance" (Hafner & Camarigg, 1992).

The change in biblical priesthood from the Old Testament to the New Testament is also comparable to the changes in library mediation. Priesthood in the Old Testament serves as a handy metaphor for librarianship prior to the digital revolution. Direct access to God was limited, and although Israel was a nation of priests, only certain special priests were able to assist the people with relating to God. However, with the death of Christ, the temple veil was torn in two, symbolizing that the heavens had been opened to a worthy human being. Jesus is the High Priest who has eternal access to the heavenly Tabernacle, but because Christians are incorporated into Him by baptism, they have access to God in a way that ancient Israelites did not. Access to God is not geographically limited and a church can gather in any place to manifest the body of Christ and worship

God in spirit and truth. Every believer in Jesus Christ is a priest from the least of them to the greatest.

When information was stored in valuable physical media and confined to geographic locations, librarians were naturally inclined to be quite protective of it and access was limited. With open stacks, inter-library networking, and the digital revolution, there is a greater degree of access to the body of human knowledge. Moreover, librarians can teach information literacy and information retrieval skills to others. Like Christians sharing the love and knowledge of God abroad, librarians delight to spread abroad their skills for learning and knowing.

Librarians as Priests of New Creation

We now turn to the greater purpose of this essay, which is to show how librarianship is an extension of Hebrew and Christian priesthood and how librarians can understand their worship and work in light of new creation. This thesis is based largely on James K. A. Smith's "liturgical anthropology," the priestly human vocation concept in the work of N. T. Wright, and the Bible's emphasis on sacred space as explained by John H. Walton. This essay continues with a discussion of the telos of Christian worship and ends with personal anecdotes about being a librarian priest of new creation.

Evangelical Interest in "Liturgical Worship"

A number of Christian writers and academics have observed in recent years that Evangelical Christians seem to be more interested now than ever before in historic Christian worship practices, or "liturgical worship" (Bratcher & Stephenson-Bratcher, 2015). Robert Webber's *Evangelicals on the Canterbury Trail: Why Evangelicals Are Attracted to the Liturgical Church* is an early example of this and it seems to have intensified since then (1985). It is true that worship in all Christian churches has some kind of liturgy, whether formal or not (Chappel, 2009). Even Pentecostal worship, which is pretty much the antithesis of the "high church" tradition, has its formative rituals and routines (Smith, 2009). However, the observation is that Christians from denominations which have not worshiped according to a formal liturgy are turning to look at the practice of those denominations with ecclesiastically ordained liturgies for worship.

Some doubt that there is a real trend, statistically speaking. Most of the denominations with formal worship liturgies remain in steep numerical decline while the evangelical megachurches grow, and actual conversions of evangelicals to "high church" traditions are few (Stewart, 2017). Moreover, stories about high profile evangelicals turning to those traditions have been emerging for decades (Stewart, 2017). Individual evangelical academics and celebrities, reflecting publicly on their own experience, are promoting the idea that Evangelicalism is experiencing an identity crisis that is driving many to look to Catholicism and Orthodoxy (Stewart, 2017). However, Kenneth J. Stewart points out in a recent book on the subject of Evangelical identity that there are more people flowing into Evangelicalism from these denominations than are going the other way, especially on a global scale (2017). If this phenomenon is real, it is a distinctly North American trend (Stewart, 2017). Interest in liturgical worship would not necessarily cause people to convert from Evangelical Protestantism to Catholicism or Orthodoxy anyway, for there are quite a few traditions in between in which one will find similar historical Christian worship which is both Protestant and Evangelical (Meador, 2014).

Nevertheless, something is afoot. Christian writers and spokespersons for churches who are exploring historic Christian liturgy often cite the same feelings and influences. In an age when people are leery of that which seems inauthentic and consumerist, evangelicals are looking for deep roots, authority, and authenticity. The Village Church, a Dallas megachurch historically affiliated with the Southern Baptist Convention, now observes the seasons of the liturgical calendar and practices weekly communion, for example. A representative for the church said that they adopted these practices because they wanted to feel rooted in church history (Sanders, 2017). Other Dallas megachurches have embraced historic Christian practices as well (Sanders, 2017). A Baptist might protest that liturgical calendars and weekly communion are un–Baptist, but this is occurring in the same city where one can find ultra-patriotic worship services complete with fireworks and American flags on civil holidays in Baptist churches.

The search for authenticity in religion is interesting in light of a resurgence of *things* in the immediate wake of the digital revolution. A 2016 book entitled *The Revenge of Analog* proposes that vinyl records and moleskin notebooks are coming back because people desire an embodied experience (Sax, 2016). Moreover, a growing number of consumers are rejecting over-processed foods and mass-produced commercial lagers in favor of sprouted grains and craft beer (Sax, 2016). Librarians can also breathe again now that it seems that eBooks have not replaced print. For many people, getting into a book is an experience which involves all the senses, even one's sense of smell.

Another factor might be decision fatigue. As librarians know, the burden of information overload weighs heaviest for the information illiterate, but it can also be lightened by thoughtful and professional curation. That which is old and trusted and enduring has also been subject to contemplation for a very long time as though vetted by our ancestors. In a culture where there are innumerable places and modes and fads for offering Christian worship, the decision of how to worship God can be quite difficult for the conscientious believer. In most major population centers, one can choose to attend any of the major denominations as well as the many non-denominational churches. Among these, there are coffee house churches, cowboy churches and biker churches in some locales. There are churches who define themselves by the political issue *du jour*. The ever-changing landscape of free worship can be exhausting on worshipers and worship leaders alike.

In certain churches, moments of personal decision are practically the telos of worship. In the revivalist tradition, in which I spent most of my life, a time for personal response widely known as an "altar call" is one of the most important parts of the liturgy. Typically, these serve as moments for people to make professions of faith in Christ, and worship has an overwhelmingly evangelistic purpose. However, these moments are not only about conversion or new birth. Every Sunday the worshiper is faced with this moment of self-examination, and there are a number of normative responses. These range from praying quietly in one's seat, to walking the aisle and asking for prayer from a pastor, to rededicating one's life to Christ. One could pray "at the altar" alone or with a friend. One could even "surrender to the ministry."

Despite the fact that these moments are perceived as "Spirit-led," it is up to the individual worshiper to interpret for himself or herself the appropriate response to what he or she is thinking and feeling in the moment. It is genuinely a moment of decision. On the other hand, all of this happens in a social context with improvised music and rhetorical pleas from worship leaders to "do business with God." Because of the social dynamic and powerful influence of worship leaders, the response of one person can lead to a response in others, even leading to a veritable cascade of people moving from their seats to draw near to God. I once heard a pastor say that he uses this social dynamic to elicit decisions from those who may be teetering on the edge of commitment. He called it "priming the pump," and would instruct certain individuals to make a move toward the altar to start the flow. The altar call is an emotionally intense moment, and it happens in almost every service.

In the "high church" traditions there are objective responses, and the main response of the baptized is communion. All desire to trust and obey God is expressed formally and concretely. Ideally, worshippers receive communion with sincerity and faith. God, to whom all hearts are open, will determine the degree of sincerity, however. A ritual of free response, such as an altar call can be navigated without sincerity and to social advantage. Perhaps people who have grown up attending liturgical services have come to take frequent communion for granted, but for those embracing liturgy today, the opportunity for an objective response is welcome in a world full of information overload and a dearth of trustworthy authorities.

To those who are not well-versed in the liturgies of "high church" traditions, it can appear that liturgical worship is a *style* of worship that may be replicated by adding a few antiphonal readings, or by adding designated moments for bodily movements such as a procession, or kneeling, or the raising of hands. Some worship leaders, having eavesdropped on a reverent and numinous liturgical service, have seen liturgy as a kind of old chest from which they can produce a few ancient worship practices that might bring that same feeling onto home turf. Done honestly, this can be endearing, but it might also indicate a kind of cultural appropriation in which free worship leaders gather up high church practices because they perceive that, for whatever reason, it *works* on the current generation. It might work to get people excited about connecting with history and the church universal, but will it work to form Christians if the telos of liturgical worship is not carefully considered?

Liturgical Anthropology

Christian philosopher James K. A. Smith has inspired Christian ministers and Christian educators alike with his *Cultural Liturgies* project, a trilogy of books on the role of desire in Christian formation, education, and politics (2009, 2013, & 2017). In line with Augustine, he shows how human beings are not merely thinking beings but desiring beings who learn to love a particular vision of "the good" by way of the habits, rituals, and routines of a particular culture or Kingdom (2009). Humans were made for worship, and Smith proposes a "liturgical anthropology," calling humans *homo liturgicus* (Smith, 2009). Thus, Christian formation and education do not occur through the intellectual acquisition of information alone, but through bodily rituals and habits or liturgy done as a part of a society (2009). So, it would not be the content of all the sermons and lectures a person hears in his or her life that determines Christian identity, but the act of assembling with other believers to hear them over and over again which would shape a Christian into a citizen of the Kingdom of God.

Inspired by Matthew Ostercamp, Director of Brandel Library at North Park University in Chicago (2014), I applied Smith's liturgical anthropology to library instruction, developing a semi-annual research and writing workshop designed to shepherd students through a liturgy of theological research. Uniting Christian practices such as a devotional service and a fellowship meal with the research habits of theological scholars, we lead students to engage in practices which are meant to inculcate in them a vision of "the good" which includes excellence in research and writing. After four years, students at BMA Theological Seminary report through feedback channels in ways which indicate that a vision of such excellence is a part of our institutional culture to a greater degree than it has been in the past.

Worship in the Ancient World

Historic Christian worship is not merely a *style* of worship because it reflects an ancient view of the world while contemporary worship expressions reflect a post-enlightenment view of the world in many ways.

The Modern Imagination

Liturgical Christian worship redefines an ancient purpose with which the people of the Greco-Roman world and the Ancient Near-East (ANE) were constantly engaged, namely, holding things together. The ancient imagination was alive with visions of cosmic activity, like in Jacob's vision of a ladder between heaven and earth or Ezekiel's vision of Yahweh's wheeled chariot throne. Modern people tend to read such things with a raised eyebrow, hoping to get beyond "the weird" to find "timeless truths." Religious worship for the ancients was direct engagement with unseen forces, forces that we *know* by our scientific instruments are not really there. Post-enlightenment demythologizing leads modern people to say, perhaps with a smirk, "They thought … but we know better." On the other hand, they also knew things *because* of what they thought and did in worship that modern people do not know. Their worship retold stories that describe in a more phenomenological way what people had been observing about humankind and the cosmos for centuries. As a result of this dismissal, modern worshipers imagine that there is little going on in the liminal space between heaven and earth. Everyone knows what a microscope can do, but Jacob's ladder has been hauled off to the cultural shed because no one knows what it can do.

What do modern people imagine is happening when they go to church? Popular conceptions of the purpose of religious worship include things like evangelism, education, experience, and exalting God (Meyers, 2003). The exact combination differs from church to church, and these are all good things, but the cosmic telos is either missing, or vague and shadowy. People are being saved and sanctified for heaven, but as the hymn goes "the things of earth grow strangely dim." Moreover, there are fewer limitations on worship media because worship is primarily conceived of as an "overflow" (Wilt, 2009) and "expression" (Kimball, 2009) from the heart of love for God. This indicates a personal relationship, and indeed that is what Christians have with God, but "personal" is not limiting enough. The relationship is covenantal, and covenants have terms (Meyers, 2003). Biblical covenants involve abstractions such as "faith" and "obedience" and "salvation," but covenants are not sealed with abstractions. The terms of biblical covenants always include specific physical media between the heart of the worshiper and God. Water is physical. Bread and wine are physical. The sound waves of speech and song are physical. The eardrums that vibrate are physical. The feet of those who bring good news are physical. God incarnate is physical.

Filling the Worship Space

Imagine a library that has nothing in it but a naked librarian. The shelves are not empty because there are none. Imagine "the Construct" from the film *The Matrix,* an endless plane of white with nothing in it but a librarian in the nude (Wachowski, Wachowski & Silver, 1999). Now, imagine the librarian attempting to complete a research consultation with a patron. Is it the patron's responsibility to fill the library with everything necessary for the librarian to meet the patron's needs? No one would let the space remain empty, but it would be very difficult for patrons to agree on what things might fill that space. What one expects is for librarians to clothe themselves and to fill the environment with *library things* so that they can help the patron to a desired outcome. One expects librarians to select and manage the objects in a library so that there are some terms for interaction already in place.

If the space that needed to be filled were the "worship space," the Bible describes what belongs there in the Old Testament much more explicitly than in the New Testament, particularly in the number of physical objects and rituals involved. These were fulfilled in Christ and one no longer needs signs pointing to the destination when one has arrived (Wright, 2018). The Calvinist and Puritan principle of only including in the worship of God that which is explicitly commanded in scripture is called "The Regulative Principle" (Chapell, 2009). It was first articulated in a time when the opposing view was not unfettered free response, but rather, worship that was, at least in the eyes of the Reformers, wrongly regulated by the magisterial Catholic Church. Some people embrace the simplicity of such a principle with open arms, and some people chafe at it from the beginning. This is not the place to argue for or against it, only to point out that one would expect a loving and responsible Father to regulate the furnishings and activities of His own house. On the other hand, if the Lord of the house is a faithful Son, one might expect the furnishings and activities to be representative of all that the Father taught Him and yet be distinctly His own. And then, of course, there is the lady of the house, who might fulfill every one of her Husband's wishes without turning to the right or to the left, yet still succeed in adding a personal touch.

Peter Leithart proposes in his little book *From Silence to Song: The Davidic Liturgical Revolution* that the origin of singing in Israel's worship is in David's reinterpretation and reapplication of the sacrificial terms given in the Torah (2011). This would be an example of a faithful son and lord who had meditated day and night on the Torah revolutionizing the liturgy of worship for a new era. David abolished nothing in the Torah but fulfilled it by giving every Israelite an opportunity to join Israel's worship through a sacrifice of praise, even while the priests continued to offer up animal sacrifices (Leithart, 2011). David effectively moved toward a more subjective kind of worship without abolishing the objective sign of animal sacrifice. Jesus, the greater David, also revolutionized Israel's worship for a new era, but Jesus' liturgical revolution would be more dramatic. David and Jesus were both saturated in the scriptures and they filled their worship with the scriptures. What will fill the "worship space" without total Bible saturation? Those who are not careful may find themselves listening to a visionary who says with Neo in the Construct, "guns, lots of guns," and end up with the ultra-patriotic nationalistic worship services mentioned above (Wachowski, Wachowski, & Silver, 1999).

Christian Worship in Light of Greco-Roman Religion

Ancient worshipers, both Jew and Gentile, imagined cosmic consequences of their worship, but not everyone in the Greco-Roman world agreed. N. T. Wright has discussed in various books and lectures the similarity between post-enlightenment deism and Greco-Roman epicureanism (2013, 2018). When people think of epicureanism they typically think of the moral dimension because epicureans see a pleasurable life as the telos of morality. Wright emphasizes the cosmological dimension of epicureanism which is that the gods and the realms of the gods are far away (2018). They do not care because they are not close. Enlightenment deism is similar in that God has wound the universe up and stepped back to let it run on its own (Wright, 2018). God might be concerned with morals, but primarily in the interest of judging humans after death, on the other side of the great gulf that separates heaven and earth (Wright, 2018). The primary difference between deists and epicureans is that the former are monotheists and believe that God created the world, whereas the latter are not and believe that the gods did not create the world (Wright, 2013).

Epicureans were at odds with the prevailing stoic view of the gods and religion. "Religion" in the Greco-Roman world referred to "the system of signs, including myths and rites, by which people were bound together as a civic unity in which gods and people both shared" (Wright, 2013). Here we assume, along with many scholars, that the English word comes from the Latin *religio,* meaning "to rebind," rather than *relego,* meaning "to go over again as with rereading, reciting, or rethinking" (Wright, 2013). *Religio* was done to keep things tied together. Make no mistake, this binding was enslavement to demons from a Hebraic, and later, from a Christian perspective, but note that these bonds keep the world turning, as it were (Wright, 2013). This called for precision in priestcraft, specifically in sacrificial offerings, to ensure that the *polis,* or city, would prosper (Wright, 2013). Stoicism was a pantheistic philosophy in which the individual pagan deities were thought to be expressions of the fact that the divine fiery *pneuma* is in all things and yet never distinct from all things (Wright, 2013).

Religion was practiced in every sphere, beginning in the home with service to household gods and with the oldest male relative, the *paterfamilias,* serving as the priest (Wright, 2013). Crucial to understanding Roman religion is the concept of the *genius* of the *paterfamilias* (Wright, 2013). This was "the deified concept of the person in his true identity, or self" (Wright, 2013). The father priest of a house was not divine, but his *genius* was an individual instance of the divine present within him (Wright, 2013). There were *genii* of persons, places, and things (Wright, 2013). The *genius* of the paterfamilias would be represented by a small statue and would be placed beside other important idols called *lares* at hearth shrines (Wright, 2013). Roman districts had such idols which they served and eventually, there was an idol representing the *genius* of Caesar Augustus in each district shrine (Wright, 2013). In 2 BC, Augustus was named "father of the fatherland," for Rome was a great house and Caesar Augustus was *paterfamilias* of that house (Wright,

2013). This is, in part, how Roman emperors came to be worshipped as sons of the gods (Wright, 2013).

The apostle Paul redefines *religio* as binding people together in Christ to the one true God so that Heaven and Earth could be united in a New Creation (Wright, 2013). Paul employs a head-body metaphor for Christ and the church to convey how essential believers are to one another. Yet, it is more than a metaphor. This is a head-body of mythic proportions. Whereas the household of Rome had a *paterfamilias* in Caesar, the declaration that Jesus Christ is Lord acknowledges that Jesus is the only mediator between God and man. The Roman empire was a great house and city, but the world is an even bigger house and city which belongs to God. Jesus is the *paterfamilias* of God's worldhouse and the city of God in which the ordinary geographic, political, and cultural boundaries are torn down (Wright, 2018). Instead of the divine fiery *pneuma* of stoicism, Jesus and His people are filled with the *pneuma* of Yahweh, the Holy Spirit (Wright, 2018). Roman emperors, convinced that their own great deeds represented the work of the gods through them, would deck themselves out as such (Wright, 2013). The kings of the earth portray themselves as mythic giants striding through the world. However, Jesus is greater than all mythic figures and all supposedly real kings.

Christian Worship in Light of Hebrew Religion

Paul supplants Roman *religio* with the Christian concept of being bound to God in Jesus, but Christian worship is a continuation of the Hebrew and Ancient Near-Eastern (ANE) understanding of religion. Thus, Paul also revolutionizes Hebrew worship by using terms of sacrifice, exodus, priesthood, and temple to describe the worship of those who follow Jesus.

Living Sacrifices

He urges the church in Rome to offer themselves in the place of animal sacrifices saying, "I appeal to you therefore, brothers, by the mercies of God, to present your bodies as a living sacrifice, holy and acceptable to God, which is your spiritual worship" (Romans 12:1, ESV). The word "present" should be taken in the religious sense as in presenting an offering for sacrifice (Wright, 2013). The word "sacrifice" is singular, indicating that it begins in the worship assembly of the saints where the people come together as a single sacrifice. They are living sacrificially as they give themselves to one another in loving service in their daily lives, but it all starts in the assembly with corporate worship. He goes on to encourage them not to be conformed to the present age, but to be transformed by the renewal of their minds. The renewal of the mind to conform to God's will seems to be linked to this presentation of the body as a living sacrifice. This is a new kind of *religio* for a new creation and prepares believers for the projects of new creation (Wright, 2013). By presenting themselves to God as a living sacrifice on the first day of the week, the liturgy of word and sacrament renews them for sacrificial living outside of the gathering in the week to come.

It is easy to flatten the sacrifices of Israel into the singular issue of payment for sin, but many of the offerings were not for atonement (Meyers, 2003). Rather, the purpose of the bloody business of sacrifice was to objectify the difficult transformation necessary for a human being to ascend into the presence of God (Meyers, 2003). Rather than renewing the mind with abstract exhortations, Israel had the sacrificial system as a way to center life on the all-consuming process of "drawing near" to Yahweh. In fact, the main word for "offering" in Leviticus refers to something that is brought near to God through the altar (Meyers, 2003). As keepers of flocks and herds, Israel's life was centered upon bringing domesticated animals from house to field and from pasture to altar. The symbolic link between the nation of Israel and its flocks runs throughout the Hebrew Scriptures (Jordan, 1988). One perfect illustration of this among many is Psalm 23, a beloved passage that brings comfort to many when faced with life's dark valleys. The Psalm moves from a pastoral scene to a festal scene. It images God's faithfulness to watch over the author at all times and to bring him to God's own house and table for rich living. The festal scene seems like an odd transition unless one compares it to the movement of a sacrificial animal from the field to the altar of the Tabernacle or Temple. The animal is then transformed by knife and fire into smoke which ascends to heaven (Meyers, 2003).

Israelites are often compared to domesticated animals in the Bible because they are set apart from all the other nations to be domestic to Yahweh (Jordan, 1988). Moreover, their responsibility to remain ceremonially pure by eating ceremonially pure animals explains this special relationship and why the food laws changed in the New Testament (Jordan, 1988). The food laws were about setting Israel apart to serve as a corporate intermediary between God and the nations. Clean animals served as the proxy for unclean people, and clean Israel served as the proxy for the unclean Gentiles. Israel failed to be that proxy for the nations, but Christ succeeded, and thus fulfilled the food laws and sacrifices.

Another illustration of this symbolic link is a piece of furniture from Solomon's temple, the bronze sea, a great water basin resting on the backs of twelve bulls (Jordan, 1988). The twelve oxen are the twelve tribes of Israel and the basin of water represents either the waters of the celestial sea (Jordan, 1988), or perhaps the waters of the Red Sea. If it is the celestial sea, it shows how Israel upholds the temple as a copy of heaven on earth through their worship (Jordan, 1988). If it is the Red Sea, it tells the story of how Israel came through a death and rebirth in the Exodus. In either case, the water represents entry into a new world, a new creation. They came up from slavery in Egypt and the waters of the underworld to serve Yahweh at Sinai. They came with their flocks and their children. They entered into a new life and constructed the Tabernacle according to the pattern that Moses received on Sinai. The bronze sea served as a place for Israel's priests to wash themselves upon entry for service into the world of the temple.

Baptismal Exodus

The Christian life officially begins with a water rite which symbolizes rebirth from the watery depths. Baptism is a retelling of the Exodus (Wright, 2013). Israel came up from slavery in Egypt at Passover, and Christ was the Passover Lamb who died to set His people free from the bondage of sin. Paul says in his first letter to the Corinthians that Israel's passage through the Red Sea was a Baptism into Moses. That event serves as a parallel to Moses' being drawn from the Nile by Pharaoh's daughter. The name "Moses" sounds like the Hebrew word for "to draw out," but is also Egyptian for "son" (Bodner, 2016). Through the faithfulness of the Hebrew Midwives, Jochebed, Miriam, and even Pharaoh's daughter, Moses receives a new birth while other sons die. When Israel passes through the Red Sea, Miriam is there once again to lead the women with the timbrel in a song of victory. She and the other women serve as midwives to bring forth the national son of God, the nation of Israel (Bodner, 2016). This passage through the sea is celebrated in Isaiah 51:9–11 as a piercing of the dragon, also known as Rahab or Egypt. This serves a near-fulfillment of the promise to woman that her seed would crush the Serpent's head. Like the Exodus, baptism brings forth the whole body of the Son of God from the waters of judgment.

Levitical Priesthood

Followers of Jesus are also a continuation of the Levitical priesthood in several ways, including baptism, preaching, dividing, and joining. Baptism signifies that Christians are priests and proceeds typologically from the lustrations that the sons of Aaron received in their ordination and for consecration upon reentry into the sacred spaces of Israel (Leithart, 2003). These washings took place at the laver outside of the Tabernacle and at the aforementioned Bronze Sea of Solomon's temple. Israel's priests washed themselves again and again as they came into the microcosm of the temple (Leithart, 2003). Christians enjoy a system that only requires one baptism because they enter the new Temple of the body of Christ and never have to leave.

The Levitical priests were preachers and teachers of Torah, known for their "true instruction," and the people of Israel were to seek true instruction "from [Levi's] mouth" (Malachi 2:6–7, ESV). Ironically, there are a number of stories where Levites have trouble with speech. Exodus opens with the story of Moses, a Levite who shies away from speaking for Yahweh. His brother Aaron, the Levite, is put forward as the official spokesman because he can speak. The New Exodus in Christ also opens with the story of a Levitical priest, Zechariah, whose mouth is closed for his lack of faith in the angelic message that he would have a son in his old age. Followers of Jesus, particularly the Apostles, are known for their preaching and instruction.

Levi is also known for the priestly task of dividing flesh with sword and sacrificial knife for the purpose of binding people to God. This is related to the fact that when God created the world good, He immediately started transforming creation through painful divisions, such as when He divided a rib from Adam to "build" Eve. To use the word "build" is no mistake, for the Hebrew word used in the construction of Eve is the same word used to describe the construction of cities such as Babel and Solomon's Temple. Levi, the father of the tribe bearing his name, used knife and sword to wrongly circumcise and then kill the men of Shechem under false pretenses of peace and a marriage between Shechem and Levi's sister, Dinah. However, the tribe of Levi came back into favor when at Sinai they took up their swords to slay the people of Israel who had broken covenant with Yahweh with the golden calf. The tribe of Levi thus became the tribe of the special priests who would enter the world of the Tabernacle and Temple and unite people to God through sacrifice.

Amazingly, this reflects what Leah said when she gave birth to Levi, "Now, this time my husband will be attached to me..." (Genesis 29:34, ESV). The name "Levi" sounds like the Hebrew word for "attach." Levi was the father of the tribe of priests that would be tasked with attaching people to God for the purpose of joining heaven and earth. Christians are called to be the priests of new creation who bind together heaven and earth. As Wright says in *Surprised by Hope*, Heaven and earth "are made for each other in the same way ... as male and female. And, when they finally come together, that will be cause for rejoicing in the same way that a wedding is: a creational sign that God's project is going forwards..." (Wright, 2010).

The New Temple

Old Testament priests entered a new world through water, and the same is true for baptized Christians because Christ and His body are the new temple. Paul tells the Corinthians that they are the new Temple of the Holy Spirit. In order to understand the significance of this statement, it helps to know more about Ancient Near-Eastern temples. John H. Walton explains throughout much of his work the importance of sacred space in the Bible, calling it "the most significant element in biblical theology," despite the fact that it has been neglected in favor of "systematic concerns, such as Christology and soteriology" (Walton, 2017). According to Walton, the creation narratives in Genesis are an inauguration of sacred space with human beings serving as guardian priests (2017). ANE temples served as the "operations hub of the cosmos," and the function of the deity dwelling in an earthly temple was to bring the order of the heavenly realm to bear upon the earth and keep the encroaching "disorder and nonexistence" at bay (Walton, 2017). This was achieved as the deity dwelt in the temple, enthroned within the house amidst faithful and ceremonially pure servants (Walton, 2017). This is why there is an emphasis on Yahweh's willingness or unwillingness to dwell in Israel's midst throughout the Old Testament, establishing "stability and security" in the community (Walton, 2017). Yom Kippur, or the Day of Atonement, was all about cleansing the place where Yahweh would set His feet. The blood which the high priest would sprinkle on the lid of the Ark of the Covenant ritually purified the house and household servants of Yahweh so that He could dwell there. Peter Leithart shows how the lid of the Ark was the footstool of Yahweh's throne and a representation of the nation of Israel who are Yahweh's subjects, His footstool people for the sake of the world (2017).

However, it is important not to lose sight of the fact that God's willingness to dwell with His people is not based upon the mechanically correct performance of temple rites and ceremonies alone. With the other ANE deities, the relationship between the deity and his or her human servants was "utilitarian codependence," but in Israel it was based upon covenant (Walton, 2017). In Israel, the rites and ceremonies are a part of the Torah, which also includes stories and commandments given to renew the minds of the children of Israel. The Torah is Yahweh's gift of wisdom for His covenant people. Moses says in Deuteronomy 4 that the Torah is meant to make the nations marvel at their wisdom and the nearness of Yahweh to Israel. On the other hand, "the Torah was contingent upon the temple, not the other way around," and so Torah was not something that was lived apart from Israel's sacred spaces (Walton, 2017).

In fact, the Jews grappled with this conundrum throughout the Babylonian exile and into Jesus' day, asking what it meant to live in accordance with Torah without the Divine Presence of Yahweh dwelling in the temple, and answering that question in several ways (Wright, 2013). Significant portions of the Torah were concerned with what to do in the Temple, and a Jew could live in accordance with Torah in the Diaspora, perhaps gaining the blessing of the Shekinah glory, if he were seriously occupied with the study of Torah (Wright, 2013). The Qumran sect believed that a "human temple" made of those who performed the works of the law could be formed, and Jews would send money from far away to pay the Temple tax and participate in the sacrifices that way (Wright, 2013). Synagogues were often built facing the direction of the temple or would point to the temple in other symbolic ways. Some Jews believed that one could participate in the liturgy of the Temple by studying the sections of Torah that pertained to it (Wright, 2013). Nevertheless, none of what could be done in the Diaspora to manifest the Temple and the Shekinah was the same as having Yahweh dwelling in their midst in the Temple. "They could produce (as it were) symbolic or allegorical equivalents of the concrete reality, but the concrete reality still mattered" (Wright, 2013).

Even though there was a rebuilt temple in Jerusalem after the return from exile, there was not a return of the Divine Presence in the form of the glory cloud. Ezekiel saw it depart and it never came back (Wright, 2013). The long-awaited return of the Divine Presence happened in the advent of Christ and for the followers of Jesus on the Day of Pentecost, however. (Wright, 2013). The similarities between the scene of the dedication of Solomon's Temple and the day of Pentecost are striking. The smoke of the glory cloud filled Solomon's temple to such an extent that the priests could not minster (1 Kings 20:10). At Pentecost there were tongues of fire coming down on each person, like the fire that once descended upon the altar to consume sacrifices. Each person in the upper room was a living sacrifice. At the dedication of Solomon's Temple there were 120 priests sounding trumpets. At Pentecost there were 120 disciples who spoke in other tongues the mighty works of God. Trumpets and fire and thunder from Mount Sinai were symbolic of the word of God coming out of the throne room of the heavenly temple. Priests in the temple blew trumpets over the burnt offerings before they were offered. The 120 "priests" of Pentecost were trumpeting the word of God.

Readers should connect this event with all of the preceding events involving sacred space from the Garden of Eden onward. However, this scene especially reminds readers of the Tower of Babel, Mount Sinai, and Solomon's Temple. The linguistic scattering of the nations that occurred at Babel was superseded by speaking in tongues. The three-thousand baptisms were a reversal of what had happened on the first Pentecost at Sinai when three thousand Israelites died for their idolatry with the golden calf. The tongues of fire and rushing wind remind readers of the inauguration of Solomon's temple. The speech of the Apostles cut their fellow Jews to the heart, the sword of the word preparing them for sacrifice as well. The new temple in Christ was dedicated that day by the indwelling of the Divine Presence through the Holy Spirit.

The New Temple and the Final City

The Romans destroyed the Second Temple in 70 AD, but the final temple remains in the church and body of Christ. Consisting of people from every tribe and tongue and nation and language, it fulfills the Ancient Near-Eastern purpose of temples such as Babel because it is an earthly body united with a heavenly head. The one language of this better-than-Babel temple is the Gospel spoken through the liturgy of Christian worship and through evangelism in the world. It is this temple that somehow becomes the Lamb's bride-city of the New Creation which comes down from heaven in Revelation 21:9–11, 22:

> "Come, I will show you the Bride, the wife of the Lamb." And he carried me away in the Spirit to a great, high mountain, and showed me the holy city Jerusalem coming down out of heaven from God, having the glory of God, its radiance like a most rare jewel, like a jasper, clear as crystal.... And I saw no temple in the city, for its temple is the Lord God the Almighty and the Lamb.

Jesus revolutionized the worship of God by demonstrating how the first Adam was meant to bear the image of God in creation by being fully human (Wright, 2018). Every object and ritual involved in Hebrew worship was meant to demonstrate what was to be true of human beings from the beginning, but also to demonstrate the transformation necessary for human beings to dwell with God. The purpose of humans is "to stand at the threshold of heaven and earth—like an 'image' in a temple, no less—and to be the conduit through which God's life would come to earth and earth's praises would rise to God" (Wright, 2018). Christian worship therefore brings all of the liturgies and objects involved in Old Testament worship to a laser focus in Christ. Everything has changed, but the change is not from the material to the immaterial, as if "spiritual" means "incorporeal." The worship space is filled with created people, priests in assembly who are filled with God's Spirit, speaking God's truth, singing God's praises, and praying for the needs of all people. Worshippers take bread and wine as symbols of Christ's body and blood, but also as a representation of creation itself, which will one day be transformed from glory to glory.

Christian Librarians and the Culture of New Creation

There are a number of theories about the relationship between human culture and the church, but it is well beyond the purpose of this essay to make a stand. The development of the body of Christ into a heavenly city on earth implies that the culture of the New Creation finds its origin in the church. What lies beyond this essay—perhaps all essays—is exactly how that comes to pass. In John's vision it is a city covered in gold and precious stones. According to the Edenic narrative in Genesis, gold and precious stones are found downriver from the garden of Eden. If the fall of Adam had not occurred, the original human priests would have worked their way downriver, mined the gold and precious stones, and processed them to build the first city while maintaining the Edenic priestly relationship with God. If the Garden of Eden was inaugurated sacred space and the first humans were priests as Walton and Wright have proposed, and if human beings are liturgical by nature as Smith has proposed, then the culture of the New Creation has its origin in Christian worship. Tragically, the first culture-makers were not Edenic priests but the children of Cain, and the first city was named after Cain's son, Enoch. The Cainite way was vengeance and violence, which led to the great flood. The first city of the post-flood world was Babel, a prideful city which God scattered by confusing its language and thus its liturgy. This is where the competing cultural liturgies of the world find their origin. In any case, when the city of God overcomes the cities of man, it will be God at work through His people in the church's worship and witness. Christian librarians find themselves with plenty of gold to refine and jewels to set in the city of God.

An Example from History

Libraries and librarians have their origin in the collection and organization of Sumerian religious texts, and the early libraries of Western European civilization were monastic libraries (Mukherjee, 1966). The earliest Christian "librarians" did not have to work hard to imagine their work as vocational service to God because they served the church as priests and scholars and copyists of sacred texts. Anastasius Bibliothecarius seems to be the first appointed librarian or archivist of the Church of Rome (Kirsch, 1914). He was highly educated, being perhaps "the most learned ecclesiastic of Rome in the barbaric period of the ninth century" (Kirsch, 1914). In a time when Western knowledge of Greek was rare, he translated a number of important works into Latin. What drove him in this task? The extant information suggests that he was interested in maintaining the bonds of the pre-schismatic church. Keeping correspondence with the deposed Patriarch Photius, "he sought to mediate between the patriarch and the pope and also to assuage the controversy over the Holy Ghost" (Kirsch, 1914). Furthermore, he sought to arrange a marriage between the son of the Byzantine Emperor and the daughter of the Holy Roman Emperor and attended the last session of the eighth ecumenical council, defending the papal cause (Anastasius, n.d.). This is not to heap praise upon him because his character and motivations might not have been stellar. Nevertheless, his work as an archivist and scholar involved him directly in important historical and cultural events.

Labor and New Creation

All Christians are priests of a new creation, so all their work is a participation in the Lamb's bride-city in at least one way. Christian worship on the Lord's Day is an assembly before the throne of the Lamb. It is effectively a manifestation of Jacob's Ladder and the saints are the new angels who go up and down in prayer and praise. Part of this worship is collecting tithes and offerings which are a tribute to the reigning King. In tithes and offerings, believers are bringing the first fruits of their ordinary labor into the service of King Jesus for the sake of the world. In the prayers, they make requests for lesser kings on earth and the rest of humankind. They also eat the bread of communion and drink the wine of the New Covenant, binding themselves together to be the body of the King. They descend to build up new creation as the body of the King and return again every seven days for renewal and resending.

Holding Things Together in the Library

Christian librarians can build up new creation in unique ways. Christians cannot simply give communion to whoever they like because it is the bread of priesthood and the cup of covenant, but they can mimic the hospitality of God by opening their own homes to their neighbor for table fellowship, rest, and evangelism. In a similar way, Christian librarians can be hospitable in the library. There are many ways that different kinds of librarians in different settings can do this, but I will focus on roles similar to my own. I am an academic and theological librarian whose primary task has been to oversee library instruction, so the following discussion will best apply in that context.

Cruciform Librarianship

As mediators between recorded knowledge and the human agents of world change, any single librarian could very well be serving others at the threshold between the world that is and the world that is to come. As a corporate body of professionals, librarians are certainly serving in the liminal space between old and new, attending to future teachers, doctors, politicians, scientists, engineers, and ministers when they are not yet fully formed. Librarians meet novices in their vulnerability, at a point of need defined by experts, and lift them up to become experts themselves. This is holding things together vertically. Furthermore, librarians are also engaged in critical work at a point of tension between the cause of preservation and the cause of access. Throughout library history, these causes have pulled in opposite directions, from books chained to lecterns to open stacks, to the advent of the Internet, digital repositories, and open access publication. This is holding things together horizontally. Reaching out horizontally to pull these causes together and bowing down to lift the fledgling agents of change into conversation with the voices of the past produces a cruciform shape. The cross is very much about the wrath of God, but it is also about being pulled and stretched as Jesus was stretched between Pilate and Herod and between earth and heaven. It can be difficult to hold things together in the library.

As Christian librarians serve in library spaces both real and virtual, they open their hearts to all kinds of students on principle while also maintaining the sanctity of the profession and serving in the mission of the overarching institution. Every research question has its place, but false assumptions will need to die. That space is like a house where growing people are nourished and disciplined. It is both bosom and crucible. Librarians have many things that they would love to *explain* to every student they serve, but few classroom instructional hours, if any at all. This is a blessing. Modern people love to explain and will overuse any platform given them unless disciplined to do otherwise. The boundaries of best practice in a reference interview or research consultation keep us from haranguing students about our own views on their research. Many students who are deep into their course of studies do not need much explanation from librarians at all. Instructional librarians want face-time with students but might not realize the importance of being present as students open themselves up to the explanations of scholars.

Word and Sacrament

The library has its own version of word and sacrament. To be open before a book is to be open to change and to be open before several books is to eavesdrop on a conversation between scholarly experts with even greater transformative potential. English philosopher Iris Murdoch argues that "moral change comes from an increased sense of the reality of someone or something…. Change of being … is not brought about by straining and 'will-power,' but a long deep process of unselfing" (Murdoch, 1993). Reading, especially in the context of uninterrupted study, is a process of unselfing; the reader's ego recedes as the writer comes to the fore. Listening to the antiphonal speech of experts from source to source is like hearing the antiphony of the academy. Academics agree and disagree at key points, but they agree on the sanctity, as it were, of the process.

Physical books filling the shelves of a library are a nonverbal sign that scholarship has happened. Perhaps the reader of this essay has occasionally read something so profound that it seemed to imbue the physical book in his or her hands with new weight and value. In this way, a book or a library full of books can operate almost like a sacrament. One might protest that only God can consecrate a sacrament, but God has made human beings in His own image and has given them the ability of speech, and there is no question about the power of human words. Perhaps human beings have a parallel to divine sacraments. A set table and a home-cooked meal could be considered a human imitation of God's divine grace and hospitality in the Eucharist. Relationships grow and change with food and table talk just as a Christian grows in his relationship with God through preaching and teaching and communion. Or, consider the function of a national flag and anthem as human nonverbal symbols which define and shape human lives (Jordan, 1988). Indicative of the power of such symbols is the fact that there is currently an ongoing public controversy over whether or not professional football players should have to stand in honor of these symbols. Like meals and flags and architecture, library *things* are a human transformation of raw creation with the power to shape and define human lives.

The Face of Knowledge

A local college went under a few years ago and one of the churches in town, having somehow come into possession of what remained of the library, held a book sale. As an academic librarian in a small town, it fell to me to go and see if, perhaps, a few books could be salvaged. Let the reader understand that this was a formality. If I only had one word to describe the situation upon my arrival at the old library building I would have said, "Ichabod," for the glory had departed. It looked like the aftermath of the Babylonian exile, the more youthful and useful vessels of that temple already carried away to Nebuchadnezzar's library. There were still large chunks of their original Dewey Decimal organization intact, but those sections were in no discernable order. I placed no blame upon the current stewards of the collection for this state of affairs. The librarian was gone. The chaos which had been so dutifully held at bay by the daily service of library staff had, after all, flooded in. Nevertheless, among the townspeople present at the sale there seemed to be a discernible reverence. The whispered conversations among them seemed to be about books, books, and the love of books. Recognizing me as a librarian, one of them came over to chat about books, and I played my part. Perhaps some of the people present were also playing their part in honoring everything that even a desolate library represents. Leaving, I saw a familiar face, the town's other academic librarian.

A librarian is the face of all this, and it is powerful to be one of the official faces that students see in connection with their academic striving and growth. In the biblical story of Jacob and Esau, after years of separation and enmity generated by Jacob's acquisition of their father's blessing, Jacob approaches Esau like a fearful worshiper. He sends impressive gifts of livestock ahead of him in three separate droves, instructing his servants to inform Esau that these are gifts from his brother. Jacob wants to soften Esau's heart to appease him. He sends his wives and servants and children and all of his worldly possessions across the Jabbok river, but he spends the night wrestling with an angel of the Lord. Victorious in the morning, he names the place Peniel because he has seen the face of God and has not died. The next day, he approaches Esau and finds, not an enemy, but a brother. Jacob tells Esau that his face is to him like the face of God because Esau has accepted him. As students engage in the tasks of research and writing, they are grappling with the forces of academia that will determine their success or failure as a student. This perhaps accounts for some of what professional librarians have called "library anxiety." The library is the gate of a necessary trial and to enter it is to willingly face that trial. However, Christian librarians can meet wrestling students with open arms and smiles in moments of profound vulnerability and fecundity, assuring them that, even though they are striving with powerful forces, they are the human agents who will transform the future with God's help.

Wrestling and Limping

I remember well the day when a student who has recently received a commission as a military chaplain was tossing and turning inside one of the library study closets, wrestling with the facts of critical biblical scholarship. He did not come to seminary to be faced with the claims of critics or unbelievers; he came to help people believe in and know God. He found himself wondering and doubting how he could subject himself to all this and keep going. I was still a student when he began his education and he asked me how I had handled the claims of higher biblical criticism. I do not remember exactly what I told him, only that I reassured him that plenty of current ministers and academics had found themselves in his shoes and that the struggle would only strengthen him. Perhaps all students walk across the stage at graduation with a personal, invisible limp that they would not trade for anything under the sun.

Some students are visibly limping along. It seems as though I rarely get to help students with higher order research and writing skills. I interact with students who are working on more advanced writing projects minimally and spend hours with students who are struggling to grasp the basics. Time after time, I have wondered how a particular student made it through the application process, and time after time, I have seen them improve and flourish. It is particularly difficult to bring heaven and earth together for these students. One student came to me in desperation, having already failed one paper, he felt that he was on his last chance. He told me his story, which I later verified, about how he had started his degree some years before but could not finish it because he had to take a job for the railroad. While he was working some men assaulted him and beat him severely, knocking out one of his eyes, and I could see upon inspection that one of his eyes was indeed made of glass. He told me that his mind did not work as well as it did before the assault, but that he wanted to complete his degree so that he could encourage his son who was also in school at another institution. At some point during his story he had to wipe away tears as he told me that his emotions sometimes got the best of him since the assault.

Based upon our initial meeting, I was unsure if he would be able to pass, but I told him that even if he did not make it, he was okay in my book. Furthermore, I told him that some people who do make it are not necessarily okay in my book because they did not have his unique challenges. I told him that he did not have to be ashamed with me. He passed that class and is still in school. At some point I realized that people of all kinds come to me because I make them feel like they do not have to be ashamed.

Standing at the Threshold of the Underworld

Sometimes the way librarians serve others can be an avenue for them back to the land of the living. My institution has a peer writing tutor program for students who need help with grammar and syntax. It creates a time-consuming conflict of interest when students need help crafting sentences for their assignments and ask faculty for help. However, I did proofread one student's papers often because English was not his first language and because he is a personal friend of mine. Over time, his English had improved enough that he no longer required my assistance. My family and his family were close enough that we would enjoy table fellowship and stay up late into the night in conversation. It is for this reason that I was utterly shocked when, weeks before he was to graduate, he told me that his wife had been unfaithful to him and that she had confessed her love for another man.

My friend had waited several weeks to tell me and appeared at my house relatively emaciated and with his hair falling out. Ichabod. I sat with him as often as I could throughout the following weeks. He went to church with me and we received communion together. At one point, he leaned into my shoulder to weep, discretely, so as not to raise alarm. I prayed that the appearance of only half this family for word and sacrament would move God to seek and save that which had been lost. His wife had gone to stay with family and he had sought the help of a pastor near her for marital counseling. The pastor asked him to read a book and keep a journal. My friend wanted me to proofread his writing. He told me that he would be confessing many of his sins as a husband and that it was very hard for him to think and write in English under the circumstances. I told him that I would help him, but I understood that he was not looking for an editor. He was looking for a mediator, someone to extend the grace of God to him that he had always heard about, but which needed to be embodied by a brother in Christ. The writer-editor relationship served as a vehicle for bringing him back from the abyss. His sins were actually fairly ordinary and not at all scandalous. When he asked me if his words were too much for me to bear, however, I told him that to him, my face was the face of God. There was a time when this would have seemed sacrilegious to both of us, but his gratitude was evident. He did not need me to *explain* God's forgiveness. He had served in ministry for years and knew all about it. He needed me to be a conduit of God's forgiveness and fatherly acceptance. It would be right and good for him to do the same for me because we are both members of the priesthood of all believers. I am happy to report that his marriage now thrives, and his family appears whole before God each Lord's Day.

Conclusion

In this essay I have sought to show how priesthood is a metaphor for librarianship. Moreover, I have shown how the worship and work of Christian librarians can be seen as participation in the New Creation brought about by the Gospel of the Lord Jesus Christ. I have relied upon the work of a number of Biblical scholars such as N. T. Wright, John H. Walton, Peter Leithart, and Jeffrey Meyers, as well as James K. A. Smith's concept of "liturgical anthropology" to argue that the telos of liturgical Christian worship is to hold things together, to bind the church to God in Jesus Christ, and ultimately to join heaven and earth together in New Creation. Christian labor is born from the matrix of Christian worship to build up the culture of New Creation. Finally, I have shown what I imagine myself to be doing when I labor as a Christian librarian. I now leave the reader with a reference to a kind of source which by definition cannot be cited. I am reminded of the proliferation of a series of memes shared on social media in recent years which show pictures of what various people think about a particular job or identity. The pictures are captioned with statements such as "What my mom thinks I'm doing," "What my friends think I'm doing," "What I think I am doing," and finally "What I'm actually doing." Perhaps librarians are just doing a job, but I believe that they are priests unto God and true royalty. Perhaps other Christian librarians can imagine themselves in this way, contributing insights from their particular jobs in other contexts.

REFERENCES

Anastasius the Librarian. (n.d.). *Encyclopedia Britannica*. Retrieved from https://www.britannica.com/biography/Anastasius-the-Librarian.
Bodner, K. (2016). *An ark on the Nile: Beginning of the book of Exodus*. Oxford: Oxford University Press.

Bratcher, D., & Stephenson-Bracher, R. (n.d.). What is liturgy? Evangelicals and liturgical worship. Retrieved August 31, 2018, from http://www.crivoice.org/whatisliturgy.html.

Chapell, B. (2009). *Christ-centered worship: Letting the Gospel shape our practice*. Grand Rapids: Baker Academic.

Ettarh, F. (2018). Vocational awe and librarianship: The lies we tell ourselves. *In the Library with the Lead Pipe*. Retrieved May 31, 2018, from http://www.inthelibrarywiththeleadpipe.org/2018/vocational-awe/

Hafner, A. W., & Camarigg, V. M. (1992). The librarian as mediator. *The Reference Librarian*, *17*(37), 3–22. https://doi.org/10.1300/J120v17n37_02.

Jordan, J. B. (1988). *Through new eyes: developing a Biblical view of the world*. Brentwood, TN: Wolgemuth & Hyatt.

Kimball, D. (2009). Emerging worship. In Duncan, J. L., Kimball, D., Lawrence, M., Dever, M., Quill, T. C. J., Wilt, D., & Pinson, J. M. (2009). *Perspectives on Christian worship: 5 views: Ligon Duncan, Dan Kimball, Michael Lawrence & Mark Dever, Timothy Quill, Dan Wilt*. Nashville: B & H Academic.

Kirsch, J.P. (1914). Anastasius Bibliothecarius. *The Catholic Encyclopedia*. New York: The Encyclopedia Press. Retrieved September 4, 2018, from http://www.newadvent.org/cathen/16002b.htm.

Leithart, P. J. (2017, March 9). Footstool of His feet. Theopolis Institute | Bible. Liturgy. Culture. Retrieved August 24, 2018, from https://theopolisinstitute.com/article/footstool-of-his-feet.

Leithart, P. J. (2003). *The priesthood of the plebs: A theology of baptism*. Eugene, OR: Wipf and Stock.

Leithart, P. J. (2011). *From silence to song: The Davidic liturgical revolution*. Moscow, ID: Canon Press.

Maxwell, N. K. (2006). *Sacred stacks: The higher purpose of libraries and librarianship*. Chicago: American Library Association.

Meador, Jake. (2014, January 16). Are Millennials joining high church traditions? Mere Orthodoxy. Retrieved January 31, 2018, from https://mereorthodoxy.com/millennials-joining-high-church-traditions/.

Meyers, J. J. (2003). *The Lord's service: The grace of covenant renewal worship*. Moscow, ID: Canon Press.

Mukherjee, A. K., & Asia Publishing House. (1966). *Librarianship: Its philosophy and history*. Bombay: Asia Publishing House.

Murdoch, I. (1993). *Metaphysics as a guide to morals*. London: Penguin.

Ostercamp, M. (2014). (Library) education of desire: Applying the pedagogical principles of James K. A. Smith in the theological library. *Summary of proceedings* (pp. 63–75). New Orleans: American Theological Library Association.

Sanders, R. (2017). Evangelical churches are embracing liturgy to make the megachurch more personal. Commentary, *Dallas News*. Retrieved January 31, 2018, from https://www.dallasnews.com/opinion/commentary/2017/12/14/evangelical-churches-embracing-liturgy-make-megachurch-personal.

Sax, D. (2016). *The revenge of analog: Real things and why they matter*. New York: Public Affairs.

Smith, J. K. A. (2009). *Desiring the kingdom: Worship, worldview, and cultural formation*. Grand Rapids: Baker Academic.

Smith, J. K. A. (2013). *Imagining the kingdom: How worship works*. Grand Rapids: Baker Academic.

Smith, J. K. A. (2017). *Awaiting the King: Reforming public theology*. Grand Rapids: Baker Academic.

Stewart, K. J. (2017). *In search of ancient roots: The Christian past and the Evangelical identity crisis*. Downers Grove, IL: IVP Academic.

Wachowski, L., Wachowski, L., & Silver, J. (1999). *The matrix*. [Motion Picture]. Warner Bros.

Walton, J. H. (2017). *Old Testament theology for Christians from ancient context to enduring belief*. Downers Grove, IL: IVP Academic.

Webber, R. E. (1985). *Evangelicals on the Canterbury Trail: Why evangelicals are attracted to the liturgical church*. Waco: Word Books.

Wilt, D. (2009). Contemporary worship. In Duncan, J. L., Kimball, D., Lawrence, M., Dever, M., Quill, T. C. J., Wilt, D., & Pinson, J. M. (2009). *Perspectives on Christian worship: 5 views : Ligon Duncan, Dan Kimball, Michael Lawrence & Mark Dever, Timothy Quill, Dan Wilt*. Nashville: B & H Academic.

Wright, N. T. (2010). *Surprised by hope: rethinking heaven, the resurrection, and the mission of the church*. New York: HarperOne.

Wright, N. T. (2013). *Paul and the faithfulness of God*. Minneapolis: Fortress Press.

Wright, N. T. (2018). *Paul: A biography*. San Francisco: HarperOne.

In a Manner Worthy of God

Hospitality and the Christian Librarian

Denise D. Nelson

Abstract

Hospitality is no doubt a hallmark of the life of faith, but it should also characterize the way we approach our work within and beyond the campus library. In the academic library milieu, such an attitude of welcome is demonstrated by hospitable people who pursue inclusive practices in the context of inviting places. When we as Christian librarians welcome our patrons with a sincere desire to help them, participate in relationship with those patrons in ways that provide for their current needs, and equip them well for the needs that lie ahead, we do so as an expression of our faith and in service to both God and our community. Both the service orientation of librarianship and the servant spirit of our faith compel us to reach toward those we have the power and the responsibility to help.

Introduction

> *Offer hospitality to one another without grumbling. Each one should use whatever gift he has received to serve others, faithfully administering God's grace in its various forms.—1 Peter 4:9–10 (NIV)*

The extraordinary generosity of God's grace and the direct instruction of God's Word compel every believer to reach toward those in need, offering the talents, blessings, and resources of our lives for the benefit of others. In this sense, extending hospitality in and through the library is an act of worship that exists "in response to God's gracious offering of hospitality. While our hospitality is not proportional to God's, nevertheless it is characterized by reciprocity and gratitude" (Oden, 2001, p. 87). Although many of the avenues by which the faithful render service to those around them lie beyond the boundaries of their professional vocation, the work of librarianship provides nearly endless opportunities to demonstrate hospitality to the communities we serve.

The daily work of academic librarianship can be overwhelming. Librarians' roles vary widely, and other important obligations can drive efforts at hospitality to the bottom of each day's list of tasks. One can easily imagine how the pressing responsibilities of research-related instruction, resource management, marketing efforts, scholarly projects, and institutional service leave little time or energy for anything else. Christine Pohl (2007) asserts much the same sentiment about the early church, explaining, "Christian leaders struggled to balance teaching and mentoring new believers with the numerous responsibilities included in hospitality" (p. 29). Despite these challenges, hospitality was required of God's people.

Although the roots of hospitality are anchored in the early church, modern perspectives—even secular ones—continue to esteem this extension of welcome and provision. Friends, family members, and even strangers are welcomed into the homes of others. The interaction is a familiar one in which "some gesture of welcome initiates hospitality" (Oden, p. 145), and that hospitality is received as a gift. Usually, the host invites guests to come in, offering them a meal, pleasant companionship, and perhaps a place to stay. This giving and receiving of hospitality depends upon generosity and often engenders deep gratitude. It promises relational care and entails some level of sacrifice in terms of the time, resources, and personal convenience of the host.

Of course, much of the hospitality that accompanies contemporary travel takes place outside the home altogether. Travelers have their choice of commercial venues for food and lodging—the inns, hotels, and bed and breakfast establishments that abound in cities and towns of every size. The welcome offered by these entities, however, is clearly of a different sort than the personal hospitality extended by one person to another. Even at the highest levels of service, commercial hospitality is characterized by its inherently transactional nature. In an attempt to articulate a clear definition for use in the then-fledgling literature of the hospitality industry, Brotherton (1999) reinforced this point, asserting that hospitality is defined in part by mutual benefit to its provider and its recipient. Although in-home hospitality may entail provision for the guest and the benefit of companionship or satisfaction for the host, Brotherton's definition fails to capture the spirit of hospitality as it is expressed in these personal relationships.

If home and hotel depict the most prevalent understandings of hospitality in our communities, it seems worth asking which of these best aligns with the kind of hospitality we seek to offer the patrons who visit our libraries. Certainly, we wish our students and colleagues to feel the relational care expressed in designing comfortable environments and welcoming visitors warmly. We want them to understand that we have the expertise required to grasp their needs and effectively identify the resources necessary to meet them. We want to offer those resources as freely as possible for the good of all who need them. For librarians of faith, we want to follow the example of Christ, who invited the needy without reservation and blessed them with resources that far exceeded their hopes.

Although the transactional definition supplied by Brotherton (1999) has limited relevance to the decidedly Christian expression of hospitality—both within the library and throughout the family of God—it conveys an important truth. Even at a hotel or restaurant, "for hospitality to exist, something more than hospitable behaviour must be evident" (Brotherton, p. 168). In other words, hospitality extends beyond mere interpersonal warmth in that the host provides for the needs of the guest or traveler. Admittedly, many proprietors succeed in anticipating such needs. Yet even the most well-appointed inns and hotels fall short of Christian hospitality in that they fail to provide for the next stage of the journey and are never entirely altruistic. They offer respite in the moment, but not the sort of preparation that "empowers the other to move on" (Oden, 2001, p. 147).

Stewart (2013) offers specificity about the unique facets of library hospitality, explaining that, for librarians, "[hospitality] is a manifestation of values, cultures, people, spaces, collections and other disparate but vitally important factors" (p. 286). This combination of individuals, attitudes, and resources yields an experience that recognizes and fulfills the distinctive needs of each library user. Patrons are guests of the library who approach its expansiveness in dependence on the librarian hosts who make its contents meaningful. The hospitable people who reach out to invite patrons into a purposeful relationship, the hospitable places where this relationship is experienced, and the hospitable practices that meet patrons' needs characterize hospitality within the field of librarianship. When love of Christ and love of others motivate these expressions of hospitality, they also characterize Christian librarianship.

Hospitable People

> *Therefore, welcome one another as Christ has welcomed you, for the glory of God.—Romans 15:1 (ESV)*

Perhaps the most essential component of hospitality is the heart of the host. In a book chapter called "Building a Place for Hospitality," Christine Pohl (2007) explains, "the character of the persons offering welcome is crucial if hospitality is to be life-giving" (p. 34). This emphasis on character is unsurprising from a Christian perspective, but it is not unique. Secular researchers (Johnson & Kazmer, 2011) agree, emphasizing the importance of sincerity and a "genuine motivation" (p. 398) to provide for patrons' needs. These authors go so far as to recommend that graduate programs in librarianship make an authentic spirit of welcome an entry requirement for admission, urging their readers to "consider means to evaluate potential students" in light of their propensity toward hospitality (p. 398).

The Reference and User Services Association (RUSA) of the American Library Association affirms the importance of being observably motivated to serve, asserting that the approachable librarian is "highly visible" (American Library Association [ALA], 2011, Guideline 1.1.1), "poised and ready to serve" (Guideline 1.1.2), and quick to show interest in the needs of the library's guests (Guideline 2.1.1). Of course, the character of a Christian librarian extends beyond readiness and apparent interest to include placing the needs of the one being served above our own. We pursue Christ's own character, understanding that true hospitality requires us to be discerning, wise, humble, and generous (Pohl, 2007, p. 34).

Particularly in the academic library, hospitality includes welcoming the guest into a community of learning and an ongoing conversation with its members. In doing so, this sort of hospitality "always presses those communities outward to make the circle of care larger" (Pohl, 1999, p. 129). Accordingly, Weaver (2012) emphasizes the need not only to love, but also to learn from, strangers. Such hospitality reaches beyond merely accommodating the presence of the stranger or guest, offering openness to the voice of the stranger, as well (Gundry, 2015). Among those counted as strangers are individuals who are strangers to our institutions, to our library facilities, or even to the research process (Weaver, 2011). Further, Weaver (2011) urges readers to consider it hospitality when we reach out to the strangers we would not otherwise encounter, pursuing them rather than awaiting their arrival. In doing so, we "[seek] reception into the lives and learning of the strangers who are our faculty and students and [love] them with Christ's love" (Weaver, 2012, final para.).

Even in Weaver's (2012) exploration of the stranger, these guests of the library are defined by an existing relationship with the community of which the library is a part. These strangers are the easily identified constituents of our libraries or institutions whom we have not yet met, but who are members of our primary community. In contrast, Iwaskow (2013) discusses the extension of hospitality beyond our core community to those described as "interested others," who are located at a variety of distances from our central service population. Among the challenges for the Christian librarian is how to extend hospitality to these interested others even when, for reasons of policy or scarcity, we are unable to serve them at the same level as members of our primary community due to any number of practical limitations (p. 291). Our resources for providing hospitality may be exhaustible; however, our spirit of hospitality can be nearly unlimited as we welcome the presence and voices of these more remote strangers despite our inability to equip them nearly as well as we would like for whatever journey awaits them.

Hospitality is expressed in relationships where a power differential is present, but it "can be provided in ways that value persons and give them a place in the community" (Pohl, 2007, p. 35). The nature of Christian hospitality is to place oneself in a position of service to each guest, not meting out care and resources as emblems of one's own power or intellect, but honoring the guest by serving with compassion and generosity. The guest is inherently dependent on the generosity of the host, who has control over access to the resources required to meet the need. Within the library, the availability of resources can pose a challenge as the host must often facilitate the needs of multiple guests simultaneously. Even the most hospitable librarian has finite resources (time, attention, logins, volumes, etc.); thus, the expression of hospitality involves a balance between generosity and stewardship (Gundry, 2015).

In the early church, the imbalances of power embodied in the roles of host and guest were ameliorated through the Christ-serving exercise of hospitality. Pohl (2007) explains, "Expressions of hospitality strengthened community bonds, guest/host roles could be fluid, and persons of different rank and status were received into the same place" (p. 32). The notion of fluid guest/host roles underscores the relational outcomes of hospitality: the guest is helped and empowered; the host is blessed and encouraged; and the host may well experience the future hospitality of the one initially received as guest. Librarians often experience this fulfilling cycle. Meeting the needs of others in the community— perhaps a faculty member with a research-related challenge—results in being invited to participate in an academic department meeting, being welcomed into the learning community of the faculty member's class, or being included in a rich conversation to which we would not otherwise have had entered. We live on both sides of the hospitality relationship, grateful for the invitations of others and fulfilled by the opportunity to serve one another in "covenant mutuality" (Berryhill, 2013, p. 88).

Hospitable Places

> *Unless the LORD builds the house, the builders labor in vain. Unless the LORD watches over the city, the guards stand watch in vain.—Psalm 127:1 (NIV)*

Generous, welcoming librarians provide the heart of hospitality in the settings where they live out their professional vocation. As essential as these hospitable people are, however, the settings themselves matter, as well. Hospitable places form the context within which welcome is extended and resources are shared, so librarians must invest themselves in creating "an environment conducive to the provision of those resources" (Johnson & Kazmer, 2011, p. 387). If hospitality is inextricably tied to "particular places" (Pohl, 2007, p. 27), then the library's spaces—whether physical or virtual—have the power to make it easier or more difficult for its guests to find help for their needs.

The embodied hospitality of the library extends beyond the people who work there to encompass the library itself. Mathews and Soistmann (2016) explain this phenomenon, contending, "We become attached to places because of what they enable us to do. They can provide us with energy and support and supply us with inspiration and comfort" (p. 24). Even when spaces are digital, they can become a meaningful source of relationship when they facilitate the interpersonal exchange of welcome, help, and provision that characterize hospitality. The RUSA Guidelines (ALA, 2011) designed to engender welcoming and effective librarian behaviors acknowledge that the library's digital space is a very real location and that our guests' experiences in that setting constitute interaction with the library as surely as those that occur within our walls.

Places become hospitable when they are offered freely to those in need. Sometimes, offering spaces in ways that make them accessible to patrons requires creativity. If welcoming guests means that we may have to "share our place, make use of what is available, or create new places" (Pohl, 2007, p. 27), then we must hold the details of those places less tightly. The details that keep patrons from encountering our space positively should be identified and resolved to the best of our ability. The *Practical Handbook of Library Architecture* (Schlipf & Moorman, 2018) mentions several of these details in regard to physical libraries and provides recommendations for avoiding or rectifying them. These challenges include poor lighting, badly designed service desks, absent or inconsistent climate control, and parking problems, among others. Even when the library "presents a sense of openness," conveying that "everyone can use it," and "all are welcome here," (Mathews & Soistmann, 2016, p. 98), uncomfortable furnishings, confusingly arranged collections, or hard-to-navigate websites may discourage students and faculty from accepting the hospitality we offer.

In the Sermon on the Mount, Christ used everyday examples to demonstrate that God's intentions for us are best fulfilled when we usefully serve God's purposes. In Matthew 5:13, he says, "You are the salt of the earth. But if the salt loses its saltiness, how can it be made salty again? It is no longer good for anything, except to be thrown out and trampled underfoot." In verse 15, he continues, "Neither do people light a lamp and put it under a bowl. Instead they put it on its stand, and it gives light to everyone in the house" (NIV). Accomplishing the purposes for which we were created is an essential component of Christian devotion. If hospitality is an expression of our faith, then the means by which we extend hospitality—not just what we do, but also where we do it—bear witness to our love for God and neighbor.

The capacity of a library to convey that those with needs are welcome, that help is accessible, and that ongoing relationships are available with both the host and other guests defines its usefulness as a hospitable place. In *Encoding Space: Shaping Learning Environments That Unlock Human Potential*, Mathews and Soistmann (2016) explain the importance of this individual connection to a space: "a space becomes a place when it rises above being a mere utility. Places have social and personal significance. They mean something to us" (p. 17). These authors assert that the way a place makes us feel is the catalyst for our attraction to it, which in turn allows it to accomplish the purpose for which it was created. This observation should combine with genuine care to encourage us to learn all we can about how our libraries affect patrons and to embrace new perspectives if necessary.

Hospitable Practices

> *Suppose a brother or sister is without clothes and daily food. If one of you says to him, "Go, I wish you well; keep warm and well fed," but does nothing about his physical needs, what good is it? In the same way, faith by itself, if it is not accompanied by action, is dead.—James 2:15–17 (NIV)*

Conveying a message of welcome and care without actually providing for the one in need is at best poor librarianship and at worst failed Christianity. Outreach to the community may draw students, faculty, or other users into the spaces of our libraries, but we must take care not to conflate simple headcounts or website traffic with meaningful connections. Rather, hospitality must be an expression of our identity as the people of Christ and as librarians. We must remember that outreach and marketing efforts are means to provide the opportunity for relationship, but that these efforts are not themselves hospitality. In fact, "to view hospitality as a means to an end, to use it instrumentally, is antithetical to seeing it as a way of life, as a tangible expression of love" (Pohl, 1999, p. 127).

Perhaps we avoid the commodification of hospitality by remembering the fullness of the Christian's role as host. Biblical references to hospitality extend the obligations of the host beyond provision for the needs of the moment, as do the professional guidelines of librarianship. The RUSA Guidelines emphasize the importance of communicating in ways that help the patron become more self-sufficient when similar needs arise in the future (ALA, 2011, Guideline 4.1.8). In Christian hospitality, guests are not only received with compassion and supplied with necessary resources, but they are also equipped for the next stage of their journey. The Pauline epistles repeatedly mention this aspect of hospitality. "After I go through Macedonia," Paul tells the Corinthians, "I will come to you—for I will be going through Macedonia. Perhaps I will stay with you awhile, or even spend the winter, so that you can help me on my journey, wherever I go" (1 Corinthians 16:5–6, NIV). Likewise, Paul writes to the Romans: "I plan to [see you] when I go to Spain. I hope to visit you while passing through and to have you assist me on my journey there, after I have enjoyed your company for a while" (Romans 15:24, NIV). Paul asks for the extension of hospitality to others, as well, instructing Titus, "Do everything you can to help Zenas the lawyer and Apollos on their way and see that they have everything they need" (Titus 3:13, NIV). In the family of God, we not only welcome the traveler and provide for the needs of the moment; we are also compelled to ease the burden of ongoing travel.

The specific practices that most effectively draw guests into a library's spaces and encourage the development of supportive relationships differ from community to community. Although the individual practices may differ, however, every practice should convey at least one of the four provisions Berryhill (2013) identifies as characteristic of a library's hospitality: comfort, protection, sustenance, and equipping. Writing specifically in the context of theological librarianship, she operationalizes these terms in useful ways. Comfort refers to the physical environment into which the guest is invited, and protection describes an intellectual environment of free inquiry. Berryhill defines sustenance as the nourishing content of the resources that librarians select, preserve, and open to the patron. Finally, equipping connotes preparation for future needs through the modeling of information literacy and the prioritization of ethical information use.

In reference to the church more broadly, Oden (2001) describes hospitality as a series of stages: welcome, in which the guest is invited to come in; restoration, when the guest's pressing needs are met; communion, a period of shared experience and relationship; and sending forth, freeing the well-supplied guest to continue with the journey that awaits (p. 145). "Hospitality," Oden asserts, "does not create systems of dependence, but empowers the other to move on" (p. 147). Successive steps of the journey become the shared responsibility of the departing visitor and the next person or institution from whom the traveler seeks assistance.

Hospitality and the Christian Librarian

> *Dear friend, you are faithful in what you are doing for the brothers, even though they are strangers to you. They have told the church about your love. You will do well to send them on their way in a manner worthy of God.—3 John 1:5–6 (NIV)*

Scripture is clear about God's intention that people of faith care for both those within and those outside the body of Christ. In Titus 1:7–8 and 1 Timothy 3:1–3, the Apostle Paul indicates that a track record of hospitality is one of the characteristics required of those who would fulfill leadership roles among the believers. Hospitality in this context is evidence of Christian character and fitness for service within the church. Not only is hospitality a requirement for service, but it is also a command for the entire community of faith. Paul admonishes the Romans, "Share with God's people who are in need. Practice hospitality" (Romans 12:13, NIV).

In the academic library, hospitality is a demeanor, a motivation, and an expression of care. A hospitable spirit is embodied in the welcoming, approachable librarian who reaches out toward those in need and removes obstacles to relationship, even the potentially transactional relationships that so often characterize our work. This generosity is motivated not by a desire for recognition or reward, but by sincere interest in "the least of these" (Matthew 25:40, NIV)—those whose relationship with us is defined by their need. In the name of Christ, we offer hospitality by meeting these pressing needs of the stranger, the novice, or the perplexed. And we continue to give. Whether face to face or at incredible distance, our hospitality provides resources beyond the need of the moment, preparing our patrons well for their continuing journey. Can librarians who have no faith commitment express hospitality to their patrons? Inarguably, yes. But when we as Christian librarians welcome our patrons with a desire to help them, participate in relationship with those patrons in ways that provide for their known needs, and equip them well for the needs that lie ahead, we do so as an expression of our faith and in service to our God.

Recommendations for Hospitality

> *God is not unjust; he will not forget your work and the love you have shown him as you have helped his people and continue to help them.*—Hebrews 6:10 (NIV)

This concluding section of this essay provides some suggestions for beginning to think more intentionally in your library about providing hospitality in pursuit of the character of Christ and in love for the people you serve. Some suggestions may be more appropriate for your library setting than others, but all of them are offered in a spirit of encouragement and in the belief that hospitality is "a practice of small gestures" (Newman, 2007, p. 174) that accumulate in meaningful ways. Embrace the conversations that allow you and your colleagues to explore with one another what hospitality may look like in your library. Work diligently to embolden hospitable people, to create hospitable places, and to initiate hospitable practices. "And whatever you do, whether in word or deed, do it all in the name of the Lord Jesus, giving thanks to God the Father through him" (Colossians 3:17, NIV).

Hospitable People

SHARED VALUES

Within your library, dialog intentionally about what it means to practice hospitality. What values provide the motivation for hospitality for you and your colleagues? If you work at a Christian institution of higher education, talk together about scriptural accounts of hospitality and what they demonstrate about the character of the host. If you work in a secular environment, share personal remembrances of instances when each person received hospitality. Each colleague might describe characteristics of the host—how that person extended welcome, recognized needs large or mundane, and expressed care. What values do these experiences suggest? How might they be relevant to the expression of hospitality within your library?

HOST'S HEART

Brainstorm with your colleagues to identify ways that your heart of hospitality could be made more visible to your community. Review your library's mission statement. Does it express your collective commitment to care for your patrons and their needs? If this component is missing from your mission statement or core values, consider revising or expanding these important representations of your priorities. If this component is present—or if you add it during revision—publicize it by including it in documents produced by your library, by posting it on your library's website, or by displaying it at service desks in the library facility.

Hospitable Places

PHYSICAL SPACES

Identify several students who do not often use your library. Invite them to enter each space within the facility and to reflect on whether or not they feel welcome. What aspects of each space draw them in and make them feel like staying? Which details discourage them from feeling like they belong in the space? Consider conducting a similar exercise with students who spend a great deal of time in your library. Why do they find it welcoming? Are there areas they believe could be made more welcoming? Reflect with your colleagues about these details to identify any areas where you have the authority or resources to address inhospitable elements of your library. Make a plan to promote the elements of your library that students identify as welcoming.

DIGITAL SPACES

Although we often evaluate our digital spaces in terms of their functionality or usefulness, librarians may not invest as much attention in considering whether these spaces are also hospitable. Review your library's digital spaces for signs of hospitality. Do they clearly convey that librarians are available to communicate via multiple media—chat, text, email, or phone—when users need help? Many libraries promote these services without necessarily emphasizing the people who provide them. Converse with your colleagues about how to convey that library personnel are friendly and approachable. As one example, you might consider using relaxed, informal photos rather than professional headshots of librarians in areas of the website that encourage users to initiate contact with the library. If your library's digital presence includes more images of facilities or resources than of people interacting with them, discuss replacing these images with photos that show how the library is actively meeting people's needs.

Hospitable Practices

DAILY PRACTICES

The daily practices that demonstrate your library's commitment to hospitality are the most influential expressions of your care for the members of your community. Collaborate with others in your library to identify a set of specific behaviors that convey warmth, demonstrate interest in your guests' needs, and ensure that those needs are met. Consider gathering a group of regular library users to ask which member of the library team makes them feel most welcome in the library, and ask clarifying questions to identify the specific practices that elicit that feeling of belonging. Perhaps other members of the team can adopt those practices, as well. For personal reflection, consider these questions: Do you introduce yourself by name to each person who seeks your help? Do you take care not to end a research consultation until you are confident the present need has been satisfied? Do you ask students or faculty about their ongoing academic work, extending an offer of support for future needs?

SPECIAL EVENTS

Special events that draw both long-standing and new patrons into the library can provide opportunities to deepen existing relationships and establish new ones. During the planning process for each special event, discuss its purpose. Events that enrich the social or intellectual life of your community may be an excellent investment of energy and other resources, but not all of these beneficial events are intentional expressions of hospitality. For any event specifically intended to enrich the library's relationships with current and potential patrons, determine ahead of time how your library will use the event to accomplish that purpose. What will library personnel do or say to demonstrate their care for guests? Communicate with your colleagues about the library's goals for connecting the special event with your ongoing hospitality efforts, and create a simple plan for making those connections visible to those who participate in the event. Use every interaction that takes place during special events to communicate a message of welcome—not just into the library's space, but into relationship with its people, as well.

REFERENCES

American Library Association (ALA). (2011). *Guidelines for behavioral performance of reference and information service providers*. Retrieved from www.ala.org/rusa/resources/guidelines/guidelinesbehavioral.
Berryhill, C. M. (2013). The guest brings the blessing: Hospitality in theological librarianship. *American Theological Library Association Summary of Proceedings, 67*, 84–89.
Brotherton, B. (1999). Towards a definitive view of the nature of hospitality and hospitality management. *International Journal of Contemporary Hospitality Management, 11*(4), 165–173.
Gundry, J. (2015). Incorporating concepts of hospitality into theological library assessment. *Theological Librarianship, 8*(1), 10–15.
Iwaskow, T. P. (2013). Second presentation: Hospitality and our broader communities. *American Theological Library Association Summary of Proceedings, 67*, 288–294.
Johnson, E. D. M., & Kazmer, M. M. (2011). Library hospitality: Some preliminary considerations. *The Library Quarterly, 81*(4), 383–403.
Mathews, B., & Soistmann, L. A. (2016). *Encoding space: Shaping learning environments that unlock human potential*. Chicago: Association of College and Research Libraries.
Newman, E. (2007). *Untamed hospitality: Welcoming God and other strangers*. Grand Rapids: Brazos.
Oden, A. G. (2001). *And you welcomed me: A sourcebook on hospitality in early Christianity*. Nashville: Abingdon Press.
Pohl, C. D. (1999). *Making room: Recovering hospitality as a Christian tradition*. Grand Rapids: William B. Eerdmans.
Pohl, C. D. (2007). Building a place for hospitality. In R. B. Kruschwitz (Ed.), *Hospitality* (pp. 27–36). Waco: Center for Christian Ethics.
Schlipf, F., & Moorman, J. A. (2018). *The practical handbook of library architecture: Creating building spaces that work*. Chicago: ALA Editions.
Stewart, D. R. (2013). Theological libraries and the "theology of hospitality": First presentation. *American Theological Library Association Summary of Proceedings, 67*, 286–288.
Weaver, J. B. (2012). The library and biblical hospitality. Retrieved from https://blogs.acu.facul/2012/10/15/the-library-and-biblical-hospitality-dr-john-b-weaver/.

Information Overload, Information Anxiety and Theological Ethics

PAUL HARTOG

Abstract

In a previous essay (Hartog, 2017), I described nine practical recommendations for librarians working with those afflicted with information anxiety. While that previous work addressed information anxiety within the framework of the professional responsibilities of librarians, this present study will address the topic within a comprehensive framework of theological ethics. We often think of information ethics applying to matters such as access equity, intellectual property, privacy protection, and the virtuous use of information. A robust theological ethic, however, can also address the personal responsibility of responding to information anxiety. The Bible condemns worry and pride, and it commends meditation and discernment. Biblical virtues like temperance, patience, contentment, and gratitude apply to one's response to information overload. Theological truths such as divine sovereignty, the Lordship of Christ, the Creator-creature distinction, God's revelatory activities, the kenosis of Christ, the *imago Dei*, human finitude, the noetic results of the Fall, and progressive sanctification can inform the Christian response. As believers think God's thoughts after him, they will be empowered to resist the transitory and consumeristic values that often induce information anxiety. They will be guided by the fear of God and the proper ordering of values. Christian librarians in particular should embody a response informed by a comprehensive theological ethic—an embodied ethic which can be "caught" as well as taught.

Introduction

We live in an information society characterized by globalization. In 2017, the Internet global penetration rate surpassed the halfway mark for the first time, as "Internet users" comprised 54.4 percent of the world population. Nearly half of those users (48.7 percent) resided in Asia (Miniwatts, 2018). According to some futurists, by 2020 information will double every seventy days, with 1.7 megabytes of new information being created every second, for every human being on earth (McDermott, 2017; compare Schilling, 2013). This information inundation affects both access and retrieval. Ironically, if one Googles "information overload," one is overloaded with 16.8 million hits in 0.37 seconds. "We're drowning in information" (McDermott, 2017).

Information Overload

While similar precursors had long existed (Bawden & Robinson, 2009, p. 182), Bertram Gross seems to have coined the term "information overload" with his 1964 work *The Managing of Organizations* (p. 856). The phrase was popularized by Alvin Toffler's *Future Shock* in 1970 (pp. 350–355). The *Collins English Dictionary* (2018) declares that "information overload" occurs when "someone has so much information that they are unable to deal with it." The *PC Magazine Encyclopedia* (2018) goes further in its definition of "information overload":

> A symptom of the high-tech age, which is too much information for one person to absorb in a world of expanding digital technology. It primarily comes from the gigantic amount of content on the Internet, including search engine results, blogs and social media.

The complicating factors of our digital age and information economy reside in the vast amount of information available in multiple formats, the speed of access, the ubiquity of connectivity, the simplicity of creating/replicating and sharing information, the increase in information channels, the flattening of information contexts, and the bypassing of traditional gatekeepers represented by presses, editors, and formal institutions (Bawden & Robinson, 2009; Feng & Agosto, 2017). The resulting information overload has been described with a bevy of negative metaphors, including "info-flood," "info-glut," "info-smog," "infoxication," "information explosion," and "information assault" (compare Shenk, 1997).

Information Anxiety

In 1989, Richard Wurman, the influential information architect (Wurman & Bradford, 1997) and founder of TED talks ("History of TED," 2016), issued a breakthrough book, entitled *Information Anxiety* (Wurman, 1989a). This seminal volume launched the phrase "information anxiety" into popular discourse (Girard & Allison, 2008, p. 111). According to Wurman, the apprehension or stress of information anxiety is caused by "the ever-widening gap between what we understand and what we think we should understand" (see Conhaim, 2001, p. 11). Janet Fox (1998) has described four contributing factors. First, "both the volume and the speed" of information dissemination are accelerating (Fox, 1988, p. 1). Second, our education and training do not prepare us "to deal with the information explosion" (Fox, 1988, p. 1). Third, "most of the systems devised for managing time and organizing and storing information and resources" do not fit "right-brain dominant" individuals (Fox, 1988, p. 1). Fourth, "well-entrenched values, habits and attitudes that once may have been useful and desirable often get in the way of learning to cope with new realities" (Fox, 1998, p. 1).

If "information overload" is the objective status of having too much information to process, then "information anxiety" is the subjective experience of the resulting stress (although many authors conflate the two). Information anxiety is the sense of stress and helplessness, losing control, being overwhelmed, not keeping up with the information available, or not succeeding at an information task. High information demands can create a sense of information burden (Horrigan, 2016). The symptoms of information anxiety include attention deficit, fatigue, frustration, irritability, confusion, and lack of focus (Hemp, 2009; McDermott, 2017; Shin, 2014). Information anxiety can freeze information seekers in indecisiveness, as they suffer from the "paradox of choice" and "paralysis by analysis" (Bawden & Robinson, 2009, p. 182; Cooper, 2000, p. 16; Davidson, 2012; Ifijeh, 2010). Info-stress can lead to trouble sleeping and in extreme cases can damage physical health (Bawden & Robinson, 2009, p. 183; Ifijeh, 2010; McDermott, 2017). In a 2001 survey, one third of managers believed that information overload had damaged their health (Bawden & Robinson, 2009, p. 184; compare Bawden, 2001). Additional studies have demonstrated that information overload also takes a toll on church leaders in particular (Larson, 1995; Miller, 2001).

In short, "information anxiety" is "the human cost of information overload" (*BusinessDictionary*, 2018). The apprehensive stress caused by information overload has been called "perhaps the most familiar of the 'information pathologies'" (Bawden & Robinson, 2009, p. 182). Other information afflictions include "info-addiction," in which "information junkies" seeking an "information fix" suffer from "information withdrawal" without the stimulus (Bawden & Robinson, 2009, p. 185; Dean, 1991). Information anxiety, however, relates to being inundated by the proliferation of information in one's society or personal life. If info-addicts are stimulated by information, then the info-anxious are stupefied by information. The former are characterized by obsession, the latter by apprehension.

While information anxiety is related to "technological anxiety" (or "computer anxiety") and "library anxiety," it distinctly concerns the knowledge content (information) rather than the means of delivery (computers or technology) or conventional location (the library) (Hartog, 2017, p. 45). Information anxiety "relates to apprehension about finding, selecting, processing, interpreting, managing, and applying information" (Hartog, 2017, p. 45). Michael McCarthy (1991) describes information anxiety as a "kind of stupor, a feeling that we simply can't keep up, can't read fast enough, don't know how to locate the information we need, don't have time to sort through or think about all the data surrounding us" (p. 12). John Girard and Michael Allison (2008) explain that "subjects are more likely to develop information anxiety as the tasks they are completing become more complex" (p. 113). A 2016 Pew Research Center survey reported that 20 percent of Americans feel overloaded by information, which is actually down from 27 percent in the decade prior (see Horrigan, 2016). This decrease may suggest that individuals are learning and implementing various coping strategies.

Coping Strategies and Tactics

Richard Wurman prescribed "coping mechanisms" for those who suffer from info-stress:

> Accept that there is much you won't understand. Plan an information strategy. Separate what you are really interested in from what you think you should be interested in. Moderate your use of technology. Minimize the time you spend reading or watching news that isn't germane to your life. Reduce your pile of office reading. You can always look it up [Wurman, 1989b, pp. 127–130, 134].

Others have compiled similar lists of tactics (McDermott, 2017; Shin, 2014), which can be simplified to the threefold strategy of filtering, withdrawing, and queuing (Feng & Agosto, 2017). Lisa Spiro (2010) alternatively speaks of selecting, sorting, and storing. In their role as information professionals, librarians can share these and other "best practices" or "strategies for intervention" (Bawden & Robinson, 2009, p. 188; Ifijeh, 2010). Therefore, information literacy is a burgeoning and vital role of professional librarianship (Burkhardt & MacDonald, 2010).

Librarians should adopt "a proactive response to information inundation" (Cooper, 2000, p. 17). Elsewhere, I have recommended nine tactics to implement, in order to assist the info-anxious (Hartog, 2017, pp. 50–55):

1. Teach coping techniques (as described in the paragraph above).
2. Create a safe environment of information inquiry, combining "high tech" with "personal touch" [compare Conner, 2014, p. 16].
3. Highlight realistic expectations, reminding patrons that a level of information anxiety is "normal" and "they are not alone" [Burkhardt & MacDonald, 2010, p.11].
4. Begin with the known, by making connections and building on what patrons already find comfortable [Wurman, 2001, p. 261].
5. Teach effective reading techniques, including skimming for key concepts and finding summary reviews [Kennedy, 2001, pp. 40–41].
6. Train in navigating and filtering the info-flood, through the proficient use of search engines and databases.
7. Share and model organization strategies, ranging from time-management tactics, to office-space orderliness, to the systematic arrangement of argumentation [Eklof, 2013, p. 251].
8. Exhibit patience, by avoiding impatient body language, complaints, criticism, and intellectual inflexibility.
9. Market information-help services, thus establishing librarians as "primary information professionals" [Biggs, 1989, p. 411].

This list of nine professional recommendations forms a basic "how-to-manual" for librarians working with the info-anxious. With this present essay, I would like to supplement these professional tactics with applicable principles from Christian ethics. In doing so, I will delve beneath the surface of coping mechanisms and responsive tactics, to foundations rooted in theological ethics.

Information Ethics

Information anxiety can be an ethical issue, and to this extent, it is a matter to be addressed by theological ethics. First, we must consider the wider context of information ethics. According to Jared Bielby, information ethics is a field of applied ethics associated with similar fields and sub-fields: computer ethics, cyber ethics, media ethics, library ethics, bio-information ethics, and business information ethics (Bielby, 2014). One could add other related disciplines, such as communication ethics, information ecology, and data science ethics.

Traditionally, information ethics encompasses such topics as privacy and security, intellectual property and copyright, misinformation and fake news, the digital divide or information divide, information integrity versus information manipulation, and the ethical organization of information. In other words, the ethical issues found within the professional field of information science reflect a wide spectrum of topics, including information collection, information organization, information access, information retrieval, information use, and information dissemination.

Information ethics addresses issues stemming from both social ethics and personal ethics. For example, information ethics attends to the economic aspects of copyright infringement, but also the ethical ramifications of a student plagiarizing from a roommate. Information ethics discusses cybersecurity and the corporate breaching of privacy, but also the unacceptability of reading a friend's private email. Information ethics addresses the political results of disseminating "fake news," but also the personal responsibility involved in evaluating information on the Web. Information ethics concerns the social implications of information organization, but also the personal ramifications of withholding pertinent information from a friend wrestling with a decision.

Information Anxiety and Biblical Ethics

As discussed earlier in this essay, information anxiety is a personal experience, yet one embedded within the social phenomenon of information overload. Information overload can afflict individuals in both educational and professional settings (Eklof, 2013, p. 247). Information anxiety can impair judgment and can negatively influence both social and political activity (Williams, 2008). It can also reduce workplace creativity and productivity (Hemp. 2009; Ryder, 2011). Yet the root of information anxiety remains a subjective, personal reaction to information inundation.

Can information anxiety, as a subject of personal ethics embedded within sociocultural phenomena, be framed and informed by theological ethics? The field of "theological ethics" examines the moral instruction and moral formation of the Scriptures as developed within the Christian interpretive tradition(s). "Theological ethics examines the interaction of religious wisdom with the most pressing contemporary moral issues, both personal and social, and addresses the important challenges related to development of faith and the life of faith in community" (Boston College, 2018). While theological ethicists have spilled much ink on business ethics, legal ethics, and medical ethics, they have engaged relatively little with the field of information ethics.

At first glance, claiming information anxiety as an ethical topic worthy of theological reflection may seem like a stretch. The biblical authors never faced the inundation of the Internet or the data-overload of the digital age. Biblical characters did not experience info-flood, info-glut, and infoxication to the degree these problems plague contemporary society. Certainly, Qoholeth declared in the Book of Ecclesiastes, "Of making many books there is no end" (Ecclesiastes 12:12, ESV). Porcius Festus, the Roman governor of Judea, charged Paul, "Much learning is driving you mad" (Acts 26:24, NKJV). Yet neither the Old Testament preacher nor the New Testament apostle faced the information explosion of the expanding digital universe (Gantz & Reinsel, 2012).

Notwithstanding, theological ethicists insist that biblical principles can address topics un-touched by the direct statements of Scripture. The Bible never mentions methamphetamines, but it does insist upon taking care of one's body, the temple of the Holy

Spirit. The Scriptures never directly address high-tech sexual encounters in a virtual reality world, but they do condemn lust. Similarly, the Bible never explicitly discusses information anxiety, but it does confront anxiety and worry in general. In the Sermon on the Mount, Jesus exhorted his audience not to worry or be anxious (Matthew 6:25, 31, 34). The solution to worry is trust in God (Matthew 6:25–34). The Apostle Paul counseled, "Do not be anxious about anything" (Philippians 4:6, ESV). He added, "but in everything by prayer and supplication with thanksgiving let your requests be made known to God" (Philippians 4:6, ESV). In a similar vein, the First Epistle of Peter encourages, "Casting all your anxieties on him, because he cares for you" (1 Peter 5:7, ESV).

The Scriptures also address the human tendency toward pride of knowledge. "God resists the proud but gives grace to the humble" (James 4:6, ESV; 1 Peter 5:5, ESV), a nugget of moral teaching surely applicable to those who pride themselves in conquering the modern information assault. By contrast, the wise person knows the limited nature of his or her knowledge (Proverbs 30:2–6). The virtuous individual prioritizes a heart of love above a mind filled with information. Indeed, if one possessed all knowledge but had not love, it would profit nothing (1 Corinthians 13:2–3). Yet the apostolic desire was "that your love may abound still more and more in knowledge and all discernment" (Philippians 1:9, NKJV). "For this very reason, make every effort to supplement your faith with goodness, goodness with knowledge, knowledge with self-control, self-control with endurance, endurance with godliness, godliness with brotherly affection, and brotherly affection with love" (2 Peter 1:5–7, CSB).

Biblical distinctions between knowledge, understanding, discernment, prudence, and wisdom may serve to prioritize one's cognitive interactions.

> We must not be hoodwinked by talk of the information age into thinking that the having of information, or worse just the bare possibility of unhindered and easy electronic access to information, is a substitute for the acquiring of productively useful knowledge, let alone the getting of wisdom [Carnley, 2002, p. 329].

As Christian library staff-members and library patrons, we do not pursue information and knowledge for our own sake (compare Fuller, 2017, p. 91). "Wisdom is supreme—so get wisdom" (Proverbs 4:7; CSB).

In practical terms, discernment and prudence are required in information "satisficing," which is defined as retrieving enough information to meet a need without being overwhelmed (Bawden & Robinson, 2009, p. 185). Proper "satisficing" positively reflects the "bounded rationality" of our human existence. "Bounded rationality thinking is limited by the available information, the tractability of the decision problem, the cognitive limitations of our minds, and the time available to make the decision" (English, 2016). "However," David Bawden and Lyn Robinson warn, "it is important to note that satisficing must be carried out rationally; there must be some clear rationale as to why decisions are being taken" (2008, p. 6).

They continue by stating that discernment and prudence must distinguish between appropriate (good) satisficing and inappropriate (bad) satisficing, because the latter merely amounts to "information avoidance, or a random and contingent selection of sources and material" (2008, p. 6). Andrew McDermott counsels, "There *is* a time to hoard information, a time to share it, *and* a time to delete information. There's even a time to ignore information" (McDermott, 2017; compare Raymond, 2005). Indeed, "there is an occasion for everything, and a time for every activity under the sun" (Ecclesiastes

3:1, CSB), including "a time to seek, and a time to lose; a time to keep, and a time to cast away" (Ecclesiastes 3:6, ESV).

Regarding biblical virtues, we are to be characterized by patience and temperance (Galatians 5:22–23). Our "endless curiosity" for information (Solis, 2012), should be tempered with proper contentment (1 Timothy 6:6). Our hearts should be filled with gratitude and thanksgiving (1 Thessalonians 5:18). Moreover, meekness, gentleness, and compassion (love) should characterize those who work with the info-anxious, including librarians or other information professionals (Galatians 5:22–23). When asked what the greatest commandment was, the incarnate Savior responded, "Love the Lord your God with all your heart, and with all your soul, and with all your mind" (Matthew 22:37, CSB). He immediately appended, "The second is like it: Love your neighbor as yourself" (Matthew 22:39, CSB). This "dual love command" forms the core of biblical ethics (James 2:8; 1 John 4:21), and its values are reflected in the "law of Christ" in Pauline moral theology (Romans 13:8; 1 Corinthians 9:21; Galatians 5:14, 6:2).

Information Anxiety and Theological Ethics

Beyond these moral imperatives and virtues, Christian theology provides the building blocks to form a comprehensive framework in response to information anxiety. The info-anxious, whose thinking is often formed by untruths and half-truths, need to renew their minds by thinking God's thought after him (Romans 12:2). God is the Lord of all—there is no facet of his entire creation over which he does not have a rightful claim. There is no human endeavor outside the pale of his authority. As Abraham Kuyper quipped, "There is not a square inch in the whole domain of our human existence over which Christ, who is Sovereign over all, does not cry, 'Mine!'" (Bratt, 1998, p. 488). He is therefore the Lord of our information creation, organization, access, retrieval, dissemination, and use.

The doctrine of divine omniscience reminds us that God knows all things perfectly well. By contrast, the Lord takes into account our human frailty and finitude. We, too, must "embrace constraints," as reflected in our finitude (Spiro, 2010). The doctrine of divine sovereignty teaches us that God superintends the world and stands over the unfolding of human events. Neither the invention of the Internet nor the development of the digital universe have taken him by surprise or caused him to wring his hands in desperation. Information professionals may recommend "*taking control* of one's information environment" (Bawden & Robinson, 2009, p. 187; italics original). Yet we do not ultimately "control our own destiny," no matter how many strategies we employ or how much information we acquire. In the 2016 Pew Research Center survey, 79 percent indicated that the following statement described them "very well": "Having a lot of information makes me feel like I have more control over things in my life" (see Horrigan, 2016). The info-stressed often sense a loss of control or feeling "out of control" (Bawden & Robinson, 2009, p. 183; Fox, 1998). The doctrine of God's sovereignty reminds us that God always remains in control.

The Lord is a God of order and design, demonstrating the inherent goodness of organization and structure. Through common grace, he allows the unregenerate to create, organize, retrieve, and disseminate meaningful and significant information. The revealing character of God reflects an information-disseminator, and the doctrine of progressive revelation teaches that he works with humans through time—not in a single download. The doctrine of God's voluntary hiddenness reminds us that God chooses when, how, and to what degree he reveals himself (Moser, 2009). One can even think of biblical characters who experienced a "revelatory overload" of sorts (Isaiah 6:1–5; John 18:6; Acts 22:6–11; Revelation 1:12–20). The sufficiency of Scripture demonstrates that God has given all we need to know to love and obey him—everything necessary for the maturity of the believer, as reflected in life and godliness (2 Timothy 3:16–17; 2 Peter 1:3).

In his kenotic humbling, Jesus grew in wisdom as well as stature and favor with God and humanity (Luke 2:52). The Son is the revelator of the Father (John 1:18), and in him are hidden "all the treasures of wisdom and knowledge" (Colossians 2:3, CSB). The Holy Spirit illuminates the understanding of the believer, so as to comprehend the things of God. The infinite-finite polarity of the Creator-creature distinction remains, even as we progress in thinking God's thoughts after him. Made in the *imago Dei*, we reflect this likeness through personality, morality, volition, rationality, and creativity (compare Fuller, 2017, p. 84). As the epitome of God's creation intended to image him on earth, humans were called to serve as royal stewards (Psalm 8:3–8). We are more than brains embedded within a physical body. The Scriptures speak of the human soul, spirit, heart, mind, conscience, and will. Yet the Bible also discusses the noetic results of the Fall—how sin corrupts the entire human person, including our minds and thus our interaction with information and knowledge. As sinners we are inclined to use information and knowledge for our own selfish purposes, thus alienating ourselves even further from God and from others.

Salvation comes by divine grace (Ephesians 2:8–9), and not by an accomplishment of knowledge (*gnosis*). Moreover, the believer becomes more Christ-like through the processes of progressive sanctification. Growth in grace begins with where we are. We do not reach perfection, including perfect knowledge, in this sphere of life (1 Corinthians 13:8–13). Scrupulous individuals and those with unrealistic perfectionist tendencies may strive for a perfection of knowledge, but such a mindset induces information anxiety (McDermott, 2017). Believers gather into local churches, with individual members using their God-given gifts and abilities for the sake of the body. One expects that these diversely gifted members will also bring distinctive knowledge bases to the common table—no member must master all the available information. The *ekklesia* forms our character not simply by disseminating information, but by shaping habits through corporate worship and spiritual formation. Finally, we are reminded that humans will not bring in the eschatological kingdom through the accumulation of knowledge or information (compare Daniel 12:4, 13). The *eschaton*, like our redemption, will come by divine initiation.

Conclusion

In the meantime, as we live in hopeful expectation of the *eschaton*, we are morally responsible for our reaction to information inundation. As Clay Shirky quipped, "There's no such thing as information overload—only filter failure" (see Solis, 2012). Will we allow the inundation to result in information anxiety? We need not only information filters, but also moral filters of virtues and values. We need to take every thought captive (2 Corinthians 10:5). Brian Solis has argued that the sense of information overload is "a symptom of our desire to not focus on what's important" and is therefore a choice (Solis,

2012). One could argue that axiological choices (choices of value) are foundational to a proper response to information anxiety. We must learn to "approve the things that are excellent" (Philippians 1:9). The training of such evaluative discernment requires training and mature experience (Hebrews 5:12–14).

The info-anxious are often "driven by relevance or the fear of irrelevance" (Solis, 2012). A fear of man often lies at the root of such drives and motivations, rather than the fear of God. According to the Bible, however, "The fear of the Lord is the beginning of wisdom, and the knowledge of the Holy One is understanding" (Proverbs 9:10, CSB). Sometimes we simply manifest what has been labeled as FOMO, or a "fear of missing out" by not engaging the information available (Palladino, 2007, pp. 118–119). Unfortunately, such a mindset is often attached to an inability to discern what is truly important—what ethicists call "moral prioritization" or "the proper ordering of values" (Littlejohn, 1993, pp. 90–91). Christians are to retain an eternal perspective in the midst of the ephemeral values of this transitory world (2 Corinthians 4:18). We should not only be aware of the dangers of the "impermanence of information," we also need to guard against "shallow novelty" and fashionable soundbites (Bawden & Robinson, 2009, p. 186).

Brian Solis maintains that "information overload is a symptom of over consumption and the inability to refine online experiences" (Solis, 2012). A consumeristic mindset, including the consumption of information, should be tempered by contentment and satisfaction in Christ. We are not to be conformed to the axiological frameworks of the world, but to be transformed by the renewing of our minds (Romans 12:2). Interestingly, information professionals recommend the cultivation of "space for reflection," and they even use the language of "quiet time" (Spiro, 2010). The Bible, of course, advocates meaningful practices of meditation upon the Word and works of God (Joshua 1:8; Psalm 1:2; 119; 143:5).

Not all Christian librarians will be able to discuss this full theological ethic with their patrons who struggle with information anxiety. Those who work in Christian environments will possess a fuller freedom to teach biblical commands, principles, and doctrines openly and directly. Nevertheless, those who are not employed in such contexts can still model a theologically informed ethic. Their lips may not be able to proclaim biblical truths and texts, but their lives can reflect biblical virtues and values. In fact, all Christian librarians should faithfully embody a robust theological ethic—an embodied ethic which can be "caught" as well as taught.[1]

Note

1. I wish to thank the Association of Christian Librarians for a President's Conference Scholarship that allowed me to attend the 2018 Annual Conference in Asbury, Kentucky, where I presented these materials. I am grateful for the refining conversations that the workshop stimulated.

References

Bawden, D. (2001). Information overload. *Library & Information Briefings*, 92, 1–15.
Bawden, D., & Robinson, L. (2009). The dark side of information: Overload, anxiety and other paradoxes and pathologies. *Journal of Information Science*, 35(2), 180–191.
Bielby, J. (2014). "Information ethics II: Towards a unified taxonomy." Retrieved from https://www.academia.edu/4896164/Information_Ethics_II_Towards_a_Unified_Taxonomy.
Biggs, M. (1989). Information overload and information seekers: What we know about them, what to do about them. *Reference Librarian*, 25/26, 411–429.
Boston College, Theology Department. (2018). Theological ethics. Retrieved from https://www.bc.edu/bc-web/schools/mcas/departments/theology/research/theological-ethics.html.
Bratt, J. D. (Ed.) (1998). *Abraham Kuyper: A centennial reader*. Grand Rapids: William B. Eerdmans.
Burkhardt, J. M., & MacDonald, M. C. (2010). *Teaching information literacy: 50 standards-based exercises for college students*. 2nd ed. Chicago: American Library Association.

BusinessDictionary. (2018). Retrieved from http://www.businessdictionary.com/definition/information-anxiety.html.

Carnley, P. (2002). The librarian and the management of information overload. *The Australian Library Journal, 51*(4), 325–334.

Collins English Dictionary. (2018). Retrieved from https://www.collinsdictionary.com/us/dictionary/english/information-overload.

Conhaim, W. (2001). Review of *Information Anxiety 2* by Richard Saul Wurman. *Link-Up, 18*(3), 11–12.

Conner, M. (2014). *The new university library: Four case studies*. Chicago: American Library Association.

Cooper, M. (2000). Coping with information overload and selecting the best search engine. *Library Talk, 13*(5), 16–17, 73.

Davidson, A. (2012). Making choices in the age of information overload. *The New York Times Magazine*. Retrieved from https://www.nytimes.com/2012/05/20/magazine/making-choices-in-the-age-of-information-overload.html.

Dean, M. (1991). Facts, statistics, and the anxiety syndrome. *Lancet, 337*, 37–38.

Eklof, A. (2013). Understanding information anxiety and how academic librarians can minimize its effects. *Public Services Quarterly, 9*(3), 246–258.

English, A. (2016). Understanding bounded rationality and satisficing. *Mediumwww*. Retrieved from https://medium.com/homeland-security/understanding-bounded-rationality-and-satisficing-175e787955d6.

Feng, Y., & Agosto, D. E. (2017). The experience of mobile information overload: Struggling between needs and constraints. *Information Research, 22*(2), 1–18.

Fox, J. (1998). *Conquering information anxiety: Relief from your data glut*. Retrieved from http://www.ibt-pep.com/articles/dataglutrelief.doc.

Fuller, S. (2017). Prolegomena to deep history of "information overload." *Journal of Information Ethics, 26*(1), 81–92.

Gantz, J., & Reinsel, D. (2012). The digital universe in 2020: Big data, bigger digital shadows, and biggest growth in the Far East. Retrieved from https://www.emc.com/collateral/analyst-reports/idc-the-digital-universe-in-2020.pdf.

Girard, J., & Allison, M. (2008). Information anxiety: Fact, fable or fallacy. *The Electronic Journal of Knowledge Management, 6*(2), 111–124.

Gross, B. M. (1964). *The managing of organizations: The administrative struggle*. New York: Free Press of Glencoe.

Hartog, P. (2017). A generation of information anxiety: Refinements and recommendations. *The Christian Librarian, 60*(1), 44–55.

Hemp, P. (2009). Death by information overload. *Harvard Business Review*. Retrieved from https://hbr.org/2009/09/death-by-information-overload.

History of TED. (2016). Retrieved from https://www.ted.com/about/our-organization/history-of-ted.

Horrigan, J. B. (2016). *Information overload*. Washington, D.C.: Pew Research Center. Retrieved from: http://www.pewinternet.org/2016/12/07/information-overload/.

Ifijeh, G. I. (2010). Information explosion and university libraries: Current trends and strategies for intervention. *Chinese librarianship: An international electronic journal, 30*, 1–15.

Kennedy, S. D. (2001). Finding a cure for information anxiety. *Information Today, 18*(5), 40–41.

Larson, C. B. (1995). Managing the information overload: With so much to keep up with, how do you decide what to read? Six leaders answer. *Leadership, 16*(2), 121–127.

Littlejohn, R. L. (1993). *Ethics: Studying the art of moral appraisal*. Lanham, MD: University Press of America.

McCarthy, M. J. (1991). *Mastering the information age*. Los Angeles: Tarcher.

McDermott, A. (2017). Information overload is crushing you. Here are 11 secrets that will help. *Workzone*. Retrieved from https://www.workzone.com/blog/information-overload/.

Miller, K. A. (2001). Capture: The essential survival skill for leaders buckling under information overload. *Leadership, 22*(2), 80–86.

Miniwatts Marketing Group. (2018). Internet users in the world by regions—December 31, 2017. *Internet World Stats: Usage and Population Statistics*. Retrieved from https://www.internetworldstats.com/stats.htm.

Moser, P. K. (2009). *The elusive God: Reorienting religious epistemology*. New York: Cambridge University Press.

Palladino, L. J. (2007). *Find your focus zone: An effective new plan to defeat distraction and overload*. New York: Free Press.

PC Magazine Encyclopedia. (2018). Retrieved from https://www.pcmag.com/encyclopedia/term/44950/information-overload.

Raymond, J. (2005). All the news that's fit to ignore: Beware information overload. *National Catholic Register, 81*(20), 13.

Ryder, B. (2011). Too much information: How to cope with data overload. *The Economist*, June 30. Retrieved from https://www.economist.com/business/2011/06/30/too-much-information.

Schilling, D. R. (2013). Knowledge doubling every 12 months, soon to be every 12 hours. *Industry Tap into News*. Retrieved from http://www.industrytap.com/knowledge-doubling-every-12-months-soon-to-be-every-12-hours/3950.
Shenk, D. (1997). *The data smog: Surviving the info glut*. San Francisco: Harper Edge.
Shin, L. (2014). 10 steps to conquering information overload. *Forbes*. Retrieved from https://www.forbes.com/sites/laurashin/2014/11/14/10-steps-to-conquering-information-overload/#48ec77557b08.
Solis, B. (2012). The fallacy of information overload. BrianSoliswww. Retrieved from https://www.briansolis.com/2012/05/the-fallacy-of-information-overload/.
Spiro, L. (2010). *Managing information overload*. Houston: Rice University, Fonden Library.
Toffler, A. (1970). *Future shock*. New York: Bantam.
Williams, C. J. (2008). Reassessing the role of anxiety in information seeking. M.A. thesis. University of North Texas.
Wurman, R. S. (1989a). *Information anxiety*. New York: Doubleday.
Wurman, R. S. (1989b). "Overcome information anxiety." *Reader's Digest, 134*, 137–140.
Wurman, R. S. (2001). *Information anxiety 2*. Indianapolis: Que.
Wurman, R. S., & Bradford, P. (1997). *Information architects*. New York: Graphis.

Scholarship as Conversation

Using a Shared Research Method (ALEA) to Help Students Seek Truth and Wisdom in a Post-Truth World

Patricia Harris, Michelle Norquist,
Dianne Zandbergen and Andrew Zwart

Abstract

How do we develop within our students a deep and abiding love for God's truth, as well as a desire to know and understand God and his creation? Can we encourage curiosity and further develop discernment in students? What role does information literacy play in stimulating curiosity and developing discernment? How does information literacy relate to the intellectual virtues? Kuyper College, a small ministry-focused college in Grand Rapids, Michigan, is attempting to address these questions and concerns through a campus-wide research process that uses a common vocabulary across the disciplines. This process, known as ALEA, is a four-stage research procedure based on the following steps: ask, listen, engage and answer. This essay describes how ALEA evolved as a result of assessment work, how it relates to one of the college's campus-wide student learning outcomes, and the role the ACRL *Information Literacy Competency Standards*, and some of the threshold concepts of the ACRL *Framework for Information Literacy for Higher Education* played in the development of ALEA. Examples are given as to how ALEA is being applied in specific assignments and courses throughout the college as well as implemented progressively in the Bible and Theology department.

Introduction

The editors of the *Oxford English Dictionary (OED)* recently selected *post-truth* as word of the year. The following article titles, which are only a small sample, seem to verify their choice:

Is Truth Dead? (2017, April 3) *Time*, cover.
Give it away: in the post-truth era, colleges must share the knowledge. (Kaufman, 2017)
College without truth. (Oshatz, 2016)
Post-truth and chaos. (Feriss, 2016)

The editors of the *OED* define post-truth as "relating to or denoting circumstances in which objective facts are less influential in shaping public opinion than appeals to emotion and personal belief" (*Living Truthfully,* p. 7). Some characteristics of the post-truth era include the following: an atmosphere of deception and chaos, blatant disregard of facts, proliferation of misinformation through the social media, and a lack of trust in all forms of news media.

In the midst of this atmosphere, perhaps few were surprised to learn a year later that both the American Dialect Society and Collins Dictionary had chosen a related term: *fake news*. Alas, this seems to be the world we now live in: one where "alternative facts" are both expected and accepted.

It could be that this reality is simply a result of the deep political divisions we face. After all, carefully listening to and engaging with another's point of view takes effort; it is much easier to decry the positions of those on the other side of the political spectrum as "fake news." But political division has always been a reality. Why have these divisions today manifested as skepticism towards truth itself?

According to Nicolas Carr (2010), author of *The Shallows: What the Internet Is Doing to Our Brains*, the answer may lie in the sheer amount of information available to us in this digital age. Many readers can relate to his personal testimony of how his online experiences have shaped the way he now digests information: "Once I was a scuba diver in the sea of words. Now I zip along the surface like a guy on a jet ski" (p. 7). If Carr's experience is not unique, then this has wider implications for the ways that we seek truth. It suggests a lack of critical engagement with the information in which we find ourselves immersed. A few pages later, Carr (2010) describes the ultimate effect of this situation: "Calm, focused, undistracted, the linear mind is being pushed aside by a new kind of mind that wants and needs to take in and dole out information in short, disjointed, often overlapping bursts—the faster, the better" (p. 19).

In other words, the problem does not lie with the truth; it lies in the superficial ways we engage with the truth.

Of course, Carr is not the first critic to lament a lack of depth in our cultural landscape. Richard Foster (1978) in his book *Celebration of Discipline: The Path to Spiritual Growth* refers to the current culture as being "hollow":

> Superficiality is the curse of our age. The doctrine of instant satisfaction is a primary spiritual problem. The desperate need today is not for a greater number of intelligent people, or gifted people, but for deep people. The classical Disciplines of the spiritual life call us to move beyond surface living into the depths. They invite us to explore the inner caverns of the spiritual realm. They urge us to be the answer to a hollow world [p. 1].

While Foster emphasizes spiritual formation and development (matters of the heart), and Carr emphasizes intellectual formation and development (matters of the mind), we, as Christian educators, are interested in both the spiritual and intellectual development and renewal of our students' hearts and minds. How can or how should Christian educators and librarians respond to a culture marked by superficiality and shallowness? How do we encourage, inspire and develop students who not only seek after truth, but who have a curiosity that enables them to become lifelong learners, who can effectively participate in scholarly conversations, and who can speak with a Christian voice that is rooted in biblical knowledge and deep reflection? How do we encourage students to "go deeper," to be curious about God and the world he has created? How do we help them to value research as a process of learning and to understand the need for evaluating the sources they use in that process? Do we as Christian educators and librarians have a moral obligation and calling to help our students seek after that which is true, noble, right, pure, lovely, admirable, excellent and praiseworthy (Philippians 4:8)? If so, how do we do this effectively?

At Kuyper College, a ministry-focused college in Michigan, the faculty and staff have wrestled with these precise questions, for these questions address our desire to equip students with a deeply rooted biblical worldview that permeates the college's entire academic curriculum. At the same time, we desire for students to see that serious academic scholarship will only enhance their understanding of God's world and word. All this to say, these questions have pushed us to consider how to teach students to engage in meaningful research as kingdom work.

Moving Towards Information Literacy

Our first step toward this vision involved thinking through how to deliberately implement a program of information literacy (IL) and research into Kuyper's curriculum. As a first step, the Director of Library Services shared the Association of College and Research Libraries (ACRL) *Information Literacy Competency Standards for Higher Education* with a committee tasked with developing a campus-wide assessment plan for student learning. These IL standards and guidelines carry authority because of their endorsement by various regional and national accrediting agencies that use them to assess the effectiveness of the library's contribution to student learning.

This presentation of the ACRL standards helped convince the committee of the need for IL instruction as a campus-wide initiative. In fact, the committee felt so strongly about this need that they suggested adopting instruction in IL as one of the five campus-wide student-learning outcomes (SLOs). In agreement, the faculty approved a new SLO that reads as follows:

> As Kuyper College equips thoughtful Christian leaders for service, students are expected to attain a level of proficiency in the following curricular student learning outcome:
> 4. Demonstrate information literacy skills that are foundational to lifelong learning:
> 4.1 Identify when research is needed
> 4.2 Locate quality information by applying appropriate evaluation methods
> 4.3 Use information ethically and responsibly
> 4.4 Develop credible messages supported by research
> 4.5 Integrate information across disciplinary boundaries to solve problems and think critically about issues [*Kuyper College Catalog 2016–2017*, p. 52].

Considering that IL had become a campus-wide SLO, the faculty would now need to assess the IL skills of students on a regular basis. The most natural place for this to happen was during what Kuyper calls "assessment week," an intentional time after our second semester when faculty meet together to assess our SLO's. During the first assessment of SLO #4, the faculty compared research papers from a lower-level course and an upper-level capstone course, evaluating the papers for how students selected their sources and implemented them to support their thesis statements or research questions. The results were not encouraging: the capstone papers showed no noticeable improvement. Most likely, this was due to the fact that up until this point, we had not been intentional about the ways we had implemented IL into our curriculum. The librarians had gone into various classes to give "one and two shot" sessions on IL instruction, but students—and sometimes even faculty—tended to see these sessions as detached from their courses.

With these results in mind, the librarians did a great deal of reading and research to determine the best practices for the most effective IL instruction programs. With no full-time instructional librarian and IL instruction being only one of the many "hats" worn by the librarians, they felt limited as to what they could do for the students. While many colleges provide a semester long course in IL and research skills, that option was not possible due to personnel and course limitations. We felt it important, however, that these constraints would not limit students' knowledge of sound IL practices.

Auspiciously, the research recommended embedding IL instruction across the existing curriculum in an intentional, developmental, and sequential manner, a model that fit best with our students' requirements. William Badke (2012), author, researcher, librarian, and instructor for over thirty years, comments, "To make research processes instruction work, it has to find a home within the curriculum, not as an elective, nor as one program among many, but as an element of the core of every student's education" (p. 104). Similarly, in Barbara Fister's essay in the book *Not Just Where to Click: Teaching Students How to Think About Information* (2015) she notes her

> strong feeling that students could not become information literate by more or less randomly scattering library sessions into their classroom experiences. Rather, it was work that would have to be intentionally embedded throughout courses and within entire programs [p. 87].

Admittedly, such an approach would require a reframing of how we thought about IL's place in the curriculum and would necessitate more intentional collaboration with administration and teaching faculty, yet according to a study of information literacy programs conducted by ProQuest in 2016 entitled *Toward an Information Literate Society*, this is exactly the right approach:

> Many [librarians] feel that the answer lies in working more closely with faculty and other instructors—learning about their needs, educating them on the importance of information literacy and the resources the library offers, and encouraging them to include more research-based projects in their coursework. "We are badly in need of an integrated presence in the curriculum," explains one respondent [2016, p. 4].

Despite the somewhat daunting task, the librarians pursued this approach for two reasons. First, as noted, the current methods for introducing students to the research process had not been as effective as they hoped. While students had become more aware of resources available to them as well as how to search and evaluate those resources, they were not regularly selecting or using those resources to investigate their research topic. Second, teaching faculty have the most influence upon students, and if the faculty promoted the need for IL skills, as well as the value of research as a learning process, students would also tend to see its value as part of their entire curriculum, and not just a "library thing."

Considering the important role that teaching faculty play in students' views of research, the next time SLO #4 was to be assessed, the Director of Assessment and the librarians decided to shift the focus from student work to our own practices. In order to implement a campus-wide IL and research program, the faculty needed to understand what was meant by information literacy, why it needed to be embedded throughout the curriculum, and what the ACRL standards were for IL. In light of this, the librarians planned a conference style assessment week that included presentations on the need for collaborative efforts in IL instruction, the ACRL standards for IL, the ethical use of information, the history of past IL instruction, and potential future models. A panel of instruction librarians from other local colleges also visited to answer questions and explain how they work with their faculty to embed IL instruction in the curriculum.

At the same time that our administration, faculty, and librarians were working on embedding information literacy and research instruction across the curriculum, an ACRL Task Force was working on revising the *Information Literacy Competency Standards for Higher Education (Standards)*. This task force released the first and second drafts of the new *Framework for Information Literacy for Higher Education (Framework)* in 2014, and its focus encouraged the direction we were pursuing at Kuyper.

The *Framework* is more conceptual and less skills-based than the former ACRL *Standards*, being based on six threshold concepts. Authority is constructed and contextual, Information creation as a process, Information has value, Research as inquiry, Scholarship as conversation, and Searching as strategic exploration. Tellingly, the *Framework* points out that it is to be used as a guide in developing an IL program that is specific and meaningful for each campus. In other words, the taskforce did not intend it to be prescriptive. Instead, they meant to inspire and encourage looking at the "bigger" picture of how IL fits into critical thinking and research skills. Accordingly, the *Framework* emphasizes the importance of integrating IL throughout a college's curriculum:

> It is important for librarians and teaching faculty to understand that the *Framework* is not designed to be implemented in a single information literacy session in a student's academic career; it is intended to be developmentally and systematically integrated into the student's academic program at a variety of levels. This may take considerable time to implement fully in many institutions [p. 10].

In light of these new guidelines and the work we were already engaged in, the Provost and Director of Assessment decided to revisit IL SLO #4 during next year's assessment week. During the upcoming year, they worked on developing a research process approach that included instruction in IL skills. In order for this approach to be effective, they determined it needed to be based on a logical sequencing of the research process, share a common vocabulary, and be intentionally embedded within the curriculum.

The Provost and Director of Assessment based this research process approach on the work of Dr. Richard T. Hughes in his book *The Vocation of a Christian Scholar: How Christian Faith Can Sustain the Life of the Mind*. They chose four key words to express this research process that aligned with the four ways, as listed below, that Hughes describes how faith expresses itself through Christian scholarship:

- Through a commitment to search for truth. Key word: ASK.
- Through engagement with a variety of conversation partners. Key word: LISTEN.
- Through critique of all perspectives, even our own. Key word: ENGAGE.
- Through the nurture of creative imagination. Key word: ANSWER [p. 8].

This research process has become known as ALEA—Ask, Listen, Engage, and Answer. This simple four-step approach is built on a logical research sequence (see the figure below) and utilizes a common vocabulary, which allows for easy and widespread implementation across the curriculum.

The ALEA research process requires that students develop specific research skills, for example, the ability to define the need for information, to find, evaluate, and organize the information, and to communicate the information effectively and ethically. Students primarily engage in such skill development through their first-year experience course, "Research and Group Development," and subsequent courses continue to reinforce this skill development.

Additionally, the ALEA research process promotes the practice of intellectual virtues (for example, courage, carefulness, tenacity, fair-mindedness, curiosity, honor, and humility [Dow, 2013]) that are founded on a love of truth and understanding. The practice of these virtues is integral in successfully accomplishing the ALEA process. Realizing this, the Provost led a faculty retreat on the topic of intellectual virtues, using Philip Dow's book, *Virtuous Minds*, and, in turn, the faculty integrated knowledge and application of these intellectual virtues into their curriculum.

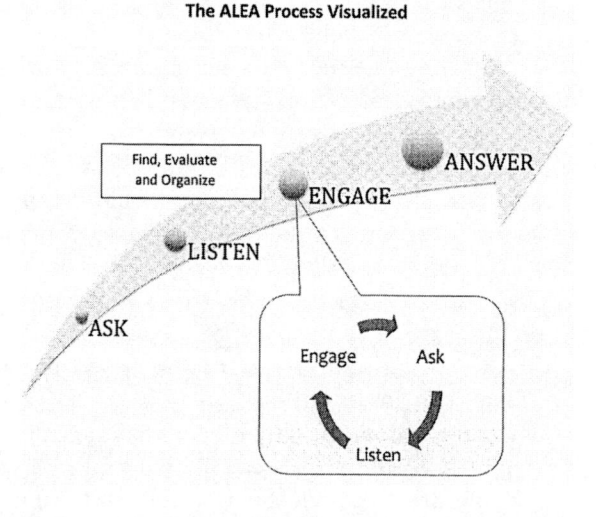

Jason Baehr, in the Foreword to Dow's book, describes the value of helping students understand and develop intellectual virtues. His thoughts align with the behaviors necessary to complete the ALEA process with integrity.

> An important part of what we want for the education of our children and students is that they develop a deep and abiding love of knowledge: a love that gives rise to curiosity and attentiveness to the world around them: a desire to continue learning about a broad range of subject matters, and to be tenacious and disciplined in this pursuit: a willingness to question their beliefs and the beliefs of others but also to have the courage of their convictions: and an inclination to treat foreign ideas fairly and respectfully [Baehr, 2013, p. 16].

During assessment week, the ALEA research method was introduced to the faculty in just this manner—a process that would cultivate in students a deep love of learning and an openness to engage in serious scholarly conversation. By the end of assessment week, the faculty had adopted ALEA along with the initiatives in teaching intellectual virtues.

In order to help faculty fully appreciate the ALEA method, each faculty member was required by the Provost to meet with one of the librarians in a one-hour "Resources You Can Use" session as part of the faculty professional development plan that summer. The librarians prepared specialized guides for each professor listing the library resources that related to them and their students.

These sessions proved to be both helpful and enjoyable for the faculty and the librarians. The librarians learned more about the faculty member's goals, objectives, and methods used to educate their students. The faculty became more aware of how the library resources and librarians could assist and support them and their students.

These sessions also helped faculty to empathize with their students' experience and led to discussion of where and why students were struggling and feeling frustrated when doing research-related assignments, but they also led faculty to think more deeply about the ways in which their own scholarship and teaching related to one another. Dr. Branson Parler (2016), a member of the Bible and Theology department, includes the following paragraph in his *2016 Reappointment Portfolio*:

> As a scholar and teacher, I listen and talk externally to the scholarly community and the wider culture. At the same time, I listen and talk internally with my students, their lives, and their concerns. Standing between these two worlds, I can make students aware of the bigger world and broader conversations that inform their own study and chosen vocation. I can draw them deeper into the big questions being asked and the knowledge and competencies needed for their chosen vocation [n. p.].

The following fall semester, Kuyper professors began putting these ambitions into practice, implementing the ALEA process into their courses, utilizing a common language and process for research.

The ALEA Process

Asking

One of the joys of teaching research occurs when we see students making an unexpected discovery, and from our observations, students are more likely to have this experience when they walk through the ALEA process. This begins with the first step: asking questions. All too often, students are asked to come up with a topic and thesis before they begin the research process, but this approach can close off discovery too quickly, and at its worst, it mirrors the contemporary trend of retreating to the news sources and opinions we know will reinforce our own views. Students sometimes unwittingly exemplify this approach when asked to explain why they find a particular source useful; we regularly used to read, "This source will back up what I want to argue," or "This article gives evidence for my point of view" when we asked students to discuss why they had chosen certain sources over others. This approach sees research as a means to expedient, even convenient, answers, rather than a yearning for wisdom and truth. In a desire to steer students away from such an approach, we considered the ACRL *Framework*'s concept of *Research as Inquiry*—the idea that rather than seeing research as nothing more than a means of locating information, students should view it as an investigation into matters that concern them, and any matter of investigation begins with a question.

Therefore, when we introduce students to research process, we begin by having them formulating their own questions. As we do so, we emphasize the need to choose a topic and a question that they are genuinely curious about and that they do not already know the answer to. To get students to see the value of such an approach, we explain that research—when done correctly—can be a means of seeing more clearly what God intends for his creation. With such a view in mind, we encourage students to view research as more than a hoop to jump through for a particular class; rather, they might begin to see it as a process they will be engaged in throughout their lives.

For a more practical approach, we also make the argument to students that if they think they already know the answer to their question, they are more likely to find themselves bored by the project quickly. This does not mean that students cannot make educated guesses or form hypotheses that they can then test as they engage in the research process, but by starting with a question, students are free to fully explore the wide range of answers any good topic will provoke. Moreover, students have a much easier time finding quality research when they do not feel pressure (self-imposed or otherwise) to find sources that support their specific point of view.

Of course, students need guidance in asking good questions for to ask a good question or identify a problem that needs solving involves the practice of identifying when research is needed and requires creative thinking about important issues. This is why students in one of our first year writing courses begin the class by reading an essay by Neil Postman that discusses the art of asking questions. Calling questions "the most important tool we have," Postman (1988) writes,

> it is meaningless to have answers if we do not know the question that produced them—whether in biology, grammar, politics, or history. To have an answer without knowing the question, without an understanding that you might have given a different answer if the questions had been posed differently may be more than meaningless; it may be exceedingly dangerous [p. 26].

With these points in mind, our students begin the first step of their research process: drafting a question that will guide them as they begin to look for sources. Often, students require help in coming up with and wording the question. In their first year Bible courses, as students carefully examine biblical passages, they receive examples of the kind of questions that promote sound biblical scholarship: What are the historical circumstances that surround that passage? Who is the author and intended audience of that passage?

In other classes, students are asked to form their own questions and then receive feedback and guidance. Recently, one student submitted the question "How does mental health affect people's everyday lives and how does it affect their Christian faith?" At first, the student failed to see that her question was too broad; such effects are far too diverse to sum up in a relatively short paper. However, after the student had a chance to receive feedback on her question, she reworded it to "How might the church minister to its members struggling with issues of mental health?"

It is worth noting, though, that this student may still not be finished with this step. Again and again, we emphasize the idea that ALEA is a circular process and so we encourage students to return to their question, to redefine and reshape it as they listen to and engage with their research materials. Ultimately, the emphasis we place on the development of good research questions should lead not only to information but also towards critical analysis and deeper reflection upon issues that students care about.

Listening

As students begin the next steps of the ALEA process—listening—we continue to encourage them to approach the research process with an open attitude. Again, before jumping ahead to their own solutions, we want students to listen carefully to how others have answered their question and attempted to solve the problem.

Towards this end, we have found Graff, Birkenstein, and Durst's (2015) book *They Say / I Say* to be of great use, so much so that it has become a required text for several classes, including two freshman courses. We assign this book because in addition to providing practical writing tips for students, it emphasizes the idea of research as a process of deep listening:

> For us, the underlying structure of effective academic writing—and of responsible public discourse—resides not just in stating our own ideas but in listening closely to others around us, summarizing their views in a way that they will recognize, and responding with our own ideas in kind. Broadly speaking, academic writing is argumentative writing, and we believe that to argue well you need to

do more than assert your own position. You need to enter a conversation, using what others say (or might say) as a launching pad or sounding board for your own views [Graff, Birkenstein, & Durst, 2005, p. 3].

Many of our students have little difficulty in boldly stating their positions (truth be told, sometimes too boldly); rather, they need to practice listening charitably and carefully to how others have already responded to our students' questions. At this point, we stress the idea that careful listening can embody the act of loving our neighbors as ourselves. In fact, through class discussion, we have found that students readily point out that their primary world of discourse—social media—encourages just the opposite: people online tend to dismiss others' ideas with little thought, even meanness. Students vocalize their disgust at such an approach even while admitting to similar behavior. Through this discussion, then, we encourage them to see the listening step of ALEA as a kind of discipline through which they can grow in the fruits of the Spirit.

Here, it might be worth pointing out that while the ALEA process will always follow the same basic principles, each professor can apply this process to best suit the course's needs. We want to provide our students with a common language for the practice of research, but we also want to help them understand that different disciplines, courses, and even professorial preference will influence the specific steps within the process.

In their Bible courses, students receive a list of reliable biblical dictionaries and encyclopedias to choose from. Then, given a list of questions, students summarize what others have written in response to these questions. For this first paper, we intentionally ask students not to go beyond the listening stage. While we do give them an opportunity to add application later, we want them to first show that they are capable of paying attention to what others have said and reporting this information accurately.

In their first year experience course and in their writing courses, students learn to use our college's databases to find their own sources. This is a crucial step; students must learn that good research requires a knowledge of the searching "tools" available to them and that there may not be a single path for exploring and engaging with the tools and the resources. The ACRL *Framework* calls this stage *Searching as Strategic Exploration*, capturing the idea that research involves both skill (strategy) and curiosity (exploration). When students begin to see research in this light, they understand that the sources they discover will reflect their own questions, interests, and approaches; there is no right answer about which sources are the *best* in answering a question. Yet, they will also understand that some sources are *better* than others. We expect students to think critically about their chosen sources, and so we ask students to assess the credibility, currency, reliability, validity, and appropriateness of the information they have retrieved.

We consider the skill of evaluating the credibility of the source to be part of the listening stage. Before students can begin to engage with a source, they must decide what sources are worth listening to. Having said that, we again want to emphasize that ALEA is not a linear process. As students begin assessing their sources, they have simultaneously moved into the next step of the research process: engagement.

Engaging

As just suggested, the line between listening and engaging is not always so clear, for engagement requires careful listening, and good listening is never a passive activity; rather, careful listening requires students to pay great attention to the details of the text.

Nonetheless, although students often move back and forth between listening and engagement, each has its own set of unique characteristics.

We might best sum up the major distinction between listening and engagement with two common phrases from rhetoric: "reading with the grain" and "reading against the grain." Reading with the grain involves an open and fair consideration of the text whereas reading against the grain occurs when students begin to wrestle seriously with what they are reading.

To put it another way, engagement happens when students begin to talk back to the text, when students ask difficult questions of the text, look for possible flaws in the author's arguments, or when they play what Peter Elbow (1998) calls the doubting game (p. 145). To be clear, though, engagement does not always mean taking an adversarial attitude towards the text. Students also engage when they observe that their text corroborates other facts they have encountered, make connections to their own experience, or formulate their own examples to illustrate an idea the text discusses. This kind of engagement maps on to the *Framework's* concept of *scholarship as conversation*. The ALEA process always aims to enable students to learn what scholarship is and invite them to become a part of that conversation.

Not surprisingly, this stage of engagement looks different in each of their courses. In their Bible courses, once students have shown that they can listen and summarize carefully, we now ask them to engage. After they have learned to locate the kind of research that helps them better understand the biblical context of a book, passage or character, we ask them to apply that knowledge, showing how a thorough understanding of that context sheds light on how the Bible speaks to us today.

For their first year research and writing courses, we have developed an assignment that helps students more fully engage with their sources. This assignment is essentially a template for annotating their sources, but rather than ask students for a general descriptive and evaluative paragraph, the template lays out a clear set of questions for students to answer for each of their sources. These include: (1) What is your current question? Has this source caused you to refocus or revise your question? (2) What is the main idea or thesis of the source read? (3) What makes this source credible? Why is it worth listening to?

To some degree, each of these questions straddles the line between listening and engagement; the final section of the template, however, asks students to respond directly to their research. In this section, the template asks students to choose a number of quotes and then react to them. They can agree or disagree with the quote and explain why, or they can explain how a particular quote helps to answer their research question.

One of the reasons we have students use these templates throughout the research process is to ensure that when they are ready to begin drafting, they already have material that they can directly incorporate into their paper, a fact that can alleviate writer's block. Certainly, they may need to reword some of their previous language to fit the context of their draft, but this method helps students understand that writing is not a process that occurs in a vacuum and that happens in one sitting. Rather, a first draft is the result of a series of rigorous steps.

Even so, to say that the first draft is the result of the ALEA process is not to say that it amounts to the culmination of their work. In fact, we encourage students to see drafting as part of the engagement phase. As students themselves often point out, it is often during the process of writing that students come upon new insights, change their minds, or discover new connections. By this point, they will have formed a tentative thesis—a first attempt at answering their question—but as they draft, they know that this answer will shift, just as their questions did earlier. Here, it is especially important to emphasize that good research requires a willingness to make mistakes and learn from them.

In some cases, we have found that students actually do change their minds as they engage seriously with the ALEA process. For example, one student began his process by asking the question "Why is race such a big deal in the U.S.?" After conferencing with his professor, he understood that his question already implied the stance that race is in fact too "big a deal." To this student's credit, though, he willingly sought out scholars who wrote about the problems of systemic racism in America. And because this student remained truly open to the process of learning both through research and through his own writing process, he ended up changing his mind on the topic. By the time that he had reached the final stage of ALEA—answering—the opening of his research paper read as follows:

> Because of the events of the Civil Rights Movement, and the various legacies of its leaders, it is difficult for many white Americans to think of racial discrimination as a present reality; but for many black Americans, racism is all too real in the areas of education, economics, and justice. This reality is not only affecting society but also the Church.... One crucial aspect for this conversation to be successful is that we "white" Americans would be able to not only look at the history of racial discrimination in the United States, but also recognize how that history has perpetuated the racial discrimination it claims to have gotten rid of. This is an important step to obtaining unity in society and in the church amongst blacks and whites.

For some, it might be tempting to steer such a student away from such a loaded issue as race, especially if the student begins with a set of presuppositions that many would view as problematic; but in this case, confidence in the process yielded great results, and not just because the student changed his mind. By the end of the process, the student had produced a compelling argument, his answer well supported by credible sources and thoughtful engagement with those sources.

To be sure, our ultimate hope is that this student—and others who have had similar experiences—would apply such a careful approach to any number of questions they encounter in the future. In other words, we want students to bring the spirit of ALEA (if not the exact methodology) to bear on their own contexts, relationships, and vocations. If taken seriously, we believe that the process of ALEA will not just make for better students, but for better citizens of the kingdom as well.

Answering

Students do not fully arrive at the answering stage until working on a second or third draft of their papers. At this point, they will have crystalized their working thesis into its clearest, most defensible form and they will be ready to defend that thesis with persuasive writing and support from their best resources.

In order to distinguish the answer phase of ALEA for our students, perhaps the biggest change we have made involves requiring multiple drafts from our students, even in some of our upper-level courses. In the past, we tended to teach editing and revision in our writing courses, but all too often we found that this resulted in poor quality work. As happens in many schools, our students tried to finish their papers at the last minute, their final projects then reading more like rough drafts than final products.

In light of this fact, as well as the ACRL *Framework's* emphasis on *Information Creation as a Process*, we decided that students really do need help breaking down the process of writing a paper into a series of steps and that this process had to include steps for multiple drafts. By the time they have finished with their first draft, we do expect students to have arrived at an answer to their question; however, students often still need help organizing (or re-organizing) their evidence, adding in logical connectors and transitions, and polishing their prose so that it reads as clearly and forcefully as possible. Through working on such aspects, students not only answer their question, but they present that answer in its strongest, most cogent form.

To this end, our faculty have developed a more in depth process for producing a finished piece. In some classes, fellow students review each other's papers. Here, though, we have worked hard to avoid the pitfalls of "peer editing" where students simply look for their partner's grammatical mistakes (and often make mistakes themselves in their revisions). Rather, we have developed different templates for students to assist them in providing feedback *as readers*. That is to say, we want each writer to have a sense of how clearly they have communicated their answers to a real audience. Therefore, our templates focus less on the minutia of writing and more on the kinds of questions their audience would be concerned with. Is the argument of the paper clear? Is it convincing? Does the paper provide enough research and evidence to support the points it makes? Are there sections that do not seem related to the rest of the material?

It is worth noting that such a process benefits more than just the writer. This kind of work also provides the peer editor—that is, the reader—the opportunity to listen and engage once again. They learn how to provide feedback that avoids the pitfalls of dismissing their fellow peer's ideas or mindlessly approving them. Again, students learn to practice the temperament needed for a larger social dialogue.

The feedback students receive does not stop with their peers, however. For each assignment that involves peer editing, students then also receive suggestions from their professors. In our students' required writing class, after the peer editing stage the professor reviews the first draft and then conferences with each student. During these conferences, students receive oral feedback on the overall strengths and weaknesses of their papers as well as written feedback on specific aspects of the paper from writing to structure. After this conference, students have two weeks to complete a thorough revision, and the final grade they receive reflects the care they have taken with this final editing process.

The work that students spend revising their papers is intended to again reinforce the idea that research is a process and that even the final stage of coming to a conclusion often involves returning to previous aspects of the research process. In fact, during peer revision or conferences, students will sometimes realize that they need to listen to a wider array of voices, find more research, or engage more deeply with the sources that they have already presented in their papers. Thus, even in the answer stage of ALEA, students find themselves circling back to earlier parts of the process.

We do recognize that an end to the process must come; at some point, the student needs to take a stand, to provide a final answer. But even here, we want students to recognize that the conclusion of their work might spark the beginning of a new conversation. To put it bluntly, our students' participation in the process does not have to end with nothing more than a final grade. Rather, we want them to see their work as adding to an ongoing dialog. In an attempt, then, to prepare students to contribute to the scholarly conversations within their discipline, each spring the college sponsors a Student Scholar

Day. Any student may apply to present a paper or participate in poster presentation, and if accepted, she will work to prepare for this presentation with a faculty member serving as a mentor. We have found this to be one of the highlights of our academic year, a chance for our students to gain some recognition for their good work, but more importantly, an opportunity for them now to engage others. We love it when the question and answer session following their presentations leads into further discussion around the lunch table.

Our decision to help students work through these steps has even resulted in unforeseen benefits. For example, by implementing information literacy skills throughout the curriculum, we came to realize that we were also doing a much better job of teaching writing across the curriculum. In fact, when it came time to revise our Writing Across the Curriculum program, we realized that much of this work had already occurred as we had been developing ALEA.

Up to this point, we have focused on ALEA in the context of research writing, but a few points are in order. First, while students often engage in the ALEA process as they work on research papers, other mediums also lend themselves to this approach. Speeches, PowerPoints or poster presentations can all benefit from students asking, listening, engaging, and answering.

Second, while many projects involve each of the four steps of the ALEA process, not *all* projects need to do so. As mentioned above, the first Bible paper that students write only involves the asking and listening stages, and this is not happenstance. This approach was the result of the Bible and Theology Department deciding to implement ALEA as a systematic process that students move through as they take successive Bible courses. In fact, in their first year Bible courses, students primarily ask and listen; and while they do begin to enter the engage stage as they write biblical applications, it is not until their second year that they move more fully into the engage and answer stages of ALEA.

In their second year doctrine classes, students begin to assemble a Faith Statement Portfolio, in which students begin with key questions about a specific theological topic. The professor selects and assigns readings for listening so that students can hear these specific voices "alone and clearly." Out of this listening, students generate a question of their own on this same theological topic and return to their readings and Scripture to listen again. At this point, students are required to find a reliable, primary source that speaks for their church or denomination on this issue and to fully engage with that source, comparing its stance with their other readings and their own ideas. Finally, the students type a preliminary answer as to what they believe regarding these theological topics.

In their third year, students develop a Spiritual Practices Reflection Portfolio. This project requires students to ask about specific spiritual practices, listen to explanations of the theology behind the practice, engage by experiencing these practices, and finally answer how they might implement this practice in their own lives.

For their final course in the sequence, students work on an extensive research paper that asks them to apply a Christian worldview to a specific cultural concern. At this point, we expect students to be proficient with the ALEA process, and we see this paper as an opportunity for them to demonstrate their proficiency. Students begin by formulating and clarifying the best way to articulate their research interest. They must then listen to credible sources that have provided answers to their own question and engage with them at a substantial level. The final paper requires multiple drafts before they finally formulate their own answer to the question that they have raised and researched thoroughly.

Applying the ACRL's threshold concepts to our own context, we have worked to help students perceive research as more than an isolated skill they will only need to survive their time in college. We even hope they regard it as more than a tool for learning the skills needed to take part in scholarly conversation and debate. Ultimately, we desire our students to become lifelong learners—to cultivate the habit of discovering, listening to, and engaging with other voices, both past and present, as a means of continually seeking and proclaiming the truth.

Moving Forward

One of the greatest challenges that remains regarding the ALEA efforts at the college is how best to assess the effectiveness of the program and its impact on student learning. How does one measure students' progress in their ability to ask good and thoughtful questions, to truly listen to the thoughts of others including those that do not agree with their own, to evaluate and engage with the resources they select, and to reflect and provide an answer or possible solutions to their question?

Up to this point, we have based much of the current assessment on direct observations from the faculty. Given our college's small size, we believe that these observations are relevant and useful, several of our professors and librarians having observed similar outcomes. In addition to these observations, though, we have begun collecting quantitative data to measure our students' facility with research. At the end of the academic year, our faculty review what we call "signature assignments," assignments that correlate with course objectives and program learning outcomes, many of which involve a research component. Using a rubric, the faculty then record the percentage of assignments that meet satisfactory criteria, and we store this information in a secure and centralized location.

Reflecting on both our direct observations and the data we have collected, as well as student evaluation forms, we have noted a number of benefits to the ALEA process as well as some new challenges. First, students seem to have a greater appreciation for research as a process and understand the essential role that information literacy skills play in that process. They understand not only the importance of locating quality resources but also the need to evaluate those resources and how they relate to their research question. More students have an appreciation for research as a meaningful way of learning (if they follow the process), and not just as "busy work" or as just a "library thing."

Second, ALEA has enabled collaboration among faculty and administration due to a shared vocabulary, method, and set of goals. In fact, one of the most influential results of this work has been greater collaboration amongst administration, faculty, librarians, and students. Such collaboration across disciplines and departments is highly valued but, unfortunately, all too rare on most campuses. The sustainability of such efforts, however, will require leadership and promotion in orienting new personnel and in assessment/evaluation efforts. Someone needs to "own" and champion the program to others. It will also require a willingness to learn from mistakes that we make along the way.

Third, the role of the librarians has evolved from general overview classroom presentations on basic IL skills to more of a one-on-one assistance with students as they come into the library for class research time. While this is helpful in that they meet with students at their point of need, the librarians have some concern as to whether or not all students are receiving basic instruction in searching and locating library resources. As professors have taken more ownership in discussing the conceptual aspects of research, our librarians have concerns about the consistency of what is being taught in regards to locating, accessing, and using library materials.

The response to the ALEA model from both faculty and students has been overwhelmingly positive. However, we understand the need to continually evaluate our work, returning to the finer points of the process. Like ALEA itself, our implementation and assessment of this model cannot be a simple linear progression. It will require that we ask hard questions of ourselves, listen carefully to our students, and engage with the data—all as we search for the kinds of answers that will help our students become committed Christian scholars.

Conclusion

ALEA is one means of encouraging students to a life of Christian scholarship. In an age marked by deception, superficiality and information overload, it requires a high level of commitment to be seekers of truth and of that which is noble, right, pure, lovely, admirable, excellent and praiseworthy (Philippians 4:18). Assisting, mentoring, and encouraging students in such pursuits is a high and worthy calling in which to invest one's life. But we can only achieve this through intentional collaboration, a willingness to spend the extra time to provide feedback and encouragement along the way, and shared values and expectations

The motto of Kuyper College is *ora et labora*—pray and work. As we work together on the ALEA method of teaching research and information literacy skills at the college, we will continue to challenge students towards lifelong learning in their search for truth and wisdom. We will encourage them to participate in and contribute to scholarly conversations, while respectfully listening to those voices from other perspectives. And in the midst of this work, we join with John Stott in his prayer that such a pursuit of truth would always find its end in Christ:

> I pray earnestly that God will raise up today a new generation of Christian communicators, who will combine an absolute loyalty to the biblical gospel and an unswerving confidence in the power of the Spirit, with a deep and sensitive understanding of the contemporary alternatives to the gospel, who will relate the one to the other with freshness, pungency, authority and relevance; and who will use their minds to reach other minds for Christ [Stott, 1972, p. 74].

REFERENCES

Badke, W. (2012). *Teaching research processes: The faculty role in the development of skilled student researchers.* Whitney, United Kingdom: Chandois.
Baehr, J. (2013). Foreword. In Dow, P. E., *Virtuous minds: Intellectual character development for students, educators, and parents* (pp. 1–6). Downers Grove, IL: InterVarsity Press.
Carr, N. G. (2010). *The shallows: What the Internet is doing to our brains.* New York: W. W. Norton.
Catalog. (2016). Vols. 2016–2017. Grand Rapids: Kuyper College.
Dow, P. E. (2013). *Virtuous minds: Intellectual character development for students, educators, and parents.* Downers Grove, IL: InterVarsity Press.
Elbow, P. (1998). *Writing without teachers.* New York: Oxford University Press.
Ferriss, L. (2016, December 16). Post-truth and chaos. *The Chronicle of Higher Education, 63*(17), B2. http://link.galegroup.com/apps/doc/A475324709/ AONE?u=lom_rbible&sid=AONE&xid=720e082e.
Fister, B. (2015). The social life of knowledge: faculty epistemologies. In T. A. Swanson and H. Jagman (Eds.),

Not just where to click: Teaching students how to think about information (pp. 87–103). Chicago: Association of College and Research Libraries.

Foster, R. J. (1978). *Celebration of discipline: The path to spiritual growth.* San Francisco: Harper & Row.

Framework for Information Literacy for Higher Education. (2015). Chicago: Association of College and Research Libraries.

Graff, G., Birkenstein, C., & Durst, R K. (2015). *They say/I say: The moves that matter in academic writing, with readings.* New York: W. W. Norton.

Hughes, R.T. (2005). *The vocation of the Christian scholar: How Christian faith can sustain the life of the mind.* Grand Rapids: William B. Eerdmans.

Information literacy competency standards for higher education. (2000). Chicago: Association of College and Research Libraries.

Kaufman, P. B. (2017, April 7). Give it away: In the post-truth era, colleges must share their knowledge. *The Chronicle of Higher Education, 63*(31), B5+. http://chronicle.com/section/About-the-Chronicle/83.

Living truthfully. (2017). *Christian Century, 134*(1), 7. http://search.ebscohost.com/login.aspx?direct=true&dlo=rfh&AN=ATLAiFZK70131001354&site=ehost-live.

Oshaltz, M. (2016). College without truth. *First Things: A Monthly Journal on Religion and Public Life, 263*, 15–17.

Parler, B. (2016). *Reappointment portfolio.* Grand Rapids: Kuyper College.

Postman, N. (1988). Defending against the indefensible. In N. Postman, *Conscientious objections: Stirring up trouble about language, technology, and education* (pp. 20–34). New York: Alfred A. Knopf.

Scherer, M. (2017, April 3). Can Trump handle the truth? (Cover title: Is truth dead?) *Time, 190*, 33–39.

Stott, J. (1972). Your mind matters. Downers Grove, IL: InterVarsity Press.

Toward an information literate society: Results from a 2016 ProQuest survey (2016). n.p.: ProQuest. Retrieved from http://media2.proquest.com/documents/ surveyresults-informationliteracy-2016.pdf.

Knowledge, Understanding, Wisdom
A Biblical Model of Information Literacy[1]

JEFF GATES

Abstract

Not satisfied with the current state of information literacy in higher education and academic librarianship, the author attempts to build a biblical model of this dominant movement which has nearly defined academic librarianship. After investigating the roots of God's original command to manage the earth and its relevance to higher education today, the author examines the biblical definitions of knowledge (the apprehension of facts), understanding (the best explanations or likely meanings of those facts), and wisdom (the best course of action that addresses those explanations or meanings) and their implications to higher education. In the next section, he examines current definitions and models of information literacy (IL) and proposes an alternative definition and model based on knowledge, understanding, and wisdom. The author concludes by applying this biblical model of IL to key players in higher education. The last application—to academic librarians—not only demonstrates the application of this model to their situation, but it also provides an example of using it to meet challenges they face in incorporating IL into higher education.

Introduction

A few years after taking my first library position, when the Association of College and Research Librarians published its Information Literacy Competency Standards for Higher Education (ACRL, 2000), I became interested in information literacy (IL). I voraciously read and attended conferences about IL and tried to present IL concepts in classes of the Bible college and seminary where I worked. I even wrote a plan to incorporate IL into the curriculum. However, I began to face challenges that caused me to question the IL model presented in the library literature. I found it difficult to explain IL to the academic dean and other faculty members. According to them, they were already doing what I described as IL. Most faculty members did not want me to do classroom presentations, let alone incorporate my suggestions for research assignments. Some even thought that helping students find resources for their assignments was doing their work for them.

My role, they assumed, was to provide access to good books and journals for assignments which they gave. All of this caused me to reflect on accepted educational practices in higher education and my role as an academic librarian. After thinking about this for another ten years as a liaison to the biblical studies faculty and student body at a different institution, another librarian challenged me to describe IL in language that faculty members in that school would understand. This essay is the result of my attempt to meet that challenge. After defining and relating knowledge, understanding, and wisdom to higher education, I show how these definitions can be used as a biblical model for IL. Furthermore, I deliberate about academic librarians working with educational administration, faculty members, students, and God to help incorporate IL into the academic curriculum.

Knowledge, Understanding, Wisdom and Higher Education

When God imagined the world, He planned to make beings like Himself to rule it (Genesis 1:26–31; 2:7, 15, 18–19; Isaiah 45:18).[2] Rather than being controlled by their environment, He wanted them to manage it. To equip people for this task, God would give them the ability to make observations, understand what they observed, and act upon that understanding. Within limits set by God, they would have the freedom to use the earth's resources to please their Maker by providing for themselves[3] and their offspring. It was a wonderful plan (Genesis 1:31).

After making the earth with its plants and animals, God made Adam. Moreover, consistent with God's plan to make him the first manager of the earth, God brought the animals to Adam to see what he would call them (Genesis 2:19–20). If Adam named the animals based upon their characteristics, this would have required him to understand them based upon what he had observed about them. Whether by the enormity of the task or his observation that there were male and female of each kind of animal, Adam realized that there was no one like him to help manage the earth. It was then that God made Eve—both to help Adam and to produce offspring with him to further assist him in his management role (Genesis 1:26–28; 2:18). Apparently, God met with them in physical form regularly (Genesis 3:8; Hamilton, 1990, p. 192). Conceivably during these times He taught them and encouraged them in this role. He also gave them and their descendants the ability to communicate along with various aptitudes and interests to excel in particular disciplines and practices. At first, Adam and Eve likely began to fulfill God's dream by adding their own observations of their garden home to the knowledge God had given to them and sharing this with each other (Genesis 3:2–3).[4] They would have heard and believed that God created everything and that obeying Him brought rewards and disobeying Him resulted in consequences (Genesis 2:17). In addition, they would have sought to understand what they had observed and used that understanding to develop techniques and tools to please God by providing for themselves and each other. However, after the Fall they fought their own evil tendency to rely solely on their own understanding and to foolishly use this for their own self-indulgence.[5] Their now dying bodies and cursed garden home also made it harder to manage the earth (Genesis 3:16–19; Romans 8:20–23).

When Adam and Eve gave birth to sons and daughters, their love toward their children would have motivated our original parents to share with them what they had learned from God, each other, and their own experience. Their grown children in turn would have shared this knowledge, understanding, and wisdom with each other and their offspring. Specialization apparently happened early in the human race. When we meet the first children of Adam and Eve, one was a shepherd and the other a gardener (Genesis 4:2). Eventually some of their progeny specialized in caring for livestock, playing musical instruments, or making metal tools (Genesis 4:20–22). According to the passage, the people with a particular skill-set had the same father. Therefore, their father likely taught them the knowledge, understanding, and wisdom needed for that skill. Yet, as people grew in this knowledge and understanding and used them to develop more techniques and tools to manage their portion of the earth, human limitations made specialization a necessity. In time, those with specialized knowledge, understanding, and wisdom formed associations for mutual support, promotion, protection, education, and furtherance of their discipline or practice among young apprentices (Simonetto, 2005, pp. 878–879; Tang, 2008, pp. 515–517).

Regrettably most of the descendants of Adam and Eve would be true to their inherited, evil tendency to forsake God and rely only on what they could collectively observe and understand (Romans 3:11–12; Ephesians 4:18). Eventually, this led to some foolish and immoral practices. Having no common frame of reference to tie these specialists together, they communicated and cooperated less and less with those in other specialties. On the other hand, specialists who embraced the God of the Bible were motivated to collaborate with those who specialized in other disciplines and practices because they saw all of them had the same ultimate source, that is, God. Yet, even many of them yielded to the temptation to interact only with others who had their interests and capacities.

Although there are exceptions, in most cultures today a majority of adolescents receive their education and training from colleges or universities. Such institutions developed in the Middle Ages around disciplines that had shown themselves valuable in addressing social issues and which were founded on Christian principles (Rüegg, 1992, pp. 26, 32–33). All of these schools teach students knowledge and understanding from experts,[6] and many of them teach students how to use that understanding to improve the situation and give them opportunity to put this into practice. Those schools that still espouse Christian values seek to underlay all of this with knowledge, understanding, and wisdom from God.

Knowledge

Knowledge of the earth's resources is necessary for us to manage them (Greene, 1998, p. 124). Here we examine the biblical definition of knowledge and its implications and place in learning within higher education to manage our world.

DEFINITION OF KNOWLEDGE

Since this essay is about IL, the reader may wonder why I do not focus on "information" instead of "knowledge." First of all, knowledge is often used synonymously with information (Riley, 2010; Sauer, 1995, p. 142; Stoan, 1984, p. 100),[7] so we can use either term. In fact, the definition of knowledge is similar to the definition of information. *Oxford Dictionary of English* defines information as facts provided or learned about something or someone, and it defines knowledge as facts, information, and skills acquired through experience or education (Stevenson, 2010a, 2010b). Another reason I use the term knowledge instead of information is because it is used much more frequently in the Bible than information. In fact, the word information is not used in some prominent versions of the Bible, such as the King James Version and New King James Version. Since I am trying to build a biblical model of IL, it seems more appropriate to use the term knowledge rather than information. In the Bible, knowledge means awareness, acquaintance, familiarity, or intelligent comprehension of the real state of objects or people through the senses or from others (Browning, 2009; Bultmann, 1964, pp. 689–692, 696–708; Johnson, 2013, p. 94; Lewis, 1980). In his study of biblical knowing, Johnson (2013) stressed the importance of the authorization of knowledge by credible sources. These designations support the definition of knowledge in philosophy, that is, justified, true belief (Ichikawa & Steup, 2018), as long as the justification comes from a credible source. While people have limited knowledge, God has all knowledge (Job 37:16; 1 John 3:20). Based on these designations, I define knowledge as the *awareness of facts*. One illustration of knowledge is my awareness of snow on my garage roof on an early spring afternoon. These definitions of knowledge also suggest some implications about its accuracy and the credibility of its sources.

IMPLICATIONS OF KNOWLEDGE

We can see many things without having an awareness of them. Yet, knowledge is not just an awareness of anything. The object of that awareness is something that is really there, that is, a fact. Therefore, knowledge requires accuracy as well as a credible source to ensure it.

Accuracy

The words "real" and "true" in the definitions above implies that knowledge is accurate. For example, being aware of the statement "The German Nazi Party said the Jewish Holocaust never happened" is knowledge because it is accurate. However, having awareness of the statement "The Jewish Holocaust never happened" is not knowledge, because it is not accurate. Furthermore, the accuracy of knowledge assumes that something cannot be accurate and inaccurate at the same time and in the same way. For example, it is a contradiction to say that all of my garage roof has snow on it now and all of my garage roof has no snow on it now. We call this the law of non-contradiction. We inherently assume this, and it has ample biblical support (Numbers 23:19; Job 4:8; Sproul, Gerstner, & Lindsley, 1984, p. 72).

Credibility

The source of knowledge, that is, our senses or others telling it to us, may be a challenge to its accuracy. For this reason, we must examine sources of proposed knowledge for credibility. If knowledge comes from our senses or from others, those sources must be reliable. We actually use our senses in both cases, since observing the world around us and receiving knowledge about them from others comes through our senses. Although we can make mistakes about what we observe and even ignore or deny it, the biblical writers assumed the general reliability of our senses to give us knowledge (John 1:46; Romans 1:20; 2 Peter 1:16; 1 John 1:1–3; Jaeger, 2016, pp. 428, 430–431; Sproul, Gerstner, & Lindsley, 1984, pp. 87–88). Tools, such as telescopes and amplifiers, also can help sharpen our senses to improve our accuracy. Consequently, I can usually trust my eyes when I see that my garage roof has snow on it—especially using tools, like my glasses.

Provided my neighbor is not legally blind, I can usually believe her when she reports what she sees, that is, snow on my garage roof.

If the source of our knowledge is people, they, like us, get knowledge through direct observation or from others—who also gain an awareness of facts directly or received them from still others. Other people may observe the same things we observe and so confirm our knowledge. Thus, for example, the witness of over 500 believers who said they saw Jesus after His resurrection confirmed what each other observed (1 Corinthians 15:3–8). However, when others tell us about something that contradicts what we observed or something that we have not observed, its accuracy depends on the credibility of the person (Browning, 2009; Jaeger, 2016, pp. 430–431; Johnson, 2013, p. xix; Lewis, 1980, 366–367). We call those with high credibility experts—who often record their knowledge for others. So, in the unlikely event that the person who sold my house to me informed me about the poor quality of the insulation under my garage roof, I acquired knowledge. It is hard for me to imagine why he would tell me this if he did not see it or hear it from a credible source. Furthermore, if I learn from a friend who has been building houses for 30 years that the brand of insulation under most of my roof is the worst brand on the market, I am even more confident about the accuracy of what the previous owner told me. Like the previous owner, my friend is not likely to lie to me, and he probably knows much more about roof insulation than the previous owner.

Another source of knowledge is God (Alston, 1993, pp. 1–4; Jaeger, 2016, pp. 429–430; Johnson, 2013, p. 30). Since He has all knowledge, is holy, and loves us, He is the ultimate credible expert. Therefore, we can count on the knowledge we get from Him to be accurate. Thankfully, He has shared some of His knowledge through the biblical authors. Since He superintended the human authors of the Bible, He insures its accuracy (John 10:35; 2 Timothy 3:16; 1 Peter 1:10–11; 2 Peter 1:20–21; Greene, 1998, pp. 123–124)—albeit we must use common principles of biblical hermeneutics to access His knowledge there. While the Bible contains limited knowledge about His creation, it does contain foundational knowledge about Himself and people which is relevant to all fields of knowledge. Although the Bible contains no knowledge about snow on my garage roof, it does contain knowledge that is relevant to this fact, that is, knowledge about those who live under my roof. Specifically, I read in the Bible about the relevant fact of my responsibility to use my resources wisely and to care for my family.

Place of Knowledge in Higher Education

Teaching knowledge obviously has a place in higher education. During a typical four year undergraduate education, students normally observe many things they have never seen, hear about many things from their instructors that they have never heard, and read about facts in their textbooks that they never knew. Since learning facts about God and His world is foundational to students' education, they need to be acquainted with basic truths in the Bible. Incorporating recognized core facts that are not found in the Bible into the curriculum is also very important for this purpose. Furthermore, they should learn how to sharpen their observational skills and add the resulting knowledge into their own knowledge base with knowledge from God and human experts. However, students and their parents would be understandably disappointed after spending so much time and money for a college or university education, if it only helped students increase their knowledge. Students also need to be taught the understanding of experts and how to develop it for themselves.

Understanding

If we are to manage our surroundings, we need more than a knowledge of them. We need an understanding of them. In this section, we look at the biblical definition of understanding and its implications and place in learning in higher education.

DEFINITION OF UNDERSTANDING

While the meaning of understanding is not always clear,[8] the biblical definition of understanding is insight, perception, or discernment. It involves distinguishing one thing from another, but the literal meaning is to bring together—perhaps to compare what is joined. Understanding also carries an ethical dimension (Blomberg, 1988, p. 945; Fontaine, 2009, pp. 709–710; Fretheim, 1997, p. 652; Ringgren, 1975, pp. 99–107). This implies seeing beyond the surface. We discover that what seems similar at first is really quite different—like identical twins after we have known them for a while. Extra-biblical sources give a similar definition of understanding, that is, comprehension, explanation, meaning, interpretation, abstraction, judgment, perspective, and empathy (Bruner, 1965, pp. 7, 31; Stevenson, 2010c; Wiggins & McTighe, 2005, pp. 37–39, 83–84, 88–92, 132). Since God understands everything perfectly, He is a source of understanding (Psalm 147:15; Proverbs 2:6). On the other hand, we are warned about relying on our own understanding (Proverbs 3:5).[9] With these designations in mind, I define understanding in this essay as *deep knowledge*. Referring to my garage roof illustration—only when I have deep knowledge of my garage roof retaining snow longer than the roof on the rest of my house, can I say I understand it.

IMPLICATIONS OF UNDERSTANDING

Closely related to understanding are the concepts of explanation and meaning. I focus on them, because the other terms are synonymous with or are included in these two notions. Explanation and meaning both involve relationships. When we say that understanding is the explanation of knowledge, we emphasize the causal relationship between what we observe and its explanation. Saying that understanding is the meaning of knowledge emphasizes the contextual relationship between what we observe and its context. Looking beyond the immediate helps us see explanations and meanings which are not always apparent. Since we can learn from others' understanding, I also address the sources of understanding.

Explanation

When we talk about the explanation of something, we generally refer to what causes it. When referring to the explanation of a child's misbehavior at school, we mean the cause of his misbehavior. Similarly, if someone asked me to explain why snow melts faster on most of my roof than on my garage roof, I would tell the person what I think causes this. Also, referring to the explanation of something infers that we believe it has a cause. We call this the law of cause and effect—which biblical writers assumed (Leviticus 26:3–4; Galatians 6:7–8; Greco, 2010, p. 9; Sproul, Gerstner, & Lindsley, 1984, p. 111). All of us were born with an inherent sense of causality and experience it every day (Bransford, Brown, & Cocking, 1999, p. 222). For example, if a child regularly misbehaves at school, we assume there is a reason for it. Likewise, I assume there is a cause both for having snow on my garage roof and not having it on the rest of my roof. Additionally, the ingrained principle of cause and effect forces us to see God as the ultimate cause of everything (Romans 1:18–19) and enables us to manage the earth.[10]

Meaning

Meaning is vitally connected to its context. Seeing the role that something plays in its larger context gives it meaning and helps us understand it (Fontaine, 2009, pp. 709–710; Riggs, 2003, p. 217).[11] For instance, seeing a letter in the context of a word helps us understand it because this gives it meaning. In other words, something takes on meaning and is, therefore, understood when we see it as a part of a group that is bigger than itself. In this way, mentally placing things that we observe into larger categories based on their similarities and differences helps us understand them.[12] When mentally placing each animal at a zoo into categories based on likenesses and differences, we put each animal into a group that is larger than itself and give it meaning. As a result, I understand the animals better. Similarly, seeing the relationship between my garage roof and other roofs in the area or mentally grouping my garage roof and other roofs that retain snow into one category, my garage roof becomes part of a group that is bigger than itself and takes on a meaning that it did not have before.

Our contextual relationship with people also has ethical implications. When seeing other people in context, we intuitively recognize that they are part of a larger group of which we are a part, that is, human beings. Therefore, we intuitively understand that we should treat other people as we want to be treated (see Romans 2:14–15). We call this the Golden Rule. Moreover, seeing people in their broadest context as image-bearers of God gives us more impetus to treat them with respect. As a result, I can see that my concern for my roof should include not only how it affects my family and me, but also how it pleases God and affects others outside of my house.

Beyond the Immediate

When first examining something, we usually focus on immediate explanations and narrow meanings and miss those which are indirect and broad. This leads to a relatively shallow understanding. Therefore, we need to look for causal relationships that are more indirect and contextual relationships that are broader. One way to do this is to think beyond the immediate situation. Are there indirect explanations for what we observe other than the obvious cause we see? Are there broader meanings other than the obvious meaning of what we experience? The immediate cause of a child's misbehavior at school, for instance, may not be the only one or even the most influential one. Besides the peer-pressure of his misbehaving friend, we should also consider his physical condition, teacher, school environment, and home life. Beyond that, we ought to take into account what the Bible says about the child and those who work with him. God is not so much the cause of the child's misbehavior, but He is the ultimate explanation and meaning for a child who can misbehave. God is also the broadest context of the child and, therefore, provides the greatest meaning of him. Since they are all finite creations of God, the child and his parents and teachers have physical and mental strengths and weaknesses. Because they are all sinners, they all have propensities to misbehave. Both causal and contextual relationships provide general explanations and broad contexts for the child's misbehavior. Similarly, the immediate context of a zoo animal only begins to show us its meaning. While we should acknowledge the animal's mother and father and other immediate explanations and meanings, deep knowledge requires us to go beyond the immediate. Finding out more about the zoo and the animal's species and natural habitat would give us a better understand of it. Focusing on the animal's Creator would help us understand it even more. As for my garage roof retaining snow longer than the roof on the rest of my house—looking beyond the roof tops to the angle of the sun on the roofs, the insulation under them, and the people who control the furnace thermostat of the rooms under the insulation gives me a better understanding of the situation. Seeing this in the light of God encourages me to consider the spiritual explanations and meanings of persistent snow on my garage roof.

Sources

While gaining understanding is necessary for us to manage the resources God has given us, it is not always easy. Therefore, we should hear what others have to say who have more understanding. Since God understands everything, we should consult what he has revealed first through the Bible (Psalm 119:34, 73, 130; Goldberg, 1980a; Johnson, 2013, pp. 67, 110–113, 194–199) and prayer (1 Kings 3:9; Psalm 119:99, 104, 125, 144, 169; Proverbs 2:2–5).[13] For example, God has shown us that He is the ultimate explanation and meaning for everything (Genesis 1–2; Nehemiah 9:6; Psalm 121:2; Isaiah 44:24; Romans 1:20; Colossians 1:16; Revelation 4:6). Through the Bible, we also have deep knowledge that a desire for relationships with God and other people is a very influential explanation for peoples' behavior (Genesis 2:18; Psalm 42:1; Ecclesiastes 3:11; Matthew 4:4), as is a desire for self-indulgence (Matthew 5:19). Additionally, finding how we fit into the life of God and others gives us meaning.

Using God's revealed understanding as a foundation, we are free and responsible to seek explanations or meaning for what we observe in our world. Yet, God gives us another gift to help us with our task of managing the earth, that is, each other. This began with God giving Eve to Adam to help him understand the earth, and it continues today with people helping each other to understand their surroundings. We can learn from other peoples' understanding, just as they can learn from ours. However, we can especially gain much understanding from experts in particular fields of study and practices—much of which is recorded so people in different times and locations may access it (Bizzell & Herzberg, 1987; Cairns, 1954, p. 342; Lockerbie, 2005, p. 11). After all, they are aware of causal and contextual relationships that have and have not been discredited. We may have enough experience in particular areas of life to informally test some proposed explanations ourselves[14] or put them into larger contexts. So, for my roof issue, it is a good idea to seek explanations and meanings for my garage roof retaining snow longer than the roof on the rest of my house from God (through prayer) and roof technicians (in library books or online videos).

Place of Understanding in Higher Education

In addition to facts, students need to be exposed in higher education to explanations that are new to them and meanings that they may never have considered. This begins by teaching them God's perspective on all subjects as revealed in the Bible, and includes having them learn about proposed and recognized explanations and meanings from experts in books and journals. In this setting, students should also learn to develop their own understanding of the world. Yet they need more than understanding if they are to manage their parcel of the earth. They must be taught how to use their understanding to determine what they should do and act upon it.

Wisdom

To manage the earth, we need wisdom to use our knowledge and understanding. In this section, we examine the biblical definition of wisdom and its implications and place in learning in higher education to manage our resources.

Definition of Wisdom

God gave Adam and Eve the ability and motivation to know and understand what they observed, but this was not just so they could explain it or find its meaning. Since God's plan and command to Adam and Eve to "have dominion" and "rule" are action verbs, the last step in fulfilling this mandate implies effort. God required them and us to act upon our deep knowledge (Sternberg, 1990, p. 152), that is, to practice wisdom (Wilckens, 1971, p. 482). In the Bible, wisdom means skillfulness, perception, judging rightly, and the ability to use knowledge rightly (Dell, 2009, p. 869). Since God has all wisdom, we should seek it from Him (Psalm 19:7; Colossians 1:17; James 1:5). Furthermore, we are not to rely only on our own wisdom (Proverbs 3:7). In non-biblical sources, wisdom is defined as good judgment, discernment, and expertise in life (Charry, 2009, p. 299; Honderich, 2005; Stevenson, 2010d). Rowley (2006, pp. 257–258) defined wisdom as the "capacity to put into action the most appropriate behaviour, taking into account what is known (knowledge) and what does the most good (ethical and social considerations)." Considering these descriptions, in this essay, I define wisdom as *skillfully-applied understanding.* If understanding leads me to believe that poor quality insulation is the most influential explanation for my garage roof retaining snow longer than the roof on the rest of my house or if this is its likely meaning, wisdom compels me to apply that understanding by replacing it with insulation under the roof of the rest of the house. However, before I proceed to improve my roof situation or act upon my understanding of anything, I need to consider the implications of wisdom, that is, expertise and ethics. I focus on them because the other terms are synonymous with, or included, in these two concepts.

Implications of Wisdom

Expertise and ethics are needed for wisdom. Expertise refers to the process, and ethics speaks of the results of that process. Expertise is what experts have. I have referred to experts above when dealing with knowledge and understanding. Experts have great knowledge and understanding, but their expertise is demonstrated by their ability to apply it. Yet one who has wisdom is also motivated toward ethical ends. Without ethics, expertise may be used for evil purposes. But we do not consider someone to have wisdom if the person does not have expertise, no matter how ethical his or her behavior is. Both are required.

Expertise

More than deep knowledge of a particular area, one with wisdom has the expertise to act upon it to bring about the best results (Birren & Fisher, 1990, p. 331). Sometimes this entails dealing with the most influential causes or factors which bring the most meaning (Kekes, 1983, p. 280). Being the ultimate expert, God possesses deep knowledge of everything and the expertise to use it in the best way (Job 12:13; Psalm 104:24; Jeremiah 10:12; Romans 11:33). Though never approaching His level of expertise, we who are in His image can develop some wisdom (Ford, 2007, p. 23; Holliday & Chandler, 1986, pp. 16, 31). Seeking wisdom is good unless we substitute human wisdom for God's wisdom or try to use it apart from His wisdom (Genesis 3:6; Proverbs 3:7; 26:12; Isaiah 5:21; Romans 12:16; 1 Corinthians 3:19–20; James 3:15–17). Yet because we can grasp some of God's wisdom and need it to manage the earth, He freely gives it to us (Proverbs 2:1–8; 4:5; James 1:5; Goldberg, 1980b, p. 283; Kenyon & McLeod-Harrison, 2016, p. 132). Being in the image of God, we also can develop wisdom through personal experience and learn it from other people (Dell, 2009, p. 874; Wilckens, 1971, pp. 492–494). Some have gained deep knowledge and expertise to become human experts from whom others seek wisdom. The biblical writers encouraged us to get wisdom from wise individuals and groups (Deuteronomy 17:9; Psalm 13:20; Proverbs 11:14; 15:22; 24:6). God had some of His wisdom recorded in the Bible, and people who have learned wisdom have recorded some of their wisdom for those in other times and locations (Wilckens, 1971, pp. 488, 492–493; see also Baltes & Staudinger, 2000, p. 122).

Ethics

Ethics is a system or theory of moral values or principles (Singer, 2018). Christians are charged with adopting God's ethics or value system in which God and people are the first and second priorities (Matthew 22:34–40). God also values the rest of His creation, but it is His third priority (Genesis 1:31; 9:15; Psalm 136:25; 145:9–10, 15–16; 147:9; Jonah 4:11; Matthew 10:29–31). Although these three priorities should guide us in our use of applied understanding, they often intersect and can be dealt with together. For example, my understanding of a misbehaving child at school should be used to enhance his relationship with God, as well as God's relationship with his parents, teachers, and fellow classmates. The effect of the child's misbehavior on animals and inanimate objects is also a concern. Likewise, I ought to use my deep knowledge of snow melting faster on most of my house roof to be a good steward of the house that God has given me and to care for my family. The condition of the roof is actually of lesser concern, though it is hardly irrelevant to the issue.

Ethics implies freedom and responsibility. Rather than rule the earth Himself, God gave that task to people. Though Adam and Eve and their descendants were accountable to Him for how they carried out this endeavor, they were free to carry it out within the limits of God's sovereign plan. As God gave Adam the freedom and responsibility to choose the names of the animals, so He gave the first couple and their offspring the freedom and responsibility to choose their actions carefully. Using their wisdom to rule would bring many benefits, but failing to take that responsibility seriously would bring dire consequences. Eventually, they failed, and their descendants followed their lead to suffer those consequences. In the case of my roof, I have the freedom and responsibility to fix my roof anyway I choose within God's big plan, but my family and I will live with the results and benefit or suffer accordingly.

PLACE OF WISDOM IN HIGHER EDUCATION

Higher education is also a place for students to learn about the wisdom of God and the insight of human experts. During this time, teachers should require them to read and hear about ways practitioners skillfully apply their understanding in their fields and practices. Additionally, teachers should show them wisdom and give them guided practice in a safe environment.

Knowledge, Understanding, Wisdom and Information Literacy

Few have written about knowledge, understanding, or wisdom in IL,[15] and, based on my research, no one has attempted to develop a biblical model of IL. Below, I define IL in light of a biblical view of these three components and begin to flesh out how they can be applied to IL within a Christian higher education setting. Knowledge, understanding, and wisdom are acquired and taught by persons interacting with other persons. Therefore, I focus on the roles of key persons involved in IL in higher education.[16] The focus here is on the role of academic librarians, but I also describe the roles of students, faculty members, human experts, and God, the Divine Expert and Teacher, in IL and end with a section on collaboration to help show how academic librarians can work with others to help students with IL.

Definition of Information Literacy

The term "information literacy" is seldom used by any faculty members, but I use the phrase here for the sake of academic librarians who work with them and are very familiar with the term. By far the most influential definition of IL among academic librarians comes from two documents by the Association of College and Research Libraries (ACRL). In 2000, ACRL defined IL as "a set of abilities requiring individuals to recognize when information is needed and have the ability to locate, evaluate, and use effectively the needed information." Recently, ACRL (2016) broadened that definition to "the set of integrated abilities encompassing the reflective discovery of information, the understanding of how information is produced and valued, and the use of information in creating new knowledge and participating ethically in communities of learning."

A major challenge in developing a biblical model of IL is the use of terms in these two definitions. Here is another example of the term information being used interchangeably with knowledge and of knowledge being used interchangeably with understanding. In these definitions, information is discovered, located, and produced. According to the biblical definition of knowledge, that is, the awareness of facts, knowledge can be discovered and located, but not produced. "Produced" may be applied to the biblical definitions of understanding and wisdom but not of knowledge. In both definitions, knowledge is used synonymously with the biblical definition of understanding, that is, the explanation or meaning of facts. We could substitute some of these words with terms that are more in line with their biblical definitions, but it is hard to imagine that those who developed the first definition intended it to apply only to the awareness of facts. Additionally, the need for knowledge and the ability to locate it suggests that it comes from someone else. Therefore, it probably refers to recorded facts, understanding, and wisdom from the community of scholars or practitioners. With these qualifications, we could rewrite the first definition this way: IL is the ability to recognize when recorded knowledge, understanding, or wisdom from the community of scholars or practitioners is needed and to effectively locate, evaluate, and use them.

114 The Faithful Librarian

Rewriting ACRL's second definition of IL using terms according to their biblical definitions also requires more than just substituting words. Again, it is unlikely that the writers of this definition wanted to limit it to the discovery of facts. Since students develop rather than discover their own understanding and wisdom, those who wrote the second definition of IL would be referring to discovering the understanding and wisdom of others. As a practical matter, this probably refers to recorded knowledge, understanding, and wisdom. Thus, we could restate the second definition in the following way: IL is the ability to reflectively discover and access recorded facts, understanding, and wisdom; to grasp how understanding is developed and valued; and to participate ethically with communities that do this. ACRL's definition of IL includes some aspects of the biblical definitions of knowledge, understanding, and wisdom, but an educational process that is based upon these components suggests an alternate definition, that is, *IL is the skillful practice[17] of acquiring recorded works from experts to develop and skillfully use understanding for God and people.*

Roles in Information Literacy

Based upon this definition, IL in higher education requires at least four types of persons, that is, students, teachers, experts, and academic librarians. Tertiary education is an opportunity for students to develop knowledge, understanding, and wisdom from teachers and experts and how to access recorded works from those experts. During this time, teachers (human and divine) show students how to develop these three areas in anticipation of them continuing to do so after graduation. Additionally, academic librarians assist students and teachers in accessing recorded works of experts to help students in this process, and, similar to teachers, they hope students will continue to access such works after graduation so they can continue to grow in knowledge, understanding, and wisdom. Below, I examine in more depth the roles of students, teachers, academic librarians, and experts in IL and use knowledge, understanding, and wisdom to suggest way of improving students' IL.

Students

Students bring their own knowledge, understanding, and wisdom with them to colleges and universities. Although some might call it ignorance and foolishness, students bear the image of God and so instinctively observe facts, try to explain or assign meaning to those facts, and endeavor to fix or improve their situation based upon that knowledge and understanding. However, students usually have relatively little knowledge or understanding outside of their own experience. Furthermore, their minds may not be developed enough to advance their knowledge and understanding, and they may not be morally mature enough to truly benefit themselves and others. Therefore, students require teachers (human and divine) to help them learn knowledge and develop and practice understanding. This involves attending and participating in their classes, doing assignments, listening to their faculty members, and seeking their help when needed. Students also need academic librarians to provide access to relevant recorded works from experts (human and divine) and to help them learn to access them. Since experts' ideas are such an important part of student development, it is critical for them to seek help and counsel from academic librarians to identify and access their recorded works. They should also seek God's assistance in developing their knowledge, understanding, and wisdom and in identifying and accessing recorded works of experts.

Teachers

God

Being omniscient, God knows each student, faculty member, human expert, and academic librarian. He knows his or her level of knowledge, understanding, and wisdom, and He is aware of what each lacks in these three areas. He also understands the best way to help each of them to grow in these components. Being omnipresent, God is always with them to help them learn and teach others. He normally does this through the Bible and His Spirit.

Faculty Members

At one time faculty members were students, and hopefully they continue to learn even after becoming teachers. In their role as students, they learned about experts in their field of study. Hopefully, they came to see God as the Ultimate Expert on every subject (Cairns, 1954, pp. 343, 345). Guided by teachers, human experts, and God (even if they were unaware of Him), students increased in knowledge, understanding, and wisdom (Ford, 2007, pp. 317–318). For this reason, faculty members are usually a good source of all three elements. They can also recommend recorded works from experts (hopefully both human and divine) to students and to academic librarians (so they can make these recorded works accessible to students and guide them to those works). Furthermore, faculty members can help students increase and develop their knowledge, understanding, and wisdom. Since faculty members were and are students, they should be able to guide their students through this process. However, many faculty members have common faults which hinder their effectiveness with others. They tend to focus only on one particular area of study and may be challenged to show or even see how it fits in broader contexts. Since faculty members are inclined to forget what it was like to be students who are new to their area of study, they may not be good at sharing what they have learned with students or guiding student in their education. Faculty members may have idiosyncrasies and biases which hinder their relationships with students, other faculty members, academic librarians, or God. Yet, faculty members need God, not only for the knowledge, understanding, and wisdom He can give them, but also for His help to work with other faculty members and academic librarians, and to guide students in learning and developing knowledge, understanding, and wisdom (Wilckens, 1971, p. 482).

Experts

God

Since God knows and understands all things, is holy, and loves us, He is an expert on all knowledge, understanding, and wisdom. Therefore, He is a credible source for students, faculty members, human experts, and academic librarians. Indeed, He is the Ultimate Expert of every discipline or practice and every person. God has shared in the Bible some of His knowledge and understanding of Himself and Creation and how we should act accordingly. He also offers these to those who seek Him in prayer (Psalm 119:66; Proverbs 1:7; 2:2–11; James 1:5). Although He has given them the freedom (and responsibility) to manage their world by increasing their knowledge and understanding of it and using that knowledge and understanding to please Him and benefit people, this should start by availing ourselves of His knowledge, understanding, and wisdom.

Human Experts

Human experts (which may include faculty members) are recognized as such because they have demonstrated that they are a credible source of knowledge, understanding, and wisdom in their particular discipline or practice. Indeed, they generally have comprehensive knowledge of their field and are familiar with prominent understandings of their subject area in the past and present. Experts usually present their own findings and ideas in their writing and lectures. Some of them develop practical principles and invent tools and techniques to fix problems and improve situations. Human experts who study the Bible and seek God have an advantage over those who do not, because they have access to God's knowledge, understanding, and wisdom. Yet even without this intentional turning to God, experts have much knowledge, understanding, and wisdom to share with students, faculty members, and academic librarians. Though they limit their sphere of knowledge, understanding, and wisdom to this world, all who are involved in the educational process can learn from them.

ACADEMIC LIBRARIANS

Because many in higher education do not see the importance of IL and do not understand the role of academic librarians in it (Badke, 2005; 2008; 2010, 136–138; Bivens-Tatum, 2011; McGuinness, 2006, 575–576; Wilder 2005; Wooliscroft, 1997, 18), I show here how using knowledge, understanding, and wisdom can help academic librarians promote IL and their role in it.

Academic librarians should start first with knowledge—knowledge of themselves and the current situation of IL in higher education. It is no exaggeration to say that academic librarians generally excel in helping students and faculty members obtain recorded works from experts (Miller & Tegler, 1987, pp. 122–123, 126). Some of them also excel in teaching students how to do this for themselves. However, some of these academic librarians feel frustrated in their work (Julien & Given, 2002, 76–80; McGuinness, 2006, 573–574). They realize that students often do not consult recorded works from experts for their assignments, in spite of the IL instruction academic librarians give to over half of them (Julien, Gross, & Latham, 2018).

Next, as academic librarians we need to dig deeper into those facts by discovering causes and seeing them in context. For instance, why do students often not consult recorded works from experts for their assignments? Also, why do academic librarians who excel in helping and teaching IL provide this to so few students? Additionally, why are some academic librarians frustrated in their work? Looking at the big picture of IL in higher education and the roles of faculty members and academic librarianship can help us find answers to these questions. Educational administrators hire faculty members to be the primary educators of student, and they hire academic librarians to support the faculty in this work. Most faculty members were above-average students and did not seek help from an academic librarian during their undergraduate and graduate education. As a result, they tend to see little need of this for their students. They greatly appreciate the books and journals that the academic library supplies, but they see academic librarians primarily as collection builders and vendor liaisons. Apart from doing what those who hired them require, they believe academic freedom gives them the right and responsibility to teach as they think best. Additionally, students who have been raised on digital technology and the Internet generally think they are good at finding the knowledge and understanding they need and do not require assistance from academic librarians. If they need help, they seek guidance from their teachers. On the other hand, due to the growth of academic librarianship into a profession; the influence of prominent academic librarians, such as Patricia Knapp, Evan Farber, Patricia Breivik, and Carol Kuhlthau; and the advancement of the Internet have convinced most academic librarians that their responsibility goes beyond providing recorded works of experts to include helping students access those recorded works from experts and teaching them to do so for themselves. In fact, this has become the chief role of academic librarianship in the minds of academic librarians. With these explanations and this context, we can see why some academic librarians are frustrated in their work.

After reviewing the current state of academic librarianship and IL in higher education and exploring their causes and contexts, we are ready to address those explanation and deal with their meanings. One potential course of action is to make our case to the provost or academic vice president, school deans, department heads, and faculty to incorporate IL into the curriculum. Providing examples of other colleges and universities that have done so and evidence that it improves student success should help bolster our case. However, educational administrators and faculty members are busy people who have their own ideas about the educational process. Faculty members may also appeal to academic freedom to resist such top-down control of their classrooms. Yet without faculty buy-in, IL may be taught poorly or not at all. Another option that may be tried in tandem with or in lieu of the first option, is to promote IL to individual faculty members. This may encourage them to incorporate IL into their courses even without administrative support. However, academic librarians have learned that this is not an easy task. Still another option is to offer an IL course to students. Since IL is arguably as necessary in higher education as writing, we could propose that every student complete the course just as they are all required to take a Composition course. Offering IL courses specifically for science, social science, and humanities majors is a related option. The challenge here is getting educational administrative and student buy-in, since administrators are already trying to reduce the number of hours in an already full curriculum and students already have a full load.

Pursuing God's wisdom and the advice of colleagues, I propose combining these approaches. Seeking the help of God and English faculty members, we can make a strong case to the academic dean for *Research Across the Curriculum* (RAC). As a part of this initiative or as an alternative (should the RAC proposal be rejected), we can recommend that this be tailored to each school or department. Appeals for such tailored IL to school deans or department chairs is surely needed, even if not met with enthusiasm by the academic dean. As part of the institution-wide or school/department-wide RAC proposals or as an alternative (should they all be turned down), we can make a case for a one-hour IL course. We should also explain to faculty members how we can help their students access recorded works from experts for their assignments and encourage those who are open to this to let us give a classroom presentation or require their student to set up a research appointment with us. While never satisfied until all students have an opportunity to receive IL teaching, we must be content with movement toward this goal. Along with these, we should devise a plan to promote IL to students directly. Since many administrators, faculty members, and students will not respond favorably to us, at least not at first, we must rely on wisdom, joy, and persistence from God and help from fellow academic librarians.

However, like students and faculty members, academic librarians have faults that can hinder their effectiveness with others. Similar to faculty members, they tend to forget what it was like as a student to be unfamiliar with accessing recorded works from experts. Since they usually do not have in-depth knowledge and understanding in particular disciplines or practices, their unfamiliarity with important works by experts in those fields may hinder their usefulness. Their limited interaction with students makes it challenging for them to help them. Even when they get those opportunities, they may be much better at accessing recorded works from experts than explaining to students and faculty members how to do this for themselves. Furthermore, the peculiarities of many academic librarians, such as introversion and obsession with organization, can hinder their ability to interact with students, faculty members, and even other academic librarians. Therefore, they need God's assistance to graciously work with students and faculty members in finding recorded works from experts for them and in teaching them to find them for themselves (Riley, 2010, p. 94).

Conclusion

Reframing IL as knowledge, understanding, and wisdom from a biblical perspective is a helpful exercise, not only for communicating IL in biblical terminology, but also for rethinking IL in a biblical way. Seeing all of this in the context of managing the earth to please God and benefit people gives IL more meaning than a secular perspective. It also potentially gives more of an incentive than a non-biblical approach for faculty members and academic librarians to collaboratively help students access recorded works by experts. Most of all, a biblical model of IL recognizes God's part in the process of training students to continue the legacy of managing the earth for God and people.

NOTES

1. I would like to thank the following people for reviewing and offering suggestions for this essay: Ed Baumann, Senior Professor of Education at Cedarville University, Sarah Ullery, a friend, and Char Gates, my wife.

2. The word "dominate" in Genesis 1:26, 28 means to tread, trample, or chastise, and "subdue" in Genesis 1:28 means to tread down and denotes subjugation of power. Adam and Eve were given the authority, attitude, and ability to make the animals and earth subservient to their use. This was only abused when Adam and Eve and their progeny became corrupted by sin (Hamilton, 1990, pp. 137–140; Mathews, 2002, pp. 168–170).

3. I discuss the importance of self-care in contrast to self-indulgence in my article "Self-Care: A Christian Perspective" (Gates, 2015); see also Csikszentmihalyi & Rathunde, 1990, pp. 36–41.

4. Although there is no record of God telling Eve not to eat fruit from the tree of the knowledge of good and evil, she knew this when talking to the serpent (Genesis 3:2–3). Apparently, she received this knowledge from Adam.

5. I thoroughly explained the difference between self-benefit and self-indulgence in my article, Self-Care: A Christian Perspective (Gates, 2015).

6. The emphasis on experts throughout this essay comes from my reading of Dru Johnson's (2013) *Biblical Knowing*, which pointed out the importance of authorized knowledge throughout the Bible.

7. Many have even used knowledge interchangeably with understanding (Sauer, 1995, p. 142; Bierly, Kessler, & Chistensen, 2000, p. 601; de Ridder, 2014, p. 44; Pearlson, Saunders, & Galletta, 2016, p.12), and some have done so with wisdom (Holliday & Chandler, 1986, pp. 17–78).

8. Many have attached the definition of understanding used here to knowledge or wisdom (Blomberg, 2007, p. 54; Brookes, 1980, p. 131; Brookes, 1981, p. 4; Davenport & Prusak, 1998, p. 3; Holliday & Chandler, 1986, pp. 13, 17–18, 31; Pearlson, Saunders, & Galletta, 2016, pp. 12, 61; Stenmark, 2001, para. 7, 19; Tucker, 2002, p. 8).

9. Popper was right when he said that human understanding (he used the term knowledge) is always provisional and open to criticism and correction (Brookes, 1980, p. 129). He used the term "verisimilitude" to refer to the best explanations or meanings that limited human beings can propose (Popper, 1972, pp. 47–58).

10. Although hard to imagine, if there were no causes for what we observe, we could never propose theories or make tools to progress beyond our current state. Rather than manage our surroundings, we would be ruled by them. Furthermore, without an intuitive knowledge of causal relationships, we would probably never explore possible causes of what we observe. Since we would not be looking for causal relationships, our discovery of them would come very slowly, if at all. Managing the earth seems to require both real causal relationships and an intuitive knowledge of them.

11. As with our in-born tendency to assume causal relationships, we also have a God-given desire to see things in a larger context—specifically, an eternal context (Ecclesiastes 3:11). As a result, we feel meaningless if we try to live only with a temporal, earthly perspective (Ecclesiastes 1–8, 11–12). As though to lead us to that eternal perspective, things around us can gain meaning if we see them in a context that is bigger than them even if not as big as eternity (Melchert, 1981, pp. 180–182, 185–186). Therefore, the broader the context in which we see things around us, the more meaning they have to us. In this way, those who believe in God have an advantage over professed atheists, because they see what they observe in a bigger context than the unbeliever. It is not hard to imagine that God put this desire in people to help them manage the earth.

12. While it is possible to artificially make up relationships that are not really there, we who are made in the image of a creative God can use our imagination to see genuine relationships that may not be obvious at first (Dykstra, 1981, p. 192; Farr, 2012, p. 265).

13. The story of God promising to explain to young George Washington Carver the mysteries of the peanut in reply to his request to understand the mysteries of the universe may be apocryphal, but his claim that God revealed the uses of the peanut and other natural products to him is not (Marr, 2011; *The New York Times*, 1943).

14. Falsification has been wrongly used to criticize theological assumptions (Flew, 1968), but it is a valid tool for discovering causal relationships once biblical assumptions are established.

15. Mandušić and Lucija (2013, p. 50) described IL as the ability to organize knowledge, and Eric Nyrose (2009a, 2009b) promoted critical thinking in IL as an aspect of wisdom. Bawden (2016, p. 297) emphasized understanding in Digital Literacy (similar to IL) and wrote that understanding resembles some aspects of knowledge construction and the sense-making approaches to information use. In her Seven Faces of Information Literacy, Bruce (1997, pp. 117–151) wrote of all three components when she identified finding and controlling knowledge, likened the concept of knowledge construction to understanding, and proposed using knowledge to gain wisdom and benefit others.

16. Polanyi (1962) was correct when he wrote that all knowledge is personal (see also Greene, 1998, pp. 122–123 and Blomberg, 2007, p. 158). The same can be said of understanding and wisdom.

17. The emphasis on skillful practice fits well with Rogers' portrayal of research as craft (Rogers, 1987, pp. 131–132; see also Charry, 2009, p. 299). She asserted that research is an intuitive, creative, and practical process carried out by practitioners, rather than an objective, rational, and impersonal method that mechanically spits out a theory. Therefore, she pointed out the need for practice based on theory, working with practitioners and interacting with their works, adaptability to various disciplines and practitioners in those disciplines, and an understanding of discipline-specific IL. All of this is compatible with the model promoted in this essay.

References

ACRL. (2000, January 18). Information Competencies Standard for Higher Education. Retrieved from https://alair.ala.org/bitstream/handle/11213/7668/ACRL%20Information%20Literacy%20Competency%20Standards%20for%20Higher%20Education.pdf?sequence=1&isAllowed=y.

ACRL. (2016, January 11). Framework for information literacy for higher education. Retrieved from http://www.ala.org/acrl/standards/ilframework.

Alston, W. P. (1993). *The reliability of sense perception*. Ithaca: Cornell University Press.

Badke, W. B. (2005). Can't get no respect: Helping faculty to understand the educational power of information literacy. *Reference Librarian, 89/90*, 63–80.

Badke, W. (2008). A rationale for information literacy as a credit-bearing discipline. *Journal of Information Literacy, 2*(1), 1–22.

Badke, W. (2010). Why information literacy is invisible. *Communications in Information Literacy, 4*(2), 129–141.

Baltes, P. B., & Staudinger, U. M. (2000). Wisdom—A metaheuristic (pragmatic) to orchestrate mind and virtue toward excellence. *American Psychologist, 55*(1), 122–135.

Bawden, D., & Robinson, L. (2016). Information and the gaining of understanding. *Journal of Information Science, 42*(3), 294–299.

Bierly, P. E., III, Kessler, E. H., & Christensen, E. W. (2000). Organizational learning, knowledge and wisdom. *Journal of Organizational Change Management, 13*(6), 595–618.

Birren, J. E., & Fisher, L. M. (1990). The elements of wisdom: Overview and integration. In R. J. Sternberg (Ed.), *Wisdom: Its nature, origins, and development* (pp. 317–332). New York: Cambridge University Press.

Bizzell, P., & Herzberg, B. (1987). Research as a social act. *The Clearing House, 60*(7), 303–306.

Bivens-Tatum, W. (2011, April 5). The myth of information literacy. [Blog post]. Retrieved from https://blogs.princeton.edu/librarian/2011/04/the_myth_of_information_literacy/.

Blomberg, C. L. (1988). Understanding. In G. W. Bromiley (Ed.), *The International Standard Bible Encyclopedia* (Vol. 4, p. 945). Grand Rapids: William B. Eerdmans.

Blomberg, D. (2007). *Wisdom and curriculum: Christian schooling after postmodernity*. Sioux City: Dordt College Press.

Bransford, J. D., Brown, A. L., & Cocking, R. C. (1999). *How people learn: Brain, mind, experience, and school*. Washington, D.C.: National Academy Press, 1999.

Brookes, B. C. (1980). The foundations of information science. Part I. Philosophical aspects. *Journal of Information Science, 2*(3–4), 125–133.

Brookes, B. C. (1981). Information technology and the science of information. In R. N. Oddy, S. E. Robertson, C. J. Van Rijsbergen, & P. W. Williams (Eds.), *Information retrieval research* (pp. 1–8). London: Butterworths.

Browning, W. R. F. (2009). *A dictionary of the Bible*. Oxford: Oxford University Press. Retrieved from http://www.oxfordreference.com.

Bruce, C. (1997). *The seven faces of information literacy*. Adelaide, South Australia: Auslib.

Bruner, J. (1965). *The process of education*. Cambridge: Harvard University Press.

Bultmann, R. (1964). γινώσκω, γινώσις, επιγινώσκω, επι γινώσις. (G. W. Bromiley, Trans.). In G. Kittel (Ed.), *Theological dictionary of the New Testament* (Vol. 1, pp. 689–719). Grand Rapids: William B. Eerdmans.

Cairns, E. E. (1954). The essence of Christian higher education. *Bibliotheca Sacra, 111*(444), 338–345.

Charry, E. T. (2009). Educating for wisdom: Theological studies as a spiritual exercise. *Theology Today, 66*(3), 295–308.

Csikszentmihalyi, M., & Rathunde, K. (1990). The psychology of wisdom: An evolutionary interpretation. In R. J. Sternberg (Ed.), *Wisdom: Its nature, origins, and development* (pp. 25–51). New York: Cambridge University Press.

Davenport, T. H., & Prusak, L. (1998). *Working knowledge: How organizations manage what they know*. Boston: Harvard Business School Press.

de Ridder, J. (2014). Epistemic dependence and collective scientific knowledge. *Synthese, 191*(1), 37–53.

Dell, K. J. (2009). Wisdom in the Old Testament. In K. D. Sakenfeld (Ed.), *The new interpreter's dictionary of the Bible* (Vol. 5, pp. 869–875). Nashville: Abingdon Press.

Dykstra, C. (1981). Understanding the place of "understanding." *Religious Education, 76*(2), 187–194.

Farr, B. C. (2012). On being theologically educated: Ten key characteristics. *Transformation, 29*(4), 260–276.

Flew, A. (1968). Theology and falsification. In J. Feinberg (Ed.), *Reason and responsibility: Readings in some basic problems of philosophy* (pp. 48–49). Belmont, CA: Dickenson.

Fontaine, C. R. (2009). Understand. In K. D. Sakenfeld (Ed.), *The new interpreter's dictionary of the Bible* (Vol. 5, pp. 709–710). Nashville: Abingdon Press.

Ford, D. F. (2007). *Christian wisdom: Desiring God and learning in love*. Cambridge: Cambridge University Press.

Fretheim, T. E. (1997). בִּין. In W. A. VanGemeren (Ed.), *New international dictionary of Old Testament & exegesis* (Vol. 1, pp. 652–653). Chicago: Moody Press.

Gates, J. (2015). Self-care: A Christian perspective. *Evangelical Review of Theology, 39*(1), 4–17.

Goldberg, L. (1980a). בִּין. In R. L. Harris, G. L. Archer, & B. K. Waltke (Eds.), *Theological wordbook of the Old Testament* (Vol. 1, pp. 103–104). Chicago: Moody Press.

Goldberg, L. (1980b). חָכַם. In R. L. Harris, G. L. Archer, & B. K. Waltke (Eds.), *Theological wordbook of the Old Testament* (Vol. 1, pp. 282–284). Chicago: Moody Press.

Greco, J. (2010). *Achieving knowledge: A virtue-theoretic account of epistemic normativity*. New York: Cambridge University Press.

Greene, A. E. (1998). *Reclaiming the future of Christian education: A transforming Vision*. Colorado Springs: Association of Christian Schools International.

Hamilton, V. P. (1990). The book of Genesis chapters 1–17. In R. L. Hubbard (Series Ed.), *The new international commentary on the Old Testament*. Grand Rapids: William B. Eerdmans.

Holliday, S. G., & Chandler, M. J. (1986). *Wisdom: Explorations in adult competence*. Basel: Karger.

Honderich, T. (2005). *The Oxford companion to philosophy*. Oxford: Oxford University Press. Retrieved from http://www.oxfordreference.com.

Ichikawa, J. J., & Steup, M. (2018). The analysis of knowledge. In E. N. Zalta (Ed.), *The Stanford encyclopedia of philosophy*. Retrieved from https://plato.stanford.edu/archives/sum2018/entries/knowledge-analysis/.

Jaeger, L. (2016). Facts and theories in science and theology: Implications for the knowledge of human origins. *Themelios, 41*(3), 427–446.

Johnson, D. (2013). *Biblical knowing: A scriptural epistemology of error*. Eugene, OR: Cascade Books.

Julien, H., & Given, L. M. (2002). Faculty-librarian relationships in the information literacy context: A content analysis of librarians' expressed attitudes and experiences. *Canadian Journal of Information & Library Sciences, 27*(3), 65–87.

Julien, H., Gross, M., & Latham, D. (2018). Survey of information literacy instructional practices in U.S. aca-

demic libraries. *College & Research Librarians, 79*(2). Retrieved from https://crl.acrl.org/index.php/crl/article/view/16606/18601.
Kekes, J. (1983). Wisdom. *American Philosophical Quarterly, 20*(3), 277–286.
Kenyon, S., & McLeod-Harrison, M. S. (September 2016). The veneration of truth: How analytic theorizing can make us wise. *Didaskalia, 27*, 115–139.
Lewis, J. P. (1980). יָדַע. In R. L. Harris, G. L. Archer, & B. K. Waltke (Eds.), *Theological wordbook of the Old Testament* (Vol. 1, pp. 366–367). Chicago: Moody Press.
Lockerbie, D. B. (2005). *A Christian paideia: The habitual vision of greatness.* Colorado Spring: Purposeful Design.
Mandušić, D., & Lucija, B. (2013). Information literacy, theory and practice in education. *Romanian Journal for Multidimensional Education, 5*(1), 47–58.
Marr, R. W. (2011). Inspiration and peanuts. *Missouri Life, 38*(1), 59.
Mathews, K. A. (2002). *Genesis 1–11:26.* In E. R. Cendenen (Series Ed.), *The new American commentary* (Vol. 1A). Nashville: Broadman & Holman.
McGuinness, C. (2006). What faculty think—exploring the barriers to information literacy development in undergraduate education. *Journal of Academic Librarianship, 32*(6), 573–582.
Melchert, C. F. (1981). "Understanding" as a purpose of religious education. *Religious Education, 76*(2), 178–186.
Miller, C., & Tegler, P. (1987). In pursuit of windmills: Librarians and the determination to instruct. *Reference Librarian, 7*(18), 119–134.
The New York Times. (1943, January 6). Dr. Carver is dead; Negro scientist. *On this day.* The New York Times. Retrieved from https://archive.nytimes.com/www.nytimes.com/learning/general/onthisday/bday/0712.html.
Nyrose, E. (2009a). The importance of wisdom in information literacy. *The Christian Librarian, 52*(3), 85–92.
Nyrose, E. (2009b). Pursuing wisdom: An investigation of the relationship between some ancient religious concepts of wisdom and current notions of critical thinking within information literacy. *Journal of Religious & Theological Information, 8*(3/4), 128–144.
Pearlson, K. E., Saunders, C. S., & Galletta, D. F. (2016). *Managing and using information systems, binder ready version: A strategic approach* (6th ed.). Hoboken, NJ: Wiley.
Polanyi, M. (1962). *Personal knowledge: Towards a post-critical philosophy.* Chicago: University of Chicago Press.
Popper, K. (1972). *Objective knowledge: An evolutionary approach.* London: Oxford University Press.
Rüegg, W. (1992). Themes. In H. de Ridder-Symoens (Ed.), *A History of the University in Europe* (Vol. 1, pp. 3–34). Cambridge: Cambridge University Press.
Riggs, W. (2003). Understanding "virtue" and the virtue of understanding. In M. DePaul & L. Zagzebski (Eds.), *Intellectual virtue: Perspectives from ethics and epistemology.* New York: Oxford University Press.
Riley, D. M. (2010). Information apprenticeship: Integrating faith and learning in the library. *The Christian Librarian, 53*(3), 88–97.
Ringgren, H. (1975). ב.ין. In G. J. Botterweck and H. Ringgren (Eds.), *Theological dictionary of the Old Testament.* (Vol. 2, pp. 99–107). Grand Rapids: William B. Eerdmans.
Rogers, S. J. (1987). Science of knowledge. In C. A. Mellon (Ed.), *Bibliographic instruction: The second generation* (pp. 125–133). Littleton, CO: Libraries Unlimited.
Rowley, J. (2006). Where is the wisdom that we have lost in knowledge? *Journal of Documentation, 62*(2), 251–270.
Sauer, J. A. (1995). Conversation 101: Process, development, and collaboration. In Fifteenth Anniversary Task Force, Library Instruction Round Table, American Library Association (Ed.), *Information for a New Age: Redefining the Librarian* (pp. 135–151). Englewood, CO: Libraries Unlimited.
Singer, P. (2018). Ethics. In *Encyclopedia Britannica.* Chicago. Retrieved from https://www.britannica.com/topic/ethics-philosophy.
Simonetto, M. (2005). Guilds. In W. H. McNeill (Ed.), *Berkshire encyclopedia of world history* (Vol. 3, pp. 878–879). Great Barrington, MA: Berkshire Publishing Group.
Sproul, R.C., Gerstner, J., & Lindsley, A. (1984). *Classical apologetics.* Grand Rapids: Zondervan.
Stenmark, D. (2001). The relationship between information and knowledge. In S. Bjørnestad (Ed.), *IRIS 24: Proceedings of the 24th Information Systems Research Seminar in Scandinavia:* Ulvik, Norway, 11–14 August 2001. Bergen, Norway: University of Bergen.
Sternberg, R. J. (1990). Wisdom and its relationship to intelligence and creativity. In R. J. Sternberg (Ed.), *Wisdom: Its origin, nature, and development* (pp. 142–159). New York: Cambridge University Press.
Stevenson, A. (Ed.). (2010a). Information. In *Oxford dictionary of English* (3d ed.). New York: Oxford University Press. Retrieved from http:www.oxfordreference.com.
Stevenson, A. (Ed.). (2010b). Knowledge. In *Oxford dictionary of English* (3rd ed.). New York: Oxford University Press. Retrieved from http:www.oxfordreference.com.

Stevenson, A. (Ed.). (2010c). Understand. In *Oxford dictionary of English* (3rd ed.). New York: Oxford University Press. Retrieved from http:www.oxfordreference.com.

Stevenson, A. (Ed.). (2010d). Wisdom. In *Oxford dictionary of English* (3rd ed.). New York: Oxford University Press. Retrieved from http:www.oxfordreference.com.

Stoan, S. K. (1984). Research and library skills: an analysis and interpretation. *College & Research Libraries, 45*(2), 99–109.

Tang, J. (2008). Professionalization. In W. A. Darity, Jr., *International encyclopedia of the social science* (2nd ed.) (Vol. 6, pp. 515–517). Detroit: Macmillan Reference USA.

Tucker, J. M. (2002). Logos, biblios & bibliotheke: Christian influences in library development. *The Christian Librarian, 45*(1), 7–13.

Wiggins, G., & McTighe, J. (2005). *Understanding by design* (2d ed.). Alexandria, VA: Association for Supervision and Curriculum Development.

Wilckens, P. (1971). σοφία, σοφός (G. W. Bromiley, Trans.). In G. Kittel (Ed.), *Theological dictionary of the New Testament* (Vol. 7, pp. 465–528). Grand Rapids: William B. Eerdmans.

Wilder, S. (2005). Information literacy makes all the wrong assumptions. *Chronicle of Higher Education, 51*(18), B13.

Wooliscroft, M. (1997, July). *From library user education to information literacy: Some issues arising in this evolutionary process.* Paper prepared at COMLA Workshop, Gabarone, Botswana. Retrieved from https://www.otago.ac.nz/library/pdf/tandlpapers_MJW.pdf.

Faith, Freedom and Information
A Christian Perspective on Intellectual Freedom
Steve Silver

Abstract

It is perhaps stereotypical to depict Christianity and librarianship as at odds over issues of intellectual freedom. Any perusal of a list of recently or most often challenged books demonstrates that religiously-based objections, even when not explicitly stated so, represent the largest category of complaint. Past literature on Christian perspectives on intellectual freedom includes challenges to the American Library Association's (ALA) approach to and understanding of intellectual freedom (e.g., Johnson, 1990/2002; Marsden, 1998; Rigenberg, 2016). The Christian librarian can, at times, feel torn between promoting Christian principles and librarianship's seeming uncompromising call for providing access to whatever the patron desires, however unsavory. Of course, as with any complex topic, and doubly so with an intersection of two complex topics, the truth of the situation is more nuanced than simple stereotypes. In fact, many Christian librarians, whether in religious or secular workplaces, actively support and promote intellectual freedom principles and find no conflict with their Christian faith in doing so. In this essay we will lay out a basic groundwork for understanding intellectual freedom from a Christian perspective, explore some key principles for a Christian approach to intellectual freedom, and examine how those principles might play out in some specific intellectual freedom issues.

Definitions

First, we should be clear what we mean when we use the phrase "intellectual freedom." The 9th edition of the *Intellectual Freedom Manual* (IFM) defines it as

> the right of every individual to both seek and receive information from all points of view and all formats without restriction. It provides for free access to all expressions of ideas through which any and all sides of a question, cause, or movement may be explored [2018, p. 251].

In concept, this definition is based on the First Amendment to the U.S. Constitution's guarantee of freedom of speech, and on the corollary right to freely access information.

This corollary right to freely access information is clearly established in various U.S. court cases (Magi & Garnar, 2015, pp. 44–45).

Three basic concepts can be seen at work. First, the right to freely seek and receive information is based on the individual. There is an interplay with community which will be explored later, but intellectual freedom at its core is seen as an individual right. Secondly, freedom of speech (or free expression) is of little value without the concomitant freedom of others to access that expression. My freedom to express my own thoughts is of little value if you are not free to hear, read, view, or otherwise receive those thoughts. Conversely my freedom to explore any and all expressions is required for your freedom of expression to have meaning. Thirdly, intellectual freedom is conceived as a right, not a privilege. It does not depend on the whim of others, on changing cultural mores, on authoritative directives, or the pressures of a peer group. The above definition from the *Intellectual Freedom Manual* and these three basic concepts essentially sum up what might be termed the "typical" understanding of intellectual freedom by the American Library Association (ALA) and its members.

However, there is an oft-overlooked context that is less obvious, but crucial for a fuller understanding of intellectual freedom. While intellectual freedom is a right inherent to the individual, it only exists within relationships. Intellectual freedom involves one individual's interaction with an idea that comes from another individual. That other individual may be across the table or across the centuries, but it is the relationship of ideas, and by inference the relationship of individuals who have those ideas, that is at the heart of intellectual freedom. This basic context gets little attention in most discussions of intellectual freedom. For the Christian librarian, of course, relationship should be at the heart of all that we do. The two greatest commandments are to love and to be in relationship (for example, Matthew 22:34–40). Ideas are important in our world, but the Christ we follow calls us to love people first and foremost. The Christian librarian can greatly enrich both the understanding and application of intellectual freedom by keeping this relational aspect firmly in mind.

Much has also been written about perceived conflicts between the ALA's understanding of intellectual freedom and a Christian worldview. Essentially most arguments boil down to variations on these two: the ALA's understanding makes the individual the sole authority for what is right or wrong for their life, minimizing the authority of God and of the community, and secondly by doing so it allows individuals to make harmful choices (for example, Johnson, 1990/2002, pp. 142–143).

Yet as stated above, many Christian librarians actively support and even promote essentially the ALA's understanding of intellectual freedom. These librarians seem to find no conflict between their Christian worldview and the ALA's definition of intellectual freedom, or perhaps they have reconceived intellectual freedom in a way that is more compatible with their Christian viewpoint. In addition to the relational aspect noted above, what might a specifically Christian perspective of intellectual freedom look like? Before we can answer that question, we must establish what we mean by the other key concept in the phrase "a Christian perspective on intellectual freedom": *Christian*. On the surface this may seem so obvious as to be overlooked. But one look around the current landscape of the Church in the United States, to say nothing of the world at large, will show a Church fractured and divided with often differing and even opposing statements of faith and belief; in essence having differing definitions of what it means to be "Christian." An examination and comparison of these various claims is beyond the scope of this essay. In an attempt to be as broadly applicable as possible, we will define "Christian" in its simplest and most inclusive manner. We understand a Christian to be one who claims to be, in whatever way they understand it, a "Christ-follower."

Some will protest that this definition does not go far enough, that there are other fundamentals which must be included. Yet this simple, inclusive definition does not preclude such ones from adding their own fundamentals for their particular expression of Christian faith. This definition encompasses their particular understanding plus the myriad of others that would add different fundamentals. This choice of definition is intentional in being as inclusive as possible. A weakness of past explorations of a Christian perspective on intellectual freedom has been the limiting of the term "Christian" to one particular expression of Christian faith, typically an Evangelical understanding. Such an approach renders a proclaimed "Christian" perspective on intellectual freedom in actuality an "Evangelical Christian" perspective, or a "Liberal Christian" perspective, or whatever particular Christian faith expression the writer in question espouses. Doing so shuts out the hundreds if not thousands of librarians with a differing understanding of Christian faith, leaving them with no articulated Christian perspective on intellectual freedom they can comfortably claim as their own. It may be that those who feel additional fundamentals should be added to "Christ-follower" may feel just as excluded by such a perspective that does not fully align with their own, but they certainly cannot claim that the term "Christ-follower" does not apply to them.

So, what might a "Christ-follower's" perspective on intellectual freedom look like, and how would it work itself out in the various issues librarians face? Rather than be seen in opposition, how can a Christian understanding actually add to and enrich the broader understanding of Intellectual freedom? We must remember first of all that ALA's understanding is largely based on legal principles established in court cases and undergirded by the First Amendment. However, that same First Amendment guarantees freedom of religion, which courts have interpreted as providing limited exceptions to those constitutional protections for religious organizations. So, while librarians working in publicly funded libraries have a certain ready-made defense for intellectual freedom principles and practices ("it's the law; I have no choice"), those working in private, faith-based libraries in some ways have a less-sure foundation. An appeal to laws that do not fully apply does not hold as much weight in those circumstances. A fully informed, well-thought out, inclusive Christian understanding can be of great help here, providing valid, cogent, and compelling arguments for practicing and promoting intellectual freedom beyond even what the U.S. Constitution and courts have to say. At the same time, a careful review of some key principles of such a view can enrich the understanding of what intellectual freedom is and should be, what the limits are where they might exist, and provide librarianship in general with a more nuanced and holistic understanding of this core value. The relational aspect of intellectual freedom has already been discussed. Keeping in mind that broader context, four key principles will be explored below: (1) All truth is God's truth; (2) Humans have inherent free will; (3) Humans are flawed and finite; and (4) Freedoms come with limits and responsibilities.

Principles

All Truth Is God's Truth

Psalms 24:1 states, "The earth is the LORD's and everything in it, the world and its inhabitants too" (CEB). If all truth ultimately leads to God, what do Christians, or any other persons, have to fear from pursuing truth as they conceive it? If God is truly sovereign, no pursuit of truth will take one outside of God's ultimate Truth. Especially, the "person whose intellect is freed—liberated—by the gospel can trust in God's sovereignty and truth" (Davis, 1985/2002, p. 133). But what if that pursuit of truth leads one to positions at odds with the accepted "truths" of their community, institution, discipline, or church? Believing that all pursuit of truth ultimately leads to God, it would seem one of two options would then be at play; either one's new belief is in fact in error and one's thinking and information needs to be more fully explored and amended, or the currently accepted teaching at that point is in fact incomplete or erroneous and needs reexamination. The latter is not often easily achieved. Maintaining the over-arching call to love one another while questioning firmly held beliefs—or while having one's own firmly held beliefs strongly questioned—is even more difficult. But if the goal is a better, clearer understanding of truth, then the freedom to question even commonly accepted "truths" becomes all the more important. The earth may truly be the Lord's, including all knowledge, but humans only perceive truth partially and imperfectly (as we shall explore in a moment). We should not fear, then, pursuit of new knowledge and ideas, nor should we fear questioning of even age-old accepted beliefs. Such questioning should ultimately lead to a better understanding of God's ultimate Truth.

Even a cursory review of human history, of course, demonstrates that humans often pursue, believe, teach, and act upon ideas that are not only plainly incorrect, but actually harmful to themselves and/or others. What are we to do with those who pursue their truth in Holocaust denial, vaccine harmfulness, or extreme, cult-like religious beliefs? Further reflection reveals that in the course of human history many "wrong" ideas have in fact been corrected. We no longer believe that planets and stars exist in crystal spheres surrounding the earth, that leeching blood cures disease, or that persons of African descent are somehow inferior to other humans. The arc of correction can indeed be long and often uneven, but if ideas are allowed to truly be free, to be explored, examined, and contested, the truest ones will eventually be demonstrated as such. As the writer of Proverbs reminds us, "iron sharpens iron" (27:17, CEB). The best way to contest incorrect ideas is not suppression, but to let them out in the open for consideration and examination, to be "sharpened" in interaction with other ideas. The Christian librarian, believing that all truth is God's truth, has even more reason to trust that the truest ideas will eventually win out if all ideas are allowed free exploration and expression. If God is sovereign, if all truth is God's truth, then God's truth will more than hold its own in the "marketplace of ideas" that intellectual freedom creates, even if it takes generations or centuries in God's patience (compare Exodus 34:6; Joel 2:13; 2 Peter 3:9).

Humans Have Inherent Free Will

The first part of Genesis 1:27 states that "God created humanity in God's own image, in the divine image God created them…" (CEB). Deuteronomy 30:19b states, "I have set life and death, blessing and curse before you. Now choose life—so that you and your descendants will live…" (CEB). In the gospel records, Jesus never imposes his will on anyone, including his closest disciples. In John 6:67, when the crowds begin to thin upon hearing Jesus' "harsh" words, he turns and asks his disciples, "Do you also want to leave" (CEB). In the Genesis account, the context in which humanity is created in "God's own image" is that of creativity, as God creates the very cosmos. Humans are created in the image of one exercising creativity, exercising free will and choice. We each are the very image of God, imbued with the same basic freedom to choose (Klassen, 2009, p. 162ff; Litfin, 2004, p. 263; Rigenberg, 2016, p. 3). Ellul (1976) reminds us that a basic condition of this freedom in Christ is an expectation that Christians will, in fact, have very differing and even contradicting opinions and actions, potentially all Spirit-led and Christ-oriented (p. 187). Additionally, those we meet and serve in our libraries, even if not Christian themselves, also carry this creative and choosing God-image. To deny them the right to freely choose for themselves denies them their God-given freedom. Yes, they will choose poorly, and have as will we. Yet to restrict access to information they might otherwise choose, even when "for their own good," removes or restricts their God-given right to choose *for themselves* life or death, blessing or curse. If our very God weeps over those who choose death and curse, but does not intervene, should we as Christian librarians do any less?

The desire to restrict and censor access to information comes from a good place (Diekema, 2000, p. 27; Rigenberg, 2016, p. 3). It comes from a desire to protect others from perceived harm. It comes from a desire to help others make good choices. It comes from a place of love for our neighbor and wanting the best for them. It even comes from a certain understanding of biblical injunctions. As one instance, Matthew 18:15–17 is sometimes cited as evidence of the authority of the church to impose correct beliefs and enforce behaviors. A closer examination, however, reveals the potential for differing interpretations (for example, Abingdon, 1994, pp. 377–379; Hagner, 1995, pp. 528–534; Simonetti, 2002, pp. 76–78). The instructions are for a situation where another believer "sins against you." It is not addressing incorrect belief, but rather behavior that has caused offense or harm. The aim of all three stages of response to that sin is repentance and reconciliation. It is, in essence, about restoring relationship rather than enforcing belief or even necessarily behavior. The final instruction for an intractable conflict is telling: "treat them as you would a Gentile and a tax collector" (v. 17). And how did Jesus and the early Church treat Gentiles and tax collectors? By loving them and seeking restored relationship between them and God and between them and their neighbors. Galatians 6:1 sums this up nicely: "Brothers and sisters, if a person is caught doing something wrong, you who are spiritual should *restore* someone like this with a *spirit of gentleness*" (CEB, emphasis added). As any parent knows, loving others sometimes means letting loved ones make their own poor choices and suffering the consequences. As Christian we are called to love all, to gently restore relationships broken by poor choices, while honoring God-given free will.

Humans Are Flawed and Finite

Romans 3:23 states, "All have sinned and fall short of God's glory…" (CEB). Though we bear the very image of God, we are also fallen creatures. We do make poor choices, and believe, promote, and act upon incomplete and erroneous "truths" because we are flawed and finite beings. One does not need a Christian perspective to recognize this aspect of the human condition. Though knowledge continues to increase at exponential rates, we still see only part of the picture, or as Paul says, "in a mirror dimly…" (1 Corinthians 13:12a, ESV; compare Johnson, 1990/2002, pp. 140–141). Recognizing our own imperfection, we should exercise humility and caution when defending what we believe to be true. Recognizing the imperfection in others, we should exercise patience and grace when we see others pursuing ideas we believe to be false or even harmful (Rigenberg, 2016, pp. 13ff). The "right" ideas the Church has vigorously defended, and the "wrong" ideas the Church has at time vigorously oppressed, have in many cases changed dramatically over the centuries: the center of the physical universe; the age of and formation of our earth; the nature of salvation; works versus grace; the proper roles and the understanding of women, or of slavery provide a small sample. Indeed, many significant issues have far from a consensus opinion among various Christian traditions today. If the Church in 2000 years of history has not been able to find or maintain a consensus on issues of even critical importance, how confident should we as individual Christian librarians be that our particular beliefs simply must be true? Rather, believing what we believe to be true, should we not rather hold open the possibility that in our limited and incomplete understanding we could in fact be wrong? And should we not practice the very grace and patience of our Lord in allowing others to make their own mistakes in choosing what information to access?

Freedoms Come with Limits and Responsibilities

The first part of 1 Corinthians 6:12 states, "I have the freedom to do anything, but not everything is helpful..." (CEB). Paul reminds us that while we certainly have God-given freedom to do (or read/view) as we please, that freedom comes with responsibility. We each individually have the responsibility to use our freedom wisely, for building up ourselves and our communities, and yes, to avoid what will harm our relationships with God and with others (George, 2009, p. xviii). If there is a weakness in the typical ALA approach to intellectual freedom it would be this: an inadequate call to use that freedom well. Such a value-neutral approach might be expected to some extent. As a secular organization with a diversity of religious and other viewpoints represented within its membership, the ALA is not in a position to make moralizing judgments.[1] Still, a call to intellectual freedom could easily be coupled with a call to exercise good judgment in that freedom while allowing each individual to decide for themselves what that "good judgment" should look like. This is an aspect of intellectual freedom that deserves further exploration, both within Christian and non–Christian circles.

A word of caution is in order. The call to exercise good judgment in freedom applies to the individual for themselves. When considering another individual, we can perhaps encourage good judgment, but we cannot impose it. Individuals still possess the God-given right to make poor choices. It is not the librarian's job to prevent bad choices. Indeed, it is not even the Christian's job to prevent poor choices made by others. All we can do is encourage wisdom in making choices. This calls for a very thoughtful and nuanced understanding by the Christian librarian. Careful and intentional thought should be given when encouragement crosses the line and becomes a pressure to conform. When a student checks out a book by a transgender protagonist, do you suggest a similar one with more traditional gender roles, or let that student tell you what they like or do not like and whether they even want a recommendation? Do you refrain from purchasing or displaying certain books to "avoid controversy"? If a patron is looking for information supporting the view that women should not teach, do you gently slip in a few resources arguing for a different understanding, or simply provide what they asked for? None of these situations have clear-cut, easy answers. Every situation will be unique and will need to be assessed on its own particular merits. When in doubt, remembering our primary calling to love and relationship and erring on the side of freedom for others to choose for themselves seems perhaps most Christ-like.

Some have argued that the individual's intellectual freedom must be balanced against the standards of the community(ies) of which one is a part (for example, Diekema, 2000, p. 14; George, 2009, p. xx, 162; Johnson, 1990/2002, p. 142). Part of exercising good judgment should, of course, include a consideration of how our choices might impact the reputation, progress, or peace of any community of which we are a member. This, too, is an aspect of relationship. Any community which does not allow individual members to pursue their own intellectual interests, however, is abrogating its members' God-given freedom to choose for themselves. Such a community is placing belief above relationship. Individuals may, indeed, make choices that lead to beliefs or behaviors that no longer conform to the community's expectations, resulting in separation (whether formal or informal, voluntary or forced) from that community. Community expectations do exist and should not be ignored as unimportant. It should not be the *librarian's* role to define or police those community expectations, however.

In fact, the librarian plays a unique role within their community, no less so (and perhaps even more so) for the Christian librarian. All communities have certain standards and expectations of beliefs and actions, some more strongly enforced than others. Communities which do not allow intellectual freedom for their members, however, including the dissent, questions, and controversy such freedom occasions, run the risk of becoming rigid, unable to grow in maturity and understanding, and overly concerned with maintaining status quo beliefs and behaviors over restoring loving relationships and continually seeking to better understand God's Truth. The Christian librarian can play a vital role in creating space for individual community members to exercise their intellectual freedom as a balance against the nearly inevitable consolidation of power and control within any community. There is a place for others to make judgments for the community. The Christian librarian's role is protecting each individual's right to make their own choices about information sought and considered. Doing so not only honors each individual's rights but respects relationship above belief and contributes to the improved health of the overall community.

Taking this unique role seriously can be a difficult position for the Christian librarian, with a certain degree of tension between community expectations and protecting intellectual freedom. But as Davis (1985/2002) reminds us, "controversy is a part of responsible Christian librarianship..." (p. 135). Unfortunately, many administrators, whether they be city managers, school principals, academic deans, or presidents, have a less-complete understanding of intellectual freedom and may often have a more strongly vested interest in maintaining or promoting a particular belief system or set of behaviors. Whether with the non–Christian manager pushing responsibility-free complete freedom or the Christian manager pushing a particular doctrinal viewpoint, the Christian librarian may find themselves at odds over intellectual freedom issues. It would behoove the Christian librarian to be well-versed in the reasons for protecting intellectual freedom and to make clear to the members and leaders of whatever community (Christian or otherwise) to which they belong what those reasons are as well as the unique position of the librarian within the community.

Even so, understanding by administrators—whether Christian or not—is not guaranteed. The Christian librarian should be clear in their own mind where their ethical "line in the sand" is regarding intellectual freedom issues in their workplace. It would be wise for the Christian librarian to be well aware of the political climate in their particular workplace. How far can a divergent viewpoint be pushed before repercussions may be felt? What are the likely repercussions? They could range from social ostracization to loss of employment. Is the Christian librarian prepared to pay the price for expressing or promoting an alternative understanding of intellectual freedom? Each librarian's situation will be unique and complex. None of us can judge for another the relative importance of supporting one's family, maintaining residence within a particular community or region, or strength of ethical concern. Fortunately, such extreme conflicts over intellectual freedom issues are rare. Still, the Christian librarian would be well-served to be prepared. Courage, clear convictions, intentionality, humility, and much prayer and communication will help keep most controversies from escalating, and will bolster the Christian librarian when controversy does come.

Summary

We have established the basic principles that (1) all truth is God's truth, (2) humans have inherent free will, (3) humans are flawed and finite creatures, and (4) freedom comes with responsibility. We understand these principles within the broader context of relationship and the supreme call to love. How then might a Christian librarian apply these principles and context within some specific intellectual freedom situations? We will briefly examine two issues: collection management and Internet filtering. There are certainly many additional intellectual freedom issues worthy of consideration. It is hoped a simple application of our core principles to these issues will provide the Christian librarian concrete examples to better understand how these principles might play out in the "real world," and how those principles might help them address the specific intellectual freedom issues with which they may be faced. We also understand that every situation and librarian is unique, and it is difficult to apply "one-size-fits-all" solutions to complex issues. Our explorations will thus be more on the line of asking what seem to be relevant questions rather than providing definitive and defining answers.

Application

Collection Management

Collection Management has been defined as "the process … that results in decisions about the acquisition, retention, and provision of access to information sources in support of the intellectual needs of a given library community" (Gregory, 2011, p. xiv). Essentially, it is the process of deciding what to make available to the library's patrons. One potential hazard regarding intellectual freedom within this decision-making process is allowing one's own biases to unduly influence those collection management decisions. This can happen in selecting or deselecting certain topics, viewpoints, authors, or publishers. Overcoming personal bias in collection management is an issue for all librarians and is well covered in MLIS courses and in the general library science literature. Is there a unique challenge, obligation, or opportunity for the Christian librarian in the call to overcome personal bias?

One temptation, it seems, is to conflate one's biases with "God's Word," and thus place them outside any consideration of personal bias. Let us be very clear. Your personal views on a particular doctrinal, moral, lifestyle, or other issue may very well represent God's intended truth on that subject. But we recall that all humans are flawed and finite, including ourselves. Seemingly indisputable Christian viewpoints in the past have been modified or called into question in the light of new evidence (the inspiration of the Latin Vulgate Bible, the earth as the center of the physical universe, etc.). Recognizing our own fallibility, should we not allow some room for contrary views? And even if our views represent God's eternal truth, would God impose that truth on another, or is the biblical record one of God allowing us humans to make our terrible mistakes over and over? Consequences suffer, yes, but access to information and the ability to make choices is not restricted. Can we trust God's sovereignty enough to select and provide information that appears to us to be contrary to God's truth?

Of course, saying it is *allowable* to choose information resources with which we disagree is not the same as saying we should *actively choose* information with which we disagree. Certainly, it would seem a direct patron request should be honored in light of the former. But outside of responding to such direct title requests, should the Christian librarian responsible for collection management actively seek and select resources that seem contrary to God's will or even potentially harmful to a patron? What does consideration of the overarching call to love and relationship have to say? Is it more loving to provide resources on topics we know our patrons may want, or to constrain resources on those same topics if we believe they may lead to error or harm? One danger is to equate our library community's needs and desires with what the majority within that community believes is appropriate, or in the case of a Christian library with what the institutional leadership believes is appropriate. Remembering the unique role of the Christian librarian within their community, we should be ever vigilant to provide the resources and information that the minority or even single voice seeks, even or especially when divergent from the accepted community standard. As in all things, a careful balance should be sought. Resources are finite, and choices must be made. Resources to support the information needs of the majority of patrons should not be ignored. But the greater danger seems to be ignoring or inadequately supporting the information needs of the minority view or dissenting community member. Christian service and love of neighbor would seem to call for ensuring the information needs of *all* our patrons are met, including those with whom we disagree.

Furthermore, believing that all truth is God's, can we trust that God can use even contradicting or erroneous information to further God's work in our world and in the lives of our patrons? We cannot predict the use a patron may make of any particular information resource. Error can best be combatted when we fully understand it. It may be beneficial to have materials in your collections that appear completely outside of God's will so that they can be studied and the errors within fully understood. *Mein Kampf* helps us understand and therefore prevent another Hitler. *The Communist Manifesto* gives us the opportunity to better understand Marx's thought, and thus to avoid simplistic reactions to communism while better understanding the thought processes of those espousing this philosophy. *Fifty Shades of Grey* gives us an opportunity to study and dissect the appeal of such a book to so many in our society rather than make simplistic assumptions. Not having resources such as these in our collections reduces our opportunity to better understand our world. What use will God make of these resources in our collections?

Including such resources certainly also represents temptation and the opportunity for being led astray from God's truth. If freedom comes with responsibility, and if love for others is our guiding principle, is there then a role for the Christian librarian in selecting or deselecting materials with the best interests of library patrons in mind? What, indeed, is the best response to "bad" information? Is it restricting access, or is it providing additional "good" information? If the *Mein Kampfs* and *Fifty Shades of Greys* are included, can resources showing the potential negatives of such resources be very well represented in our collections as well? Are there resources which no amount of "good" information can counteract, and which should simply never be included? Where is the line? Acquisition of pornography videos or hardcore erotica are probably inappropriate for a library connected to a Christian school or college.[2] What about "soft porn"? *Sports Illustrated* swimsuit issue? Steamy romance novels? It is a slippery slope. To recognize the slippery slope is not to say that there are not resources at one end that are wholly inappropriate for your constituency, even taking into account minority views. But it is important to recognize the slippery slope, and in the interests of protecting the intellectual freedom of our patrons, especially the minority or dissenting patron, to seek to be more rather than less inclusive of differing viewpoints in our collections.

The Christian librarian working in a secular or non–Christian library may have additional challenges. Your personal views about what is inappropriate to select may very well be at odds with your supervisor, library leadership, or your patrons' desires. What is the best response? Is it a better witness to take a stand for your beliefs, or to place relationship and service above belief and provide resources on the topics sought by your patrons or directed by library leadership even though you view them as highly problematic? Is it a better witness to be a "leavening" presence (for example, Luke 13:20) within a non–Christian setting, or on principle to refuse to compromise your beliefs even at the risk of your employment? Every librarian and every situation will be unique. Each one will need to answer these questions for themselves.

Internet Filters

Many reading this will not be in a position to make decisions about whether to apply Internet filtering software on public access computers in their libraries. However, every librarian must deal with the consequences of whatever decision has been implemented regarding Internet filtering, and every librarian can be an advocate for changes to policy. It seems worthwhile, then, to think carefully about a Christian perspective on this complex topic.

Some might be tempted to view installing Internet filtering software on public access computers as just another aspect of collection development. Key differences, however, place the decision to provide Internet access on public workstations in a different category, with unique intellectual freedom issues. Collection development is proactive. The librarian selects from among many choices what materials to make available. Providing Internet access, on the other hand, is mostly an all-or-nothing proposition. One does not proactively choose from what is available through the Internet to provide to library patrons, but simply makes access to the entire universe of choices available. There is no active selection. Filtering software uses "some combination of the domain, IP address, keyword, and file type" to prevent certain websites from being viewable on the filtered workstation (Houghton-Jan, 2010, p. 26). Installing filtering software, then, is a reactive or restricting approach to providing resources. Rather than selecting what to include, filtering software restricts access to what is otherwise already available. Furthermore, while nearly all collection development selection involves choices made by human librarians,[3] filtering software "is like entrusting the entirety of your collection development to a single proprietary, black-box, artificial intelligence that uses private rating schemes" (Magi & Garnar, 2015, p. 110). Companies that provide filtering software vigorously protect their proprietary filtering algorithms, white lists,[4] and black lists.[5] "As a result, no one can know what is being blocked and why without extensive testing and trial and error" (Magi & Garnar, 2015, p. 106). In short, filtering software reactively restricts rather than proactively selects, and furthermore takes those access decisions out of the hands of local librarians, applying unknown one-size-fits-all largely computer-generated processes that cannot be discovered or questioned.

Another way to state this is that filtering software entirely removes the relationship element from decisions regarding resource provision. When making selection decisions, the collection development librarian does so with an understanding of the needs and desires of the community their library serves. As established above, this should also be done with an understanding of the needs of those holding or seeking information about minority views. Doing so implies and requires some level of relationship with the community. Filtering software precludes any insight gained from such relationship, instead imposing decisions made by automated software algorithms and opaque processes created by for-profit companies applied universally.

One could argue, and perhaps rightfully so, that simply providing Internet access has already removed the relationship aspect to resource provision decisions. As stated earlier, Internet access is pretty much an all-or-nothing proposition. There is no selection decision, merely a decision to either make everything available or none of it. What providing unfettered access to the vast array of resources available through the Internet does do, however, is place the choices about what Internet resources to access squarely with the patron. This is in keeping with honoring each patron's God-given free will, without imposing or restricting decisions about what information to seek. Providing (unfiltered) Internet access can be seen, then, as an intellectual freedom activity, honoring free will, and allowing each person to make their own choices. Just as in accessing other forms of information, flawed and finite humans will make poor choices (and suffer the consequences). And as we have argued above, it should not be the Christian librarian's job to police those choices, whether on the Internet or otherwise.

It is true that for most filtering software systems local librarians and administrators do have some control over what categories to block or unblock, and can usually list specific websites to block or leave unblocked. Requests to unblock otherwise blocked websites, however, generally come from patrons brave enough to request a site be unblocked. It is unknown how many incorrectly blocked websites go unreported due to the "chilling effect."[6] Otherwise legitimate sites thus remain blocked not only for the initial user, but for all other Internet users in that library as well. The ability to select specific categories to block or leave unblocked does give the local library some level of control. But the definitions of the different categories are opaque at best, and effects on specific domains or websites can only be determined by laborious trial and experimentation. The local librarian still has little if any idea what, exactly, is being blocked or left unblocked, even when selecting from a menu of categories.

Furthermore, as has been implied above, filtering software remains far from perfect.

Filters both over block (i.e., incorrectly block something unobjectionable) and under block (i.e., incorrectly allow something objectionable).

> Filters on the market today employ artificial intelligence, image recognition, and complex algorithms. Yet with all of these advanced tools and techniques, filters still cannot successfully evaluate and determine the actual content, context, and intent of text, still images, audio, or video. As a result, filter performance is highly variable [Magi & Garnar, 2015, p. 106].

The available research suggests that, "on average, software filters over-block legitimate content or under-block sexually explicit imagery approximately 15 to 20 percent of the time" (Batch, 2014, p. 18). And these results are only based on text-based filtering. The one study to consider image-based filtering found a 54 percent error rate. That is, the image filter incorrectly identified images slightly more than half the time. Non-English language sites are also routinely overlooked and unblocked as most filtering products only work with English-language sites (Magi & Garnar, 2015, p. 107).

Few follow up studies on filter efficacy have been conducted in recent years, but other recent studies point to the inability of filtering software to effectively prevent viewing of the content they are designed to block. A 2008 study on the effectiveness of various strategies by parents to reduce the exposure of their adolescent children to online risks concluded that "software-based strategies (filtering and monitoring)" were not found to be effective in reducing such risk, "challenging future research to identify the benefits, if any, of such practices" (Livingstone & Helsper, p. 596). A 2011 doctoral dissertation examining Internet pornography usage among male students at three mid-west Evangelical Christian colleges found that 61 percent of these students viewed pornography weekly, despite Internet filters being in place on the campus networks at all three colleges (Chelsen, 2011, p. 135).[7] A 2018 analysis of two studies in the United Kingdom found that Internet filters on home networks had, at best, a 0.5 percent positive effect on preventing children from viewing what parents considered inappropriate websites. That is, 99.5 percent of the parameters influencing whether a child saw inappropriate material on the Internet came from factors other than the installed filters. Considering the "nontrivial economic, informational, and human rights costs associated with filtering" this analysis concluded that "filtering does not play a practically significant protective role" (Przybylski & Nash, 2018).

Internet filtering products, then, have been demonstrated to be largely if not completely ineffective in preventing viewing of the kinds of materials they purport to block. Filtering products have also clearly been shown to block otherwise legitimate content a statistically significant 15–20 percent of the time, imposing real-world constraints on the intellectual freedom of effected Internet users. Internet filtering products also largely take local and human control away from the librarians charged with relating with their local community(ies), instead applying impersonal, automated, universal, and opaque procedures. Many processes in the new Information Age have been automated to achieve significantly greater efficiency, accuracy, consistency, and/or cost savings. Internet filters seem to fit none of these categories of improvement over human processes and decisions. They are not terribly accurate or consistent. While they may achieve some purely economic cost savings over librarians or other human agents making local decisions about the appropriateness of specific websites within the rapidly expanding universe of the Web, factoring in the intellectual freedom costs calls the overall cost effectiveness into question as well.

And yet, there are clearly websites and information accessible through the Internet that have no redeeming qualities and can potentially cause or incite real harm. Blocking or eliminating these sites, it seems, would be good for our individual library patrons and good for society, for example: violent hardcore pornography, militant religious extremists recruiting for their cause, and white supremacists spreading hate and bigotry. If Internet filters are incorrect 15–20 percent of the time, then they are also correct 80–85 per cent of the time. Is this error rate simply a small price to pay for protecting our patrons—especially our younger ones—from material that is more than just inappropriate, but could do real damage? This seemingly simple question will have complex answers unique to every library and librarian. If God is sovereign and all truth ultimately leads Godward, where do such sites, and the potential viewing of such sites, fit in God's sovereignty? Within God's sovereignty, humans possess free will. To abrogate that free will is a serious issue that should perhaps only happen in extreme circumstances. If a decision is made to filter, does this principle call for filters and policies that are as least restrictive as possible? How far down the slippery slope of harmful websites does one draw the line, saying this is acceptable while the other is not? How best do we honor the reality that our patrons are flawed and will make poor choices, while recognizing our own fallenness and potential for error in understanding? Are we convinced of the harmfulness of certain websites or categories because of real evidence, or merely because our faith or a faith leader leads us to believe so? Is it a more responsible response to protect our patrons by restricting access, or, recognizing the apparent ineffectiveness of filters to provide this protection, to provide education and awareness? Is it more loving to restrict access to a swath of websites, knowing that legitimate and perhaps needed information will be blocked as a result, or to leave it open, providing alternative information, support, and prayers where needed? Where is the balance between providing what our communities want versus giving them what we believe they need (or rather, restricting their access to what we believe will be harmful to them)?

Much more could be written on this topic. What questions need to be asked around hostile work environment issues, for instance, when library staff are exposed to deeply offensive or disturbing sites due to patron use of unfiltered Internet access? Are there different questions for Christian librarians working in faith-based institutions versus those working in secular organizations? Are there different answers in those situations? Are there different questions for librarians working within a library versus those in positions of leadership and decision-making? The Children's Internet Protection Act (CIPA) requires Internet filtering for school or public libraries receiving certain federal funding. What should be a Christian librarian's response to this requirement? Assuredly additional questions can be imagined or will come to light in response to future developments. It is hoped that this basic exploration and application of the basic principles and the context of love and relationship will point in fruitful directions for reflection and consideration.

Certainly, additional intellectual freedom issues could and should be considered. The privacy of patron records plays a significant role in protecting their intellectual freedom. How does the principle of responsibility apply within that context when patrons access information that could lead to criminal activity or self-harm? Most libraries provide displays highlighting resources available on particular topics or in particular genres. Are there topics or categories that the principle of responsibility would deem off-limits for such display? Or does the Christian librarian's unique role within their community call for specifically targeting controversial topics in displays? If your library provides meeting spaces for community groups are the rights of all community members to peaceably assemble fully protected in your library's policies and procedures, or are certain groups excluded? Should they be? Is it a curtailment of your own intellectual freedom to be prevented from sharing your faith at work? Is the answer different if sharing with co-workers versus patrons? On social media? Is labeling resources with age or content appropriateness a helpful aid to patrons, or does it lead to restriction of access or a chilling effect for some patrons? How best do we protect the intellectual freedom of children in school or public libraries while responsibly recognizing both their developmental stages and the wishes of their parents or guardians?

Conclusion

The questions could go on. Indeed, the questions should go on. Intellectual freedom is at heart a simple concept, but how it plays out in real life situations is anything but. Intellectual freedom is and should be a core value for Christian librarianship. But it is not the only core value. When different values are at cross purposes, difficult questions are raised. No value can be applied as an absolute without doing damage to other values. How such value conflicts are negotiated and compromised constitutes much of the hard work of living as intellectually authentic Christ followers. The Christian librarian will need to balance the value of intellectual freedom for library patrons with the value, for example, of combatting evil in our world, both individually and societally, with the value of remaining holy (set apart from the world, pure), and with the value of evangelization. The converse is equally true. The value of combatting evil in our world needs to be balanced with the value of intellectual freedom. The value of holiness or purity needs to be balanced with intellectual freedom. The value of evangelization needs to be balanced with intellectual freedom.

The four basic principles discussed here will provide help in understanding and applying the value of intellectual freedom to our work as Christian librarians. Remembering that all truth is God's truth we can trust that within God's sovereignty all intellectual pursuits will ultimately lead to God's truth. Understanding that humans possess God-given free will, we resist curtailing or restricting that free will, knowing that such restriction reduces the humanness and the image of God all humans bear. Recognizing that all humans are flawed and finite, including ourselves, we practice humility and caution regarding our own, even deeply held, beliefs, and exercise grace and patience with the perceived errors of others. Realizing that with freedom comes responsibility we encourage and educate others and ourselves to use our freedom in ways of belief, behavior, and information seeking that increase benefit and good in our society and in individuals.

And in all things, love. As the value of intellectual freedom inevitably crosses purposes with other core values for the Christian librarian, remembering and applying as best we can the context of love and relationship will provide direction and healthy perspective as we balance competing values. It will not necessarily make such values balancing acts easier, but holding love for others within relationship as the context within which all such values decisions are made will help us make such decisions better. Intellectual freedom is, indeed, a core Christian value. It deserves our full attention, promotion, and defense, as librarians and as Christians. With God's help and guidance, may the principles outlined here help us all to do so.

Notes

1. Some have argued that the ALA does exactly this in insisting that all members abide by its own interpretations of intellectual freedom, somewhat ironically suppressing differing viewpoints on intellectual freedom itself. While a topic worthy of some consideration, exploration of this question is beyond the scope of this essay. The basic premise still stands: the ALA cannot and should not expect specifically moral or religious stances to unilaterally apply to all its members.

2. Although it could be a very responsible Christian action to seek such resources for the sake of study and better understanding of their dangers. This would likely come as a very specific collection development request.

3. Aggregator packages of journal articles or electronic books, and various forms of patron driven collection development, blur this line, of course. Even in these instances, however, a librarian (or team) is still making choices about which package(s) to select or which patron driven program to implement.

4. Lists of urls or domains that will always be unblocked.

5. Lists of urls or domains that will always be blocked.

6. "1. Constitutional law. The result of a law or practice that seriously discourages the exercise of a constitutional right, such as the right to appeal or the right of free speech. 2. Broadly, the result when any practice is discouraged" (Garner, p. 293).

7. Chelsen (2011) is careful to point out that his research did not determine whether these students were accessing pornography on campus network computers or on off-campus networks.

References

Abingdon Press. (1994). *The New Interpreter's Bible: General articles and introduction, commentary, and reflections for each book of the Bible, including the Apocryphal/Deuterocanonical books.* Vol. VIII: *New testament articles. Matthew. Mark.* Nashville: Abingdon Press.

Batch, K. (2014). *Fencing out knowledge: Impacts of the Children's Internet Protection Act 10 years later* (Policy Brief No. 5, June 2014). American Library Association: Office for Information Technology policy; Office for Intellectual Freedom. Retrieved August 7, 2018, from http://www.ala.org/aboutala/sites/ala.org.aboutala/files/content/oitp/publications/issuebriefs/cipa_report.pdf.

Chelsen, P. (2011). *An examination of Internet pornography usage among male students at Evangelical Christian colleges.* Accessed August 8, 2018, at https://ecommons.luc.edu/luc_diss/150/.

Davis, D. G., Jr. (2002). Intellectual freedom and evangelical faith. In G. A. Smith (Ed.), *The Christian librarian* (pp. 131-138). Jefferson, NC: McFarland. (Original work published 1985.)

Diekema, A. J. (2000). *Academic freedom and Christian scholarship.* Grand Rapids: William B. Eerdmans.

Ellul, J. (1976). *The ethics of freedom.* (G. Bromiley, Trans. and Ed.). Grand Rapids: William B. Eerdmans.

Garner, B. (Ed.) (2014). *Black's law dictionary.* St. Paul: Thomson Reuters

George, F. C. (2009). Introduction. In P. A. P. Aguiar and T. Auer (Eds.), *The human person and a culture of freedom* (pp. xiii-xxii). Washington, D.C.: American Maritain Association: Distributed by Catholic University of America Press.

Gregory, V. (2011). *Collection development and management for 21st century library collections: An introduction.* New York: Neal-Schuman.

Hagner, D. (1995). Matthew 14-28 (Word biblical commentary; v. 33B). Dallas: Word Books.

Houghton-Jan, S. (2010). Internet filtering. *Library Technology Reports* (No. 8, pp. 25-33). ALA TechSource. DOI: http://dx.doi.org/10.5860/ltr.46n8.

Johnson, J. R. (2002). A Christian approach to intellectual freedom in libraries. In G. A. Smith (Ed.), *The Christian Librarian* (pp. 139-164). Jefferson, NC: McFarland. (Original work published 1990.)

Klassen, David (2009). Jacques Maritain and natural rights: The priority of metaphysics over politics. In P. A. P. Aguiar and T. Auer (Eds.)., *The human person and a culture of freedom* (pp. 162-175). Washington, D.C.: American Maritain Association: Distributed by Catholic University of America Press.

Litfin, A. D. (2004). *Conceiving the Christian college.* Grand Rapids: William B. Eerdmans.

Livingstone, S., and Helsper, E. (2008). Parental mediation of children's Internet use. *Journal of Broadcasting and Electronic Media, 52*(4), Dec. 2008, pp. 581-599.

Magi, T., & Garnar, M. (Eds.). (2015). *Intellectual freedom manual* (9th ed.). Chicago: ALA Editions.

Marsden, G. M. (1998). *The outrageous idea of Christian scholarship.* New York: Oxford University Press.

Przybylski, A., & Nash, V. (2018). Internet filtering and adolescent exposure to online sexual material. *Cyberpsychology, Behavior, and Social Networking, 21*(7), 405-410. https://doi.org/10.1089/cyber.2017.0466.

Ringenberg, W. C. (2016). *The Christian college and the meaning of academic freedom: Truth-seeking in community.* New York: Palgrave MacMillan.

Simonetti, M., & Oden, T. (2002). *Matthew 14-28* (Ancient Christian commentary on Scripture. New Testament; 1b). Downers Grove, IL: Intervarsity Press.

Communities of Scholarship, Communities of Faith
The Academic Library as Place

NANCY FALCIANI-WHITE

Abstract

A Christian college or university comprises two concurrent and yet unique communities: the Christian community, which is concerned first with the spiritual formation of its members and the support of their pursuit of a close relationship with God, and the scholarly community of learning, teaching, research, and publication. These communities have different purposes and different needs, but they share some fundamental essentials: in order to thrive each needs to have both togetherness and solitude. In addition to acknowledging that these two communities are striving to exist within a single institution, it is necessary to recognize the importance of providing a place where each of these communities can meet both of these needs. While most Christian campuses provide places for communal worship and even private prayer, little thought is often given to the need to provide intentional place for all facets of academic practice. This paper will explore the dimensions of and similarities between Christian community and academic practice, and suggest that the academic library has a significant role to play as the *place* in which academic practice can be carried out to its fullest extent.

Christian Community

It is common within Western Christian circles to be confronted with the idea that we, as Christians, should live "in community." We are part of a "community of saints," a "cloud of witnesses," a "body of believers," and should participate in "intentional community." But what does it mean to live in community? What does this community look like? Dietrich Bonhoeffer defines community for Christians as visible fellowship with other believers (Bonhoeffer, 1993). Community is not optional for Christians. We are created in the image of the triune God, and thus are created as relational beings (Bilezikian, 1997; Gorman, 2002). As the Trinity is three distinct persons of Father, Son, and Holy Spirit and yet one God, so Christians should live as distinct individuals who are part of one body of Christ.

That there may be no division in the body, but that the members may have the same care for one another. If one member suffers, all suffer together; if one member is honored, all rejoice together. Now you are the body of Christ and individually members of it [1 Corinthians 12:25–27, ESV].

Because of salvation through Jesus Christ and membership in the body of Christ, all Christians are members of a community of believers, whether they wish to be or not, regardless of how they choose to engage with that community. Thus a Christian who sporadically attends church, reads her Bible, prays, and rarely engages with others about her faith is just as much a part of the community of believers as the Christian who is extremely devout, prays and reads her Bible daily, is engaged in her church, and serves her community for Christ. They are united under the shared purpose of glorifying God.

When the idea of "living in community" is discussed, however, the popular understanding is that this can only be fulfilled when Christians live, eat, serve, witness, and experience life with other Christians. This view stems from the belief that "the primary application of [the] biblical mandate for communal life can only take place in a context of closeness and togetherness" (Bilezikian, 1997, p. 54). This understanding of community has a strong biblical basis, in both the Old and New Testaments (for example, Psalm 133:1–3; Ecclesiastes 4:9–12; Matthew 18:20; Acts 2:44–47; Romans 12:5; 1 Corinthians 10:17, 12:27; Galatians 3:28).

Dietrich Bonhoeffer suggests that a day lived as part of a successful Christian community includes time spent with others (Bonhoeffer, 1993). He suggests that time spent with others should include common worship at the beginning and end of each day, including Scripture reading, song, and prayer. The fellowship of the table follows morning worship and occurs at other times during the day, and involves giving thanks to God for His gifts and provision. Bonhoeffer describes the fellowship of the table as festive, a celebration during which we enjoy our respite from work and remember that God nourishes and sustains us both physically and spiritually, and that He also rested after creation. He also sees it as a reminder of our obligation to others in our community, in that it is "our bread" that is being consumed, not "my bread," and as long as it is eaten together and not hoarded, no one goes without. Bonhoeffer also describes work as one of the significant responsibilities of the communal life, because work requires an outward focus on material, impersonal things that help the individual find objectivity and liberation from herself. Work is also significant because of the perfect relationship that exists between work and prayer. Bonhoeffer holds that when done properly, work and prayer are inseparable, and each is only fully understood when experienced with the other.

The campus of a Christian college or university works hard to promote community among its members. Students and faculty may come from a variety of ethnic, socioeconomic, cultural, and (often) denominational backgrounds, and campuses strive to create a sense of unity that centers around Jesus Christ as the first commonality of purpose, and academic work as the second.

Opportunities for engaging in and building community are numerous. Time spent in classrooms, laboratories, or music rehearsals encourages dialog, questioning, technique development, reading, listening, writing, and collaboration, all intended to create a learning community, a group of people with a common goal of learning certain material. Student government and student life organizations want to foster a sense of community outside of class, hosting activities intended to promote health and balanced living, connect like-minded individuals, raise awareness of social issues, and provide opportunities for off-campus ministries. Chapel services are an opportunity to worship in community;

and concerts, plays, lectures, panel discussions, and poetry readings invite participants to further engage in the life of the community, a community of learning, experiences, and appreciation.

This plethora of opportunities for community experiences is a blessing in many ways. But it can result in constant busyness, constant engagement, and constant socializing, with little chance for reflection upon those experiences. At its most extreme, this can lead to "physical, mental, and spiritual exhaustion" (Nouwen, 1978, p. 13). True community requires trust, time, and effort (Gorman, 2002). Trust means vulnerability and openness, both to God and to other members of the community, and the time and effort required mean that community will not occur when groups of people simply spend time together doing things. It requires investing in getting to know one another personally and spiritually, in ways that make many people today uncomfortable. Interestingly, trust, time, and effort are three things that are particularly challenging for college students. Trust is difficult because students are in a new environment with individuals they have only just met. Time and effort are difficult to manage because both are already being extensively expended in multiple directions. Thus the thing that could potentially have the greatest benefits for a Christian college is the thing that is the hardest to attain. "Much hope and healing can come through participation in true Christian community, but only if we relate to the community in a receptive and investing way" (Wilhoit, 2008, p. 184). In order to get the most out of the "togetherness" that so often and easily occurs within Christian communities, it is important to take the time to reflect upon the experiences and interactions regularly, so that they can contribute formatively to spiritual and personal growth. True community also requires solitude.

Solitude in Community

According to Davies (1996), when confronted with being alone, most people tend to enter into one of two states: that of loneliness or that of solitude. Loneliness occurs when an individual has less social interaction than he wants, and experiences an "inner emptiness" (Foster, 1988, p. 96). In contrast, solitude can be defined as "a journey inward that seeks to strengthen the individual's relationship with self and/or with God" (Davies, 1996, p. 3). Solitude is a choice that we make to explore ourselves as we are when we are not under the influence of others (Willard, 1988). It is the intentional pursuit of unity with God, which Richard Foster describes as a state of mind and heart, an "inner fulfillment" (Foster, 1988, p. 96). Bonheoffer, in addition to his recommendations for living together (above), which for many Christians are the recognized activities within a Christian community, also recommends that those engaged in community spend time alone in solitude and silence, specifically for the purposes of meditation, prayer, and intercession. He does not view time in solitude as an occasional need, one that should be indulged when a community member is struggling in a particular way. Rather, Bonhoeffer believes that both time together and time alone are essential components of community life, noting that "the day together will be unfruitful without the day alone, both for the fellowship and for the individual" (Bonhoeffer, 1993, p. 78). Bonhoeffer describes the silence of a Christian as a listening silence and a humble stillness, in which the Christian is waiting for God's Word.

This definition of silence as a time of waiting is supported in scripture, when Elijah is waiting for God on Mount Horeb:

And behold, the Lord passed by, and a great and strong wind tore the mountains and broke in pieces the rocks before the Lord, but the Lord was not in the wind. And after the wind an earthquake, but the Lord was not in the earthquake. And after the earthquake a fire, but the Lord was not in the fire. And after the fire the sound of a low whisper [1 Kings 19:11–12, ESV].

The need for solitude is likewise made clear in the actions of Jesus himself:

Immediately he made the disciples get into the boat and go before him to the other side, while he dismissed the crowds. And after he had dismissed the crowds, he went up on the mountain by himself to pray. When evening came, he was there alone [Matthew 14:22–23, ESV].

Henri Nouwen describes solitude as a "deep human need," and argues that without solitude, life spent together in Christian community is doomed to fail, as the pressures of community living can often cause members to leave, either temporarily or permanently (Nouwen, 1978, p. 14). He presents two misunderstandings that many have about solitude. The first is "Solitude over against community," in which solitude and community are set in opposition to one another, creating a false dichotomy between individual rights and needs and community rights and needs. According to this perception of solitude, any time taken for solitude is taken for oneself, and gives preference to the individual, a preference that is in competition with the goals and ideals of community life. Feelings of guilt, irritability, frustration, and nervousness which result from a legitimate need for solitude being repressed in submission to the needs of the community can quickly become destructive to the community as a whole.

The second misunderstanding that Nouwen identifies is "Solitude in service of community" (Nouwen, 1978). In this view, solitude is valued, but only for what it can do for the community as a whole. Solitude is seen as a place of recuperation and rejuvenation, often remedial, and thus it is often associated with weakness. It is often believed that strong members of the community, or those who are living their lives properly centered on Christ, have no need of solitude. Nouwen suggests that these infusions of solitude are insufficient to sustain long-term commitment to life in community.

Nouwen goes on to identify three perspectives that can lead to a healthy understanding of solitude: intimacy, clarity, and prayer. First, solitude allows members of a community to grow closer to one another and gain perspective that is not possible when constantly in one another's presence. Second, it allows members to discern between what should be shared and what should be kept to oneself, reminding us that we are valued and loved by God first, and that His eternal acceptance is of greater significance than that of the community of which we are a part. This allows us to have more realistic expectations of the community and its individual members. Finally, solitude also frees us from the demands of action and response that are a constant part of any community, and allows us to come before God in prayer as "useless" beings, recognizing Him as our only true source of strength and security (Nouwen, 1978).

Solitude is neither self-indulgence nor narcissism, but rather a way of opening the self to the presence of God in a way far beyond that which can be attempted when surrounded by noise and distraction (Barton, 2004; Merton, 2007). It can provide an opportunity to purge the soul of the desire for the things of this world that usually distract from God, so that "when this desire is quenched ... the soul ceases to feed upon its pleasure in all things and thus remains in darkness and without any object" (John of the Cross & Reinhardt, 1957, p. 11). St. John of the Cross identifies this state as the "dark night of the soul." This state allows the soul to reorient itself away from the world and toward the Divine, and achieve true transformation.

Spending time in solitude can allow one to experience freedom from worldly distractions, pressures, and views, as well as peacefulness, fulfillment, calmness, and a sense of being "in rhythm," or in touch with oneself (Davies, 1996, p. 6). It can allow an individual to deal with issues that they would rather avoid, and can lead to stronger self-identity and self-confidence. It can also benefit problem solving, because "solitude is the space people need to think deeply about things" (Davies, 1996, p. 7).

In addition to these benefits to the individual, time spent in solitude allows individual members of a community to be healthy contributors to that community, recognizing that a community whose members fail to thrive cannot itself be successful. Bilezikian suggests that "in order to be attuned to each other in oneness, humans must be individually attuned to God because he is himself oneness and the designer of human oneness" (Bilezikian, 1997, p. 27), focusing on the oneness of the body of Christ. Philosopher George Grant focuses more on the integrity of the individual as part of the larger whole, arguing that

> if the community is to be more than a beehive it must be made up of individuals who are in themselves something. A group is not by definition good.... For nothing plus nothing plus nothing (even a million times) is still nothing.... We must cultivate our aloneness so that when we come to a group, we come as somebody [Grant & Davis, 2002, p. 180].

Why is it so difficult for members of a Christian community to accept solitude as an essential component of life together? Bonhoeffer suggests that people participating in community do not spend time alone in part due to fear of being alone, and that these individuals are active in community for the express purpose of avoiding spending time alone (Bonhoeffer, 1993, p. 76). These individuals have possibly experienced loneliness when alone, rather than true solitude. Nouwen points to "the often all-pervasive mood of urgency and emergency" (Nouwen, 1978, p. 23). Personal preference is also a factor (for example, introverts and extroverts may prefer different levels of social engagement and time spent alone [Burger, 1995; Larson, 1990; Leary, Herbst, & McCrary, 2003]).

Reluctance to insist upon time for solitude may also be in response to rhetoric condemning Western individualism. Individualism is the tendency of someone to prioritize the self and goals of the self over the group and the goals of the group (Triandis, 1989). If the misunderstanding described by Nouwen (above) that sets community and solitude in opposition to one another is the common understanding of solitude within a Western Protestant Christian community, then the desire for solitude is associated with selfishness, a search for personal gain, and narcissism. Well-known verses condemn these things as sin (for example, Galatians 6:9–10; Philippians 2:3–4), and when this is coupled with reminders such as "the self-sufficiency and personal independence that characterizes [our Western] evaluation of success are totally foreign to the Godhead that exists in interdependent oneness of community" (Gorman, 2002, p. 27), it is possible that constant engagement in "togetherness" in the community is done as a defense against the sin of individualism. And yet "[h]ow does one attend to the heart's desperate longing for God in the midst of so much religious activity?" (Barton, 2004, p. 28).

For Christian community to be successful, both togetherness and solitude must exist in balance. But these components are necessary in other community settings as well. In an examination of Bonhoeffer's *Life Together* and how its principles of community living can be applied within the context of a Christian university, Dan Caldwell (1992) observed that he was

> struck with how much these observations about [Christian] community apply to the academic life, whether for students or faculty. Much, if not most learning goes on when a person is by him- or herself. But, the best learning cannot take place without interacting with others.

Recent research exploring academic practice supports this idea that the guidelines for a successful community can also apply to academia.

Academic Practice

In looking at academic communities and their needs, it is important first to fully understand what occurs in these communities. The phrase *academic practice* refers to all activities comprising the life of an academic (Falciani-White, 2016). The term *academic practice* describes the practice of academic work, often also called scholarship. This stems from Ernest Boyer's definition of *scholarship*, and Alasdair MacIntyre's definition of *practice*. Boyer (1990) includes four functions in his description of scholarship: discovery, integration, application, and teaching. *Discovery* is the work that contributes to human knowledge and the intellectual climate on a college or university campus, but that is also valued for the process and the passion involved. *Integration* involves making connections across disciplines, focusing on interpretation and providing new insights to research being conducted. *Application* is the work of applying what has been discovered and interpreted to the real world problems, and *teaching*, whereby the work of a scholar can be understood by others, and how future scholars are "educated and enticed."

MacIntyre (1984) defines *practice* as

> any coherent and complex form of socially established cooperative human activity through which goods internal to that form of activity are realized in the course of trying to achieve those standards of excellence which are appropriate to, and partially definitive of, that form of activity, with the result that human powers to achieve excellence, and human conceptions of the ends and goods involved, are systematically extended [p. 187].

Scholarship in any discipline fits this definition of a practice, as each discipline has an established and coherent identity, is socially cooperative, results in internal goods (defined as being good for its own sake rather than for the sake of profit), and has standards that must be achieved.

A recent study described the academic practice of faculty as fitting into two primary categories: inputs and outputs (Falciani-White, 2016). Inputs include any information that a scholar takes in, while outputs are what the scholar produces, either formally or informally. Solitary and social components permeate both the inputs and the outputs, of academic practice. MacIntyre (1984) envisions any practice as being inherently social, and thus academic research must have a social component. He suggests that joining a practice means that one "enter[s] into a relationship not only with its contemporary practitioners, but also with those who have preceded us in the practice, particularly those whose achievements extended the reach of the practice to its present point" (p. 194). That suggestion is consistent with dominant views of collaboration that have existed within various fields of academia for many years.

Katz and Martin (1997) suggest that the word "collaborators" needs to be defined broadly as (1) individuals working together for the entirety or a significant part of a research project, or those contributing frequently or in a major way; (2) individuals named in the research proposal; and (3) individuals providing leadership in one or more significant areas of the project, such as the design of the methodology or the data analysis. "Collaborators" might also refer to (4) those individuals responsible in some way for a key part of the project, such as the person who had the initial idea or proposed the hypothesis; or (5) an individual who initially proposed the project, even if that person did not contribute to the actual research project itself (pp. 7–8).

Research by de Solla Price and Beaver (1966), focusing on scientific research particularly, describes a phenomenon known as the "invisible college" comprising an "ingroup" that claims to stay in touch with everyone who is involved in research in a particular area, both nationally and internationally. A study by van Rijnsoever, Hessels, & Vandeberg (2008) identified four networks that a scholar might belong to that could result in collaborations: the faculty network, which includes relationships within the faculty member's own department; the university network, which includes connections within the scholar's university, but outside of his or her own department; the external network, which includes any contacts with scholars working at other universities; and the industrial network, which includes interactions with private companies (p. 1257).

Reasons for collaboration vary among disciplines and individuals, but can include gaining knowledge, access to methods, and access to equipment or resources. Collaborations can also develop out of existing relationships such as friendships, previous collaborations, and those between a student and a supervisor (Melin, 2000). Katz and Martin (1997) add to this list the improving ease and cost of travel and communication, and the increasing specialization that is found in many fields. The benefits of collaboration also vary, but those identified by Melin (2000) include increased knowledge, higher scientific quality of completed research, the generation of new ideas, and the development of connections for future projects.

Beyond direct collaborations on projects, however, the social nature of scholarly practice manifests itself in other ways. In a study focusing on the humanities, Bulger et al. (2011) suggest that scholars within that division "have for long situated themselves within larger intellectual communities," through participation in conferences, workshops and seminars for the purposes of sharing research with their peers and receiving feedback on their work prior to publication (p. 71).

Social interactions do not simply exist within the research being done by a scholar, but also include engaging with others through attending or presenting sessions at conferences, teaching or interacting with students, or even critically reading a text.

Despite this social context, academic work is acknowledged to be a very solitary affair, often painfully so (Wilson, 2006). This is because what social interactions occur are often narrowly within a department or discipline, and the nature of research and creation, and subsequent publication or performance, requires focus and concentration, often in isolation, though this can vary widely by discipline. This isolation is necessary because without time spent in solitude, thinking, analyzing, writing, waiting for ideas, testing theories, reflecting on the words and ideas of others, one will simply reiterate the work of others without adding one's own unique contribution or interpretation. As sociologist Andrew Abbott (2004) describes a scholar's solitude:

> There is no surer truth than that much of an intellectual's life must be spent alone.... For the academic intellectual much of solitude is filled with work neither whimsical nor critical, but simply laborious.... At the same time, much of an intellectual's work is filled with hard critical thinking, with judgment, with juggling of categories and arguments until there is something reasonable to say.... Sustained whimsy is also a solitary matter. One cannot navigate the floating haze of insight when there are others around.... Too many tiny disagreements and misunderstandings disturb the aimless concentration that is necessary for deep thinking [p. 121].

Academic practice, like Christian community, requires a balance of engaging in the community of the discipline and solitude. Both are essential for high quality scholarship and intellectual vitality.

The Coexistence of Academic Practice and Christian Community

At a Christian college or university, two distinct communities are striving to coexist: the Christian community and the community of academic practice. As Christians operate inherently within the community of the body of Christ, so scholars and others engaged in academic pursuits operate inherently within the community of their discipline. Both of these communities need their participants to engage in both solitude and togetherness in order for the individuals and the communities to thrive, and yet these communities have very different tendencies. The Western Protestant Christian community tends to emphasize, encourage, and reward togetherness, often to the neglect of solitude and reflection. The community of academic practice, likely due in part to the individual reward system of tenure and promotion prevalent in Western systems of education, lends itself most naturally to solitude, often to the neglect of togetherness.

There are two complexities in examining Christian academic communities. First, it is tempting to examine these communities and assume that the success of one cancels out the failing of the other: because scholarly communities succeed at solitude where Christian communities struggle with solitude, members of a Christian academic community likely spend appropriate amounts of time in solitude, and there is nothing about which to be concerned. Second, there is a particular challenge for Christians who are engaged in academic pursuits, as scholars or students, because academia, like Christian community, requires solitude to be successful, and Christians, who may feel pressure to be in constant community, may find it difficult to justify solitude spent in the pursuit of scholarship. Students in particular may struggle to spend appropriate amounts of time in solitude and reflection on their academic work because of the often competing expectations of purpose felt by students at a Christian institution. Is their purpose while at college to engage in academics taught from a Christian perspective? Is it to develop strong relationships with other students and their professors and intentionally engage in the physical community of which they are a part for a limited period of time? Should they engage in the many social justice causes of which they have recently become aware? Many would likely reply "yes" to all three questions.

The danger here, of course, is equating scholarly solitude with prayerful solitude. These two solitudes must be nurtured separately, with appropriate focus given to each so that both spiritual formation and scholarship can mature. If a single period of solitude is set aside with the expectation that both will develop, then one will be developed while the other languishes. Both require too much concentration to support such a bifurcation of purpose. If academic solitude and prayerful solitude are developed separately until maturity is reached, then a merging of the two can occur, in a way that facilitates the potential of Christian scholarship. It is assumed here that Christian scholarship and the Christian intellectual life are valued by a Christian college or university, and thus space will not be devoted here to defining, defending, or justifying them. This has already been extensively and expertly addressed by many (for example, Henry & Agee, 2003; Noll, 2011; Williams, 2002).

Ultimately, as Mark Noll (2011) suggests,

> for scholarship that is Christian the essential ingredients are the same as for family life, politics, community service, economic activity, medical care, or any other activity that would be Christian. Those ingredients are prayer that returns to the source of forgiveness and hope, service that goes into the world in Christ's name, Bible reading or preaching or catechesis that rehearses the story of salvation, sacraments that instantiate the presence of Christ, fellowship that draws believers to each other and to their Lord, singing that inspires love of God and neighbor, sympathy that turns hearts toward the suffering, and meditation that draws the mind to God [p. 148].

For either scholarship or spiritual formation to be fully developed, the heart and the mind must be aligned. It may be helpful to think of solitude as we think of prayer as it is defined by the Russian Orthodox monk Theophan the Recluse—"as standing in the presence of God with our mind in our heart" (Theophan the Recluse, as cited in Nouwen, 1978, p. 21).

Academic practice can provide a lens through which solitude in Christian community can be better contextualized. Likewise, Christian community can provide insight into how "togetherness" in academic practice can be better understood.

Time spent in solitude as an academic is essential for reflecting on and processing inputs. Without reflection and without time spent apart with limited stimulation or engagement, there is no opportunity to take ownership over the ideas that have been encountered. This limits creative thinking and problem solving, and increases the chance of regurgitation, or even plagiarism. A scholar needs to "make up her own mind" about a topic or an idea, weighing it against her knowledge and experience, so that when she responds, her contribution is relevant, thoughtful, and original.

These same principles apply in a Christian community. Significant numbers of inputs are taken in, taking the form of causes, needs, requests for assistance, contribution, or engagement, challenges to theological principles, alternatives to familiar interpretations of scripture. Time must be allowed for processing and reflecting on them. Time spent in prayer is essential, as is time spent reading and reflecting on scripture. Prayer and scripture, together with knowledge and experience, serve as additional inputs that can inform a Christian's response or course of action, so that it, like that of a scholar, is relevant, thoughtful, and original, and above all, steeped in an understanding of God's will.

That response or course of action is the reengagement in community that can flow naturally from time spent in solitude. Nouwen suggests that there is a more specific relationship between solitude and togetherness than simply that they are both necessary for successful community (Nouwen, 1995). In fact he suggests that the proper order for these is solitude first, time spent alone, prayerfully seeking the will of God. This then naturally leads to togetherness, community with people that share a calling. This is then followed by ministry, which Nouwen describes as not limited to a specific and intentional act of ministry, such as pastoring a church or serving lunch at a soup kitchen, though those are certainly ministries. Once again, he sees this final piece of a Christian's life as naturally following. If you have spent time in solitude developing that closeness with God, and if you are successfully living together in community and sharing struggles and victories, ministry is something that simply happens. You cannot help but impact those around you.

How does this relate to academic practice? Scholars who spend time in solitude thinking, reflecting, and writing, have an outlet for the results of this time investment. They teach, present, publish, and dialog with others about their ideas. College students are being mentored into academic practice, with their undergraduate and graduate school experiences potentially preparing them for full entry into that community. However, students typically lack a sufficient outlet for their research efforts. The very limited opportunities that they do have (for example, a short presentation to their class about their project), do not allow them to fully develop their thinking, and engage in the academic community in a meaningful way that can test and refine their ideas. It is in this refinement that true learning is able to occur.

College students frequently struggle to see their research projects within the context of the larger scholarly conversation that is taking place. Students select a topic, ask a research question, collect sources, and write what they have found from those sources. They do not see how their project fits in to their major or discipline, and frequently see it as having no real purpose. The idea of engaging "the literature" is largely a foreign one—they are primarily focused on finding resources that talk about their topic narrowly. They work alone, or occasionally with classmates, to develop a document or presentation that never goes beyond that class, is never read by anyone other than that professor. No wonder students lack motivation to research and write well: their only incentive is a grade. There is a natural desire, once the investment in solitude has taken place, to move into community. It is only when that individual effort is placed within the context of the greater body of knowledge that it begins to have meaning. The individual effort is important, as solitude is important. And yet what is the purpose behind our solitude? It is to be physically, spiritually, and psychologically healthy, so that we can reach the fullness of what we were created in God to be. Then when we do participate in community, we are able to do so "as somebody" (Grant & Davis, 2002, p. 180). Those individual academic efforts enable full participation in a community of scholars, because it has allowed thoughtful reflection. If only the faculty members of an academic community are able to fully participate in academic practice, the college campus is not a true scholarly community for students, and they will not reach their fullest potential in that environment.

In order for students to thrive academically and spiritually, opportunities for togetherness and solitude in academic practice and Christian community must be made available to them. More important than just the availability and opportunity for these components, however, is that there must be *places* for academic practice and for Christian solitude on the college campus. There needs to be a place where the focus, atmosphere, and resources are centered on the support and facilitation of the entirety of academic practice for the academic community. There needs to be a place where an individual can be alone to pray, meditate, and listen for God.

The Importance of Place

Place is important to us as people, a fact born out in the many contexts in which it is discussed. Discussions of place occur in anthropology, architecture, higher education, library science, literature, psychology, sociology, theology, and others. In his work on land as a symbol for the people of ancient Israel, Brueggemann defines "place" as

> space which has historical meanings, where some things have happened which are now remembered and which provide continuity and identity across generations. Place is space in which important words have been spoken which have established identity, defined vocation, and envisioned destiny.... It is a declaration that our humanness cannot be found in escape, detachment, absence of commitment, and undefined freedom [Brueggemann, 1977, p. 5].

Bartholomew describes place as central to our humanness, ubiquitous, socially and culturally defined, and historical (Bartholomew, 2011), also in ethnographic work among the Western Apache, Basso experiences place as socially constructed, strongly associated with stories and memories, and ultimately home to wisdom that is passed down through generations via remembering (Basso, 1996). Throughout scripture the idea of place plays a prominent role, including the use of memorials to remember individuals and successful battles (Bartholomew, 2011; Schmitt, 2009; 1 Samuel 7:12), stones set up as alters to define a place as holy, or sacred, often as the result of a direct encounter with God in the Old Testament (Ross, 1985; Genesis 28:10–22; Genesis 35:1–15) as well as the focus on the land of Israel and the division of that land (Joshua 13–22). Less obvious, but still present, are references to place in the New Testament, such as Jesus' reference to preparation of "a place" (John 14:1–4; Bartholomew, 2011).

Jeff Malpas (1999) suggests that place has an impact on human identify formation, agreeing with Edward Casey that "where we are—the place we occupy, however briefly—has everything to do with what and who we are (and finally, *that* we are)" (Casey, 2010, p. xiii).

Thus place is culturally significant, and plays an important role in preserving memories, representing history, and shaping identity. Several authors also suggest that considering place and place-making is particularly important today, when our Western culture has become less settled, less conscious of place, more conscious and bound by time, and often more at home in cyberspace than invested in place (Bartholomew, 2011; Burton-Christie, 2009; Casey, 2010; Schneekloth & Shibley, 1995). This is problematic because if place is not considered, people can begin to lose those pieces of memory, history, and identity that are intrinsically bound to location.

Thinking intentionally about place on a college or university campus is important, as the Association of College Unions International (2012) found during their summit on building community:

> In an increasingly diverse society, it is critical that college students have multiple opportunities to practice productive interaction and constructive disagreement, experience high-quality socialization, and learn to live productively in community with one another. Especially important to ensure are opportunities and places for students to experience different perspectives, life experiences, and world views, while developing in themselves a sense of self as part of a community, with concomitant responsibilities to others.
>
> All too often, however, such experiences are limited to pedagogical, cognitive, or curricular considerations, with less intentionality given to physical spaces that might serve as laboratories for practicing the behaviors and perspectives necessary for living in community [p. 7].

Interestingly, this quote also demonstrates the narrow definition of community as "togetherness" frequently subscribed to in higher education. As critical as it is to provide those opportunities for togetherness, it is equally critical to provide opportunities and places for solitude.

Having places on the college or university campus that are set aside for the important work of both academic and spiritual community is essential to that work being done to its fullest potential. On a Christian campus, some attempt has usually been made to provide prayer chapels and places for communal worship. But where can students gain experience with the entirety of academic practice? How can they contextualize their research within the conversations that are already taking place within their own and related disciplines? Some of this can and should take place in classrooms under the guidance of faculty who model academic practice in its fullness. Outside of class time, however, there is really only one place on campus where academic practice is fully embodied and where students can learn to contextualize their work: the library.

Library as Place

The library of a Christian college or university is a unique place. It is, first, the tangible representation of the intersection of heart and mind, where intellectual gifts are applied to the glory of God, for His purposes. It is, second, the epitome of interdisciplinarity, where disciplines, majors, and programs coexist and intermingle on equal terms. No discipline is dominant. It is, lastly, the exemplification of the dual roles of community and solitude. A cacophony of information and knowledge exists within an atmosphere of reverence and quiet study. There are spaces for group projects, conversations, poetry readings, and other activities engaged in "together," but also individual study carrels and rooms and an atmosphere of quiet that allows for reflection and study. It is one of the few places, particularly on a residential campus, where one can be alone. In fact, it is one of the few places where being alone is accepted, and even expected. It is one of the few places in which a friend might think twice about disturbing you.

Changes in available technologies, including the World Wide Web, Google, wireless Internet access, Google Books, Google Scholar, Internet Archive, Amazon.com, and many others, have forced libraries to begin thinking of themselves and their mission more broadly than they have historically. The historic focus of most libraries has been the collection, preservation, and access of print collections of materials, making those institutions about resources, the *things* that are located within the buildings. With the technological developments of the last twenty years, being a place in which an individual can get resources is no longer sufficient, for the simple reason that many resources are now accessible in other ways. It is important for libraries to acknowledge this shift and reconsider their purpose and mission.

The academic library is the one place on campus where all aspects of academic practice come together. A library that is fully engaged with the whole of academic practice does not focus solely on its resources, though resources are essential to academic practice in most disciplines. Such a library partners with faculty and students to support and provide opportunities for academic practice from beginning to end. Such a library provides or partners with other organizations or groups on campus to provide

- opportunities for experiences that allow scholars and students to discover, explore, and test ideas with colleagues, faculty and peers. These could include facilitated sharing or discussion times or more informal opportunities to discuss work over coffee.
- quiet areas, where scholars and students can withdrawal from company to

contemplate and reflect on ideas and their implications. These could be study rooms, or areas of the library specifically designated as "quiet zones."
- support and opportunities for the pursuit of ideas and creation of a final product in which those ideas are argued and presented, and opportunities to share those arguments and findings, and receive feedback that can further learning and conversation. This could include support and training in research and research-related software, hosting poster sessions or research awards, book discussions, seminars, and workshops.

Because of the role it plays in this endeavor, the library is a place of significance in an academic community.

If we return to the Brueggemann quote defining place (above), we can see how easily the academic library fits into this definition of place. In its collections of resources, the library brings together historical meaning and important words, and provides continuity, serving as the memory of a people, an institution, or a civilization, recording the discoveries, theories, and thoughts for future generations. However the library is also a place where "things" *continue* to happen, furthering the current generation's contributions to continuity and identity. Whether engaged in a conversation (in person or with a source), or sitting in quiet contemplation, the library serves as a reminder that we are not alone. We cannot, as human beings, escape or deny the intellectual community of which we are a part, and we cannot fully realize either our intellect or our spirituality unless we acknowledge that context and commit to it.

In a qualitative study exploring the library as place in the life of a scholar, Antell and Engel (2007) interviewed faculty of varying ages to ascertain their perceptions and use of their academic library. These faculty viewed the library as a place to do sustained, uninterrupted intellectual work, and, despite convenient electronic access, a place that is "conducive to scholarship"—the atmosphere contributes to their academic endeavor. One particularly interesting quote from their research provides insight into the significance that such a place can have for an individual:

> Comfortable chairs and couches, elegantly bound volumes, and encapsulating solitude are a necessary escape.... Nothing can compare to the sensation of walking into a building and being surrounded by the physical sensation of knowledge: seeing books, feeling each page as it turns, smelling the aging paper and ink, and so forth. For me, the physical space of a library creates an environment that has been specifically designed to give a physical and spiritual sensation of knowledge, past experiences, and hope for the future. Electronic resources, no matter how useful, cannot duplicate this experience [Antell & Engel, 2007, p. 176].

Thus the library is a *place* of significance, both in a college or university context and outside of it. The library is also an intellectual sacred space. One common definition of sacred is simply that it is something "set apart." Eliade suggests that sacred space is "qualitatively different" from other space (Eliade, 1959), while Theissen and McAlpine (2013) define it as "identifiable space that is demarcated from its surroundings and that holds religious significance and/or meaning particularly with respect to the divine to those who use it" (p. 133). Theissen and McAlpine found that visiting sacred space (a church, in their study) served to "center" their participants with meaning and direction, and made those participants feel closer to God. This "centering" orientation is also a significant characteristic of sacred space for Eliade (1959). If, as Hervieu-Leger (2000) suggests, religion is a "chain of memory," dependent upon the authority of a tradition that is "constituted, maintained, developed and controlled" (p. 82), then the library on a Christian campus, as a place in which that religious tradition is maintained, studied, continued, and recorded, takes on greater significance.

A library is a sacred space because of its role in bringing order from chaos, as it organizes and maintains the intellectual work of millennia: "The sacred reveals absolute reality and at the same time makes orientation possible; hence it *founds the world* in the sense that it fixes the limits and establishes the order of the world" (Eliade, 1959, p. 30). The library is also a sacred space because of how it is perceived, as the "heart" of a college or university, and as a place in which it is easier to participate in the higher calling of academia (Council on Library and Information Resources, 2005; Gyure, 2008). In a study that explored individuals' reactions to libraries, Jackson and Hahn (2011). found that many of their participants viewed and engaged with libraries as they would view or engage with a church: as sacred. They suggest that an academic library is sacred because, as a church allows attendees to feel closer to God, salvation, and other abstract ideas, an academic library allows users to feel closer to the academic mission of the college or university (Jackson & Hahn, 2011).

The academic library thus serves multiple purposes. It is a place for academic togetherness and a place for academic solitude. If the vision of Christian scholarship is attained, the library also becomes a place of religious togetherness and prayerful solitude. In a place of Christian higher education, these things should not be separated. For experienced scholars, the academic and the religious are inextricably intertwined. Among students, scholars-in-training if you will, the academic and the religious need to be clearly associated and modeled. Not just in applying a religious worldview to academic problems, but approaching scholarship prayerfully, as an act of worship.

Conclusion

In a world in which more and more resources are available online and both instruction and learning can take place on-the-go, 24/7, the physical library connotes the higher purposes of learning and higher education, and can positively contribute to those engaged in academic practice. In addition, the library is one of the few places on campus in which community members can engage in both togetherness and solitude, making it a vital place for the health of the community.

Christian colleges attempt to support a healthy Christian community that encourages the spiritual formation of its members, as well as a community of robust academic practice. In attempting to encourage both of these communities to thrive, it is essential to recognize that togetherness and solitude must exist in both contexts, as in both academic practice and Christian community, solitude is essential for full and informed participation in togetherness. If both solitude and togetherness are valued for both spiritual formation and academic practice, then both need to be actively encouraged and resourced. Place is an important part of this resourcing. The place set aside for activities communicates the memories and traditions of those who have been there before, and can have a positive impact on learning. Not encouraging and creating places for both solitude and togetherness is deleterious to an individual's spiritual life, the Christian community as a whole, and the scholarship being done at an academic institution, because "solitude and community belong together; each requires the other as do the center and circumference of a circle. Solitude without community leads us to loneliness and despair, but community without solitude hurls us into a "void of words and feelings" (Nouwen, 1978, p. 17).

REFERENCES

Abbott, A. (2004). Academic intellectuals. In *The Dialogical Turn* (pp. 115–137). Lanham, MD: Rowman & Littlefield.
Antell, K., & Engel, D. (2007). Stimulating space, serendipitous space: Library as place in the life of the scholar. In *The Library as Place: History, Community, and Culture*. Westport, CT: Libraries Unlimited.
Association of College Unions International (ACUI). (2012). *Physical Place on Campus: A Report on the Summit on Building Community*. Association of College Unions International.
Bartholomew, C. G. (2011). *Where mortals dwell: A Christian view of place for today*. Grand Rapids: Baker Academic.
Barton, R. R. (2004). *Invitation to solitude and silence: Experiencing God's transforming presence*. Downers Grove, IL: InterVarsity Press.
Basso, K. H. (1996). *Wisdom sits in places: Landscape and language among the Western Apache*. Albuquerque: University of New Mexico Press.
Bilezikian, G. G. (1997). *Community 101: Reclaiming the church as community of oneness*. Grand Rapids: Zondervan.
Bonhoeffer, D. (1993). *Life together*. San Francisco: HarperSanFrancisco.
Boyer, E. L. (1990). *Scholarship reconsidered: Priorities of the professoriate*. Princeton: Carnegie Foundation for the Advancement of Teaching.
Brueggemann, W. (1977). *The land: Place as gift, promise, and challenge in Biblical faith*. Philadelphia: Fortress Press.
Bulger, M. E., Meyer, E. T., Flor, G. D. la, Terras, M., Wyatt, S., Jirotka, M., & Madsen, C. M. (2011). Reinventing research? Information practices in the humanities. SSRN eLibrary. Retrieved from http://papers.ssrn.com/sol3/papers.cfm?abstract_id=1859267,
Burger, J. M. (1995). Individual differences in preference for solitude. *Journal of Research in Personality, 29*(1), 85–108. https://doi.org/10.1006/jrpe.1995.1005.
Burton-Christie, D. (2009). Place-making as contemplative practice. *Anglican Theological Review, 91*(3), 347–371.
Caldwell, D. (1992). Bonhoeffer's Life together and the Christian university. *Faculty Dialogue, 17*, 27–38.
Casey, E. (2010). *Getting back into place: Toward a renewed understanding of the place-world* (2d ed.). Bloomington: Indiana University Press.
Council on Library and Information Resources. (2005). *Library as place: Rethinking roles, rethinking space*. Washington, D.C.: CLIR.
Davies, M. G. (1996). Solitude and loneliness: An integrative model. *Journal of Psychology and Theology, 24*(1), 3–12.
de Solla Price, D. J., & Beaver, D. (1966). Collaboration in an invisible college. *American Psychologist, 21*(11), 1011–1018.
Eliade, M. (1959). *The sacred and the profane: the nature of religion*. (W. R. Trask, Trans.). New York: Harcourt, Brace.
Falciani-White, N. (2016). Understanding the "complexity of experience": Modeling faculty research practices. *The Journal of Academic Librarianship, 42*(2), 118–126. https://doi.org/10.1016/j.acalib.2016.01.003.
Foster, R. J. (1988). *Celebration of discipline: The path to spiritual growth*. San Francisco: Harper & Row.
Gorman, J. (2002). *Community that is Christian*. Grand Rapids: Baker Books.
Grant, G. P., & Davis, A. (2002). *Collected works of George Grant Vol. 2*. Toronto: University of Toronto Press.
Gyure, D. A. (2008). The heart of the university: A history of the library as an architectural symbol of American higher education. *Winterthur Portfolio, 42*(2/3), 107–132. https://doi.org/10.1086/592058.
Henry, D. V., & Agee, B. R. (2003). *Faithful learning and the Christian scholarly vocation*. Grand Rapids: William B. Eerdmans.
Hervieu-Léger, D. (2000). *Religion as a chain of memory*. New Brunswick: Rutgers University Press.
Jackson, H. L., & Hahn, T. B. (2011). Serving higher education's highest goals: Assessment of the academic library as place. *College & Research Libraries, 72*(5), 428–442.
John of the Cross, & Reinhardt, K. F. (1957). *The dark night of the soul*. New York: F. Ungar.
Katz, J. S., & Martin, B. R. (1997). What is research collaboration? *Research Policy, 26*(1), 1–18. https://doi.org/10.1016/S0048-7333(96)00917-1.
Larson, R. W. (1990). The solitary side of life: An examination of the time people spend alone from childhood to old age. *Developmental Review, 10*(2), 155–183. https://doi.org/10.1016/0273-2297(90)90008-R.
Leary, M. R., Herbst, K. C., & McCrary, F. (2003). Finding pleasure in solitary activities: desire for aloneness or disinterest in social contact? *Personality and Individual Differences, 35*(1), 59–68. https://doi.org/10.1016/S0191-8869(02)00141-1.
MacIntyre, A. C. (1984). *After virtue: A study in moral theory*. Notre Dame: University of Notre Dame Press.

Malpas, J. (1999). *Place and experience: A philosophical topography*. New York: Cambridge University Press.
Melin, G. (2000). Pragmatism and self-organization: Research collaboration on the individual level. *Research Policy, 29*(1), 31–40. https://doi.org/10.1016/S0048-7333(99)00031-1.
Merton, T. (2007). *New Seeds of Contemplation*. New York: New Directions.
Noll, M. A. (2011). *Jesus Christ and the life of the mind*. Grand Rapids: William B. Eerdmans.
Nouwen, H. J. M. (1978). Solitude and community. *Worship, 52*(1), 13–23.
Nouwen, H. J. M. (1995). Moving from solitude to community to ministry: Jesus established the true order for spiritual work. *Leadership, 16*(2), 81–87.
Ross, A. P. (1985). Studies in the life of Jacob, pt. 1: Jacob's vision: the founding of Bethel. *Bibliotheca Sacra, 142*(567), 224–237.
Schmitt, R. (2009). "And Jacob set up a pillar at her grave…": Material memorials and landmarks in the Old Testament. In *Land of Israel in Bible, history, and theology* (pp. 389–403). Leiden: Brill.
Schneekloth, L. H., & Shibley, R. G. (1995). *Placemaking: The art and practice of building communities*. New York: Wiley.
Thiessen, J., & M., Bill. (2013). Sacred Space: Function and Mission from a Sociological and Theological Perspective. *International Journal for the Study of the Christian Church, 13*(2), 133–146.
Triandis, H. C. (1989). The self and social behavior in differing cultural contexts. *Psychological Review, 96*(3), 506–520. https://doi.org/10.1037/0033-295X.96.3.506.
van Rijnsoever, F. J., Hessels, L. K., & Vandeberg, R. L. J. (2008). A resource-based view on the interactions of university researchers. *Research Policy, 37*(8), 1255–1266. https://doi.org/10.1016/j.respol.2008.04.020.
Willard, D. (1988). *The spirit of the disciplines: Understanding how God changes lives*. San Francisco: Harper & Row.
Wilhoit, James C. (2008). *Spiritual formation as if the church mattered: Growing in Christ through community*. Grand Rapids: Baker Academic.
Williams, C. (2002). *The life of the mind: A Christian perspective*. Grand Rapids: Baker Academic.
Wilson, S. (2006, March 24). The isolated academic. *Inside Higher Ed*. Retrieved February 2, 2018, from https://www.insidehighered.com/views/2006/03/24/isolated-academic.

Loving Your Co-Worker as Christ Expects
Personnel Practices Through the Eyes of Faith

Esther Gillie

Abstract

Christian librarians can approach their workplace relationships with the advantage of Christ-like compassion and love as they collaborate with, supervise, manage, socialize and mentor the staff and librarians in their institution with whom they work. From the simple act of praying for those with whom they interact daily, to the complex task of dealing in a Christ-like manner with the inevitable problem behaviors and dysfunctionalities encountered, faith teaches Christians to love their neighbors (and their co-workers) as they love themselves and as Christ has loved them. Allowing the grace of Christ to be mediated through daily actions and attitudes can be challenging and transformative, helping to define and model best practices for human resources (HR). This essay outlines how these approaches to working with others in a faith based way might play out in either faith based institutions or secular institutions.

Introduction

"Christian librarians' view of truth should be reflected in their *management activities*." So stated Gregory Smith (2002) in his chapter "A Philosophy of Christian Librarianship" (p. 79). In particular, Smith points to the need for using both scriptural insight and general revelation (that is, knowing God through natural means) in dealing with matters of organizational behavior. He recommends further research on the integration of faith and management. In response to his invitation, this essay will examine ways in which both scriptural insight and general revelation might encourage Christ-like practices in personnel management and supervision in libraries.

Background

Human resources are a vital part of all libraries. Most library budgets, whether for public or academic libraries, allocate about 50 percent of their budget to personnel costs

(Lewis, 2016, p. 57). Decisions concerning areas such as benefits and employment policies are generally handled on an institutional level. Librarians ought to seek to have a voice at the table where human resources (HR) policies are discussed, if at all possible, and also to raise awareness about HR issues that should be examined. That being said, this discussion will address mostly the day-to-day, down in the trenches interactions of direct interaction and personnel supervision.

Many librarians, at some point in their careers, will need to supervise other people, particularly as they advance in their career path. Learning to be a good supervisor is distinct from learning to be a competent librarian (Fitsimmons, 2014). Supervisors need to know how to manage complex interrelationships and create a positive, friendly work environment that is sustainable, and one in which people can be engaged, satisfied and productive.

While not generally stated on job descriptions, personnel management soft skills such as good communication, project management, team building expertise, and conflict resolution are highly valued and much in demand (Dishman, 2017). Arns and Price (2007) provide a thorough list of the kinds of supervisory skills and managerial competencies most valued in library supervisors. Even if supervision is not part of a librarian's responsibilities, knowing how to interact well with others is a major component of working in any library whether the organizational structure is hierarchical or team-based. As well, it sometimes happens that a librarian who is extremely competent at their professional duties is appointed to a supervisory role and is not gifted at supervising.

Librarians gain their supervisory expertise from a variety of sources, including life experience, graduate coursework, and continuing education, especially through professional organizations such as the Library Leadership & Management Association (LLAMA), a branch of the American Library Association (ALA). Because personnel management and workplace collegiality are vital to librarianship, there are many opportunities to engage in coursework about personnel management from a library perspective. The Kent State University School of Information offers a program in Library Management, for example. ALA sponsors the Library Leadership Institute, directed by Maureen Sullivan and Kathryn Deiss. The Harvard Graduate School of Education offers the Harvard Institutes for Higher Education (HIHE) Leadership Institute for Academic Librarians (LIAL). Siena College provides training in business acumen, including personnel management, for library directors through their Leadership Institute for Academic Library Managers. The Association of College and Research Libraries (ACRL) hosts the College Library Director Mentoring Program (CLDMP), now in its 25th year. Expertise specific to Christian library directors is offered by the Council for Christian Colleges & Universities' (CCCU) Snezek Library Leadership Institute.

Although some librarians who step into supervisory roles feel they lack formal training (Arns & Price, 2007), in addition to the opportunities already mentioned, there are a number of excellent publications dealing with human resource management, such as *The Fundamentals of Library Supervision* (McNeil, 2017), *Practical Tips for Developing Your Staff* (Pratchett & Young, 2016), and the forthcoming *Cultivating Engaged Staff: Better Management for Better Libraries* (Law, 2017). My own background in library personnel management has been a combination of trial-by-fire experiences in a variety of academic library settings, both Christian and secular, public and private, and large and small, as well as using resources and attending trainings.

The Integration of Personnel Management and Faith Principles

For the Christian librarian, guidance on interpersonal relationships should stem from a deep understanding of Christian faith principles as found in Scripture. These principles hold true regardless of the particular work environment, be it public or private, academic or government, secular or Christian. There are solid benefits that come from creating a work culture based on scriptural principles.

Debra Dean (2017) enumerates the benefits of a wholesome spirituality in the workplace environment. These benefits include improved employee health, reduction of stress, more job involvement, increased job satisfaction, higher levels of commitment, less frustration, and enhanced work performance (p. 4). Christian spirituality encourages values, attitudes and behaviors that contribute to a sense of hope, a trust in the vision of the institution, and a corporate culture of altruism where courage, empathy, compassion, forgiveness, honesty, humility, kindness, patience, trust, and loyalty are valued. Dean's (2017) research showed altruistic love to be the most important factor in developing a sense of wholeness, harmony, and well-being through care, concern, and appreciation for self and others (pp. 75–76).

Whether working for a Christian organization or not, integrating faith into the workplace is a desirable benefit. Such integration goes beyond merely praying for those with whom you work. The integration of faith begins with a basic difference in how Christians view others. Genesis 1:27 states that "God created humankind in his image, in the image of God he created them" (NRSV). If people are created in the image of God, then a faith integrated approach to personnel management begins by seeing the image of Christ in others, even those who seem un–Christ-like.

Gary Roberts (2014) points out that many organizations view employees as resources, one piece of the cost of production that must also be financially managed. Supervisors refer to their staffing levels as needing the fat trimmed or being too thin, a mindset that reduces people to mere production components. In the current desperation climate of financial pressure, downsizing, competition, changes in required skillsets driven by technology, and performance pressures, it is easy to adopt a survival-of-the-fittest mentality. For the Christian, as Roberts states, "employees are not just 'resources,' but human beings with emotions, families, and souls" (p. 93).

Jim Collins (2001), author of the seminal business book *Good to Great: Why Some Companies Make the Leap … and Others Don't*, purports that the vision and strategy for moving a company from being a good company to becoming a great company, demands getting the right people on the bus, as he puts it, getting the wrong people off the bus, and then getting the right people in the right seats (p. 13). The bottom line for Collins includes not just ensuring that the company remain financially productive (his basic definition of what makes a company great), but that the organization thrives and continues to be a vibrant and enjoyable place to work. However, he maintains that you can't repurpose a person wrong for a job into someone who will be great at it, especially if they do not believe there is a problem. Hiring mistakes are made, and must be corrected. Letting the wrong people hang around drives away good employees.

For Christians, there can be friction between our understanding of how to treat people with dignity and respect, and ensuring that the organization flourishes, especially in the financial realm. As good stewards of the resources with which we are entrusted, we want to be wise and to help the organization fulfill its stated mission and vision. Personnel management does involve investments of time and money. First Corinthians 4:2 tells us "moreover it is required in stewards that one be found faithful" (NKJV). Financial abundance may or may not be the most important goal personally, but library supervisors are still responsible to deliver superior performance, to make a distinctive impact and to achieve lasting endurance for their organizations.

Balancing excellent business acumen and faithful stewardship with Christian compassion and teachings can be challenging. It is often difficult to discern where our loyalty should lie between our commitment to the institution and the person to whom we report, and our commitment to the people we supervise. For Christians, this is the crux of personnel management, the balancing of consumeristic expectations with treating people in loving ways that encourage them to be all that they are designed to be, without enabling less than desirable work habits. Knowing when to be tolerant and turn the other cheek, and when to take a firm stand and curse the fig tree, so to speak, requires divine guidance.

Mark 9:33–35 relates Jesus' response to his disciples when they were arguing about who was the greatest or most important disciple. He said, "If anyone desires to be first, he shall be last of all and servant of all." Later, he reinforced the importance of serving when he chose to wash the disciples' feet at the Last Supper, as related in John 13. Servant leadership is an important concept to explore. Any servant leader will need to make moral and ethical decisions based on weighing deontological (principle-based ethics), teleological (greatest good) attributes, and virtue-based reasoning. How does one resolve conflicts between servanthood principles and utilitarian stewardship objectives?

Gary Roberts (2014) provides an excellent example of an organization that made an intentional choice to adhere to deontological principles, in this case, the commandment to observe the Sabbath, irrespective of the cost. Chick-fil-A founder Truett Cathy made the decision to close his stores on Sunday, which, as Roberts states,

> strongly conflicted with the prevailing retail and marketing wisdom. By choosing to honor the Sabbath, Mr. Cathy demonstrated both his faith in God and his care for the well-being of employees with a guaranteed day of rest. Chick-fil-A is now one of the most profitable fast-food franchises [p. 18].

Roberts (2014) continues:

> When we obey God's commandments in spite of the obstacles, we are demonstrating our obedience and faith in a powerful God who moves mountains, transforming lives and bringing order out of chaos. It is important to understand that following the correct path does not always lead to short-term or long-term success. Oftentimes, our obedience produces failure as the world defines it, but from the ashes rise God's perfect redemptive plan, resurrecting good from the trials and tears [p. 18].

This conflict between faith and common practice is often the reason why so many personnel issues, less than desirable behaviors, and toxic environments are allowed to go unaddressed for lengthy periods until they erupt in hurtful and damaging ways. Finding the godly approach between doing what we are asked to do by our employer while at the same time treating those we supervise with love and respect requires us to be in continual prayer and remain sensitive to the guidance of the Holy Spirit.

The library supervisor who is a Christian might consider viewing persons they supervise as a flock under their care, needing shepherding, nurture and love. Such a perspective provides the foundation necessary to develop a wholesome spirituality in the library, in accord with Dean's (2017) emphasis on altruistic love. Focusing on treating others according to Matthew 7:12, commonly referred to as the Golden Rule, allows the development of a sense of wholeness, harmony, and well-being through care, concern, and appreciation for others. At the same time, as in the parable of the talents listed in Matthew 25:14–30, we need to be accountable and trustworthy with what we are given.

Christians dealing with these challenges can maintain an awareness of human dignity and welfare. By God's grace, Christian librarians can approach their workplace relationships and personnel management tasks with the advantage of Christ-like compassion and love as they collaborate with, supervise, manage, socialize and mentor the staff and librarians with whom they work. Christians can draw from faith-based assumptions and use techniques consistent with their faith, even though the supervisee and the administration may be unaware of the application of Christian principles (Impellizzeri, 2012, pp. 55–56).

Key Faith Principles

In Matthew 22:35–40, Jesus, in responding to the Pharisees' question about what is most important to God, provides excellent guidelines for accomplishing the integration of our faith with our workplace relationships with others. Scripture states:

> One of them [Pharisees], an expert in the law, tested him [Jesus] with this question: "Teacher, which is the greatest commandment in the Law?" Jesus replied: "Love the Lord your God with all your heart and with all your soul and with all your mind. This is the first and greatest commandment, and the second is like it: 'Love your neighbor as yourself.' All the Law and the Prophets hang on these two commandments."

This Scripture provides a two-fold strategy to a Christian approach to personnel management. First, work towards having a right and deepening relationship with God. That enables a person to better interact with others, seeing them as Christ sees them. As Father Ron Rolheiser (2017) stated, "No one can love unless he or she has first been loved" (para. 6). When I applied for my current position, I was asked to write about how I integrate my faith with my profession. My opening paragraph reflects this sentiment:

> My Christian faith informs who I am, who I am becoming, what I do and how I do it. This involves both working at keeping my relationship with God in good stead, and continually learning to love others. If I am in right standing with God and listening to the guidance of the Holy Spirit, then hopefully what I do will help move the world in the direction of God's design, the strengthening of his kingdom [Gillie, 2016, para. 1].

Developing a Right Relationship with God

Developing a vibrant relationship with God, one that is transformative, is a lifelong endeavor. As Christian library supervisors and employees, it is imperative to keep connected to the source of our faith regardless of our setting. There are many excellent resources available to help develop healthy spiritual habits that feed your soul. Dallas Willard's (1991) *The Spirit of the Disciplines: Understanding How God Changes Lives*, Richard Foster's (1988) *Celebration of Discipline: The Path to Spiritual Growth*, and Adele Ahlberg Calhoun's (2005) *Spiritual Disciplines Handbook: Practices That Transform Us* are wonderful primers filled with practical suggestions. In addition to regular fellowship with other Christians through small group Bible studies and church attendance, devotional literature such as Phyllis Tickle's (2007) *Divine Hours* manuals and Barbara Cawthorne Crafton's various works such as *Living Lent: Meditations for These Forty Days* (1998) and *Meditations on the Psalms!* (2003) bring a daily diet of reflection on the Word of God. Every denomination offers materials such as these to encourage people to draw close to God and to experience God's love and transformative power in their personal lives.

Learning to Love Your Co-Worker as Christ Expects

Having a focus on your relationship with God spills over into your relationships with others. Psalm 23:5 indicates that when you have been at the table God prepares for you, you are not only filled, but anointed to reach out to others. Your cup will simply overflow with love. "You prepare a table before me in the presence of my enemies; you anoint my head with oil; my cup overflows" (NRSV).

When you have experienced the love of God, you find you are much more capable of loving others. It is less about striving hard to achieve the desired behaviors and more about experiencing the freedom to live a loving life. The apostle Paul lists some of the characteristics of how people act towards others when they are in right relationship with God:

> Love is patient, love is kind. It does not envy, it does not boast, it is not proud. It does not dishonor others, it is not self-seeking, it is not easily angered, it keeps no record of wrongs. Love does not delight in evil but rejoices with the truth. It always protects, always trusts, always hopes, always perseveres. Love never fails [1 Corinthians 13:4–8].
>
> But the fruit of the Spirit is love, joy, peace, forbearance, kindness, goodness, faithfulness, gentleness and self-control. Against such things there is no law. Those who belong to Christ Jesus have crucified the flesh with its passions and desires. Since we live by the Spirit, let us keep in step with the Spirit. Let us not become conceited, provoking and envying each other [Galatians 5: 22–26].

Another key passage in developing a Christian approach to personnel management is Ephesians 4. The opening verses (1–6) enumerate the importance of unity and peace, and list the attitudes that permit such an environment: lowliness, gentleness, longsuffering, love, all the work of the Holy Spirit.

Verses 11–16 remind us that we all have different gifts, and that we should not behave like children, tossed about by deceit or cunning, but that we learn to speak the truth in love in order to grow up in Christ. The particular importance of speaking the truth to each other in love is emphasized by the repetition of that skill (verse 15 and verse 25).

In verse 26, we are also instructed not to let bad feelings linger, but to settle them quickly. We are told not to let the sun go down when we are angry about something, but to take care of it.

Verse 29 instructs us that our words must be good for edification and impart grace to the hearers.

Following these principles, one can envision developing ways to enable people to use their particular skills and gifts to the best advantage so that there is unity and purpose, and everyone is focused on the vision and mission of the library and the institution, developing and maturing in relationship with each other as we fulfill the vision of our leaders.

Addressing Personnel Challenges in a Faith-Based Way

It is apparent from the Scriptures how we ought to behave towards others. It is more challenging to live according to those guidelines. While Christian attributes are desirable, they can be challenging to apply in situations involving people. Good employee attributes include the ability to perform the job with excellence, but also to endure trials patiently, to learn from mistakes, to be teachable, to obey policies, to accept responsibility, to solve problems, to exercise initiative, to help co-workers even when inconvenient or contrary to personal interests (Roberts, 2014). Unfortunately, people rarely fulfill such lofty expectations, even Christians. People sometimes think that working in a Christian organization where everyone is a Christian means that everyone gets along well. Unfortunately, just because someone is a Christian does not necessarily mean that they will be mature in their faith, have a close relationship with God, or behave in ways consistent with Christian standards.

Mother Teresa (n.d.) said of people, "Each one of them is Jesus in disguise." But sometimes it is challenging to see Christ in those we supervise. God may seem indiscernible, unrecognizable. To see the immanence of God through such a distorted presentation requires divine intervention. People are complex. Each one brings a unique set of backgrounds, characteristics, and experiences.

Library supervisors who truly love the people they work with will want to see them prosper and succeed. They have a responsibility to know and understand their employees, to mentor them in positive ways, to provide the kind of exposure that will help them mature spiritually and emotionally as well as in their areas of expertise, and to encourage them to let go of destructive behavior and embrace healthy habits. Christian librarians have at their disposal numerous resources about developing and improving skills to become servant leaders. There are many excellent resources encouraging the adoption of servant leadership, not the least of which are Robert Greenleaf's many works such as *Servant Leadership*, *On Becoming a Servant Leader*, and *The Servant-Leader Within*. Excellence in servant leadership requires both solid character and competency.

Gary Roberts' book *Servant Leader Human Resource Management: A Moral and Spiritual Perspective* provides a detailed view of the impacting factors and the considerations of working with people. Roberts (2014) emphasizes the importance of a balanced Christian-oriented approach that incorporates both grace *and* accountability, both forgiveness *and* discipline, both autonomy *and* clear boundaries (p. 9). So often the Christian perspective emphasizes grace, forgiveness and autonomy, but the Bible is just as clear about accountability, discipline and boundaries. Finding the right balance between these seemingly conflicting perspectives is important. The challenge for library supervisors is to learn how, as a Christian, to unfold accountability, discipline and boundaries with grace and genuine caring.

There are many good resources about positive mentoring skills. ALA resources cover a broad spectrum of mentoring scenarios and goals, from helping academic librarians achieve promotion to helping librarians gain proficiencies with cataloging. These are important pieces of helping librarians grow in their professional development. Equally as important, though less popular, is helping people work well together.

Lisa Hussey (2013) states that conflict is part of life, and that it is common for people not to want to deal with it out of fear (p. 229). Kerry Patterson (2002) describes conversations necessary to deal with uncomfortable personnel issues as crucial, in that the stakes are high, opinions will vary, and emotions run high (pp. 2–3). She states that "unfortunately, it's human nature to back away from discussions we fear will hurt us or make things worse. We're masters at avoiding these tough conversations" (p. 2). This is especially true for introverts, many of whom work in libraries. Christians are well posed to learn to address these issues well, and have at our disposal good, biblical instruction and models.

Libraries are not exempt from conflict. Every library has experienced the difficulties that arise from interpersonal problems. Every position I have held as both supervisee and supervisor has required learning how to address disagreements, dysfunctional workers, and prickly people. In many discussions with other librarians and library directors, inevitably when the topic comes up, everyone has a story to share or a problem to present. Despite the widespread commonality of personnel issues, there is a certain reticence to talk about them. Some reticence is due to privacy concerns and rightly so. Sometimes reticence is due to a Christian concern not to gossip or create additional strife by talking about people behind their backs. While, of course, it would be imprudent to connect a situation with a particular person, there is room to discuss common challenging behaviors without betraying confidences. Proverbs 3:11–12 tells us that the Lord corrects those that he loves, just as a father corrects a son in whom he takes delight. Supervisors can share strategies in setting a positive environment of providing non-threatening feedback focused on lovingly helping to encourage growth, learning and emotional maturity. Learning how to give and to receive corrective feedback in a transforming way is an important skill to develop.

Scriptural Instruction

God surely understands how difficult it is to address problem behavior! Scripture provides help. Hebrews 4:16 instructs us to boldly go before the throne of grace to find mercy and grace to help in time of need. Before addressing performance issues in someone else, we are instructed in Matthew 7:1–5 to make sure we are in a right place, that we have removed the plank from our own eye before addressing the splinter in someone else's eye. Once we are in right relationship with God, then we can humbly approach our co-worker about problems. Supervisors must understand their own contributions or failings with regard to performance issues or relationship issues when working toward resolving conflicts. Scripture provides instruction for how to proceed here as well. Matthew 18:15–17 tells us that if we have something against a fellow employee, we are instructed to talk directly to that person and try to resolve the issue. It takes courage to speak to another employee about a problem, but it is the quickest and most effective way of taking care of problems.

Often, supervisors act as mediators in situations where someone wishes to effect a change in the behavior of a co-worker, but lacks the courage to directly confront the other person. Hussey (2013) points out that by the time personnel conflict reaches the manager, people are often no longer actually seeking solutions for the present incident, but that the issue involves a deeper and longer standing conflict (p. 234). Much time and energy could be saved if, when there is an issue, the offended or affected person would just go talk with the other person as soon as the offense occurs. Here again scriptural principles can prevent damage. Ephesians 4:26–27 instructs people to deal with issues that cause anger quickly, before the sun goes down, so that the devil is not given a foothold and no further problems can develop. When anger festers, not only does it cause physical harm to the person who is angry, but it also escalates the perception of the impact of the incident, which then becomes more difficult to address.

Human nature being what it is, Scripture allows that the first attempt to settle something can be ineffective, and provides a second method of resolving issues. This involves speaking to the person again with the support of others. Here is where the supervisor who desires to be a good steward of time and resources has an opportunity to play a role.

One of the most important negotiation skills is to listen deeply without immediate response. Listening is different from hearing. Hearing registers sound. Listening reflects on what is heard and strives to understand what is meant. Listening is registering more than just the words. It is hearing what is not said. Active listening includes an awareness of the tone of the content, of body language and other cues. A good listener stays in the moment, resisting judgmentalism or working on forming a response while the other person is still speaking. Many businesses recognize the importance of listening as a skill important to managing people. The Christian has an advantage in this area, because we can seek the help of the Holy Spirit in truly understanding. Psalm 111:10 tells us that the fear of the Lord is the beginning of wisdom, especially for situations beyond our human ability to comprehend. It is more loving to seek the Lord who helps us hear and understand what is not being said, and to wait on the Lord before forming a response or making any decisions.

In my seminary coursework, students participated in an exercise called Faith Sharing. We were assigned groups and we sat together on a regular basis and listened to each other share what was on our hearts. The rules were simple. We could not respond verbally either during the session or afterwards. We simply listened and prayed for the person silently. Many of the situations that were shared were complex and heartbreaking. When people described their circumstances, my mind would race ahead and come up with what I thought was a good solution. If they just did x or y, they could overcome the problem. When the situations were resolved, however, it was clear that God had created a path that simply was not visible to me as a solution, and that took into account impacts of which I was unaware. God's ways were so superior to anything I could have imagined. My faith in God and my respect and awe for the sovereignty and divine nurture grew and deepened based on the evidence of God's involvement in people's lives that I observed in those sessions. Jeremiah 33:3 encourages us that when we call on God, God will answer us and show us things we do not know.

Working Out Our Faith

Every library has "that person"—the one with whom everybody is frustrated because they are not doing their job. The one who is making their own workload increase. The person who once was a productive employee but either did not evolve with the changes in paradigm or technology, or feels they have arrived and can sit back on their laurels and coast. The one who is prickly and obstinate, who objects to everything, who inserts toxicity into the environment. Some libraries have more than their fair share of difficult people.

There are numerous reasons why poor employee performance may be allowed to go unaddressed by supervisors. Henry Cloud (2010) enumerates the following:

- being convinced that the dysfunction is normal and not really all that bad;
- covering for another person's dysfunction to ensure that the work happens in spite of the dysfunction;
- not wanting to fail, so continuing to try and make things work;
- having a false concept of loyalty to the person;
- believing that nothing can be done about the situation, so just accept it;
- being afraid of hurting the person and causing them suffering; and
- "fear of man" in terms of anger and damage to the relationship [pp.60–69].

Realizing that a situation is not going away on its own is the first step in addressing the situation. Once a supervisor realizes that they must take action, the place to begin is prayer. James 1:5 instructs us that if we are lacking in wisdom, we should ask God, who gives to all generously and ungrudgingly. Solomon asked God for wisdom and the whole earth sought his wisdom (1 Kings 10:24). Empowerment from the Holy Spirit can provide insight and intervention in difficult situations. Obvious ways of integrating faith with personnel interactions includes things like prayer before and after a meeting (either with people if they are open to prayer, or privately before and after meeting with them), using Scripture to inform the direction of the conversation, using faith principles such as confession and forgiveness when dealing with undesired behaviors. Another source of support is to seek advice discreetly from other Christians and supervisors who evidence wisdom in handling challenging situations.

Every library employs people in various states of productivity and fitness. It is much easier to address a problem immediately than to wait until it becomes entrenched. Often it is tempting to hope simply that the issue will resolve itself, but that is seldom, if ever, the case. Proverbs 25:11 says that a word fitly spoken is like apples of gold in settings of silver, beautiful and valuable. Being willing to immediately bring something to a person's attention may avoid months of agony later on. By addressing the situation truthfully, you are providing the person a chance to address the problem and improve. This can be accomplished in a caring and empathetic manner, with kindness but also truth. Because the goal is to encourage people to be all that they can be, to get along well, to take care of small impediments, then speaking the truth in love becomes part of mentoring others, not punitive.

Sometimes good mentoring requires having the person observe similar positions in other organizations to gain an understanding of what their job should entail. They should be able to recognize what doing the job well looks like. Sometimes it is a simple matter of putting the person in a role that plays to their strengths. Instruments such as the Myers-Briggs Type Indicator (MBTI) or the Clifton Strengthsfinder can help both the employee and the supervisor gain a better understanding of a person's skills. By understanding how a person functions, it is less likely that a person will be asked to do something they are neither skilled at doing, nor passionate about. It often happens that someone who is stellar at the work for which they were hired gets promoted to a position for which they are ill-suited. While it is difficult to transition someone from a higher position to a less prestigious position, often that solution brings relief to the person struggling to do a job for which they are not skilled as well as to the people impacted by the lack of accomplishment. Sometimes additional training is required or developing new habits that will enable them to function better. Sometimes good mentoring includes exposing the person to new experiences, good reading, webinars, and people who are highly functional.

Other times, for whatever reason, the person decides not to change or simply is incapable of making the desired change. In that case, the person will need to leave. At this juncture, you have reached a point where what you are doing to change the situation is not working and it is clear that there is no hope of resolution (Cloud, 2010, p. 86). After all avenues of addressing the situation have been exhausted, not executing a necessary ending causes more pain than it solves (Cloud, 2010, p. 83). Allowing the situation to continue wastes time, resources, and energy. Love by itself has never caused a resistant person to change (Cloud, 2010, p. 88). Cloud (2010) offers lists of traits which can help assess where a person is in the process of effective change (pp. 12–130, 134–136, 143).

The hope is that through various means, peace can be restored and people will be content to work together in unity. Sometimes that simply does not work out. If our focus is on the success of the institution to which we have been called, then we must sometimes make hard decisions about the people who are part of the team and how they are functioning. If however, we insist on taking responsibility for the lives of others, and supporting them regardless of their ability or desire to do the job, then the work of the library may sink to a level of mediocrity and dysfunction that will affect everyone on the team and ensure that the work will not move forward as it should.

We confuse relationship and compassion towards others with work requirements. One can still care about and nurture a relationship with someone even while severing work ties. We often feel that letting someone go who is not performing well is dooming them to a life of financial ruin and homelessness. We forget that we cannot save people. Only God can do that. We also forget that God does have a plan for each person's life, and that by enabling them to continue in a position that is, in all likelihood, not God's best for them, we are preventing them from something more suited to their calling and from finding a position where they will be respected for the gifts and skills that they bring to the table. Just because a person is not right for one setting does not mean that they are wrong for all settings.

This becomes more challenging when a person has been allowed to continue in a position and evidence poor work behavior for a long period of time, especially when the person is aging out of the workforce but is not quite ready to retire. We fear that they will not find another position, and that they will suffer because of our actions. We are torn between being good stewards and being compassionate Christians.

As Cloud (2010) stated, sometimes we need to make decisions that are not good for someone in the short term; people are ultimately responsible before God for their own lives (p. 66). Enabling others' bad behavior because we are compassionate Christians is actually destructive for the person being enabled and for the entire team. It prevents them from growing up. Cloud (2010) rightly points out that there is a vast difference between the Christian injunction to care for the marginalized, the disabled, and the infirm (which, I might add, is not the purpose of a library), and extending compassion to someone who resists growing up and being a responsible adult (p. 67).

As Christians, we do not have to put up with bad performance, but are instructed to speak the truth in love (Ephesians 4:15, 25) and to correct wrong behavior even as Jesus worked with his disciples to bring them to a place of greater maturity, fit for the work of the kingdom. While the goal is to help people change and become productive, sometimes the person either cannot or will not change. Keeping someone on who is not performing well is destructive not only to the person and to their supervisor, but also to those who do perform well, to morale, to initiative, to the library, to the organization, and to the culture. Often there is pain and bleeding when you cut out a cancer (Cloud, 2010, p. 163). When termination is necessary, the process must take into consideration the dignity of the person being impacted. To show proper respect in an honoring way, work with HR to find a gentle means of exiting. Proper advance notice, counseling, job search assistance, adequate transition time and privacy are important factors in easing a difficult termination.

Some resources that will be helpful in learning how to hold challenging conversations of this nature include Patterson's (2002) *Crucial Conversations*, Cloke and Goldsmith's (2011) *Resolving Conflicts at Work: Ten Strategies for Everyone on the Job* and Elgin's (1980) *The Gentle Art of Verbal Self-Defense*. Counselors from HR are equipped to coach these kinds of conversations and will assist in identifying what needs to be said and how to say it. They allow you to practice the conversation in advance, and are usually willing to sit in on such conversations as a neutral third party witness to what is said and meant. It is very important and scriptural for supervisors to include a witness in difficult conversations, and to record in writing afterwards a summary of what was said. I have found collaboration with HR essential in dealing with awkward and challenging situations, both in union and non-union establishments.

Additional Considerations

As mentioned earlier, supervising involves managing complex interrelationships. Other factors such as generational expectations may play a role in how people relate to each other. Library staff are increasingly a mix of Baby Boomers, Generation X, Millennials and Post Millennials. Each of these age groups grew up in significantly different environments and cultures that drive their sense of what is normal and what the standards are. Each of them is in a different season of life. Much has been written to help understand people from different generations. One example is Jolie Graybill's (2014) article "Millennials Among the Professional Workforce in Academic Libraries: Their Perspective on Leadership."

One consideration for the Boomer generation, those born between 1940 and 1965, is the looming reality of entering a new season of life. Our culture does not address or model transitioning to a season of late life. Boomers are often reticent to retire for any number of reasons. While it is true that the Bible does not talk about retiring, Ecclesiastes 3 tells us that there is a season for everything and every season has its purpose. Our culture is more familiar with the seasons of infancy, childhood, the teens, young adults, parenting, and middle age. At some point, no matter how we resist the idea, it is inevitable that people will begin to think about a season of aging.

James Hillman (1999) writes extensively on this transition, which he calls a major paradigm shift, from lasting and hanging on to leaving or letting go. His work addresses many of the fears involved in making that transition from working to retiring and living life to the full for that season. What remains challenging is identifying where that line lies, and it will differ for each person. Just as with every season, there are inevitable changes that happen and which must be acknowledged. Fritz Coleman (2014) delivers a humorous look at some of the physical changes.

Boomers who are still working are focused on what they generate, what they are contributing. Many of them are welcome employees, wonderfully gifted and sources of knowledge and expertise. Helping Boomers understand the changes they are experiencing will help them decide the right course of action for them. If they choose to continue working, it is important to recognize if the person is still aligned well with their current position. Many Boomers are working well into their seventies and eighties. Sometimes transitioning to a different position enables them to continue productive contributions at work when their skills are not current for a position which they have held long term. The focus is not on the age of the person, but on their ability to meet the demands of the job as it currently exists.

Most libraries have staff who have worked for the institution for more than a decade. These people are sometimes referred to as legacy staff. When they were hired, they were capable and dedicated and may even have helped establish the library. Over time the nature of the work evolved, moving to newer paradigms requiring different skill sets. Sometimes, legacy staff, whether they are part of the Baby Boom generation or not, are no longer a good fit for their position, even after retraining. Larry Sternberg (2014) outlines a variety of ways to address this situation: transition them to a job they are able to do, terminate them either with or without severance and help; carry them and have others compensate for their deficiencies; provide opportunity for them to meet expectations. Many organizations now encourage a phased retirement system to help retirees adjust gradually to the changes that come with retirement. *The Chronicle of Higher Education* has a publication entitled *Greasing the Retirement Wheel* that outlines a number of initiatives to assist people in making the transition.

One important piece in addressing the loss of long time employees is to ensure that there are measures in place to capture institutional history and knowledge. Helping someone get their processes and work flows out of their head and documented in significant ways will assist those who may need to address queries about past projects or take over some of the responsibilities of those exiting. Embedding this into the routines before someone is about to retire will ensure that it does not become a pre-retirement overwhelming task.

For Christians who respect and value the dignity of each person, the ultimate goal, as it should be for all employees, is to see a legacy staff person prosper and be blessed. We want to show them a purpose and a future. However, when a staff person is unable to do their job, it means others have to shoulder the workload. Resentment often builds. The entire department is affected and morale is low, even though they may acknowledge the past contributions and legacy of the person. Providing support during a time of transition in a caring way is important.

Naturally, age plays a role in these matters. If a person is nearing retirement age, they may be trying to just ride it out until they reach the magic age when they can collect their pensions. Depending on the severity of the inability to do the work, and the closeness of the retirement date, that may be one approach. However, in many cases, retirement is still several years off. Can the team sustain carrying them over a longer time period? Can the person find a position of lesser impact, a transitional position to retirement? Providing counseling to help someone understand and transition to retirement may be appropriate and helpful.

When a situation in which an employee has not been performing well begins to be addressed, there are often many roadblocks to overcome. Sometimes the annual performance evaluation, if there are any, has not indicated that there are concerns. Of course, the person has assumed that all is well. It takes time to speak the truth, documenting with examples. The employee can undergo a series of responses such as denial that there is a problem, blaming other people, lashing out in anger, etc. Each reaction must be met with love, truth, and hope, but a firm commitment to finding a resolution to the situation. These interactions must be covered in prayer and guided by the wisdom and inspiration of the Holy Spirit. Some will understand and do their best to change. When progress happens, even if the person is not able to embrace totally their work, their honest efforts go a long way in helping the team support where their ability falls short.

This is not to say that every prickly person is a candidate for discipline. Some people have an important role to play in representing alternate perspectives and standing up for something that has not been properly seen from all viewpoints, playing the devil's advocate. You want these voices on your team. Generally, they are not incompetent or dysfunctional in their daily duties. The key is to understand when their view has enough merit for consideration, and when the alternate voice, though necessary, will not bring added value to decisions.

There is an excellent metaphor in the description of spiritual gifts that also applies to employment situations. First Corinthians 12 describes the unity and diversity of the body of Christ. It states that the body (think team) is made up of many members, and that they are called to different work. We are not all created to accomplish the same work. If you are expecting an eye to do the work of a hand, you will continue to be disappointed. To punish the eye for not meeting goals meant for a hand would be unjust. While every work team needs a variety of members and different perspectives and voices represented at the table, it is important that each member be assigned the work their skills and gifts fit them for.

Behaviors such as emotional immaturity or passive-aggressive actions can be addressed in healthy and productive ways. There are a number of good resources for measuring and improving emotional intelligence or addressing particular types of undesirable behaviors. Dr. Les Carter (n.d.) of the American Association of Christian Counselors, for example, offers both descriptions of passive-aggressive behaviors and ways to address the undesired behavior. However, due to the increase in the numbers of people experiencing challenges such as learning disabilities, autism, anxiety disorders, depression, and mental disorders, it is important to know when a situation ought to be referred to a professional. One challenge in knowing when to refer a person for counseling is that not everyone has been diagnosed with a particular disorder, even though it is clear to others that they are exhibiting behavior common to people with a particular disorder such as autism or bipolar. When a person is unaware that they may need help, it can be difficult to find a constructive path to a good solution. In this age of unpredictability about employee response to work situations, it is important to err on the side of caution rather than risk being blindsided by an unexpected reaction.

Having an awareness of warning signs for behavior that extends beyond simple corrective encouragement will help initiate appropriate conversations with HR. Websites such as WebMD or the National Institute of Mental Health provide lists of signs and symptoms of bipolar disorder, for example. *Personnel Today* offers a list of traits common to autism and provides strategies for dealing with autism in the workplace. Generally, HR departments are equipped to deal with such situations, and many organizations offer counseling and support as a benefit to employees.

Conclusion

Christians are called to live according to the Word of God. Christian librarians can rely on their faith to provide a solid foundation from which to interact with those with whom they work. First Corinthians 16:14 says, "Let all that you do be done with love" (NRSV). If we are integrating our faith with our work, then we can replace an environment of fear with love and trust, which will enhance communication, learning and growth. Seeing in others the value Christ has placed on humanity, treating them according to Christian principles, praying for and with them, mentoring them, disciplining them, addressing undesirable behavior quickly and truthfully, being willing to have difficult but crucial conversations, learning how to unfold a necessary ending with grace, and trusting God to direct through wisdom and innovative solutions all speak to integrating faith and personnel management in librarianship.

References

ACRL College Library Director Mentoring Program. Retrieved from http://acrl.ala.org/dirmentoring/.

ALA Library Leadership Institute. Retrieved fromhttp://www.ala.org/tools/librariestransform/ala-leadership-institute American Library Association. http://www.ala.org/.

Arns, J. W., & Price, C. (2007). To market, to market: The supervisory skills and managerial competencies most valued by new library supervisors. *Library Administration & Management,* 21(1), 13–19.

Calhoun, A. A. (2005). *Spiritual disciplines handbook: Practices that transform us.* Downers Grove, IL: IVP Books.

Carter, L. The passive-aggressive always wins. *American Association of Christian Counselors.* Retrieved from http://www.aacc.net/the-passive-aggressive-always-wins/.

Clifton Strengthsfinder. http://www.strengthsfinder.com/home.aspx.

Cloke, K., & Goldsmith, J. (2011). *Resolving conflicts at work: Ten strategies for everyone on the job.* San Francisco: Jossey-Bass.

Cloud, H. (2010). *Necessary endings: The employees, businesses, and relationships that all of us have to give up in order to move forward.* New York: HarperBusiness.

Coleman, Fritz. (2014). *Senior conference on aging: Part two.* Retrieved from https://youtu.be/LR2qZ0A8vic.

Collins, J. C. (2001). *Good to great: Why some companies make the leap—and others don't.* New York: HarperBusiness.

Crafton, B. C. (1998). *Living lent: Meditations for these forty days.* Harrisburg, PA: Morehouse.

Crafton, B. C. (2003). *Meditations on the Psalms: For every day of the year.* Harrisburg, PA: Morehouse.

Dean, Debra. *Religion and spirituality in the workplace: A quantitative evaluation of job satisfaction and organizational commitment* (PhD dissertation). Retrieved from ProQuest Dissertations & Theses Global (10260968).

Dishman, L. (2017, July 26). Five skills you'll rarely see in job postings (but definitely need). *The Future of Work.* Retrieved from https://www.fastcompany.com/40444120/five-skills-youll-rarely-see-in-job-postings-but-definitely-need.

Elgin, S. H. (1980). *The gentle art of verbal self-defense.* New York: Dorset Press.

Fitsimmons, G. (2014). On being a good library supervisor. *The Bottom Line,* 27(1), 14–16. doi: 10.1108/BL-01–2014–0001.

Foster, R. (1988). *Celebration of discipline: The path to spiritual growth* (rev. ed.). San Francisco: Harper & Row.

Gillie, E. (2016). *Perspective of integration of Christian faith with my philosophy of librarianship.* Unpublished.

Graybill, J. O. (2014). Millennials among the professional workforce in academic libraries: Their perspective on leadership. *The Journal of Academic Librarianship,* 40(1), 10–15. doi: doi,org/10.1061/j.acalib.2013.09.006.

Greenleaf, R. K., Spears, L. C., Covey, S. R., & Senge, P.M. (2002). *Servant leadership: A journey into the nature of legitimate power and greatness.* New York: Paulist Press.

Greenleaf, R. K., Spears, L. C., & Frick, D.M. (1996). *On becoming a servant leader.* San Francisco: Jossey-Bass.

Greenleaf, R. K., Spears, L. C., Beazley, H., & Beggs, J. (2003). *The servant-leader within: A transformative path.* New York: Paulist Press.

Hillman, J. (1999). *The force of character and the lasting life.* New York: Random House.

How to recognize bipolar disorder. *WebMD.* Retrieved from http://www.webmd.com/bipolar-disorder/guide/bipolar-easy-to-recognize.

Hussey, L. (2013). Understanding and resolving conflict. In D. Velasquez, *Library management 101: A practical guide* (pp. 229–240). Chicago: ALA.
Impellizzeri, J. (2012). *A Phenomenological study of supervisee experiences of Christian integrative supervision* (PhD dissertation). Retrieved from ProQuest Dissertations & Theses Global (3536188).
Kent State School of Information. Library Management. Retrieved from https://www.kent.edu/iSchool/librarymanagement.
Law, M. Z. (2017). *Cultivating engaged staff: Better management for better libraries*. Westport, CT: Libraries Unlimited.
Lewis, D. (2016). *Reimagining the academic library*. New York: Roman & Littlefield.
Leadership Institute for Academic Librarians. Harvard Graduate School of Education. Retrieved from https://www.gse.harvard.edu/ppe/program/leadership-institute-academiclibrarians.
Library Leadership and Management Association (LLAMA). http://www.ala.org/llama/about.
McNeil, B. (2017). *Fundamentals of library supervision* (3d ed.). Chicago: ALA Editions.
Mother Teresa. (n.d.) "Each one of them is Jesus in disguise." Retrieved from https://www.brainyquote.com/quotes/quotes/m/mothertere163850.html.
Myers Briggs Foundation. Retrieved from http://www.myersbriggs.org/my-mbti-personalitytype/mbti-basics/home.htm?bhcp=1.
Patterson, K. (2002). *Crucial conversations: tools for talking when stakes are high*. New York: McGraw Professional.
Pratchett, T., & Young, G. (2016). *Practical tips for developing your staff*. London: Facet.
Roberts, G. (2014). *Servant leader human resource management: A moral and spiritual perspective*. New York: Palgrave MacMillan.
Rolheiser, R. (2015). Lacking the self-confidence for greatness. *OMI Newsletter*. Retrieved from http://ronrolheiser.com/lacking-the-self-confidence-for-greatness/#.WU1n7OsrJhF.
Siena College Leadership Institute for Academic Library Managers. Retrieved from https://www.siena.edu/centers-institutes/institute-for-leadership-development/leadership-institute-for-academic-library-managers/.
Smith, G. (2002). A philosophy of Christian librarianship. In *Christian librarianship: Essays on the integration of faith and profession*. Jefferson, NC: McFarland.
Snezek Library Leadership Institute. Retrieved from https://ppslli.wordpress.com/ https://www.cccu.org/cccu_event/2017-snezek-library-leadership-institute/.
Sternberg, L. (2014). *How should you deal with legacy employees?* Retrieved from http://talentplus.com/talent-plus-viewpoint-blog/35-leadership/450-how-should-you-deal-with-legacy-employees.
Tickle, P. (2007). *The divine hours*. Oxford: Oxford University Press.
Willard, D. (1991). *The spirit of the disciplines: Understanding how God changes lives*. San Francisco: Harper.

Discerning and Following Christ's Call to Leadership

NADINE P. ELLERO

Abstract

This essay tells the story of my personal experience of discerning and following Christ's call to leadership and a serendipitous discovery of Greenleaf's servant leadership model. This model encourages the personal and virtuous growth of others as well as the leader. My journey as a servant leader follows a winding path of deepening faith and reliance on Christ, witness to the fruit of just in time grace, and a wealth of support from daily prayer and the writings of others practicing servant leadership.

The Setting

I was close to finishing my dossier for my third year review toward tenure and serving as the serials acquisitions librarian in the unit of electronic resources and serials services at Auburn University Libraries, when my boss announced her retirement on April 7, 2014. This news sent waves of concern across several units and library management as she held oversight for essential technical services operations. There was little prior preparation for succession and to intensify this situation, there was little documentation of her work. She held a wealth of institutional knowledge and experience, the transfer of which would not be quick or easy. I had less than two months' time to secure as much of this information as I could.

Before long, I was invited to apply for a position as head of technical services, with a charge to lead and merge the two separate units of electronic resources and serials services and monographic services. These separate areas included responsibilities for monographic and serials acquisition, cataloging and metadata, physical processing, bindery, and all aspects of electronic resources management, including licensing. I was not seeking any position of rank or power, and being a professed Secular Franciscan, I was certainly not seeking higher monetary remuneration. More importantly, I did not desire the intensity and pain of simultaneously working toward tenure and taking on the responsibility of head of a newly forming department. My work responsibilities would more than double as I imagined sacrificing a great number of personal hours in order to fulfill the research and writing requirements for tenure, in addition to assuming various other responsibilities in this new department. Wrestling with the question of whether to apply or not, I turned to prayer and entered an intense journey of discernment.

This essay is my experience of discerning and following Christ's call to leadership, discovering Greenleaf's servant leadership model, growing deeper in faith, witnessing the fruit of just in time grace, and helping others to grow as persons and employees. Msgr. Chester, my former Spiritual Director from 1997 through 2011 and author of *Arise: A Christian Psychology of Love*, was an inspiration and passionate advocate of personal growth of self and others as followers of Christ. In Fr. Chet's (1981) words:

> Because Jesus is the tangible, audible, visible expression of God in human flesh, he is the way by which we on earth can encounter God. Every association with the life of Jesus brings the grace to enable us to overcome our human weaknesses and rise to the high level of life required for maturity. Every word and action of Jesus is a sacrament which has the power to put us in direct contact with God and thus bring divine grace to our struggle against the obstacles along the path of life [as cited in Michael and Norrisey, 1981, p. 51].

I owe a lot to him for his care and guidance in my formation during those years and now as I frequently consult his writings.

The Summons

The question before me was "Do I apply for this position, a middle management position, incorporating two units that needed a lot of help, not the least of which would involve tensions from above and below?" As a leader and manager, time is not your own and there are multiple demands for your attention. I was seeing this opportunity more as a heavy cross to bear as a cascade of questions flooded my mind. Was I growing slack in spirit? What or who am I truly following in life? Am I following the will of God, a fear of not having a job, or other people's desires? I confess to being a worrier and people pleaser, character traits that I have been trying to change for quite some time, yet knowing well only Christ can set us free from these bondages through his transforming power of love joined with our willingness to follow him and humbly let go of our ego centered desires and fears.

On the other hand, could this be a golden opportunity for deeper relationship, service, and witness to God? With that thought I launched into an intense process of prayer and soul searching. A book by Marko Ivan Rupnik (2006), entitled *Discernment: Acquiring the Heart of God*, was extremely helpful during this time of contemplation and discernment. I realized that I needed more than ever to deepen my relationship with Jesus and spend even more time in periodic prayer throughout the day to keep myself focused and connected to God. Rupnik (2006) writes, "My vocation is not an automatic fact but a process of maturing in relationships, beginning with the foundational relationship with God" (p. 21) and "Discernment thus leads us to acquire and maintain an attitude of docility, which is a dimension of authentic humility" (p. 87). Despite encouragement from library management to apply, I wrestled with actually applying for this position. My prayer, recorded in my prayer journal of April 17, 2014, was *"Dear Jesus: I don't have a clear sense of this being in your Will. I wait in silence for your voice of direction."* No sense of an answer was appearing and only silence prevailed. Earnestly writing in my journal on May 10, 2014, I petitioned, *"Dear Jesus, do I apply for head of technical services?"*

While praying and waiting in silence, I completed one of the exercises that Rupnik (2006) suggests in his book. For this exercise I imagined how taking this position would affect my relationship with Jesus, my personal growth as a Christian, and desire to make his presence known in the world. I created the following discernment table (Table 1) in my journal and continued waiting for some sign of blessing or confirmation from God.

Table 1. Discernment Table

Growing Closer to Jesus (Perceived Advantages)	Growing Away from Jesus (Perceived Disadvantages)
Model Servant Leadership*	Ego Inflation
Bring light of Christ to the examination of jobs, duties, and attitudes in the department	Workaholism
Bring a vision of unity, common purpose, truth, and healthy practices	Division and less family and church community time
Encourage relationship building and restoration of healthy attitudes/spirits	Isolation, less time in prayer, little cultivation of fruits of the Spirit

*Servant Leadership listed as in Jesus' example with foot washing, since I was not aware of Greenleaf's model at the time I made this discernment table.

Despite not sensing a call from God or receiving any other sign of confirmation, I chose to move forward and submitted my application and letter on May 12, 2014. Three days later I was invited to interview with the customary full day itinerary and a 20- to 25-minute presentation. This gave me essentially a week to prepare. Feeling overwhelmed as I was also working on a substantial addition, re-analysis, and re-write for a recently submitted paper, I asked to postpone the interview and was granted the extra time. Once again, I entered into a two month period of intense prayer and struggle with discernment, seeking and desiring concrete confirmation from God for the right direction to take.

Then, totally out of the blue, on the morning of July 24, 2014, as I was arising from sleep, I heard the call, *"Shepherd my people."* I immediately thought, "Does this mean that I am supposed to go through with this interview?" There was no question in my mind that I would heed and obey God's call and considering that I was not officially leading anyone at work or Church at the time, I concluded this must be the answer to my prayer—the substantive sign I was awaiting. It would be some time later that I realized the vast majority of the people I am leading are believers and faithful Christians, a privilege that I held and hold dearly. Following God's call, I interviewed on September 9, 2014, and was offered the position soon after, with an official start date of October 1, 2014. However due to preparations for the fiscal year rollover (September 30–October 1 fiscal year cycle) I effectively began acting as head of the new department upon my boss' retirement in late June 2014.

The Servant Leadership Model (Discovering Greenleaf)

True to what I imagined, the responsibilities and demands of this head position in conjunction with work for tenure intensified. The newly formed department consisted of three faculty librarians, eleven staff, and two student assistants. Our materials budget was close to seven million dollars with at least eighty percent expended on electronic resources. The first major goal, after my first solo fiscal year rollover, was to begin unifying the two separate units of electronic resources and serials services and monographic services and integrate work operations where feasible. After two months, my optimism began fading as waves of retirements rolled in. First, the acquisitions/accounting specialist announced her retirement, effective February 2015. No one else in the department could assume her acquisitions/payment voucher preparation so a staff person from library administration temporarily assumed this responsibility. Next to retire in March 2015 was a staff cataloger, followed by a faculty librarian, the coordinator of monographic acquisitions in June 2015. The staff cataloger position was not replaced and I personally assumed responsibility for the monographic acquisitions faculty librarian's duties. Compounding these retirements were other inter-departmental changes challenging our thinly covered operations in technical services. Several key persons were feeling the mounting stress and strain. On top of all this, I was keenly aware that I must become a good role model for functioning well under pressure and maintaining composure. Slowly, I was realizing this tension as fertile ground for my growth in temperance, a virtue I long sought.

At this time and for a variety of reasons, faculty and staff required much of my attention. I was without both a work mentor and a spiritual director, resources that I had in plentiful supply earlier in my life and career. There were a few colleagues and friends that I could call upon and I am thankful for those conversations, but they were too few and far between. I moved to Auburn in September 2011 after having spent twenty-one years in Charlottesville, Virginia, where I cultivated several close friends and built a trusted community. In Auburn at this time I was still feeling new and building both close friendships and a trusted community. The cross seemed almost unbearable as work at the library, tenure, and general life challenges were mounting. Where would I find tangible support to grow and thrive?

In early 2015 I providentially recalled a used book that I purchased at a Methodist church Christmas bazaar in December 2014. This particular book caught my attention because of the prominence of the word leadership on the cover. Thinking that this book might be useful in the coming months, I made the purchase and placed it on a bookshelf at home, never giving it another thought until one Saturday in early March 2015. Retrieving the book *Reflections on Leadership: How Robert K. Greenleaf's Theory of Servant-Leadership Influenced Today's Top Management Thinkers* (1995) from my bookshelf, I began reading and becoming immediately absorbed and fascinated with the chapter essays by prominent business writers. As I was reading, it felt as if the authors were speaking directly to me and this book helped to fulfill some of the support and validation that I was seeking. More importantly, this book revealed to me for the first time Greenleaf's vision and notion of "servant as leader" as well as the *servant leader/leadership* body of literature. In particular, the chapter by Dennis L. Tarr (1995), "The Strategic Toughness of Servant-Leadership," especially captivated my attention as it was there that Greenleaf's gold standard test of a servant leader: "Do those served grow as persons? Do they, while being served, become healthier, wiser, freer, more autonomous, more likely to become servants?" began to make sense to me (p. 80). Leading is hard work, especially when desiring to do what is right and true with respect to facilitating personal growth for my faculty, staff, and self while accomplishing the work of the department. I found consolation in Tarr's (1995) words: "The servant leader is a listener, is task-oriented, has a strategic sense, is eager to understand, to empathize and to collaborate, but does not escape becoming the target of many challenges and tests" (p. 81). One is frequently faced with holding sensitivity or compassion along with maintaining a strong constitution fostering healthy attitudes and good works, when working with both individuals and the collective (team or department) to achieve the organization's mission. It is true as Autry (2001) states, "Your ability to face these perplexing and dispiriting challenges will be tested and will often strain your deepest reserves of emotional, psychological, and spiritual stamina" (p. 100).

At this point I was only seven months into this new head position, working toward filling two vacant positions and completing work on a research paper for publication. Nearing exhaustion, I began questioning if I had made the right choice. Did I discern God's call correctly? How am I going to survive, let alone thrive? Then it happened again. On the morning of May 13, 2015, I awoke to the clear call, "*Have a shepherd's heart.*" What did this mean? Sometime after hearing this second call, I discovered a small yet powerful book, *The Way of the Shepherd: 7 Ancient Secrets to Managing Productive People* by Leman and Pentak (2004). This book further illuminated my understanding of the growth processes needed to support my faculty and staff, and how the hard work of true love, especially in the form of patience and correction are vital nutrients for fostering growth, temperance, and maturity. Transformation works from the inside with one's heart, attitude, and relationship with Jesus, which then pours into relationships with others. For me this is a moment to moment learning from and leaning on the Holy Spirit in trust and faith, for just in time grace. Essentially this work is about sincere caring and serving. Leman and Pentak (2004) write that

> the quality of your return is based on the quality of your investment. If you want your people to return loyalty and trust to you, you first have to invest your loyalty and trust in them. That's why it's called a return. If you give your people halfhearted leadership, you'll get a halfhearted following. But if you invest yourself in them, if you have a heart for them, your people will return your investment with a heartfelt following [p. 106].

It is my experience and belief that during times of exhaustion and discouragement, like fear, we are given the opportunities to exercise expectant hope for God's grace to appear—just in time. One such experience for me was an evening in March 2016 after Bible study, when I shared my new discovery of Greenleaf's servant leadership model with Mike, a retired U.S. Air Force officer. His eyes lit up and he said, "this is an excellent model but very hard to do." He loaned me a book that he used when learning and applying servant leadership principles, by Blanchard and Hodges (2003), *The Servant Leader: Transforming your Heart, Head, Hands, & Habits.* This book became an indispensable prayer companion, helping to sustain me through the trials of 2016. Needless to say, I now have my own copy. What I found most helpful was the way in which this book pointed out the differences between a serving versus a self-serving leader. Also helpful was Blanchard and Hodges' (2003) advice: "To successfully combat temptations to be self-serving we need daily to surrender our motives and actions to Christ as our guide and role model for how we should lead" (p. 23). In addition this small but powerful book includes just the right scripture passages to combat a host of fears and temptations along with helpful lists for reference, such as Richard Foster's ways to cut back on distractions.

Another illustration of God's just in time grace came when a staff person approached me with a desire to tackle a new area of responsibility in acquisitions. I saw this as the hand of God, lifting a huge burden from me and the department, in addition to giving her a renewed sense of purpose and vitality in her job. Receiving permission to fill two of three positions was a second instance of grace and provided the opportunity to engage in a reflective process to determine immanent and future personnel needs of the department. Persons with business oriented skills and experience were needed, such as accounting and negotiating licenses. Thus, the acquisitions/accounting specialist with skills and experience spanning a variety of acquisitions business processes was the first position filled in April 2015. Soon after, in June 2015, an electronic resources librarian was hired to concentrate on licensing, converting print to electronic journal subscriptions, and coordinating all aspects of electronic resources management work. This electronic resources librarian position replaced my former position of serials acquisitions librarian and was the first electronic resources librarian for this library. Much later, the faculty position for the coordinator of monographic services, vacant since July 2015, was filled by a new hybrid position, the metadata librarian and coordinator of monographic acquisitions, in June 2017.

These real experiences of God's just in time grace encourage me to continue ascending the mountain of becoming a servant leader and to investigate servant leadership in the library literature. While the volume of library literature on servant leadership is small, it is significant and a good source of information and support. I was surprised to find as early as 1980, Merikangas (1980) referencing Greenleaf and servant leadership in his article "Leadership by Nonadministrators in Academic Libraries" with a focus on persons who are naturally inclined to help, interested in the growth of persons, and who are conversant in interpersonal dynamics especially with conflict resolution. These leadership aspects, Merikangas (1980) suggests are instrumental in instituting or influencing effective change and developing group cohesion to achieve goals. With respect to leadership and technical services, Riggs (1988) highlights the differences between leadership and management with sections on "positive self-regard," "compassion," and "inspiration," all aspects reflecting servant leadership qualities. Furthermore, Riggs (1988) concludes that "the proof of leading is in the qualitative growth of those being led in technical services, as individuals and as a group" (p. 39).

Highlighting transformation and aspects of beingness, Doncevic (2003) summarizes Greenleaf's inspiration and conception of the *servant leader* and introduces Autry's (2001) "five ways of being" which are the desire to be "authentic, vulnerable, accepting, present, and useful" (p. 10) that is so instrumental in the day-to-day life of a true servant leader. A true servant leader according to Doncevic (2003) follows a natural calling and not one focused on self-gain. Writing on servant leadership for law library leaders, Anzalone (2007) addresses Spears' "ten essential characteristics which are listening, empathy, healing, awareness, persuasion, conceptualization, foresight, stewardship, commitment to the growth of people, and building community" (p. 797) and also emphasizes leadership as "way of being" (p. 805). Evoking Christian philosophy, Olson (2010) points out a plethora of servant leadership attitudes such as "wanting to serve" (p. 48), having a "sense of God's calling" (p. 49) and incorporating "sacrifice" (p. 49). Above all, Olson states that as a Christian librarian "it is about God"(p. 48).

More recently, Frey's (2017) *Reflections on Being a Servant Leader* addresses spirituality and connecting with people in a meaningful and compassionate way. Frey also found Spears' characteristics of servant leadership helpful as she practices servant leadership and has "aspiration towards the first two degrees of humility—refraining from that which may cut me off from God, and detachment from worldly security, and honors that may distract me from God" (p. 248). Additionally, Frey confronts ways in which the servant leadership model can be misunderstood and seen to lack depth in some areas, such as "conflict resolution" (p. 248). She illustrates servant leadership in action with two real-life scenarios; one involving her personal experience with a "difficult employee" and another showcasing a colleague's empathic patron encounter (p. 248). Autry (2001) makes an important observation in his chapter on conflict, by noting that "servant leaders must realize that they cannot make people like one another ... [but to] ... care about one another in the context of what they do together, because in context they are mutually interdependent whether they personally like one another or not" (p. 172).

Synthesis

While my experience and practice of the day-to-day work of servant leadership has not become easier and often comes at a high cost or, as Anzalone (2007) states, "not the comfort of the servant leader" (p. 799), the fruits of this labor are plentiful and seen in the people one serves, the department as a whole, and in opportunities for deep growth as a Christian in the workplace. Riggs (1988) notes, "The proof of leading is in the qualitative growth of those being led in technical services, as individuals and as a group" (p. 39). When several of my faculty and staff expressed gratitude in having me as their leader I realized I truly earned their trust. I saw evidence of my faculty and staff's personal growth by their honest self-reflection, appraisals, openness, and desire to do their best. Receiving a compliment from a colleague who said how impressed they were to see our department work together to create and execute a successful open house, replete with posters and activities, exemplified the quality of our teamwork. Teamwork is community building where persons are enabled to bloom with their particular and diverse talents and skills for the good of the organization's mission. I am humbled by being a part of this growth process, which, while painful has led me to pause and pray more. My relationship with the Lord is more intimate and dependent upon his word in order to receive the gifts of just in time grace. The virtues of patience, integrity, fortitude and wisdom, for which I have been aspiring are shaping my thinking and actions as I make efforts to exercise them in the work of leading technical services and incorporate them in my very being. Leadership involves many sacrifices for the good of persons and the organization. In particular, building teamwork and upholding truth comes with challenges and costs. Lencioni (2012) describes this well as he writes, "And they [leaders] must be the first to do the hardest things, like demonstrating vulnerability, provoking conflict, confronting people about their behavior, or calling their direct reports out when they're putting themselves ahead of the team" (p. 191). Likewise, Blanchard and Hodges (2003) emphasize the necessity of honesty and truth in the leader as they note that

> a servant leader in the image of Christ must be by nature a truth-teller and a realist. Honesty in communicating the price to be paid for serving and living out the values of servant leadership is a crucial test of the integrity of the leader [p. 59].

Following the call to servant leadership is not easy. Leading technical services is full of surprising challenges and triumphs and I know that as I stay close to Christ in continual prayer, He will be beside me in the work of leadership service and bringing out the good in others. Just as Olson (2010) states, "Without sacrifice, there is no ministry." Trying to find the time to write this essay has been a struggle, but I desire to point to Christ who is the source that provides support and guides me in the moment of need and sustains my spirit when being tempted to quit or to collapse into cynicism.

Like Solomon in the Old Testament, I desire wisdom so that I can better discern

God's will and become more Christ like in attitude and action both as a person and as I fulfill this call to leadership. Most especially, I seek the ability to model calmness under pressure and radiate joy. Rupnik's (2006) book, which I read several times, helped to deepen my understanding and need for temperance which, as he writes,

> brings us to surrender our entire beings to love and thus brings about our real integration, a progressive unity, in which the different dimensions of our persons and the various facts of our lives are no longer lived as separate pieces that cause us unbearable suffering and confusion [p. 114].

Msgr. Chester Michael always encouraged his directees to "give your best to God, first," and for me this means beginning my day with God in thanksgiving and supplication. When fed on the Word of God I am better able to set my foot in the right direction. Discernment is a never ending process and as Rupnik (2006) encourages, "Prayer is a conscious relationship with God" (p. 184), which sustains us as we cultivate a "state of continuous attitude of discernment" (p. 199).

God is ready to transform daily struggles, just in time, into the courage, conviction, or counsel needed in the moment whenever we make earnest petition. I can now say that this time of leadership has proven to be a golden opportunity and pearl of great price for encountering God more intimately as I engage in the work of leading the people performing the work of technical services in a medium sized academic library. For you, dear reader, it is my desire that you find hope in Christ and follow His call knowing that you will be supported and that you will grow in glorious ways.

References

Anzalone, F. M. (2007). Servant leadership: A new model for law library leaders. *Law library Journal*, 99(4), 793–812.
Autry, J. A. (2001). *The servant leader: How to build a creative team, develop great morale, and improve bottom-line performance.* New York: Three Rivers Press.
Blanchard, K., & Hodges, P. (2003) *The servant leader: Transforming your heart, head, hands & habits.* Nashville: J. Countryman.
Doncevic, J. (2003). Servant-leadership as a model for library administration. *Catholic Library World*, 73(3), 171–178.
Frey, S. M. (2017). Reflections on being a servant leader. *Catholic Library World*, 87(4), 243–253.
Leman, K., & Pentak, B. (2004). *The way of the shepherd: 7 ancient secrets to managing productive people.* Grand Rapids: Zondervan.
Lencioni, P. (2012). The advantage: Why organizational health trumps everything else in business. San Francisco: Jossey-Bass.
Merikangas, R. J. (1980). Leadership by non-administrators in academic libraries. *Journal of Library Administration*, 1(4), 21–39.
Michael, C. P., & Norrisey, M.C. (1981). *Arise: A Christian psychology of love.* Charlottesville: The Open Door.
Olson, N. J. (2010). Refreshing your philosophy of servant leadership as a Christian librarian. *The Christian Librarian*, 53(2), 48–55.
Riggs, Donald E. (1988). Leadership versus management in technical services. *Library Management and Technical Services*, 9(1), 27–39.
Rupnik, M. I. (2006). Discernment: Acquiring the heart of God. Boston: Pauline Books & Media.
Spears, L. C. (Ed.). (1995). Reflections on leadership: How Robert K. Greenleaf's theory of servant-leadership influenced today's top management thinkers. New York: Wiley.
Tarr, D.L. (1995). The strategic toughness of servant-leadership. In L. C. Spears (Ed.), *Reflections on leadership: How Robert K. Greenleaf's theory of servant-leadership influenced today's top management thinkers* (pp. 79–86). New York: Wiley.

Recommended Reading

The following books provided additional information, guidance, and support in my journey of servant leadership.

Greenleaf, R. K., Spears, L. C., Covey, S. R., & Senge, P.M. (2002). *Servant leadership: A journey into the nature of legitimate power and greatness.* New York: Paulist Press.

Greenleaf, R. K., Spears, L. C., & Frick, D.M. (1996). *On becoming a servant leader.* San Francisco: Jossey-Bass.

Greenleaf, R. K., Spears, L. C., Beazley, H., & Beggs, J. (2003). *The servant-leader within: A transformative path.* New York: Paulist Press.

Keller, W. P. (2007). *A shepherd looks at psalm 23.* Grand Rapids: Zondervan.

Maxwell, J.C., & Elmore, T. (Eds.). (2014). *The Maxwell leadership Bible.* Nashville: Thomas Nelson.

O'Brien, W. J. (2008) *Character at work: building prosperity through the practice of virtue.* New York: Paulist Press.

Spears, L.C. (Ed.). (1998). *The power of servant-leadership: Essays by Robert K. Greenleaf.* San Francisco: Berrett-Koehler.

Townsend, J. (2009). *Leadership beyond reason: How great leaders succeed by harnessing the power of their values, feelings, and intuition.* Nashville: Thomas Nelson.

Christian Faith and Its Impact on Library Interpersonal Relationships and Professionalism

Dana M. Caudle

Abstract

As Christians and librarians, we are called to live out our faith in the workplace. Not only must we do our jobs with excellence to the best of our ability, but we must do them in a way that brings glory to God. We need to be people of integrity. Excellence on the job is not enough if it is not coupled by love. We are commanded as Christians to take the love we receive from God and the lessons we are taught in how to live out that love and bring it into our interactions with the people we encounter, particularly the ones we work with on a daily basis. We need to act with humility, respect, and openness instead of the arrogance that can creep in when we are at the top of the hierarchy. Our Christian faith should guide us to love and support our colleagues on both a professional and personal level, desiring their success as much as we desire our own. It should lead us to be team players and, if necessary, peacemakers. We need to be supportive of our administrators as the people in authority even when we respectfully disagree with them. We need to be the ones who push for diversity and inclusion in both hiring and in changing our library cultures. We need to be the ones to practice forgiveness when relationships are damaged in the workplace. The Christian teachings we receive on love and living in community inform our actions in all of these interpersonal and professional areas and enhance our interpersonal relationships and ultimately our professionalism.

Introduction

This essay grew out of my thoughts over the years on the importance of relationships and the Christian's command to love God with our whole being and to love our neighbors as we love ourselves. I became a Christian my junior year in college and with much prayer, evaluating of skills and talents, and talking to those who knew me, felt a call to librarianship as my vocation and avocation. So from the very beginning in graduate school studying to get my Masters of Library and Information Science, the idea of integrating my faith into my professional life was something I strove to do. God has used my job as the largest factor in growing my faith. Living out my faith at work has had the largest positive impact on my career. The one thing I have learned as a Christian and a librarian over my 28-year career is that people matter. Relationships are at the heart of every successful human enterprise. Loving my colleagues is every bit as fulfilling and more lasting than the technical aspects of my job. None of my ideas are unique as other authors have been saying the same message over the years but I hope to extend on their work on what it really means to love our neighbor as ourselves in the workplace.

Where Faith Meets Work

As Christians and librarians, we seek to integrate our faith with every aspect of our lives including work (Smith, 2002b). We cannot separate our faith from our work because it is an integral part of who we are and to do so would be to live a dichotomous life (Irish, 2002; Smith, 2002b). Faith is more than attending Sunday morning worship services. What we learn on Sunday needs to be lived out the rest of the week in our workplaces where we spend the majority of our time (Davis & Tucker, 2002). To be the whole people we were created to be, we cannot forsake our faith when we walk in the doors of our libraries even if the American Library Association (ALA) Code of Ethics tells us to lay personal beliefs aside (American Library Association [ALA], 2008). We are to put God before professional standards (Irish, 2002; Smith, 2002b). In fact, the Bible makes it clear that "whatever you do, whether in word or deed, do it all in the name of the Lord Jesus, giving thanks to God the Father through him" (Colossians 3:17, NIV). My church teaches the concept of the life of the mind in service to God which is intellectual labor for him. Physical and intellectual labor were part of God's creative work and passed down to Adam before the fall of humanity (Davis & Tucker, 2002). Education and the acquisition of knowledge are, therefore, sacred pursuits (Smith, 2002b). Librarianship in particular, with its emphasis on providing knowledge to further the pursuit of the truth, whether in a secular or religious setting, is sacred work (Smith, 2002b; Davis and Tucker, 2002; Kaehr, 2008). Ephesians 2:10 states that "we are God's handiwork, created in Christ Jesus to do good works, which God prepared in advance for us to do." Seen in this light, as Christians, we can view our work as a vocation, a calling by God where we use our gifts and skills to provide for our physical needs and to work toward the development of God's kingdom under the inspiration of the Holy Spirit (Trott, 2010). Our work then becomes our service to God, not a means to an end (Trott, 2010).

Work to the Glory of God

Not only must we do our jobs with excellence to the best of our ability, but we must do them in a way that brings glory to God. We need to be people of integrity (Smith 2002b; Trott 2010). We should strive to "live a life worthy of the Lord and please him in every way, bearing fruit in every good work, growing in the knowledge of God" (Colossians 1:10, NIV). The first challenge for Christians as workers is to work responsibly and productively (Davis & Tucker, 2002), doing our jobs with honesty, diligence, and humility in an ethical manner. The Bible warns us not to be idle but to work for what we eat (2

Thessalonians 3:10–11). We are being paid to accomplish certain tasks in the workplace. Slacking off and other poor employee behaviors not only cheat our employers, but they bring no honor to God, who is our true employer. We are to be an example to those around us by doing what is good, showing integrity, seriousness and soundness of speech (Titus 2:7–9)

Love and Relationships Matter

Our Christian faith can lead us to be better employees, but being a good employee is only half the equation. Excellence in librarianship is not enough if it is not coupled by love because our work is relational in nature (Smith, 2002c). Relationships touch on every aspect of our work (Kaehr, 2008). Our God is a relational God. Jesus himself quoted the Jewish Shema: "Hear, O Israel: The Lord our God, the Lord is one" (Mark 12:29). However, as he commissioned his followers to make disciples, he instructed them to baptize them "in the name of the Father, and of the Son, and the Holy Spirit" (Matthew 28:19, NIV). So in the form of the Trinity, God encompasses relationship within himself. Moreover, he desires a relationship with humanity and this is the work that Jesus came to do:

> For God so loved the world that he gave his one and only Son, that whoever believes in him shall not perish but have eternal life. For God did not send his Son into the world to condemn the world, but to save the world through him [John 3:16–17, NIV].

God is love and love comes from God and that the way to know God and to live in God, is to live in love (1 John 4:7–31). Jesus considered love so important that his greatest commandments were to love the Lord our God with heart, soul, strength and mind; to love our neighbors as ourselves (Matthew 22:34–40; Mark 12:28–34; Luke 10:25–28); and to love our fellow Christians as he loved us (John 13:35; Smith, 2002a). Since the nature of God is relational and Christian relationships reflect his nature, loving relationships are central to the life of a Christian. This Christian lifestyle of taking human relationships seriously should set us apart (Davis & Tucker, 2002). How we treat people matters. We love because God first loved us and we are to love others in return (1 John 4: 11, 19). Jesus' commandments to love God, neighbor and other Christians are the core virtue at the heart of librarianship so our highest calling as librarians is to promote the love of God (Smith, 2002a). To love God with heart, soul, mind and strength is to love him with every aspect of our being, the physical, emotional, and rational, and to allow that love to flow to others (Kaehr, 2008). We should love our patrons and served them by offering information resources to help them become everything that God wants them to be in every aspect of their lives (Smith, 2002c). In addition to loving our patrons, we need to do the same for our colleagues as well, loving them, desiring the best for them, helping them grow as people and find their way to Jesus and achieve a more fulfilling life (Davis & Tucker 2002a; Kaehr, 2008; Smith, 2002a). We should "do nothing out of selfish ambition or vain conceit. Rather, in humility value others above yourselves, not looking to your own interests but each of you to the interests of the others" (Philippians 2:3–4, NIV).

> Individuals who look to the needs of others will emerge inevitably as spiritual resources for colleagues and library users who express fear and anxiety in times of personal need.... To function in this manner is the honor and obligation of Christian service [Davis & Tucker, 2002, p. 42].

In summary, we are commanded as Christians to take the love we receive from God and the lessons we are taught in how to live out that love and bring it into our interactions with the people we encounter, particularly the ones we work with on a daily basis.

Hope, Life and Courage

The prayer below is from the early to mid–1990s. It was one of those anonymous emails that was circling the globe like so many others at the time. What struck me about it was how it beautifully expressed what the Christian life should look like in the workplace, both performing the work itself and our relationships with the people we encounter.

Workplace Prayer
Lord Jesus, as I enter this workplace I bring your presence with me. I speak your peace, your grace, and your perfect order into the atmosphere of this office. I acknowledge your Lordship over all that will be spoken, thought, decided, and accomplished within these walls. Lord Jesus, I thank you for the gifts you have deposited in me. I do not take them lightly, but commit to using them responsibly and well. Give me a fresh supply of truth and beauty on which to draw as I do my job. Anoint my creativity, my ideas, my energy so that even my smallest task may bring you honor. Lord, when I'm confused, energize me. Lord, when I am burned out, infuse me with the light of your Holy Spirit. May the work I do and the way I do it, bring hope, life, and courage to all I come in contact with today. And, oh Lord, even in today's most stressful moments, may I rest in you. In the name of our Lord and Savior Jesus Christ, I pray. Amen [Workplace Prayer, n. d.].

The first part of the prayer acknowledges the Lordship of Christ over the workplace. It goes on to talk about using our gifts "responsibly and well" and asks the Lord to anoint us "so that even our smallest task will bring him honor." This is a good summary of my first two points about integrating our faith with our work and seeking to do our jobs to the best of our ability to bring honor to God. But the phrase that really stands out to me is "may the work I do and the way I do it bring hope, life, and courage to all I come in contact with today." It is this point I wish to focus on for the rest of this essay. Bringing hope, life and courage to the people we come in contact with is a good way of saying we love everyone we meet and act in ways that support and encourage them out of that love. We become vessels channeling God's love, mercy, and grace to those we encounter in the workplace. All of us are in need of love, mercy, and grace on a constant basis. Kelly (2016) states that everyone is carrying a heavy burden and a heavy load. We all have our problems and challenges. We may or may not know what challenges our colleagues are facing, but we can be certain they are facing something hard. But, if we are open, approachable, and trustworthy, we can engage in the ministry of thoughtful listening as our colleagues talk about their anxieties and burdens (Davis & Tucker, 2002). With empathy, kindness, compassion, absolute confidentiality, and authenticity, we invite confidences (Smith and Tucker, 2002). Some might say it is not appropriate to talk about personal issues at work, but as Christians, we value our colleagues as whole people with lives beyond the job and want to ease whatever burden is keeping them from being their best selves or doing their best work. When we listen to another, we allow God to bring truth to a troublesome situation by asking thoughtful questions and offering advice which may include referring them to a professional (Davis & Tucker, 2002). Authentic mutual burden-bearing is a powerful ministry (Davis & Tucker, 2002). Another way we bring hope, life and encouragement is to see interruptions as opportunities from God to minister to our colleagues. This runs counter to the usual advice on how to get things done. But to a Christian, human needs are of utmost importance in every situation and a keen awareness of the feelings and well-being of others is as important as efficiency in doing our jobs (Davis & Tucker, 2002). Through our interactions with our colleagues and others we encounter, we become part of a network of personal relationships that form a community (Davis & Tucker, 2002). The caring relationships we establish can even foster resilience which allows people to manage change and transform into more mature people (Wilson & Ferch, 2005).

Living Witnesses

Responsible life in community means loving our colleagues over time without trying to specifically evangelize them (Davis & Tucker, 2002). Our biggest witness to our colleagues is how we treat them and how we do our jobs. It is easy to wonder what kind of witness we are making when we fail to love our colleagues (Kaehr, 2008). Authenticity and being willing to show our faults and vulnerabilities makes us human to our colleagues. Instead of trying to put on this mask of the perfect employee, we need to be professional but also personal and real. The truth is that people can see through our masks quite easily whether we realize it or not. We know each other's work habits and triggers through long familiarity with each other, both the good and the bad (Kaehr, 2008). If we truly wish to make an impression on our colleagues that advances Christ's kingdom, we need to let them see how we deal with failure and mistakes and trials. That is a far more powerful witness to the working of God in our lives than pretending to be perfect.

Ways to Live in Love

Here are some ways of loving our neighbors as ourselves. "Love does no harm to a neighbor" (Romans 13:10). The Bible is clear that egotism, elitism, pride, jealousy, perfectionism, fear, and looking out for yourself first have no place in the life of a Christian. We are to rid ourselves of anger, rage, malice, slander, and filthy language, refrain from lying (Colossians 3:8–9), and put away hatred, discord, jealousy, fits of rage, selfish ambition, dissensions, factions and envy (Galatians 5:20–21). Unfortunately, our libraries are rife with such behaviors as is every endeavor involving humans. We have all got some of these or other negative qualities to some degree. My church calls our less than stellar qualities and actions "showing our humanity." Putting these aside to focus on our colleagues can be difficult indeed. To do so, first we must acknowledge and accept our own humanity and realize we need the help of the Holy Spirit to act in loving ways toward our colleagues. For "the fruit of the Spirit is love, joy, peace, patience, kindness, generosity, faithfulness, gentleness, and self-control" (Galatians 5:26–27, NIV). In this way, we can clothe ourselves with compassion, kindness, humility, gentleness and patience, forgiving each other when we have grievances, living in peace and surrounding it all with love (Colossians 3:12–15). We can be devoted to each other and honor others above ourselves (Romans 12:10). In any situation where we are unsure if an action is loving, we can check it against the characteristics of love in 1 Corinthians 13:4–7. We can ask ourselves: is it envious, boastful, proud, dishonoring of others, or self-seeking? Love is none of these things. Instead it is not easily angered, keeps no record of wrongs, does not delight in evil but rejoices in the truth, protects, trusts, hopes, and perseveres (1 Corinthians 13:4–7). We are to be quick to listen, slow to speak, and slow to anger (James 1:19). Love is a verb, not a feeling. Our actions do the most to demonstrate the love we need to have for our colleagues and our patrons. We are to love not with words or speech, but with actions and truth (1 John 3:18) and faith without deeds is dead (James 2:26). Practically speaking, we should not use sarcasm or take things personally (Kaehr, 2008) and serve cheerfully (Davis & Tucker, 2002) without worrying about our status (Terhune, 2006). Even in confrontations we are to be strong but loving and tactfully confront unethical or improper attitudes (Kaehr, 2008).

When interacting with any of our colleagues, it helpful to remember the Golden Rule: "Do to others what you would have them do to you" (Matthew 7:12, NIV). We all crave kindness and respect. We want to be forgiven when we have done something wrong or damaged the relationships we have with our colleagues. We want to be acknowledged for doing a good job. We want someone to listen to us empathetically when there are problems or when we think we have a good idea that will forward the mission of our workplace. Since this is how we all wish to be treated, that is how we should strive to treat our colleagues. I believe that this is the essence of how the Golden Rule should be applied in the workplace. Whether or not we are supervisors, we are leaders, and servant leaders at that. We need to oppose power games and lead by prayer and by example with humility and obedience (Delivuk, 2002).

Desiring the Success of Our Colleagues

Our Christian faith should guide us to love and support our colleagues on both a professional and personal level, desiring their success as much as we desire our own. We also need to get rid of selfish ambition and the desire for personal glory (Philippians 2:3). Looking out for number one runs counter to the command of Jesus to love God wholeheartedly and love our colleagues as much as we love ourselves. I have learned over the years to desire the success of my colleagues as much as I desire my own success. Yes, I have career goals, but so do my colleagues. When I am thinking about their success as well as my own, we all succeed together and everybody wins. One practical way to do this is mentoring which can include letting them know of career opportunities and passing along sources of information and research ideas (Davis & Tucker, 2002). Another is looking for opportunities to affirm them for a job well done and celebrating their successes (Davis & Tucker, 2002). When someone starts a job, we need to give them all the resources they need to succeed. Training offers many opportunities to support our colleagues. Our staff strive for excellence and we can give them training to do their jobs well or move them to jobs which are better fits (Kaehr, 2008). I have discovered that patience during training leads to more successful learning and successful, happy staff. It is a wonderful feeling to know that I helped someone succeed in their career. And the time I spend listening to my colleagues and supporting them in their careers often returns as good to me in several ways. One is genuine respect and another is having those same colleagues support me when I need it.

The Workplace as Community

Work is a communal enterprise. The workplace is a community with a particular purpose and the Christian faith has a lot to say about how to live in community with each other (1 Corinthians 12, Romans 12). Our interactions do much to create this community and our colleagues can become like family (Davis & Tucker, 2002). First Corinthians 12 and Romans 12 both speak of the community of believers as being a single body with many interdependent parts. Everyone has gifts and talents that are a gift from the Holy Spirit and we are to use our various gifts to uphold the community. This analogy of one body with many parts can be extended to our work communities (Trott, 2010). Our talents applied to a specialized aspect of our jobs are a spiritual gift (Trott, 2010). It is easy to love colleagues that we share similarities with but it can be quite challenging to love colleagues who are very different from us in personality or culture. But in Christ there is no Jew, or Gentile, male or female, slave or free (Galatians 3:28; Colossians 3:11). Just as our gifts and talents are useful to the community, so too our cultural and linguistic backgrounds are gifts that can build up the community as a whole (Delivuk, 2002). We need to be the ones who push for diversity and inclusion in both hiring and in changing our library cultures. Our workplaces should be safe spaces free from discrimination and bullying.

Respect Everyone

Our workplaces should be places of equality and respect (Trott, 2010). We must treat everyone with loving respect and concern from our administrators to the janitorial crew (Smith, 2002a; Davis and Tucker, 2002). The Bible admonishes us not to be proud or conceited, but to be willing to associate with people of low position (Romans 12:16). We need to act with humility and openness instead of the arrogance that can creep in when we are at the top of the hierarchy. Most of our egotism, elitism, and pride for librarians in academic environments revolves around the emphasis on education and credentials, particularly the Master of Library Science (MLS) degree. When tasks once done by librarians are being shifted to paraprofessional staff, it is difficult to clarify the respective roles and jurisdictions of responsibility between librarians and paraprofessionals (Applegate, 2010). The possession of an MLS becomes the distinguishing mark of who is a professional and who is not (Applegate, 2010). One of the things I learned early in my career was that my colleagues who did not have advanced degrees were no less smart or capable than I was. Yes, the MLS is a requirement for the majority of professional library positions, but to a Christian all it should mean is that we have a certain level of training in the theory and history of librarianship that helps us better understand the big picture (Applegate, 2010). It does not make us better than our paraprofessional colleagues. We need to treat each of our colleagues with the dignity and respect we wish to receive no matter where they fall in the library hierarchy (Matthew 7:12). Library staff may lack our credentials, but they are vital in doing the work that keeps our libraries running. We each have our roles to play in the workplace community and 1 Corinthians 12 and Romans 12 make it clear that no one role in the community is more important than another. When we see every aspect of librarianship from a Christian perspective, we value the talents and giftings of others and therefore eliminate much of the pride that comes from hierarchies (Trott, 2010). It should lead us to be team players and, if necessary, peacemakers.

Jealousy can be a common problem in our workplaces when too much praise is heaped on certain individuals by the administration while others are virtually ignored. We are not to show favoritism. (James 2:1, 9; 1 Timothy 5:21; Trott, 2010). We are also not to judge anyone (Luke 6:27). We need to be supportive of our administrators as the people in authority even when we respectfully disagree with them. Our administrators are the established authority and we are to give them the honor and respect due their position (Romans 13:1–6). This means not slandering them in public even if we disagree with them. We are to submit to their authority and not cheat them and also to set an example of integrity so that they can find no fault with us (Titus 2:7–10). We are to oppose power games but confront our administrators in a loving manner (Delivuk, 2002). We need to continually keep those in power in our prayers.

Christian Love and Prayer

Christians are not the only ones capable of showing love in the workplace, but what makes us as Christians different from others is that we love because Christ loves us (1 John 4) and we pray and have the indwelling of the Holy Spirit to help us (Kaehr, 2008). Christian librarians are dependent on the Lord, not intuition or the current literature (Davis & Tucker, 2002). We are called by God as agents of reconciliation and grace (Davis & Tucker, 2002). One way to see our colleagues as people in need of love, mercy and grace, instead of rivals, is to pray for them. Through prayer we invite the Lord to bless and direct each aspect of our lives, including our professional activities (Smith, 2002c). We may not like everyone we work with and sometimes personality types clash, but everyone deserves respect and we should try to get along, especially with those people who rub our fur the wrong way. This is a huge reason to pray for our colleagues and administrators. Prayer truly does change us for the better, especially in dealing with those sandpaper colleagues who irritate everyone around them. Praying for our colleagues helps us to see them as hurting people and to have patience with them. We become sensitive to the needs of our patrons and colleagues (Smith, 2002c) and this naturally leads us to be in regular prayer for their difficult situations (Davis & Tucker, 2002).

Long-Term Dangers

When working for decades at a relentless stressful pace in the face of incredible change, it is easy to let the stress lead to burnout and subsequent disengagement from work (Baird & Baird, 2016). Another factor that affects our work is low morale caused by some instance of abuse from a colleague or supervisor (Kendrick, 2017). Such low morale often leads to a similar disengagement and poor work behaviors as a result (Kendrick, 2017). For the Christian, the answer to both burnout and low morale is the renewing work of the Holy Spirit in our lives, bringing new life and putting to death the behaviors of the flesh (Romans 8:1–17). The other necessary ingredient is the practice of interpersonal workplace forgiveness (Aquino, Grover, Goldman & Folger, 2003). We should seek to support our colleagues who suffer from burnout or low morale so that they are healed and able to continue in our work and we need to lovingly confront bullies on their behalf.

Forgiveness and Reconciliation

All human communities including our workplaces are full of volatile human interactions and relationships (Aquino et al., 2003). We have endless opportunities to hurt or offend others, intentionally or unintentionally (Aquino et al., 2003). The health of our libraries and how well they function depends on the ability to heal broken relationships through interpersonal workplace forgiveness (Aquino et al., 2003). Forgiveness is necessary to relationships where colleagues have to continually to work with each other (Aquino et al., 2003). It is a way to repair damaged workplace relationships and release debilitating thoughts and emotions resulting from injury (Aquino et al., 2003).

> Interpersonal workplace forgiveness is a process whereby an employee who perceives himself or herself to have been the target of a morally injurious offence deliberately attempts to (a) overcome negative emotions (e.g., resentment, anger, hostility) toward his or her offender and (b) refrain from causing the offender harm even when he or she believes it is morally justifiable to do so [Aquino et al., 2003, p. 212].

This is not resignation or condoning the offence but investing the emotional and cognitive energy to understand offender's motives, engage in constructive dialogue, give time or attention to the offender, and acknowledge one's own role in causing or contributing to an episode (Aquino et al., 2003). Interpersonal workplace forgiveness can lead to reconciliation (Aquino et al., 2003). The Bible also has much to say on the subject of forgiveness. We are to forgive as the Lord forgave us (Colossians 3:13). In fact, Jesus said in several places that forgiveness of our sins depends on our ability to forgive the sins of others and to act with mercy (Matthew 6:14–15, 18:21–25; Mark 11:25; Luke 6:37–42). We are to forgive anyone anything (Kaehr, 2008) and the power to do this comes from prayer and the Holy Spirit. In the Lord's Prayer, Jesus taught his disciples to pray "forgive us our debts, as we also have forgiven our debtors" (Matthew 6:12, NIV). When we forgive someone we no longer judge them and we act kindly toward the offender (Kaehr, 2008). The Christian's commandment to forgive is not just words and if the conflict is with a non-believer, the burden to forgive is on the Christian (Kaehr, 2008). We are to follow the definition of interpersonal workplace forgiveness and not engage in retaliation. In fact, we are warned not to take revenge but to do good to those who harm us (Romans 12:19–21).

None of this is easy. If it were, the Bible would not spend so much time talking about it. We need to keep at it and keep praying and listening to God. Some of my worst and most hurtful mistakes on the job have come when I have failed to listen to that still, small voice inside. In some ways, this essay was hard to write without feeling like a hypocrite since I know full well how short I can fall of these principles. We are all works in progress, especially when it comes to living out our faith. And when I am the one doing the hurting out of my own pain, I need to forgive myself and do everything I can to restore the work relationship and make amends, starting with a sincere apology. The words "I was wrong and I will not do it again" hold tremendous power. It is also important to learn from one's mistakes, especially when it comes to interpersonal relationships. We are called to be peacemakers. Forgiveness of ourselves and others leads to reconciliation.

Conclusion

The Christian teachings we receive on love and living in community inform our actions in all of these interpersonal and professional areas; they enhance our interpersonal relationships and ultimately our professionalism to the degree that we follow them. Allowing God to love us and love through us is as much our mission as being a good employee.

In fact, it makes us better employees. I hope this essay has shown some of what it means to "bring hope, life, and encouragement to all you encounter today" (Workplace Prayer, n.d.).

REFERENCES

American Library Association. (2008). Code of Ethics [Website]. Retrieved from http://www.ala.org/tools/ethics.

Applegate, R. (2010). Clarifying jurisdiction in the library workforce: Tasks, support staff, and professional librarians. *Library Trends, 59*, 1–2, 288–314. Retrieved from http://muse.jhu.edu/article/407819.

Aquino, K., Grover, S. L., Goldman, B., & Folger, R. (2003). When push doesn't come to shove: Interpersonal forgiveness in workplace felationships. *Journal of Management Inquiry, 12*(3), 209–216.

Baird, T., & Baird, Z. M. (2016). Running on empty: Dealing with burnout in the library setting [Blog post]. Retrieved from http://www.liscareer.com/baird_burnout.htm.

Davis, D. G., Jr., & Tucker, J. M. (2002). The master we serve: The call of the Christian librarian to the secular workplace. In Smith (Ed.), *Christian Librarianship: Essays on the Integration of Faith and Profession* (pp. 40–47). Jefferson, NC: McFarland.

Delivuk, J. A. (2002). Multiculturalism and libraries: a Biblical perspective. In Smith (Ed.), *Christian Librarianship: Essays on the Integration of Faith and Profession* (pp. 100–110). Jefferson, NC: McFarland.

Irish, D. E. (2002). And ne'er the twain shall meet? personal vs. professional ethics. In Smith (Ed.), *Christian Librarianship: Essays on the Integration of Faith and Profession* (pp. 120–130). Jefferson, NC: McFarland.

Kaehr, R. E. (2008) Being a Christian librarian: A partial definition. *The Christian Librarian, 51*(3), 125–131. Retrieved from http://digitalcommons.georgefox.edu/tcl/vol51/iss3/4.

Kelly, M. (2016). *Resisting Happiness*. North Palm Beach, FL: Beacon.

Kendrick, K. D. (2017). The low morale experience of academic librarians: A phenomenological study. *Journal of Library Administration, 57*(8), 846–878.

Smith, G. A. (2002a). The core virtue of Christian librarianship. *Faculty Publications and Presentations* 1. Retrieved from http://digitalcommons.liberty.edu/lib_fac_pubs/1.

Smith. G. A. (2002b). A philosophy of Christian librarianship. In Smith (Ed.), *Christian Librarianship: Essays on the Integration of Faith and Profession* (pp. 69–84). Jefferson, NC: McFarland.

Smith, G. A. (2002c). The role of the library in the character formation of the Christian college student. In Smith (Ed.), *Christian Librarianship: Essays on the Integration of Faith and Profession* (pp. 181–190). Jefferson, NC: McFarland.

Terhune, S. (2006). The impact of the Christian faith on library service. *The Christian Librarian, 49*(2), 91–100. Retrieved from http://digitalcommons.georgefox.edu/tcl/vol49/iss2/16.

Trott, G. (2010). M.L.S. or ABC? A Christian critique of professionalism. *The Christian Librarian, 53*(2), 38–47. Retrieved from http://digitalcommons.georgefox.edu/tcl/vol53/iss2/2.

Wilson, S. M., & Ferch, S. R. (2005). Enhancing resilience in the workplace through the practice of caring relationships. *Organization Development Journal, 25*(4), 45–60.

Workplace Prayer (n.d.) [Electronic mailing list message]. Retrieved from http://www.beliefnet.com/prayers/protestant/work/workday-prayer.aspx.

The Relational Interaction
A New Look at Glorifying God through a Reference Interview

Garrett B. Trott

Abstract

The reference interview (RI) is a common and foundational tool for librarians. However, it is often seen through pragmatic and objective lenses. RIs serve the purpose of providing the patron with the information that he or she needs. This essay argues that the RI should be seen through the lens of Saccone's relational intelligence (RQ). When seen through this lens, the RI moves from an objective transaction meeting merely the surface level needs of the patron to a relational encounter where fellowship and community can be manifested and the deep needs of the patron can be identified and met. This essays shows how Carol Kuhlthau's model can be utilized to truly utilize RQ to holistically meet the information needs of the patron.

Introduction

Many have written about faith and its intersection with Christian higher education (Beers, 2008; Claerbaut, 2004; Dockery, 2007; Jacobsen, 2004; Marsden, 1997). Throughout these writings, scholars argue that Christian institutions of higher education (IHE) need to rejoin what has been disconnected: "a comprehensive educational vision which unites knowledge, virtue, faith, and service" (Beers, 2008, p. 34; cf. Clark, 2003, loc. 7167; Jacobsen, 2004, p. 10). The holistic nature of the gospel aligns with this ideology, often phrased "faith and learning integration" (Smith, 2002, p. 18).

While theory undergirds some of these discussions related to faith and learning integration, application is critical as well. Librarians working in Christian IHEs can play a critical role in the integration process. Librarians not only integrate faith into the theories behind their various services, but the services themselves are often excellent venues to manifest their faith. Reference interviews (RI) play a key role in the services librarians offer in IHEs (compare Igbinovia, 2015).

The RI is a key component through which Christian librarians can manifest a key element of their faith: its relational nature. Two particular elements of this relational nature are the trinity and fellowship. Studying the trinity and fellowship manifest four themes critical to relational development and subsequently relational intelligence (RQ): authority, authenticity, humility and joy. When displaying RQ in a RI, particularly, but not exclusively, in a face-to-face context, a librarian not only manifests their faith, but models for the patron a level of confidence in both current and future information pursuits. This essay argues that RQ utilized in a RI can be a powerful entity, clearly modeling the gospel to the patron.

Reference interviews are common for librarians. A standard definition of a RI is

> an interpersonal communication that occurs between a reference librarian and a library user to determine the person's specific information need(s), which may turn out to be different than the reference question as initially posed. Because patrons are often reticent, especially in face-to-face interaction, patience and tact may be required on the part of the librarian [Reitz, 2007].

Theological Foundations for a Reference Interview

The Trinity

When one thinks of a theological foundation for a RI, the concept of the trinity is not the first idea that comes to mind. However, the trinity has a strong relational component as does the RI. Subsequently, the trinity serves as the grounding for a theological understanding of the value of relationships and is instructive as to how Christian librarians should practice the RI.

Historically, when referring to the concept of the trinity, the ideas of an economic trinity or an immanent trinity have taken precedence. The immanent trinity is the way God exists in himself. The economic trinity is the way in which God revealed himself in the history of salvation (Letham & Karkkainen, 2009, p. 907). With these vague differentiations, studies on the trinity throughout church history have not availed much distinction (Erickson, 2015, p. 112). Even Karl Rahner (1997), in his work entitled *The Trinity*, famous for this distinction between the two, notes the ambiguity in the differentiation when he states, "the 'economic' Trinity is the 'immanent' Trinity and the 'immanent' Trinity is the 'economic' Trinity" (pp. 21–22).

However, the second half of the 20th century has seen a remarkable resurgence in scholarship in relation to the trinity, leading to the development of the concept of a social trinity.[1] With a variety of nuances, the concept has four common elements. First, unlike much of the tradition, the social trinity does not give priority to the one divine substance over the three persons in God. The three persons are irreducible. Secondly, scholars advocating for the social elements of the trinity understand the three persons to be acting and relating subjects. They are not simply three modes of being of a singly personal subject. Thirdly, these theologians argue that there is a certain kind of relationship among the three persons of the trinity and that this relationship is a key element to unity. The last common element in the social trinity is a correspondence between the relations within the trinity and relationships among human beings (Bauckham, 2015, p. 37). Scholars advocating the concept of the social trinity argue that one should look at interactions between the trinity as a model for how individuals should interact with others (Grenz, 2001, pp. 4–5).

While the social trinity has direct theological components applicable to relationships, two additional elements of the trinity need to be addressed: the three-fold nature of the trinity and authority.

When it comes to relationships, Scripture often utilizes marriage as the ideal scenario: in marriage, two become one (Genesis 2:24; Mark 10:8), and the love between a husband and a wife portrays God's love for the church (Ephesians 5:23). While marital relationships often manifest the love of Christ, and subsequently can be an ideal model for relationships, the concept of the trinity takes it one step further. To attain a scenario where three individuals can work together in absolute harmony, accomplishing a common task takes remarkable humility, unity, and passion. The trinity reflects this:

> The three individual and distinctive Persons of the Godhead, with each member setting about his own work joyful to labor and support and yield and command, according to the eternal *taxis* that is intrinsic to the life of triune God. Whether submitting, serving, and obeying, or whether leading, sending, and commanding, each divine person accepts his respective roles and responsibilities with complete and unabashed delight [Ware, 2005, p. 157].

There is still much mystery behind the doctrine of the trinity (Bloesch, 1995, p. 167), and yet it is clear that the three-fold nature of the trinity displays relationships serving a united purpose with authenticity, humility, and joy (Bloesch, 1995, pp. 186–188). These elements play a foundational role when serving a patron through a RI.

In the 21st century, authority and submission are often looked upon critically and with disdain. However, authority and submission play critical roles in the relationships of humans and the relationships within the social trinity. At times, a resent of authority is a manifestation of an individual's sin nature. God's trinitarian nature embodies a submission to authority (Ware, 2005, p. 137).

In stating this, a differentiation between authority and authoritarian is critical. Authority has a relational tone, indicating a right to rule. Statements and claims often express authority, and compliance and conformity often acknowledge it. However, the exercise of authority does not necessarily manifest authoritarianism. Authoritarianism is authority corrupted. Authoritarianism occurs when individuals misuse authority for personal gain. Any form of human authority can easily degenerate into authoritarianism (Packer, 1981, pp. 7–8).

The trinity's authority is a critical component of the Christian faith. Likewise humility, necessary for true authority, begins for man with the acceptance of the trinity's authority as expressed in God's word (Packer, 1981, p. 15). Joyful submission is the result of the humble acceptance of authority (Lawrence, 1987, p. 329).

The relational nature of the trinity calls for relationships to manifest godly characteristics. How godly characteristics are displayed and for what purpose are critical elements to these relationships. Fortunately, Scripture provides several insights into how authority, authenticity, humility and joy function within the concept of fellowship.

Fellowship

Fellowship is a critical element of relating to God and one another and therefore to the faith of an individual. Evangelicalism expressed this idea through the defining phrase of "having a personal relationship with Jesus Christ" (Price, 1993, p. 53) and it is also echoed throughout Scripture.[2] Subsequently, relating plays a critical role for a Christian librarian desiring to model her faith through a RI. While the Bible speaks to relationships, the concept of fellowship is a key element in Scripture that speaks specifically to what a relationship should look like.

A common Greek word often translated as "fellowship" is *koinonia*. The idea expressed in this word is not that of simple association with another individual or group (Campbell, 1932, p. 353; O'Brien, 1993, p. 294). The idea articulates participation in something (Campbell, 1932, p. 353; O'Brien, 1993, p. 294; George, 1953, p. 239; Martin, 1979, p. 36). The participation required for fellowship can be immense, often much more than just being physically present, as it involves the development of shared experiences that goes beyond just a casual greeting. Steve Saccone (2009) cultivates this idea in his work *Relational Intelligence*.

Relational intelligence (RQ) is a key venue through which fellowship is established. An individual with RQ develops relationships simply for the sake of relationships. It is often difficult, particularly in 21st-century America, to completely disjoin relationships with entities such as work or projects. However, RQ puts the relationship as the ultimate priority. RQ is "the ability to learn, understand, and comprehend knowledge as it relates to interpersonal dynamics" (Saccone, 2009, p. 20). Saccone (2009) notes seven traits of RQ: self-awareness, story-collector, energy carrier, compelling relator, conversational futurist, likeable hero and disproportionate investor. While each of these elements is unique, each is critical to developing relationships manifesting the four elements of the trinity: authenticity, humility, joy, and authority.

Self-Awareness

Humility and authenticity are critical to developing self-awareness. Self-awareness is knowing oneself: having a deep understanding of one's own emotions, strengths, weaknesses and drives (Goleman, 2004, p. 7). An individual is self-aware when she is able to assess herself and readily accept, even long for, the constructive criticism of others (Goleman, 2004, p. 7). Self-awareness is one element of RQ endowing individuals to have a firm grasp of who they are and what they can do. It enables an individual to have self-confidence, subsequently utilizing her self-confidence to empower others.

Saccone takes this concept one step further, however, by pointing out that believers in Christ have a desire and an invitation to see themselves clearly. Christianity builds upon the assumption that regardless of how many deficits or dysfunctions an individual has, God's love for that individual never changes (Psalm 136; Romans 8:38–39). God's love plays a key role in this perspective of humanity. Believers in Christ have a dynamic tension between being blatantly honest about the fallen nature of all human beings, yet in the same breath, having confidence in whom God created humanity to be (Saccone, 2009, pp. 30–31). It is through this tension that RQ allows mankind to hear the brutal honesty of their sinful nature and yet feel confident in God's love. (Saccone, 2009, pp.30–31, compare Hagner, 1983, p. 170).

An individual with deficient self-confidence often lacks authenticity and cannot truly invest in fellowship and contribute to her unique contribution to the community. Likewise, even if it is not intentional, an individual lacking self-awareness often develops relationships solely for collaboration on tasks or self-gratification. Unfortunately, neither context enables relationships to flourish.

Story Collector

A second element of RQ, critical to both the RI and fellowship, involves collecting stories. Collecting stories takes conversations beyond conventional questions, such as

"How are you?" or "Where do you work?" Questions of this nature are often common in our culture and answers to them are part of an individual's conversational ability. However, these kinds of question seldom drive conversations to deeper levels (Saccone, 2009, p. 59). In order to be relationally intelligent, one must ask questions that discover the dreams, life history and passions of an individual. Asking good questions, or story collecting, is the primary skill needed to do this.

Story collecting fosters authenticity, and it is often a key component to generating good fellowship. The art of story collecting invites fellowship as it encourages individuals to share about themselves, and invites them to be part of a community (Joset, 2016, p. 65). A story collector, with a passion to know and understand how God has worked in the lives of others, not only strengthens her RQ, but also provides a warm space in her own life, empowering her relational ability.

Energy Carrier

An angry patron comes to the reference desk. The librarian at the reference desk decides how to react. While there are several options available, Saccone notes that in a context like this, librarians typically either manifest themselves as a thermostat or a thermometer. A thermometer is an individual who is responsive to her setting. In this context, a thermometer may respond with a spirit of anger or fear, allowing the patron to control the context. A librarian who is a thermostat, on the contrary, understands their authority and, with a tone of humility, sets the environment for the RI. When being a thermostat in this manner, the librarian is an energy carrier. The librarian carries energy by being emotionally present and utilizing her emotions authoritatively to influence the context (Saccone, 2009, pp. 79–80).

Saccone argues that two elements counter the ability of an individual to carry energy: the appearance of alertness or being emotionally unavailable. These elements can negatively affect others and diminish the librarian's authority. While being alert and available to the patron can be indicators of a good listener, they also model the love of Christ (McCartney, 2009, pp. 114-115; McKnight, 2011, pp. 135-136). The librarian's ability to be authentically present supports her ability to change a setting (that is, a thermostat) by enhancing the influence she has on those around her. A patron will listen and respect what a librarian says when the patron is aware that the individual will respectfully meet her with a listening ear.

Compelling Relator

In 2011, Nancy Colier (2011), a psychotherapist, in a *Huffington Post* blog noted that boredom has become an epidemic in the 21st century. Colier's (2011) comments align with how individuals interact with technology. For example, users get bored quickly with web pages. After only 10–20 seconds, if people do not find what they want, they will move on (Nielsen, 2011). In order for a web site to have a successful visit, the web site must clearly communicate its value proposition in ten seconds or less (Nielsen, 2011). In response to the boredom epidemic, Saccone argues that librarians need to manifest humility by becoming compelling relators.

Saccone points to an excellent example of what it means to be a compelling relator in John 4, Jesus and the woman of Samaria. In this context, Jesus is alone at a well during the middle of a very hot day and a woman from Samaria comes to get water. Jesus is thirsty and subsequently asks this woman to give him a drink. While there may not be any difficulties with a gesture like this in the 21st-century Western world, this gesture raised several issues in first-century Israel (Michaels, 2010, p. 239). Jesus uses this controversial context and humble request for help, to display his need and build a relational bridge with the Samarian woman (Saccone, 2009, pp. 116–17).

Likewise, controversy or cognitive dissonance can play a critical role in developing RQ and can subsequently empower the librarian to be a compelling relator. RQ invites one to use dissonance to build relationships, not just for the sake of being contrary; but, to challenge a patron's normal patterns of thinking (Saccone, 2009, pp. 107–108).

For example, a patron inquires about finding resources related to video games and its impact on the learning ability of a child, giving implications that she feels that the impact is minimal. Regardless of the position held by the librarian, the librarian could manifest humility and ask some fundamental questions, suggesting additional possibilities to the patron's position. Doing so is not simply to argue or prove a point; but, to develop a relationship with the patron and strengthen and/or challenge the position of the patron. The challenges that take place in a RI often increase the ability of an individual to be interesting to those around them, and potentially, earn the right to be heard by others (Saccone, 2009, p. 123). Using dissonance humbly can empower a librarian to become a compelling relator and, when called for, can break the epidemic of boredom, which at times dominates a RI.

Another element for a compelling relator is to activate passion, a manifestation of joy. Interesting people have passion. Passion is critical in creating a compelling relator. Individuals desire to follow those they discern as having passion and subsequently, passion enables relationships to thrive (Saccone, 2009, p. 123).

Conversational Futurist

Conversational futurists think before speaking, they listen with one ear to earth and one ear to heaven. The ear towards the earth listens to the individual (compare Katz, 2002, p. 135). The ear towards heaven subsequently listens to God, listening for God's direction and guidance in the RI (Saccone, 2009, p. 133).

As noted earlier, listening is a key element in being an energy collector. Listening in this fashion is similar, but includes listening to God. Dual listening is critical in the RI and enables the librarian, while hearing the information need of the patron, to prayerfully assess the non-verbal cues, the tone of voice, and many other elements which speak to the need of the patron. Dual listening also enables the librarian to pray in the midst of the RI, allowing the RI to take place with the best interest of the patron at the heart. Service done in this manner is humble, respectful, and honoring to God.

Service at this level, at times, requires an invitation for change. For example, a librarian in a RI understands the context of the assignment for which a student is pursuing assistance. However, the initial interest of the student is too broad to fit the parameters of the assignment. Subsequently, the librarian invites the student to consider narrowing or changing her area of interest, while praying that God would enable a tone of humility, authenticity, and authority. When this is the case, a conversational futurist can invite a context where relational dialog can thrive and the ability to change is possible (Saccone, 2009, p. 143).

Likeable Hero

Likeability is not about becoming a people pleaser or trying to be all things to all people. It is, however, a critical component to RQ. Saccone suggests that individuals enjoy the camaraderie of a likeable hero (Saccone, 2009, p. 151). According to Saccone (2009), the five elements of likeability are: approachability, stickiness, rapid trust formation, friendliness, and flexible optimism (p. 153). Saccone argues that likeability is important in the context of developing RQ and therefore would affect the RI. These elements help to support the values of the individual (Saccone, 2009, p. 152).

Likeable librarians are approachable. A likeable librarian is not only open to getting to know others, but she has an ability to draw individuals into her life and subsequently, open doors to the reference services of a library. A librarian with an enthusiastic posture aimed at developing authentic connections with others can speak volumes to a patron seeking help (Saccone, 2009, p. 154).

Likeable librarians manifest joy. They are enjoyable to be around; they are sticky. Subsequently, the relationships developed create loyalty. Stickiness and loyalty often counter turnover. If a patron experiences frequent relational turnover, they often feel adrift or unsupported (Saccone, 2009, p. 159).

Saccone's third element of likeability is rapid trust formation. The more likeable an individual is, the faster others trust them. It is often through rapid trust formation, particularly in quick interactions, such as a RI, that individuals are able to trust the words of a newly acquainted individual (Saccone, 2009, p. 162).

Friendliness is a fourth dimension of likeability. Many times individuals look at their personality type to determine whether they are naturally friendly. While some individuals do have an innate ability to develop relationships, Saccone's aspect of friendliness goes further. Friendliness is a way of interacting with others, regardless of the context and irrespective of an individual's demeanor. Likeable people manifest joy and authenticity and subsequently convey warmth (Saccone, 2009, p. 164).

The last element of a likeability which Saccone develops is flexible optimism. Flexible optimism considers the risks when assessing a scenario and the subsequent outlook. It is not an optimistic perspective regardless of the scenario, but it utilizes wisdom and knows when a pessimistic perspective is necessary. Flexible optimism can provide a realistic and joy-filled perspective on life. This kind of outlook is often contagious, and supports the likeability of the librarian (Saccone, 2009, p. 166).

Disproportionate Investor

In an era of consumerism, it is easy to seek relationships with the intention of "What can this person do for me?" Often times, relationships are pursued when a need is present and it is perceived that the identified individual can provide for that need. Saccone argues that instead of having a consumer mindset when it comes to relationships, one should look at relationships as a disproportionate investor. A disproportionate investor is an individual investing into relationships, for the sake of investing, not for the sake of returns. A disproportionate investor sees every relationship as a gift from God, and decides to invest in others as an honor and a privilege from God, regardless of who the individual is, her background, or her status in society.

Saccone notes six characteristics of true investors including generative, grateful, teachable, missional, strategic, and resilient. These six traits involve a combination of willingness, humility, purpose, and intentionality. Utilizing these six traits in relational encounters empowers individuals to be contributors in every facet of another's life. It is when an individual develops as a disproportionate investor approach that RQ grows, nurturing one's ability to influence others and impacting their own ability to make a difference through a RI.

Summary of Saccone's Seven Traits of RQ

Saccone's seven traits of RQ are powerful when it comes to relationships. They enable relationships to be free from hidden agendas. They direct the focal point of relationships to the needs of others and subsequently manifest Christ-likeness. They manifest the four traits seen in the trinity: authority, authenticity, humility, and joy. In this context, relationships develop and thrive. Subsequently, RQ empowers a RI, enabling a librarian to serve the needs of a patron holistically. Integrating RQ into a RI enables the librarian to discover and meet the true needs of the patron, glorifying God in the process. The next portion of this essay will explore the way in which a librarian can manifest the gospel through this application. Carol Kuhlthau's insight into how patrons seek meaning serves as an excellent foundation through which one can apply RQ to a RI.

Application: Carol Kuhlthau's Seeking Meaning

While there are many lenses through which one can assess a RI, few align with RQ and the theological themes of fellowship and the trinity like the works of Carol Kuhlthau. Kuhlthau (2004, 2002, 2001, 1999) has published several works concerning the affective component of library services. In a more recent work, a second edition of a book entitled *Seeking Meaning*, Kuhlthau (2004) provides an understanding about the needs of patrons when it comes to seeking information.

Librarians, while they are often well trained in comprehending the information needs of a patron, frequently lack an understanding of the related affective components aligning with research endeavors (Kuhlthau, 2004, p. 8). The affective component, Kuhlthau (2004, p. 8) argues, has a significant impact on the ability of a patron to truly learn through a RI. Fostering the elements of Saccone's RQ enables the librarian to develop a strong relationship with the patron and creates a relational foundation from which they can apply Kuhlthau's model. This empowers the librarian to not just meet the information needs of a patron, but do so in a way that glorifies God.

Kuhlthau (2004, p. 8) points out that certainty and order serve as a basis for many library structures and instruction. Services in a library function with an element of certainty. For example, it is difficult to lead a patron to a book or an area of the library that contains a certain topic when a patron lacks certainty regarding the topic she is pursuing (Kuhlthau, 2004, p. 8). Kuhlthau's (2004, p. 8) research shows that reference services often rest upon a foundation that requires the patron to know with some certainty their area of interest or concern. Kuhlthau's research also shows that patrons often do not truly know what they need when they initially contact a librarian. Subsequently, Kuhlthau develops a method, which, she convincingly argues, enables a RI to begin with a principle of uncertainty and truly meet the needs of a patron lacking certainty in her research endeavors. Kuhlthau's (2004, p. 8) research argues that many RIs begin in this manner. Her model provides an application that utilizes RQ through the RI. The model emphasizes similar relational elements displayed in biblical fellowship and the social dynamics of the trinity.

Kuhlthau's Model of a Reference Interview

When a patron comes with a reference question, one often assumes that the patron is inquiring about resources needed for her research (Brown, 2008; Jennerich and Jennerich, 1997, pp. 1–2; Kern and Woodard, 2016, pp. 63–64; Mulac, 2012, p. 57). While this is the case at times, Kuhlthau (2004, p. 8) argues that in order to truly help a patron with her needs, the librarian should not assume this is true in all scenarios. Instead, Kuhlthau (2004) applies a number of studies (Bates, 1986, p. 357; van Rijsbergen, 1996, pp. 221–231; Wilson, Ellis, Foster, and Spink, 2002, pp. 704–15; Whittermore and Yovits, 1973, 221–231) to develop an uncertainty principle for Library and Information Science. Per Kuhlthau's (2004) model, uncertainty is

> a cognitive state that commonly causes affective symptoms of anxiety and lack of confidence. Uncertainty and anxiety can be expected in the early stages of the information search process. The affective symptoms of uncertainty, confusion, and frustration are associated with vague, unclear thoughts about a topic or question. As knowledge states shift to more clearly focused thoughts, a parallel shift occurs in feelings of increased confidence. Uncertainty due to a lack of understanding, a gap in meaning, or a limited construct initiates the process of information seeking [p. 92].

The pursuit of information is rarely a simple linear progression. Uncertainty about the topic or method often accompanies an information pursuit, which commonly causes symptoms of anxiety and lack of confidence (Kuhlthau, Heinström, and Todd, 2008, para. 2). A patron often manifests this anxiety through uncertainty, confusion, and frustration, which often display themselves through lack of clarity on a research endeavor (Kuhlthau, Heinström, and Todd, 2008, para. 2). Confidence about research endeavors often parallel clarity of focus and thoughts (Kuhlthau, 2004, p. 103). Kuhlthau developed a paradigm for understanding one's transition from uncertainty to understanding. She highlights three levels of experience in her paradigm that portray when a patron is at the beginning (uncertainty) to the final stages (understanding) of her research: thinking, feeling, and acting.

A RI should bring the thoughts of a patron, Kuhlthau (2004, p. 105) argues, from vague to clear. Research pursuits often begin with a broad idea of a topic or interest. The initial stages of research often include the narrowing or development of a topic. Part of this stage involves seeing if the individual can fully pursue her topic within the research parameters allotted for that particular project. A patron can be identified in the initial stage of research when they ask a broad question, such as "Can you point me to resources on biomechanics?" Clarifying questions, such as "Is there any particular context for which you need information on biomechanics?" enable the librarian to discover where the patron is beginning.

In asking these questions, the librarian aims to address the feelings and actions of the patrons as well. This can be done by reducing confusion and supporting the patron as they develop the skills and abilities to locate the needed information. The reduction of confusion and the lessening of uncertainty enable the patron to pursue research.

Saccone's insight in developing a story collector can influence the uncertainty principle and the subsequent feelings of inadequacy and confusion directly. Saccone argues that a story collector asks questions that move beyond the traditional queries in conversation (that is, "How was your weekend?"). The purpose of this is to pull out three distinct elements of an individual in a conversation: dreams, life history, and personhood. Understanding the way in which a person's selection of topics relates to their growing sense of purpose, passion or dreams for self can help the patron make connections and therefore adjust uncertainty.

When practicing story collecting in a RI, a vague reference inquiry, such as "I need information on cerebral palsy," can mark the beginning of a relationship instead of a simple transaction. For example, the librarian can begin to ask some questions to discover scenes from the patron's life enabling the librarian to understand the needs of the patron more completely (Saccone, 2009, p. 68). Understanding the context of the assignment or personal need driving a patron's need for information provides some, although limited, insight into the patron's story. Understanding the story undergirding the patron's current information pursuit, can also aid in narrowing a patron's inquiry. While there are situations where a patron does research on a topic just because she was told to do so, many patrons pursue research areas in which they have personal interest. For example, a student may seek information on a particular disease or ailment because it runs in their family. The librarian's ability to garner and respond to this level of personal information with appropriate sensibility builds a relationship between the librarian and the patron. The connection perceived by the patron reduces the feelings of inadequacy and confusion, subsequently reducing uncertainty and enabling thoughts to be clearer and more focused (Kuhlthau, 2004, p. 69). The perceived connection also establishes an initial level of trust, reducing the relational anxiety that often comes when a student makes initial interaction with a librarian (Kuhlthau, 2004, p. 69).

Utilizing a RI as a means to develop a relationship and subsequently serve the patron better is a clear manifestation of the gospel (Mohrlang, Comofort, and Borchert, 2007, p. 192). While library services do tend to be user-focused, to truly minister to the information needs of others, the librarian should strive to understand the often unspoken needs of the patron. RQ can play a role in so doing by focusing on the elements of fellowship modeled by the trinity.

Kuhlthau (2004, p. 95) posits that a RI has the potential to impact uncertainty in another way: moving a patron from a feeling of anxiety to a feeling of confidence. Kuhlthau's idea of moving a patron from uncertainty (which often is frustrating) to a realm of certainty echoes the role a librarian can play in encouraging a patron. By being sensitive to the affective manifestations of the patron, the reference librarian can utilize the RI as an opportunity to build up the abilities and information-seeking skills of the patron, providing support and clarity as the patron develops both her research skills and more certainty on her topic (compare Best, 1986, p. 220; Morris, 1991, p. 163).[3]

A RI is often a component of information literacy. Librarians teach this literacy within the context of the students' assigned research projects. Students often begin their process with a librarian at the request of their professor. The initial interaction of the RI offers the librarian an opportunity to model the fellowship of the trinity as well as the opportunity to move the patron along Kuhlthau's continuum of uncertainty to a place of certainty.

One component of information literacy, the idea that information creation or meaning making is a process (Association of College and Research Libraries [ACRL], 2017) is exemplified by Martin Luther and his understanding of Romans 1:17. While Luther's transformation had several elements, one of them was his discovery of this verse in a new light. He had always looked at this passage with confusion and distaste, primarily because he understood it in the light preached by the Catholic Church: an individual cannot live by faith because she is not righteous. When reading this text again, his understanding of it changed:

> For a long time I went astray [in the monastery] and didn't know what I was about. To be sure, I knew something, but I didn't know what it was until I came to the text in Romans 1 [:17], "He who through faith is righteous shall live." That text helped me. There I saw what righteousness Paul was talking about. Earlier in the text, I read "righteousness." I related the abstract ["righteousness"] with the concrete ["the righteous One"] and became sure of my cause. I learned to distinguish between the righteousness of the law and the righteousness of the gospel. I lacked nothing before this except that I made no distinction between the law and the gospel. I regarded both as the same thing and held that there was no difference between Christ and Moses except the times in which they lived and their degrees of perfection. But when I discovered the proper distinction—namely, that the law is one thing and the gospel is another—I made myself free [Luther, 1967, pp. 442–443].

Martin Luther's new understanding of this text subsequently transformed his thinking. Luther's new thinking played a critical role in his development and personhood, subsequently playing a critical role in changing the world. There was significant power that came when Luther moved, in Kuhltahu's words, from uncertainty to certainty. This transition empowered, at least in part, his impact upon the world.

Kuhlthau (2004, p. 103) argues that the initial feelings of uncertainty, confusion, and frustration are often associated with vague unclear thoughts about a topic. As patrons gain a better understanding of their topic, this increased understanding correlates with an increased confidence in their research abilities. Kuhlthau's (2004, p. 103) zones of intervention serve as instructive guide posts for the librarian to better serve the patron by supporting the patron appropriately in the RI. Kuhlthau's model aligns with the idea that a RI can embody one of the two greatest commandments: loving your neighbor (compare Matthew 22:37–40), which entails understanding and serving the patron and seeking her well-being (Turner, 2014, p. 537).

Kuhlthau's Zones of Intervention

Kuhlthau's model of zones of intervention integrates RQ into reference services. There are different types of reference questions and each type of reference question requires a differing type of intervention. An individual pursuing a statement of fact (that is, "What year was John F. Kennedy assassinated?") requires services that differ dramatically from an individual requesting assistance with a research agenda (that is, "I am doing research on the development of the printing press and how it played a role in the Reformation"). The latter question requires thinking about: the impact the printing press played on the distribution of Luther's 95 theses; how this distribution changed the scope of the Reformation; the financial and cultural impacts Luther's ideology had upon European culture; and the role the printing press played in this impact; just to name a few.

Kuhlthau divides reference inquiries into differing levels of mediation. These levels of mediation take into consideration both the patron's stage of research and the often related complexity of the patron's problem (that is, the further a patron is in her research endeavors, the more complicated research inquiries often become). Kuhlthau identifies five levels of mediation: organizer, locator, identifier, advisor, and counselor.

Level one, organizer, provides no direct intervention. The system of an organized collection and an online catalog are able to meet the needs of the patron (Kuhlthau, 2004, p. 115). For example, when a patron is looking for a particular book, enters data into a search query and finds the book for which she is looking, level one mediation has taken place. This is the only level of mediation that does not require some direct human intervention.

The second level, locator, assists the patron in finding a single fact or aids the patron in finding a single resource to answer her question. An underlying assumption when serving at this level of mediation is that there is one right answer and one single source that will match the user's inquiry (Kuhlthau, 2004, p. 116). The intervention done by the librarian is simply locating that single source (Kuhlthau, 2004, p. 130).

While Kuhlthau's third level of mediation, identifier, states that the patron comes with an inquiry more extensive than a simple reference question, this level only leads the patron to sources based upon her initial inquiry. In this level of mediation, the librarian typically formats the patron's inquiry into phrases of words that a database will understand, finds results related to the patron's inquiry and considers the RI complete (Kuhlthau, 2004, p. 117). The librarian aids the patron to some degree, but typically does not address the complexity of the learning process nor the true needs of the patron (Kuhlthau, 2004, p. 117). Kuhlthau (2004, p. 130) labels the zone of intervention of this level of mediation "group of sources," because the librarian typically finds multiple sources for the patron.

The fourth level, advisor, adds one additional step to the role of identifier. While an advisor definitely aids the patron in finding relevant resources, she also walks them through some of the basics of research protocol: starting with a general inquiry and progressing to a narrow topic from what is learned in the general inquiry (Kuhlthau, 2004, p. 118). For example, if a patron came looking for resources on violence in video games, an advisor would take the patron through a sequence of resources, likely beginning with a discipline-specific encyclopedia. Utilizing the same call number range of the encyclopedia, the librarian would take the patron to the general collection of a library and find similar, but more specific resources. The advisor would then show the patron the bibliography in the resource, and pull an article from it that related to her inquiry (Kuhlthau, 2004, p. 130).

Kuhlthau entitles the last and highest level of mediation as counselor. A counselor takes the inquiry one step further. The counselor provides intervention in the research process of the patron. Levels one through four base mediation upon the idea that a patron has a good idea of what she needs for her research endeavors. In these contexts, librarians provide definitive answers (specific resources) to queries about a vague topic or unfocused problem (Kuhlthau, 2004, p. 119).

The level of counselor contrasts with levels one through four. In levels one through four, certainty serves as the basis of mediation. At the level of counselor, the uncertainty principle underlies the librarian's intervention. The RI, when done at the level of counselor, involves inquiries by the librarian to determine not just what resources the patron needs, but this level of inquiry goes to the root of where the patron is with her research endeavors.

The level of counselor enables the manifestation of RQ in the RI. Rapid trust formation functions as an excellent foundation for a librarian serving at the level of counselor. The first time a patron approaches the librarian for a RI, sufficient time to develop a firm relationship between the patron and the librarian is often lacking. However, as this essay suggests, relationships are critical to providing good RIs, particularly when done at the level of counselor. Subsequently, rapid trust formation, a trait common in RQ (Saccone, 2009, p. 162), is important for interactions at the level of counselor.

Kuhlthau (2004, p. 120) elaborates that at the level of counselor the librarian establishes a dialog leading to developing a research process. While this is the purpose of a first encounter, at the level of counselor, the reference librarian becomes a partner whom the patron periodically visits to refine and revise her search strategy (Kuhlthau, 2004, pp. 120, 130). Relationships, a key component of a RI at this level, are the medium of influence. It is often through relationships that influence and education takes place (Saccone, 2009, p. 20). Subsequently, if a librarian desires to affect a patron in a RI, the relationship is key.

Several elements of RQ enable a librarian practicing reference interviews at the level of counselor to flourish. Reference librarians are seldom the first stop for an individual when it comes to looking for information or help on an assignment (Kern, 2015, p. 62). Saccone (2009, pp. 80–81) argues that anyone can be either a thermostat, an individual who can change the climate of any context, or a thermometer, someone who adapts to the culture around him or her. If a librarian strives to be a thermostat, or an energy carrier, empowering and influencing patrons utilizing a RI, she can change the tone of the library making the library a first stop for research problems. This, aligned with the fact that RQ involves traits that anyone can develop and learn (Saccone, 2009, p. 23), can have tremendous impact on enabling a librarian to practice RIs at Kuhlthau's level of counselor.

Saccone points out two elements that would aid any librarians in becoming an energy carrier. First, one must ask of themselves, "What kind of a tone do I set in the library? Do students come to the reference desk intimidated because of non-verbal cues?" Perhaps the geospatial context of the reference area itself intimidates patrons. Being aware of the tone the individual and the context provides a starting place to utilize RQ into a RI (Saccone, 2009, p. 80).

It is critical that one learn to externalize internal energy. Everyone has internal energy of some sort. Everyone has things they enjoy doing, things they enjoy talking about, and stories of their life they are passionate to share. An ability to externalize those passions plays a critical role in being a thermostat. If a librarian is driven to discover truth and serve her community, these two passions can be externalized by the tone of conversation and the passion expressed in a RI. Saccone (2009) states:

> The more passionately you care about what you're saying, the more people will desire to listen to you, be around you, and take part in your mission. More than anything else, your passion is what convinces people that what you are talking about matters and people want to connect to something that matters [p. 123].

Passion, the externalization of internal energy, applied to a RI not only changes the tone of the conversation, but also has the potential to direct the passion of patrons. Another element Saccone ascribes to RQ is that of a conversational futurist. A conversational futurist has more than the ability to simply diagnose a reference question, Conversational futurists are able to see where a RI is going and they know how to get ahead of the RI, outrun it, and lead both the RI and the patron in the proper direction (Saccone, 2009, p. 128).

Kuhlthau's (2004, p. 92) uncertainty principle argues that lack of clarity often brings with it anxiety and a lack of confidence. By becoming a conversational futurist, reference librarians empower themselves to counter the uncertainty principle by listening with one ear to earth and one ear to heaven. The ear to earth truly listens to the patron. The ear to heaven is listening to how and where God is guiding the RI (Saccone, 2009, p. 133). It is with both of these ears attentive that the librarian can listen to the questions of the patron even when the questions are not articulated in question form. For example, at times a patron will ask a straightforward question. At first glance, this may seem to fall under Kuhlthau's level of locator. However, after the patron makes this brief inquiry the ear to earth listens to the patron, interpreting her non-verbal cues of confusion and frustration. The conversational futurist is able to project that unless something changes in the conversation, the patron is going to leave lacking the services desired. Sensing what is about to happen, the librarian implements RQ in the RI by listening to heaven, asking God for wisdom. After whispering a short prayer, the librarian, empowered by the Holy Spirit, displays empathy and moves the RI forward with wise and loving interaction by asking questions to clarify the needs of the patron. In so doing, the librarian is able to minister to the patron, serving her true needs and subsequently manifesting the gospel (Saccone, 2009, p. 136).

Saccone (2009) closes this chapter on conversational futurists by noting a critical element in any RI: "Maybe as much as anything, we must remember that being a conversational futurist is all about serving people's best interest with humility, honor, and respect…" (p. 136). Otherwise, the patron often responds with resistance, pride, and an unwillingness to accept any assistance (Saccone, 2009, p. 143). Because of this, a tone of fellowship must accompany the task of the conversational futurist in the midst of a RI.

Saccone (2009, pp. 107–108) notes that controversy plays a critical role in RQ. Subsequently, it can play a key role in a RI, particularly when done at the counselor level. RQ demands that the librarian utilize controversy not just for the sake of controversy, but also to challenge normal patterns of thinking in order to minister to the patron by getting her to think through the various intellectual aspects of her topic (Saccone, 2009, pp. 107–108). For example, often times, patrons come to a topic with many preconceptions based on her own experience. It is often easy for a librarian to see these in a RI, but it can be difficult to address them. This is a place where raising a question about a false preconception can be critical to the research endeavors of the patron. However, if done without a relational foundation, the patron often does not take the question seriously.

Utilizing RQ and being a counselor, enables the librarian to be an effective devil's advocate, getting the patron to think about her topic and subsequently perform better research. However, it is critical that this style of interaction occur at the level of counselor, when a relationship of trust between the patron and librarian has developed. Otherwise, being contrary can often serve ulterior purposes.

Saccone notes that a refusal to be irrelevant is another necessary element in order to be a compelling relator. This influences an effective RI. This can be manifested when the librarian talks to someone, rather than at someone. At the level of counselor, this style of transaction of talking to someone is not necessarily natural. Whereas, talking at someone is more commonplace for the other four levels of reference services (Kuhlthau, 2009, p. 120). For example, when a librarian directs a patron to resources that she found for the patron, instead of instructing the patron how to find the resources themselves; the librarian is talking at the patron. In comparison to a librarian truly inquiring to learn what circumstances hinder the patron from finding resources (Kuhlthau, 2009, p. 120). In this context, the librarian is talking with the patron, instead of at them. In order to be a compelling relator, relevance is critical. One way relevance can be a part of dialog is to strive to be talking to individuals, not at them.

Conclusion

The RI is a service offered by libraries of all shapes and sizes. It serves a fundamental and foundational purpose to patrons and libraries: aiding patrons to find the information for which they are looking. For many years, librarians have seen this service as task-based: help the patron find what she needs and the RI is complete. While this is the case for some scenarios, Kuhlthau's research shows a strong affective component that must be aligned with library services and especially the RI.

It takes more than mere information to move a patron from nervousness and confusion to certainty and confidence. In fact, more information can cause even more confusion at times. Subsequently, the RI must be relationally clothed in order to truly be effective.

This relational component involves more than just asking the patron a few questions about her topic, but looks back to two biblical models of relationships: the trinity and fellowship. These two models provide examples of relationships that are truly focused on the needs of others, passionately desiring the information needs of the patron be met, with understanding, clarification and context of the needs, empathy, and passion. It is when a RI can manifest these traits that the RI not only becomes more effective by truly meeting both the affective and information needs of the patron, but it also has the potential of drawing the patron to utilize the library services more frequently and even draw the patron closer to God.

When a librarian utilizes RQ in the RI, it not only provides the patron with the services she needs, it also enables the librarian to practice love for her neighbor by truly providing the patron with what she needs.

NOTES

1. While there are a number of theologians who have explored this concept, theologians such as Wolfhart Pannenberg, Jurgen Moltmann, Miroslav Volf, John Zizioulas, and Catherine LaCunga really led the way in this development.

2. While the Bible does not use the term "relationship with Jesus Christ," the concept that relationships play a critical role in the kingdom of God is common throughout Scripture, for example, Romans 5:8, 10–11; 2 Corinthians 5:18–19; Galatians 4:5–6; Ephesians 2:16; Colossians 1:21; 1 John 3:1–2.

3. In the context of 1 Thessalonians 5:11, Paul encourages the audience to strengthen others through their words. A RI, done in light of RQ, can be utilized as a manifestation of this passage.

REFERENCES

Association of College and Research Libraries. (2017). *Framework for Information Literacy for Higher Education*. http://www.ala.org/acrl/standards/ilframework.

Bates, M. J. (1986). Subject Access in Online Catalogs: A Design Model. *Journal of the American Society for Information Science 37*(1), 357–376.

Bauckham, R. (2015). *Gospel of Glory: Major Themes in Johannine Theology*. Grand Rapids, MI: Baker Academic.

Beers, S. (Ed.). (2008). *The Soul of a Christian University: A Field Guide for Educators*. Abilene, TX: Abilene Christian University Press.

Best, E. (1986). *A Commentary on the First and Second Epistles to the Thessalonians*, Black's New Testament Commentary. Peabody MA: Hendrickson Publishers.

Bloesch, D. G. (1995). *God the Almighty: Power, Wisdom, Holiness Love*. Downers Grove, IL: InterVarsity Press.
Brown, S. W. (2008). The Reference Interview: Theories and Practice. *Library Philosophy & Practice*. Retrieved from: http://libr.unl.edu:2000/LPP/willenbrown.htm
Campbell, J. Y. (1932). KOINŌNIA and Its Cognates in the New Testament. *Journal of Biblical Literature* 51(4), 352–380.
Claerbaut, D. (2004). *Faith and Learning on the Edge: A Bold New Look at Religion in Higher Education*. Grand Rapids, MI: Zondervan.
Clark, D. K. (2003). *To Know and Love God: Method for Theology*. Wheaton, IL: Crossway Books.
Dockery, D. (2007). *Renewing Minds : Serving Church and Society through Christian Higher Education*. Nashville: Broadman & Holman.
Erickson, M. J. (2015). *Introducing Christian Doctrine*. 3rd ed. Grand Rapids, MI: Baker Book House.
George, R. (1953). *Communion with God in the New Testament*. London: Epworth Press.
Goleman, D. (2004) What Makes a Leader? In *HBR's 10 Must Reads on Leadership* (pp. 1–22). Boston, MA: Harvard Business Press.
Grenz, S. J. (2001). *The Social God and the Relational Self: A Trinitarian Theology of the* Imago Dei. Louisville, KY: Westminster John Knox Press.
Hagner, D. A. (1982). *Matthew 1–13*. Word Biblical Commentary. Dallas, TX: Word Books Publisher.
Igbinovia, M. O. (2015). Shining a Light on the Reference Librarian Role as Reference Services Adapt to Users' Needs. *Library Connect*. Retrieved from https://libraryconnect.elsevier.com/articles/shining-light-reference-librarian-role-reference-services-adapt-users-needs.
Jacobsen, D. (2004). *Scholarship and Christian Faith: Enlarging the Conversation*. New York: Oxford University Press.
Jennerich, E. Z., & Jennerich, E. J. (1997). *The Reference Interview as a Creative Art*. Englewood, CO: Libraries Unlimited.
Joset, T. (2016). The Church as a Counter-Cultural Eschatological Fellowship: What is the Church and Why Does it Matter? *European Journal of Theology* 25(1), 64–72.
Kern, M. K. (2015). The Reference Interview Revisited. In D. A. Tyckoson & J. G. Dove (Eds.), *Reimagining Reference in the 21st Century* (pp. 61–74). Charleston Insights in Library, Archival, and Information Sciences. West Lafayette, IN: Purdue University Press.
Kern, M. K., & Woodard, B. S. (2016). The Reference Interview. In L. C. Smith and M. Wong (Eds.), *Reference and Information Service: An Introduction* (5th ed.) (pp. 57–88). Santa Barbara, CA: Libraries Unlimited.
Kuhlthau, C. (2005). *Seeking Meaning: A Process Approach to Library and Information Services* (2d ed.). Westport, CT: Libraries Unlimited.
Kuhlthau, C. (2002). *Teaching the Library Research Process*. Lanham, MD: Scarecrow Press.
Kuhlthau, C. (July, 2001). *Rethinking Libraries for the Information Age School: Vital Roles in Inquiry Learning*. Keynote address presented at the International Association of School Librarianship Conference, Auckland, New Zealand.
Kuhlthau, C. (1999). The Role of Experience in the Information Search Process of an Early Career Information Worker: Perceptions of Uncertainty, Complexity Construction, and Sources. *Journal of the American Society for Information Science* 50(5), 399–412.
Kuhlthau, C., Heinström, J., & Todd, R. J. (2008). The 'Information Search Process' Revisited: Is the Model Still Useful. *Information Research* 13(4).
Lawrence, W. D. (1987). Distinctives of Christian Leadership. *Bibliotheca Sacra* 144(575), 317–329.
Letham, R., & Karkkainen, V.-M. (2009). Trinity, Triune God. In *Global Dictionary of Theology* (pp. 901–913). Downers Grove, IL: Inter-Varsity Press.
Luther, M. (1967). *Luther's Works*. Vol. 54. (H. G. Lehman, Ed., & T. G. Tappert, Trans.). Philadelphia: Fortress Press.
Marsden, G. M. (1997). *The Outrageous Idea of Christian Scholarship*. New York: Oxford University Press.
Martin, R. P. (1979). *The Family and the Fellowship: New Testament Images of the Church*. Grand Rapids: William B. Eerdmans.
McCartney, D. G. (2009). *James*. Baker Exegetical Commentary on the New Testament. Grand Rapids: Baker Academic.
McKnight, S. (2011). *The Letter of James*. The New International Commentary on the New Testament. Grand Rapids: William B. Eerdmans.
Michaels, J. R. (2010). *The Gospel of John*. The New International Commentary on the New Testament. Grand Rapids: William B. Eerdmans.
Mohrlang, R., Comfort, P. W., & Borchert, G. L. (2007). *Romans, Galatians*. Carol Stream, IL: Tyndale House Publishers.
Morris, L. (1991). *The First and Second Epistles to the Thessalonians*. Grand Rapids: William B. Eerdmans.
Mulac, C. (2012). *Fundamentals of Reference*. Chicago: American Library Association.
O'Brien, P. T. (1993). Fellowship. In *Dictionary of Paul and His Letters* (pp. 293–295). Downers Grove, IL: IVP Academic.
Packer, J. I. (1981). *Freedom and Authority*. Oakland, CA: International Council on Biblical Inerrancy.

Price, R. M. (1993). *Beyond Born Again: Toward Evangelical Maturity.* Upper Montclair, NJ: Apocryphal Books.
Rahner, K. (1997). *The Trinity.* New York: Crossroad Publishing.
Reitz, J. (2007). Reference Interview. In *Online Dictionary for Library and Information Science.* Santa Barbara, CA: ABC-CLIO. Retrieved from https://www.abc-clio.com/ODLIS/odlis_r.aspx.
Saccone, S. (2009). *Relational Intelligence: How Leaders Can Expand Their Influence Through a New Way of Being Smart.* New York: John Wiley & Sons, 2009.
Smith, G. A. (Ed.). (2002). *Christian Librarianship: Essays on the Integration of Faith and Profession.* Jefferson, NC: McFarland & Co.
Turner, D. L. (2014). *Matthew.* Grand Rapids, MI: Baker Academic.
Van Rijsbergen, C. J. (1996). Information, Logic, and Uncertainty in Information Science. In *Proceedings of CoLIS Conceptions of Library and Information Science* (Vol. 24) (pp. 221–231). Copenhagen, Denmark, 1996.
Ware, B. A. (2005). *Father, Son, and Holy Spirit: Relationships, Roles, and Relevance.* Wheaton, IL: Crossway Books.
Whittermore, B. J., & Yovits, M. C. (1973). A Generalized Conceptual Development for the Analysis and Flow of Information. *Journal of the American Society for Information Science* 24(3), 221–231. doi:10.1002/asi.4630240308
Wilson, T. D., Ford, N. J., Ellis, D., Foster, A. E., & Spink, A. (2002). Information Seeking and Mediated Searching: Part 2. Uncertainty and Its Correlates. *Journal of the American Society for Information Science and Technology* 53(9), 704–15. doi:10.1002/asi.10082.

The Information Therapist Is In[1]

ROBIN R. HARTMAN

Abstract

Communication technology has gotten a lot of press these days leading up to and following the 2016 U.S. Presidential Election. Social media and popular websites have taken the place of previously trusted news sources for many people. The ability to publish information is no longer the exclusive privilege of a few established media empires. Easily accessible technology has enabled anyone with a passion for telling their stories to do so for little cost and sometimes for great profit. Combined with a growing acceptance of post-truth—or subjective truth—in the wider culture, Christian college librarians find the task of teaching students how to evaluate sources increasingly more complex. Judging the credibility of a source must take into consideration motivation and inherent bias of the publisher. Fact checking sources are suspect. Integrity and humility are hard to come by. As librarians we aim to equip our constituents to become lifelong learners, capable of using new media to discover truth. However, finding the enormity of seemingly credible information is too much for us to process. Even our efforts to inform add to the digital overload which results in an inability or unwillingness to thoroughly evaluate information. We see a preference for willed ignorance rather than doing all that is necessary to fully understand an issue. Librarianship is at its core a helping profession. In this essay I recommend a new role for librarians to be that of information therapist. As information therapists we can assist our patrons in becoming healthy problem solvers—setting personal boundaries while maintaining the integrity of truth.

The Information Therapist Is In

Therapy is something that moves a person forward past a difficult problem: physical therapy, behavioral therapy, or psychiatric therapy.

Dr. Laura Steele, the dean of Psychology and Counseling at Hope International University, believes that therapy utilizes a "growth" approach where a client draws on personal resources to solve problems unique to them (Steele, 2017). This means that the therapist must listen to the client's story, evaluate their problem as they see it, and help them to see ways to move past it. In this way the therapist takes the present situation, helps the client see how their past experiences may have had an effect on them, and then see how they can make decisions and inform their future.

One way that Steele (2017) likes to look at past experiences is as a shoebox full of photographs. We might open the lid, get overwhelmed by the contents, shut the box, and put it away (Steele, 2017). Eventually, the therapist helps the client to open the box and sort out the photos and categorize them to make some sense of them, to see what is really there (Steele, 2017).

I believe there are close parallels for librarians encountering researchers who come to a particularly troubling point in the information seeking process. Just as the therapist has good listening skills, empathy, and seeks to empower the client to move forward, the reference librarian needs to exhibit similar interpersonal skills to help the patron move forward in their research.

Although Librarianship is not typically listed among the helping professions, I believe that a case can be made for its inclusion. If a helping profession is one "that nurtures the growth of or addresses the problems of a person's physical, psychological, intellectual, emotional or spiritual well-being" (Wicktionary.org), I propose in this essay that librarianship can stand alongside nursing, psychological counseling, social work, education, and ministry as a helping profession. Further, when compared to a mental health therapist as a professional who provides "services to individuals seeking guidance and assistance in addressing their social, emotional, and mental needs" (OnlineCounseling-Programs.com), then we can see librarians operating as "information therapists" in the context of the information seeking process.

As the world we serve changes, we must regularly revisit our role as librarians (Horley, 1999; Tyckoson, 2016), specifically if librarianship is envisioned as a helping profession. Academic librarians who serve institutions of Christian higher education today must think about the cultural context we find ourselves in, our role in academia, and the greater mission of the church in the world. How can we best support our constituents and further the goals of our profession and parent institutions? Information overload—a term popularized by Alvin Toffler in his book, Future Shock (1970)—is a very real problem that has only grown since its introduction to the popular lexicon. It has contributed to what Richard Saul Wurman first calls information anxiety which is "produced by the ever-widening gap between what we understand and what we think we should understand" (2001, p. 14). Both terms continue to be topics of discussion and study today. Over the years people have learned to cope with this in various ways—not all positive. Increasingly, librarians see the effect of information anxiety on students who are learning to engage in the research process. We understand that as information professionals we can have a significant role in helping students to develop healthy thought processes and practices that may alleviate some of this anxiety.

Contributors to Information Anxiety

Some contributors to the current climate of information anxiety include social media, a lack of confidence in journalistic integrity, the myriad of choices presented by information abundance, and post-truth relativism.

Social Media

There are many factors that create social media and its myriad uses. As with any medium, the message is influenced not only by the owners, publishers, and distributors of the content, but by the way it is shared and received—by its pathways to us. The evolution of new media formats and the acceptance of new sources and pathways say something about our evolving culture. Many in the developed world see ourselves as prosumers, as capable as the next guy to produce information as well as consume it. In fact, we encourage students to take this role for themselves. Once they gather information, synthesize it and are ready to present it, we would be encouraged to see them take the initiative to use new media to share their new conclusions with their peers and even the world. Think of the efforts to use student research to populate our institutional repositories. It is something to be proud of.

But, as anyone who has been around social media knows, it is also a new challenge for teaching information literacy. The traditional rubrics for evaluating sources need updating to incorporate new information sources.

Facebook is one example. When an article pops into a Facebook feed, we learn to ask how it got there. Is it there because a Friend Likes the sponsor? Or because a Friend that you follow posted it on their own timeline? Did your Friend specifically post it on your timeline to get your attention? We do not necessarily need to understand Facebook algorithms but an information literate person should be prepared to ask some critical questions. If a "friendly" post is shared by an actual friend (in real life and virtual), is this friend an expert on the topic? Are they likely to have vetted the information and its source? Can you vet the source yourself to confidently use the facts reported in the article before passing it along as true?

Most of us do not have time to read all news that is published, posted, or broadcasted. I confess that I have relied on my social media communities to alert me about what is worth looking into. But as an information professional, I realize that headlines can be misleading. I take time to fact check, corroborate stories with other news sources and do some research on the reporting organization to tell me more about a source that is new to me. I look at their parent or partner organization(s), who follows them and who quotes the source (finds them reputable). These factors will lead me to make judgments about potential biases and conclusions about the veracity of their claims.

What about ads that are placed in your Facebook feed by paying sponsors? Why do some stories appear in your feed and not others? As we know, complex algorithms are employed to deliver information that seems relevant to you. It is a good thing. If they did not filter information based on your demographic data (as reported "about" you in your profile), your circle of friends, your "likes" and comments, you would see an endless list of posts that you really do not care about. Facebook, like television, needs you to be happy so they can deliver your eyeballs to advertisers. But Facebook can go beyond the Nielsen ratings of television in terms of targeting content to a specific audience. Nielsen monitors and analyzes demographics—age, gender, race, socioeconomics, and location. Facebook (and other social media) gathers information about your personality, values, opinions, attitudes, interests, and lifestyle based upon your participation. The science of predictive analytics and trust prediction is applied accordingly.

Even innocuous search engines can steer a researcher in a direction they might not expect because of its programming. How a search engine makes suggestions or autocompletes a search is based on such analytics (Badke, 2018; Cadwalladr, 2016; Chen, Jeon, & Kim, 2014; Noble, 2017; Olmstead, Mitchell, & Rosenstiel, 2011b, 2011a). Technology may seem sterile, but it is not neutral.

Journalistic Integrity

Journalists see themselves as playing a significant role in democracy. They hold that an informed public keeps those in power accountable to the values of the Constitution. So long as journalists hold to their code of ethics, the public tends to trust them. Particularly in the days of print news, a common belief was that if it is in print, it must be true. However, one might recall reading about the prevalence of yellow journalism in the 1890s. Sensationalism sells papers. News is big business and advertisements, sponsors, and subscribers will have an effect—directly or indirectly—on what is reported and how it is presented. But beyond that, even long-standing reputable news organizations have been found to engage in sloppy journalism.

This alone is reason to believe that criticism of mainstream news sources may have some credence. The current president famously criticizes and discredits the mainstream news. Today popular terms like "fake news" and "alternative facts" are used to cast doubt on any story that is in conflict with one's presumptions. Trust in American news sources is dwindling. A 2016 Pew research report shows that a relatively small percentage of Americans hold a lot of trust in professional news sources: 18% national; 22% local (Mitchell, Gottfried, Barthel, & Shearer, 2016). Another Pew study revealed that 23% of those surveyed admitted to sharing a made-up news story—either knowingly or not—with others (Barthel, Mitchell, & Holcomb, 2016).

Another aspect of the current journalistic environment is the diversity of voices and perspectives that are now being seen in the public domain. These "new" ideas may not have ever occurred to the mainstream population before new media allowed them to be shared with our "local" virtual communities. These new perspectives give voice to many who felt that they had no voice in the mainstream. More people are recognizing that fresh perspectives off the beaten path have validity and veracity and that there are many ways to look at the truth. But are resource evaluation rubrics being stretched to include alternative truths in the name of diversity and cultural tolerance (Levinovitz, 2017)?

The Role of Librarians

The American Library Association's (ALA) Freedom to Read Statement (2006, July 26) charges librarians to protect the freedom to read as an issue closely tied to the First Amendment and essential to democracy. It states that "publishers and librarians have a profound responsibility to give validity to that freedom to read by making it possible for the readers to choose freely from a variety of offerings" (para. 6). Furthermore, "It would conflict with the public interest for [librarians] to establish their own political, moral, or aesthetic views as a standard for determining what should be published or circulated" (para. 11). Librarians have been taught to value neutrality in order to encourage discovery of truth where ever it may be found. Although librarians have personal biases, we are taught to deny them in professional application.

Within this document, however, are the implied "political, moral, or aesthetic views" (American Library Association [ALA], 2006, para. 11) of the ALA and the Association of American Publishers. For example, librarians are to deny their own biases in favor of the values of the professional association. Further, Critical Librarianship calls librarians to a more activist role—"to be transformative, empowering, and a direct challenge to power and privilege" (Garcia, 2015, para. 1). This may be admirable and noble, but it is not neutral (ALA, 2006; Farkas, 2017; Garcia, 2015; Schlesselman-Tarango, 2017). So, how do we reconcile professional neutrality with our values?

We generally believe that it is in the best interest of the community to encourage users to consider a broader range of perspectives rather than rely on preformed conclusions to solve problems or make sense of the world. Librarians take responsibility to give users (often undergraduate students) the freedom to discover outlier non-mainstream viewpoints regardless of the potential incongruences with prior beliefs. In fact, librarians might take these risks especially *because* they could cause cognitive dissonance among our impressionable students, which we hope will spur intellectual growth. Is it any different for librarians of faith supporting faith-based institutions?

What Is Truth?

There is a growing acceptance of subjective truth in our society. Science historian, James Burke (1986), explains in the British documentary television series and book by the same name, *The Day the Universe Changed*, "science seeks the truth defined by the contemporary structure" (p. 308). Burke (1986) also states that "[p]olitical motivations of scientific research and discovery can affect its meaning" (p. 326). Burke (1986) uses Post-World War I Germany as a case in point when he states that "[e]xact science could never be objective. Causality was dangerous and destructive. It had failed Germany" (p. 333). Burke (1986) concludes his argument by stating that, "science ... is not objective or impartial, since every observation it makes of nature is impregnated with theory" (p. 336) and subsequently concluding that truth is relative. Relativism is based on values such as diversity, coexistence, and tolerance, all highly esteemed in American culture.

Philosophically speaking, truth has been in question from the beginning of human history in the Garden of Eden. It is probably the most popular topic discussed, defined, and debated from the earliest recorded philosophers to contemporary thinkers.

Truth, of course, is of central importance to the Bible and Christian faith. Jesus was born and came into the world to testify to the truth. But the Truth Incarnate met with opposition himself. When Jesus told Pilate that "everyone on the side of truth listens to me." Pilate retorted, "What is truth?" (John 18:37–38, NLT).

Even among his followers, Jesus experienced firsthand how difficult truth is to accept. After feeding the five thousand he teaches his disciples that he is the bread of life. But this did not fit with what they knew to be true. Bread is for eating. Human flesh is not. How could it be true that everyone has to eat his *body*—his flesh and blood—in order to have eternal life? Many of his disciples said, "This is a hard teaching. Who can accept it?" and many no longer followed him (John 6: 25–70).

Later, there was division among his followers over who Jesus was. Some argued that according to Scripture, "when the Messiah comes, no one will know where he is from." But his followers knew where Jesus was from (or so they thought), so it logically followed that Jesus could not be the Messiah. On the other side of the Jesus identity argument were those who pointed to the evidence of what Jesus had been doing in front of them. What else would the Messiah have to do to prove he was the one they were waiting for (John 7:25–31)?

Jesus told people the truth even though it was hard to hear. Our students will come across information that they find hard to fully understand. This can cause uncertainty and anxiety during the research process. We librarians want to assure them that it is worth continuing the information seeking process in pursuit of truth.

So, what do we mean when we refer to truth in the context of research? Is it something that is discoverable? There are two common theories of truth: correspondence and coherence. Each theory has a distinct answer to this query.

The correspondence theory of truth relates to facts and data that correspond to consensual reality. Examples include claims such as I am listening to music, it is daytime, and twenty-seven people responded to my survey. These claims can be found to be true or false based on independent observation. And, in the digital age, we can easily find "proof" of reality in various formats such as digital photos, videos, sound recordings, data, statistics, as well as other irrefutably scientific evidence in abundance. Yet, we know that these things can be faked, edited, modified, enhanced, manipulated, shown from different distances, angles, and lighting. Even unedited representations are perceived differently by different people. This is evident in popular internet controversies—Is the dress blue or gold? Is the girl's name Yanni or Laurel? Close calls in professional sport contests are regularly challenged, implementing reviews of different camera angles to overturn an official's decision that can result in fairly significant changes in the final outcomes.

Then add alternative facts, fake news and conspiracy theories to the mix. We are being told that things are not really what they seem. And fact checking services cannot be trusted to present an unbiased truth. These mixed messages make for great drama but not for confident information gathering for research. The correspondence theory of truth is only as reliable as our agreed upon perceptions of reality.

The coherence theory of truth requires more than reporting of facts and data but includes analysis and interpretation. For example, in the aforementioned survey, I would go beyond reporting the number of respondents and determine a course of action based upon my interpretation of the results and/or make a judgment about the methodology used.

For the purpose of this essay, we will focus on the coherence theory of truth as it fits with the ACRL *Framework for Information Literacy for Higher Education* (ACRL, 2015). Information literate people should be able to recognize appropriate expertise and credibility, including different types of authority, and to evaluate sources based on context. Only then will the information seeker be able to determine whether any given statement fits with all of the other claims they believe to be true or their presuppositions. If the new information fits with what they already "know" (and is relevant), it can be incorporated it into their research findings. No problem.

But newly discovered truth claims can also call into question what they already "know" (as in the biblical examples mentioned above). By the time they reach college age, most students have experienced plenty of such challenges. As children we learn new things every day and some can be traumatic. I still remember seeing my uncle leaving presents under the Christmas tree after my sister and I were supposed to be in bed. Was he pretending to be Santa Claus? He didn't even try to dress the part. I could have rejected the notion that Uncle Dale was Santa Claus because I knew the difference between them. I had a choice to make. I could have continued to believe in Santa Claus but that would mean that Uncle Dale was not to be trusted. (Why would someone pretend to be Santa Claus?) But my nine-year-old brain was unable to accept that my uncle, who was working two jobs to provide for his sister's kids, was untrustworthy. I decided that it was more likely that he just was not very good at playing a game (because he got caught) that all adults had been playing my whole life.

We make decisions to make sense of the world. This is true in the research process. As librarians, we help provide our students with an overabundance of reputable information sources to choose from and we hope to teach them to differentiate between them. But as we know, this abundance is not as wonderful as we might think. It takes a toll on our mental capacities. Much has been written about the problem of having too many choices (Schwartz, 2005) and how we make decisions in the digital information age (Baron, 2007; Gladwell, 2007; Jones, 2010; Manheim, 2014; Pescosolido, 1992; Schwartz, 2005; Weinberger, 2007). Simply being faced with the mountain of information available on any given subject causes information anxiety, and then when sifting through it reveals a plethora of conflicting information it is too much for the human brain to process. This is why librarians need to see ourselves as information therapists.

Effects on Research

Although students are encouraged to use peer reviewed resources that are available to them in our library's subscription databases, their thinking process can very likely be affected by the popular culture. Further, as we will see, the information search process is wrought with anxiety in general.

Barriers to Research

The information seeking process is complicated. Research takes time. People often do not take the time to do it justice. Barry Schwartz (2005) writes in *The Paradox of Choice* about two kinds of choosers of information. The maximizer will not rest until the best possible option is found. This requires looking into all possible options and comparing all variables of what constitutes the "best" (Schwartz, 2005). Satisficers are those who have certain criteria in mind and are on a quest to fill the criteria as reasonably as possible (Schwartz, 2005). They consider the time involved in choosing among all of the options and decide on something that fits the criteria whether or not something better is out there (Schwartz, 2005). They have made a decision and will stick with it for peace of mind (Schwartz, 2005).

While satisficing works for buying a pair of jeans or finding a suitable apartment, it may not be adequate to pursue a research project. Manheim (2014) observes that in a review of literature, satisficing has been identified as one of the pathologies of information "non-seeking" behavior, along with avoiding and filtering. She ultimately argues, however, that it might not be all bad in terms of understanding information seeking behavior holistically (Manheim, 2014).

I was introduced to the concept of satisficing in the first semester of my Library and Information Science program. A wise professor taught her eager information loving students that we cannot use all of the information relevant to any information problem. We eventually must stop gathering and start to analyze, synthesize, and make sense of it. It was a valuable lesson that provided me with the mental and emotional freedom to actually finish the degree.

Avoiding is a coping mechanism often seen in medical information seeking. Studies show that when one is diagnosed with cancer they are likely to ignore information that may be beneficial to their health (Case, Andrews, Johnson, & Allard, 2005). People do not always act rationally when seeking information. Knowing the unknown might be worse for us than not knowing, so we avoid it.

Focusing on seeking medical help to make decisions, Bernice A. Pescosolido (1992) looks at it from a sociological perspective. If we do persist in seeking information that we find uncomfortable to know, we do not necessarily follow a strictly rationality-based decision-making process (Pescosolido, 1992). As social beings, it is in our nature to rely on our social networks to cope with uncertainty and to make decisions about what is right or wrong (Pescosolido, 1992). We use our social networks to help filter information that is worth considering (Pescosolido, 1992). Pescosolido (1992) argues that in this context, relevance is a social concept.

Filtering is fed by our natural desire to avoid pain and reduce emotional tension. Another form of filtering is motivated by the principle of least effort (Zipf, 1949). On the one hand, seeking information is a way to resolve a feeling of uncertainty. On the other hand, we want to minimize the effort required to come to the answers we seek. The principle of least effort "predicts that seekers will minimize the effort required to obtain information, even if it means accepting a lower quality or quantity of information" (Case, 2009).

Inspired in large part by Carol Kuhlthau's work, Bilal and Nahl (2017) collected a series of writings in their work entitled, *Information and Emotion*, which explores the role of emotions in information behavior. This involves our motivations for selecting certain information as well as our assigning value to it. As much as our library systems and services are designed to lead users down a logical path of information seeking, they miss the affective part of the human psyche. Librarians, as fellow human beings, have a much better capacity to read and respond to these cues.

The Information Search Process

Carol Kuhlthau's Information Search Process (ISP) model will serve as the structure and framework for understanding our role as information therapists. It reveals a process in which a person is "seeking meaning in the course of seeking information" (Kuhlthau 2008, p. 67). This six-stage model is based on years of longitudinal studies observing patterns of different types of users in educational and workplace environments. In each stage, Kuhlthau observes cognitive thought process, affective influences, and psychomotor activities that are common to all. She follows users through the process from their perspectives rather than the library systems. This way, we can see what motivates and demotivates information seekers and how we might be able to intervene at appropriate times with appropriate assistance.

For our role as information therapist, it is important to make a diagnosis regarding which stage the user is in. Three domains; cognitive (thoughts), affective (feelings), and psychomotor (actions), will be observed with special interest in the affective/emotional domain of the process. We will look for symptoms that deter effective research behavior and then consider effective intervening strategies.

Kuhlthau's first stage of the ISP is initiation. This is when the information seeker first becomes aware of a lack of knowledge or understanding. The thoughts, actions and feelings that align with Kulthau's first stage are as follows:

- Thoughts—recognizes the need for new information to complete an assignment.
- Actions—thinks more about the topic, discuss it with others, and brainstorm.
- Feelings—apprehension and uncertainty are common.

The second stage of Kuhltahu's ISP is selection. In this stage a general search area, topic, or problem is identified. The following thoughts, actions, and feelings are typically expressed when an individual is in Kulthau's second stage:

- Thoughts—starts to think about how to proceed with the information search.
- Actions—retrieves some information and reformulates queries.
- Feelings—uncertainty often fades and is replaced with a sense of optimism.

In the third stage of Kuhlthau's ISP, information on the topic is gathered and a new personal knowledge is created. The following thoughts, actions, and feelings align with Kulthau's third stage of ISP:

- Thoughts—locates new information and starts to fit it in with their previous understanding of the topic.
- Actions—retrieves new (often inconsistent, incompatible, or incomplete) information.
- Feelings—uncertainty, confusion, and doubt frequently increase and people lose confidence in their abilities. Anxiety is common.

The fourth stage of Kulthau's ISP is entitled formulation. It is when a focused personalized perspective begins to form from the general information gathered in the exploration phase. The following thoughts, actions, and feelings are typically displayed when an individual is in Kulthau's fourth ISP stage:

- Thoughts—starts to evaluate the information that has been gathered.
- Actions—reviews the information gathered so far; chooses a particular focus from within the information already gathered.
- Feelings—uncertainty diminishes as confidence begins to increase.

Kulthau's fifth ISP stage is entitled, "collection." It when information that is pertinent to the focused perspective is gathered. During this phase the following thoughts, actions, and feelings are commonly displayed:

- Thoughts—knows what is needed to support the focus.
- Actions—searches for and collects relevant information.
- Feelings—uncertainty subsides, interest deepens in their personalized topic and they experience greater confidence in their research process.

Search closure is the final stage in Kuhlthau's ISP. At this point, the individual has completed the information search. The thoughts, actions, and feelings that align with this stage are as follows:

- Thoughts—summarizes and report on the information that was found.
- Actions—presents or explains learning to others or in some way put the learning to use.
- Feelings—relief and, depending on the outcome, either satisfaction or disappointment.

Formulation is considered to be the most important stage of the process and often identified as the crucial "zone of intervention." This is when the seeker is most likely to be ready for help when experiencing uncertainty, confusion, doubt, and anxiety.

Levels of Mediation

However, Kuhlthau (2004a) recommends five levels of mediation for librarians to assume along the entire ISP with strategies for appropriate intervention at each stage. These levels of mediation include (1) Organization, (2) Locator, (3) Identifier, (4) Advisor, and (5) Counselor. The first level of mediation is the organization of the library systems including cataloging and the design of self-service interfaces. This level underlies the entire set of library services but does not require any direct human interaction with users. Levels two through four are familiar library reference roles that each serve different information needs along the search process. They are source-based, aimed at providing the appropriate resources for the information problems common to many users at a given time.

These go hand in hand with five levels of library education which, for her purposes, are defined as "any planned instruction related to the use of sources found in a library as well as the use of information in the broader context of learning." (Kuhlthau, 2004a, p. 120). The levels of education include 1) Organizer, 2) Instructor, 3) Lecturer, 4) Tutor, and 5) Counselor. Similar to the levels of mediation, the first level does not require intervention. Levels two, three, and four correspond to traditional library instruction activities, such as single session library orientations and strategic use of a complex set of information resources.

In both mediation and education, the first level of intervention requires no intervention. Levels two through four correspond to familiar source-based library reference and instruction services that each address different information needs within the search process. They focus on providing the appropriate resources for the information problems common to many users at a given time. Only the fifth, counselor role, provides a holistic process-based intervention over time.

The counselor "provides process intervention that accommodates the user's thoughts, actions, and feelings in each stage of the information search process" (Kuhlthau, 2004a, p. 124). Providing encouragement and support is important as it goes beyond finding the right sources to address the more complex activities of interpreting, seeking meaning, and gaining understanding.

> At the counselor level the two forms of intervention, mediation and education, merge into one service of guidance. The counselor's challenge is to provide a new kind of intervention that is becoming essential in the technological information age. The vast increase in the amount of information calls for intervention into the process of information seeking that leads to meaning. The process of information seeking with the object of accomplishing a meaningful task need not require access to all of the information relevant to the topic but only to that which pertains to the particular focus the person has formulated. The focus formed in the early stages of the ISP enables choices of what is relevant, pertinent, and enough to accomplish the task in the later stages. The counselor guides and supports the user, offering encouragement, strategies, depth, format, and redefinition through exploration and formulation in preparation for collection and presentation. (Kuhlthau, 2004a, p. 126).

Zones of Intervention

From the information user's perspective, Kuhlthau (2004a) identifies five "zones of intervention" during the ISP as areas in which the user can benefit from a mediator's advice and assistance. Each information task or problem will fall into one of these five zones (Z1–Z5). The librarian must interview the user to correctly diagnose which zone the problem fits into in order to apply appropriate intervention strategies. "The first few minutes of the interview are crucial for determining the zone of intervention. Based on professional experience and theory, the librarian makes a diagnosis as to whether the problem is a source problem or process problem" (Kuhlthau, 2004a, p. 131).

The zones of intervention that users may cross through in the ISP correspond with the appropriate roles that librarians may assume according to the five levels of mediation and education. Zones of intervention range in complexity beginning with self-service (no intervention needed) in zone 1 to focusing on a single source for Z2, a group of sources in Z3, and advising on a sequence of sources in Z4. All of these call for traditional source-based librarian interventions.

Kuhlthau (2004a) outlines symptoms of these zones and specific professional skills and services that would be useful in each. By and large, she concludes that librarians have done well in addressing zones 1 through 4 over the years. Classification systems, customized pathfinders, LibGuides, and video tutorials apply to zone 1 (Kuhlthau, 2004a). Library tours, single session workshops, basic group bibliographic instruction, and individual consultation appointments focused on using sources sequentially are examples of successful intervention techniques routinely used to address zones 2 through 4 (Kuhlthau, 2004a).

In zone 5, however, librarians enter into new intervention territory as counselors. It is because of the proliferation of information available, particularly in the digital environment, that users are likely to become overwhelmed, confused, and uncertain as they seek meaning in the information search process. The problem of information overload and information anxiety has been well documented since Alvin Toffler's *Future Shock* (1970) and Richard Saul Wurman's *Information Anxiety 2* (2001). The current post-truth, fake news, alternative facts environment adds another anxiety-producing layer to the information search process.

Within the academic library context, college students have been found to experience what is called "library anxiety" (Mellon, 1986). Library anxiety has to do with the users' feelings of inadequacy in navigating and using library resources in comparison to others. As Erin L. McAfee reports (2018), the biggest problem identified in library anxiety studies is that student users perceive librarians as intimidating and aloof. This perception may simply be imagined, but librarians may, in fact, contribute to this unapproachable or inhospitable perception due to their own feelings of inadequacy. McAfee (2018) concludes that shame and guilt are the basic causes of library anxiety. For example, we know that procrastination is a common problem among college students, and it is frustrating to try to meet the resulting desperate information needs. Users feel guilty for not starting their research earlier and ashamed to ask questions exposing what they do not know. Librarians feel inadequate because we cannot help these users as we know we could (under different circumstances) and because we know that we are contributing to a negative perception of librarians. But since these feelings are difficult to identify, they continue feed on each other and perpetuate library anxiety.

The counselor's role in the Z5 intervention is strongly associated with the principle of uncertainty—"a cognitive state that commonly causes affective symptoms of anxiety and lack of confidence" (Kuhlthau, 2004b, p. 3). The librarian-counselor learns to recognize these symptoms by listening for clues of uncertainty in the seeker's vague descriptions of their topic. They become aware of the subtle indicators of mood in comments and questions that are signs of confusion, frustration, and doubt.

Similarly, McAfee (2018) suggests that librarians should become attuned to the user's perspective, demonstrating genuine understanding and, particularly when it is in the case of anger, leveling or validating the user's feelings. She further recommends confessing one's own feelings of inadequacy to help develop a safe environment to ask questions (McAfee, 2018).

Once the ISP stage is recognized, librarians pursuing a process-based intervention will be able to employ strategies appropriate to encourage users in that stage. Kuhlthau suggest six ways a librarian-counselor may address the negative aspects of the ISP, in no particular order.

The first way a librarian-counselor can address the negative dynamics of an ISP is collaboration. Collaborating with others tends to help the user realize that they are not alone in the search learning process. When librarians collaborate with the user, showing interest in their project is a natural way to engage in the process. We can gain insight into the stage they are in. Collaboration is also a valuable skill for students to take with them to the work environment after leaving the academic institution.

A second way that a librarian-counselor can address negative aspects of the ISP is by continuing. The idea here is to instill in the user that a meaningful understanding of a complex topic takes time and "enough" information. Each zone offers opportunities for counselors to employ strategies to help users recognize where they are in the information search process and offer suggestions for proceeding to the next stage. With proper guidance, students learn that the difficult transition from the exploration stage to formulation is essential to their personal understanding of the topic.

Some users may be quick to settle for information gathered in the early stages without truly understanding the complexity of the topic. Librarian-counselors will be sensitive to clues that point to reasons for the user's reluctance to continue the search process and offer suggestions for proceeding with the particular issue they are confronting.

Here is where librarians may need to help users decide what is "enough" information to make sense of the topic. In today's information abundant world, "maximizers" who are not ready to proceed unless they have exhausted every possible resource may need to be encouraged to "satisfice" (Schwartz, 2005). Librarians can help them recognize when they know enough to formulate a sensible perspective on which to focus.

Another way librarians can address negative aspects of the ISP is by what Kuhlthau calls "choosing." During the ISP patrons make a number of choices. Although choosing may be difficult for some, it helps develop their own perspective and understanding based on their personal interests. At each stage, librarians can guide users in making choices by having them to ask themselves four questions:

- How much time do I have?
- What am I trying to accomplish?
- What do I find personally interesting?
- What information is available to me?

Counselors can help users see their range of choices at each stage of the ISP but some choices are more important than others. In the early stages selecting a topic to determine what is generally relevant is key to moving forward. Later, formulating a focus from the initial results will be necessary to identify what information is pertinent in the final stages of collection. And counselors must remember to respect the user's choices as valid so long as they serve their present information need.

Charting though conceptual mapping techniques is another way librarians can rise to the service of counseling. This is a way that illustrates the ISP for users so it can help them diagnose for themselves the stage they are in. It enables users to acknowledge their feelings and clarify the task before them and helps them understand their part in the ISP. It is also a creative way to organize ideas for the final presentation stage.

Conversing, another way to empower Kuhlthau's counselor, gives the counselor an opportunity to listen to the user and diagnose the stage they are in. This may seem obvious, but the user may be reluctant to engage in conversation or unable to articulate the information problem they are having. Counselors may need to encourage dialogue through invitational exploratory questioning. Counselors may also point out feelings that are common in the patron's current stage.

The counselor may recommend a means of documenting and organizing their thoughts throughout the ISP. Journaling, outlining, free association writing can be useful to enable users to articulate thoughts, identify gaps, and clarify inconsistencies they find along the way. Composing promotes thinking. Composing and Conversation enables the user to focus or formulate a point of view.

In Kuhlthau's model, the counselor's overall purpose is to develop strategies and techniques for enabling the user to apply basic information literacy abilities. This requires guiding the user to recognize their own worldview or presuppositions in order for them to be self-aware of the fact that this will influence their selective remembering of information and judging the significance of ideas encountered that convey meaning for themselves. It will have an impact on their filtering of what is important, pertinent, significant, and salient to formulation of their new perspective. For instance, counselors will encourage summarizing and paraphrasing information as a means of understanding and guide users to value their part in the academic conversation as well as that of others—while guarding against plagiarism.

Kuhlthau's model takes into consideration the affective as well as cognitive and psychomotor domains of the user's experience in seeking information. The mission of Christian higher education incorporates a similar holistic approach to student development but includes a spiritual formation aspect as well.

Students who enroll in a Christian college or university have a deep desire to know God's will for their lives. The institution seeks to help them develop a worldview that will serve them in the continuing quest to do God's will throughout their post-academic career.

With this in mind, we must consider higher stakes than information literacy for life-long learning. We must understand that each assignment is intended to play a part in helping the student integrate faith and learning. Each task can be seen as a piece of the worldview development. Each course is designed to enhance their spiritual formation. As with many students in secular institutions, when a Christian college student comes to the library with an information problem to solve, there very well may be an underlying question that is unarticulated. In faith-based institutions, we take the very important issues of faith, theology, and biblical truth into consideration in every aspect of the educational process—including research.

As Kuhlthau and others agree, people seek information in order to solve a problem and ultimately make sense of the world. Librarians working in secular institutions, which may not align with a mission related to transformative learning, do not necessarily have the call to shape lives, unlike many of their Christian counterparts (Fish, 2017). In the case of many Christian librarians, the principle of "uncertainty" may have eternal ramifications obligating us to see our professional responsibilities as a calling from God.

From studying models of human development such as Piaget's (1932) stages of cognitive development, Kohlberg's (1971) stages of moral development, and James Fowler's (1981) stages of faith we understand that college students may be in a vulnerable place of maturity development on which information seeking will have a dramatic impact. Worldview development decisions will be made in the course of the traditional four-year college career.

Fowler identified six stages of faith on a continuum from imitative childhood faith through a conventional faith (where most people spend their adult lives) to a more independent personalized faith to the universalizing, self-transcending faith of full maturity. M. Scott Peck developed a simplified version that may also be consulted for diagnostic purposes ("Chart of James Fowler's Stages of Faith | psychologycharts.com," n.d.; Fowler, 1981; Hartman, 1990; Peck, 1998).

Besides correctly diagnosing the stage of our users regarding their ISP, we must also be sensitive to their cognitive, moral, and faith development stages. In order to apply a truly holistic approach to intervening in their information needs we must recognize the whole of the individual. It is because of this distinction that I propose that we must be prepared to go beyond the counselor role in Kuhlthau's model to "Information Therapist" when necessary.

Using Kuhlthau's ISP model, focusing on the counselor role for intervention, information therapists also listen for clues of maturity and readiness to engage in the learning process. We can attempt to challenge students to challenge their presuppositions but understand that they may not be able to make a change in thinking without inner turmoil. This inner turmoil, if connected to faith, may prevent them from wanting to continue with dialogue on the subject. Their community of faith and perhaps even their eternal lives may be at stake. It may be as dramatic in their own experience as changing religious convictions from Muslim to Christian with all of the cultural identity and familial ties associated with that. We cannot take these moments lightly. We want to gently guide them toward maturity in Christ with each encounter recognizing that they may be the "weak brother or sister" (1 Corinthians 8:9–13) or one in need of "having the way of God explained more adequately" (Acts 18:18–28).

In this way, we might be more in need of being equipped with pastoral counseling skills. Christian librarians often discuss ways to integrate faith and librarianship to address student information needs at a deeper level. Ken Badley and Jane Scott (2011) promote the idea that the fruits of the Spirit (Galatians 5:22) could be called upon to equip students to reduce research anxiety. Nancy Warwick (2017) approaches the issue from a broader perspective. She argues that Christian librarians should view our roles in terms of discipleship. She points out that "our impact on our community is probably greater than any other profession. As librarians, we are charged with building a collaborative learning community that meets the information of both today and the future" (Warwick, 2017, p. 182). "God centered people seek to be sensitive to the needs of others while exhibiting genuine care. Sincere listening helps to build one another up. Ideally, even the vulnerable should thrive, instead of merely survive, in a remarkable community" (Warwick, 2017, p. 185).

Taking an even broader view, the late Christian philosopher and author of *All Truth Is God's Truth* (Holmes, 1983), Arthur Holmes, communicated the idea of the integration of faith and learning in many academic disciplines. In regards to librarianship, he asserted that the library should have a significant part in developing a "climate of faith and learning" in the Christian College (Holmes, 1995, p. 1). Librarians must be able to articulate what the integration of faith and librarianship means in practice. All information is interdisciplinary and we must develop a Christian worldview understanding everything. As with academic disciplines, librarians must examine the values and understand the foundational assumptions of our profession and recognize how they may conflict with Christian theology (Holmes, 1995, p. 3). Finally, librarians, like classroom teachers, have the opportunity to mentor our student's moral as well as their intellectual development (Holmes, 1995, p. 5).

For Christian academic librarians to contribute to the creation of a climate of faith and learning we must understand our role in the educational process. The Christian college curriculum is designed to integrate faith and learning into a holistic experience which incorporates spiritual formation as well as intellectual development. Librarians can support the curriculum well when they understand its intended outcome. Although our colleges differ, for our discussion, we may turn to the Council of Christian Colleges and Universities for a general agreement on a definition of a Christian higher education. We all intend to graduate students who value academic research and can relate it to biblical truth (Council of Christian Colleges and Universities, 2016).

Conclusion

In the current climate of information overload, post-truth, fake news, and ever-evolving digital information formats, a new level of librarianship is needed to address the types of information anxiety this brings on our constituents. An information therapist goes beyond basic reference interviewing skills to employ greater sensitivity to the emotional aspects that influence the information search process. They recognize the stage of the seeker by listening intently and being attentive to even unarticulated communication cues and recognize emotional and irrational barriers to healthy research behaviors. They see their role in relationship to the overall information seeking process in the context of the outcome of the assignment or problem presented as well as the ultimate goals of the parent institution. They understand that teaching information literacy to prepare students for lifelong learning requires more than the ability to accurately evaluate sources. It requires the courage to view different and conflicting perspectives with integrity and the ability to recognize their own presuppositions and how they may influence their information seeking behavior. An information therapist seeks to equip students to seek the truth by guiding them through the uncertainty and the fear of the unknown. They encourage students to grapple with differing perspectives with humility to give them confidence that they can do so in the future, regardless of how this information is presented.

NOTE

1. Thanks to the administration of Hope International University for sabbatical release time and to the Council for Christian Colleges and University Scholars Retreat grant, funded by the Issachar Fund, for the resources to complete this project.

REFERENCES

American Library Association. (2006, July 26). The freedom to read statement. Retrieved from http://www.ala.org/advocacy/intfreedom/freedomreadstatement

Association of College & Research Libraries. (2015, February 9). *Framework for Information Literacy for Higher Education.* Retrieved from http://www.ala.org/acrl/standards/ilframework.
Association of College & Research Libraries. (2015, May 19). Keeping up with.... Critical librarianship. Retrieved from http://www.ala.org/acrl/publications/keeping_up_with/critlib.
Badke, W. (2018, February). Search tips from a seasoned searcher. Retrieved from http://www.infotoday.com/OnlineSearcher/Articles/InfoLit-Land/Search-Tips-From-a-Seasoned-Searcher-123091.shtml.
Badley, K., & Scott, J. (2011). Fruitful research: A Biblical perspective on the affective dimension of research. *The Christian Librarian, 54*(2). Retrieved from http://digitalcommons.georgefox.edu/tcl/vol54/iss2/3.
Baron, J. (2007). *Thinking and deciding* (4th ed.). Cambridge: Cambridge University Press.
Barthel, M., Mitchell, A., & Holcomb, J. (2016, Dec. 15). *Many Americans believe fake news is sowing confusion.* Pew Research Center. Retrieved from http://www.journalism.org/2016/12/15/many-americans-believe-fake-news-is-sowing-confusion/.
Bilal, D., & Nahl, D. (Eds.). (2007). *Information and emotion: The emergent affective paradigm in information behavior research and theory.* Medford, NJ: Information Today.
Burke, J. (1985). *The day the universe changed* (1st American ed.). Boston: Little, Brown.
Cadwalladr, C. (2016, December 4). Google, democracy and the truth about internet search. *The Guardian.* Retrieved from https://www.theguardian.com/technology/2016/dec/04/google-democracy-truth-internet-search-facebook.
Case, D. O., Andrews, J. E., Johnson, J. D., & Allard, S. L. (2005). Avoiding versus seeking: The relationship of information seeking to avoidance, blunting, coping, dissonance, and related concepts. *Journal of the Medical Library Association, 93*(3), 353–362. Retrieved from https://library.hiu.edu:2206/docview/203518629?OpenUrlRefId=info:xri/sid:wcdiscovery&accountid=41006.
Case, D. O. (2009). Principle of least effort. In K. E. Fisher (Ed.), *Theories of information behavior* (3d ed.). Medford, NJ: Information Today.
Chart of James Fowler's Stages of Faith. (n.d.).| psychologycharts.com. Retrieved February 4, 2018, from http://www.psychologycharts.com/james-fowler-stages-of-faith.html.
Chen, Y., Jeon, G. Y., & Kim, Y. (2014). A day without a search engine: an experimental study of online and offline searches. *Experimental Economics, 17*(4), 512–536. Retrieved from http://library.hiu.edu:2097/10.1007/s10683-013-9381-9.
Council of Christian Colleges and Universities. (2016, July 26). About: Our work and mission. Retrieved from https://www.cccu.org/about/.
Counseling vs. Therapy vs. Psychology—What's the difference? (n.d.). [Education]. Retrieved April 25, 2018, from https://onlinecounselingprograms.com/resources/helping-professions/.
Farkas, M. (2017, January 3). Never neutral: Critical librarianship and technology. Retrieved from https://americanlibrariesmagazine.org/2017/01/03/never-neutral-critlib-technology/.
Fish, S. (2017, January 17). Citizen formation is not our job. *The Chronicle of Higher Education.* Retrieved from http://www.chronicle.com/article/Citizen-Formation-Is-Not-Our/238913.
Fowler, J. W. (1981). *Stages of faith: The psychology of human development and the quest for meaning* (1st ed.). San Francisco: HarperCollins College Division.
Garcia, K. (2015, June 19). Keeping up with ... critical librarianship. Retrieved from http://www.ala.org/acrl/publications/keeping_up_with/critlib.
Gladwell, M. (2007). *Blink.* New York: Back Bay Books.
Hartman, E. M. (1990). *An introduction to James Fowler's faith development theory* (Unpublished thesis). Emmanuel School of Religion, Johnson City, Tennessee.
Helping profession. (n.d.). *Wikitionary.org.* Retrieved from https://en.wiktionary.org/wiki/helping_profession.
Holmes, A. F. (1983). *All truth is God's truth.* Downers Grove, IL: InterVarsity Press.
Holmes, A. F. (1995). Faith, learning & libraries (pp. 1–6). Presented at the CCCU New Faculty Workshop, unpublished.
Holtzen, W. C. (2018, April 20). Truth.
Horley, N. (1999). Nick Horley looks at changing perceptions: How librarians understood their professional purpose and values between 1960–1997. *Christian Librarian, 23.*
Jones, W. (2010). *Keeping found things found: The study and practice of personal information management.* Burlington, VT: Morgan Kaufmann. Retrieved from http://site.ebrary.com/lib/alltitles/docDetail.action?docID=10206107.
Kohlberg, L. (1971). *Stages of moral development as a basis for moral education.* Cambridge: Center for Moral Education, Harvard University.
Kuhlthau, C. C. (2008). From information to meaning: Confronting challenges of the twenty-first century. *Libri: International Journal of Libraries & Information Services, 58*(2), 66–73.
Kuhlthau, C. C. (2004a). *Seeking meaning: A process approach to library and information services* (2d ed.). Westport, CT: Libraries Unlimited.
Kuhlthau, C. C. (2004b). *Zones of intervention in the Information Search Process: Vital roles for librarians.* PowerPoint presented at the Library Orientation Exchange Conference, Ypsilanti, MI. Retrieved from http://wp.comminfo.rutgers.edu/ckuhlthau/presentations-lectures/.

Levinovitz, A. J. (2017). It's not all relative: Can a devotion to cultural tolerance lead to the triumph of alternative facts? *The Chronicle of Higher Education*. Retrieved from http://undefined/docview/1883624245/abstract/C73F8AE1B34E402FPQ/1.

Manheim, L. (2014). Information non-seeking behavior. In *Proceedings of ISIC, the Information Behaviour Conference, Leeds* (Vol. 19). Retrieved from http://InformationR.net/ir/19–4/isic/isic18.html.

McAfee, E. L. (2018). Shame: The emotional basis of library anxiety. *College & Research Libraries*, 79(2). https://doi.org/10.5860/crl.79.2.237.

Mitchell, A., Gottfried, J., Barthel, M., & Shearer, E. (2016, July 7). *The modern news consumer*. Pew Research Center. Retrieved from http://www.journalism.org/2016/07/07/the-modern-news-consumer/.

Noble, S. U. (2017). Google and the misinformed public. *The Chronicle of Higher Education; Washington*. Retrieved from https://library.hiu.edu:2206/docview/1867003369/abstract/B9CFC2CE84474DF4PQ/17.

Olmstead, K., Mitchell, A., & Rosenstiel, T. (2011, May 9). *Google drives most users*. Pew Research Center. Retrieved from http://www.journalism.org/2011/05/09/google-drives-most-users/.

Olmstead, K., Mitchell, A., & Rosenstiel, T. (2011, May 9). *Google: Parasite or provider?* Pew Research Center. Retrieved from http://www.journalism.org/2011/05/09/google-parasite-or-provider/.

Peck, M. S. (1998). *The different drum: Community making and peace* (2d Touchstone ed.). New York: Touchstone.

Pescosolido, B. A. (1992). Beyond rational choice: The social dynamics of how people seek help. *American Journal of Sociology*, 97(4), 1096–1138. Retrieved from http://www.jstor.org/stable/2781508.

Piaget, J. (1932). *The moral judgement of a child*. London: Kegan Paul, Trench, Trubner.

Schlesselman-Tarango, G. (2017). Critical librarianship in a post-truth age. SCELCapalooza 2017. Retrieved from http://scholarworks.lib.csusb.edu/library-publications/36.

Schwartz, B. (2005). *The paradox of choice: Why more is less* (1st Harper Perennial ed.). New York: HarperCollins.

Steele, L. (2017, April 6). Therapy as a term applied to library reference work.

Toffler, A. (1970). *Future shock*. New York: Random House.

Tyckoson, D. A. (2016). History and functions of reference service. In L. Smith & M. Wong (Eds.), *Reference and information services: An introduction* (5th ed.).

Warwick, N. (2017). Librarians as disciples and disciple-makers. *The Christian Librarian*, 60(2). Retrieved from http://digitalcommons.georgefox.edu/tcl/vol60/iss2/8.

Weinberger, D. (2007). *Everything is miscellaneous: The power of the new digital disorder*. New York: Times Books.

Wurman, R. S., Leifer, L., Sume, D., & Whitehouse, K. (2001). *Information anxiety 2*. Indianapolis: Que.

Zipf, G. K. (1949). *Human behavior and the principle of least effort: An introduction to human ecology*. Cambridge, MA: Addison-Wesley.

Holy Listening in Reference Work
A Sacred Aspect of the Christian Librarian's Calling

Cynthia Strong

Abstract

Along with all Christians, I live out a vocation—both a general and a missional calling. More specifically, as a Christian who is a librarian, my missional calling is to serve my patrons. In my experience, the best way that I can fulfill this service is by listening. As Dietrich Bonhoeffer (1954) writes in *Life Together*, "[t]he first service one owes to others in the community involves listening to them" (p. 97). Many pastors and spiritual directors write on the practice and importance of listening for the work they perform. The listening they do is shaped by their faith, as well as their professional practice. A number of librarians (Christian or not), write about the intersection of listening with their work. There is scant literature, on how a Christian librarian's faith and calling shape our listening as librarians. In this essay, I will suggest a new model for reference work with patrons at a Christian university. By examining literature from librarianship and from two Christian helping professions, I will pose a model for holy listening as a Christian librarian. I am particularly addressing librarians who are employed at Christian universities, where our faith shapes and informs the work we do as reference librarians, but the ideas presented here can also apply to the work of any librarian who is a Christian. Examples gleaned from my practice as an academic librarian are provided.

Introduction

"Let everyone be quick to listen."—James 1:19

"Encourage one another and build up each other."—1 Thessalonians 5:11

Beth[1] walked in the door of my office, as she had many times before. She entered tentatively, unsure of herself—not unusual for a doctoral student at the end of her first year. I welcomed her back to this space, a safe space that she visited often during her initial year of study. The lighting and the placement of a comfortable chair were intentionally arranged to provide a warm, barrier-free setting. Beth and I sat face to face. As she settled in, I asked her some open-ended questions. I used key non-verbal cues to express my continuing interest in her research (Jennerich, 1980; Reference and Adult Services Division [RASD], 1996, 2.2 & 2.4). I also took notes, while making sure that I maintained regular eye contact (Jennerich, 1980; RASD, 1996, 1.3 & 2.2). I smiled frequently. I mentally prayed and asked God to be with me during the interaction. Beth's voice was thick with tiredness. She started to cry as she described her time spent in the PhD program and the crushing emotional nature of doctoral work. I listened to the details of her journey, including her thoughts about possibly dropping out of the program.

Every summer, the doctoral faculty at Seattle Pacific University ask me to teach a one-hour session for new doctoral students, to introduce them to some of the library resources. At the end of those all-too-brief sessions, I gather a list of email addresses from the students and then ask them to arrange a meeting with me for a more in-depth reference interview about their research interests. This is how I first became acquainted with Beth. Over the course of Beth's visits that followed her first reference interview, our times together became more personalized. In addition to assisting her with the particular topic of her research, we also came to see each other through the eyes of our mutual faith.

During the visit described above, I eventually set my pad of paper and pen aside and leaned forward to listen more intently to Beth. Before she left my office that day, I asked if I could pray with her. Beth would share that the time I spent listening and praying with her during that dark hour played a part in her continuation in the program. She went on to graduate with her PhD in education. The exchange was a gift to both of us. I offered her the gift of listening, and she offered me the gift of her story (Hart, 1980). It was a holy interaction.

As a Christian, I live out a vocation—both a general and a missional calling (Koskela, 2015). As a librarian, one of the core parts of my job is to serve my patrons by assisting them to develop the skills they need to find, evaluate, and use information (American Library Association [ALA], 2017). And as a Christian who is a librarian, my missional calling is to spend time working closely with patrons to guide them with their research needs while pointing them to God. One of the best ways I can fulfill this service is by listening. As Dietrich Bonhoeffer (1954) wrote in *Life Together*, "the beginning of love for the brethren is learning to listen to them" (p. 97).

Many pastors and spiritual directors have written on the practice and importance of listening in the work they perform. The listening they do is shaped by their faith, as well as their professional practice. Meanwhile, many librarians write about the intersection of listening and reference work, but not through the lens of faith. There is scant literature, on how a Christian librarian's faith and calling shape our listening as librarians. By examining literature from librarianship and from two Christian helping professions, I will pose a model for holy listening as a Christian librarian. I am particularly addressing librarians who are employed at Christian universities, where our faith explicitly shapes and informs the work we do as reference librarians, but the ideas presented here can also apply to the work of any librarian who is a Christian.

Librarians as Listeners

Even a cursory examination of library literature indicates that listening is an essential part of a librarian's skill set. As early as 1876, Samuel Green, Worcester Public Librarian, called for librarians to listen to their patrons. He wrote: "A hearty reception by a sympathizing friend, and the recognition of someone at hand who will listen to inquiries even although he may consider them unimportant, make it easy for such persons to ask questions, and put them at once on home footing" (Green, 1876). Margaret Hutchins (1944) built on the description of a librarian's work when she wrote that listening through to the "end of a patron's speech" is a minimum courtesy that should be offered a patron in a reference interview (p. 22). Hutchins (1944), who was an assistant professor at Columbia University, maintained that not only should reference librarians be physically available, they should also be approachable in an "intellectual and spiritual" way (p. 22). Being approachable intellectually and spiritually involves listening. Listening is an essential part of a reference interview.

Expanding the role of the librarian, David Maxfield (1954), former librarian and associate professor of library science at the University of Illinois Library School, introduced the term "Counselor Librarianship" (p. 2). Maxfield (1954) advocated that counselor librarians should invest in reference interviews that offer more than pieces of information. Rather, reference interactions should include an interview in which the librarian, trained in counseling techniques, would show an interest in the "total individual development" of patrons (Maxfield, 1954, p. 21). Counseling techniques involve listening skills that are necessary for a robust interview process.

Building on Maxfield's (1954) counseling model, Patrick Penland (1970) recommended going beyond merely furnishing information to engaging in an exchange during which "library counseling tries to facilitate human development as an interaction between the individual and his environment" (p. 71). In his work, entitled *Interviewing for Counselor and Reference Librarians*, he posited a new emphasis in librarianship termed "advisory counseling for librarians" (1970, p. 4). As part of the advisory counseling role, Penland (1970) encouraged librarians to use specific counseling skills such as listening and empathy. Penland, and others, apply theories of interpersonal communication, such as Carl Rogers' "Client Centered Therapy," to the work of the reference librarian (1970, p. 33; Bunge, 1999; Radford, 1999; Tibbets, 1974). Penland (1970) proposed that these same skills should be used in an "interview encounter" with library patrons in order to be more "effective in serving the individual patron" (p. 5). He also asserted that library schools should provide more instruction on the interview encounter. His scholarship pushed librarians to focus on the "human relationships of the librarian and his interpersonal communications" rather than "emphasizing the mechanical" (p. 4). Further, Penland (1970) said that librarians should "establish a relationship of frankness ... where the librarian listens carefully to understand what is said." (p. 8). Other scholars (Jennerich & Jennerich, 1976; Klipfel, 2015; Peck, 1975) have sought to apply counseling skills to the reference interview. Peck (1975) wrote: "Many similarities exist between counseling and reference work." More recently, Kevin Klipfel (2015) suggests that employing counseling skills will help librarians to engage authentically with students so as to understand them as unique persons, resulting in an "ideal informational transaction" (p. 27).

In addition to applying counseling skills to librarianship, a few scholars borrow concepts from the "helping relationships" literature and apply them to reference work (Bunge, 1999; Jennerich, 1980; Lukenbill, 1977; Penland, 1976). Bernard Lukenbill (1977) used the work of Naomi Brill, social worker and professor, to reform reference work. Brill (1973), in her book *Working with People: The Helping Process*, wrote about the need for empathy, attentive behavior, and active listening when working with people. Lukenbill (1977) proposed using Brill's ideas to guide librarians in reference work. He went so far as to design a library school course, entitled "Helping Relationship Instructional Unit" (p. 115). As part of the course, he listed five teaching objectives. One of the objectives is "to introduce students to some of the basic helping relationship concepts and skills such as empathy, attentive behavior, active listening, and to help students to apply these skills to the reference process" (p. 116).

In a seminal article, Robert Taylor (1967) described the practice of "question negotiation" and applied it to the patron-librarian interaction. Taylor (1967) asserted that "negotiation of reference questions is one of the most complex acts of human communication" (p. 253). He insisted that trying to figure out what a patron wants is, ultimately, a communication problem.[2]

Also, taking librarianship to a level beyond mechanical aspects, Nancy Maxwell (2005), former library director at Miami Dade College, equates library work with the work of clergy. In her book *Sacred Stacks: The Higher Purpose of Libraries and Librarianship*, she writes about the sacred/spiritual dimension of the work librarians perform and mentions that some see their work as a calling and a way of serving a higher purpose. Maxwell (2005) identifies active listening as a key part of the "higher calling" of librarianship. She shares that some librarians feel called by something or someone they cannot describe. She falls short, however, of naming God as the One who calls.

In 1996, the Reference and Adult Services Division (RASD), a subdivision of the American Library Association (ALA), realized the need for a set of specific guidelines addressing patron-librarian interactions. The RASD (1996) listed five key facets of reference services—Approachability, Interest, Listening/Inquiring, Searching, and Follow-up. With the goal of emphasizing the importance of the reference interview, RASD (1996) developed "Guidelines for Behavioral Performance of Reference and Information Service Providers." The Guidelines state that "the success of the transaction is measured not by the information conveyed, but by the positive or negative impact of the patron-librarian interaction" (RASD, 1996). Three of the five facets include a number of interpersonal communication skills that require listening. For example, to be approachable, the verbal and nonverbal responses of the reference librarian should make it clear that he or she is "available to provide assistance" (RASD, 1996, 1.0). To do this, the Guidelines assert that conversing with patrons is key in setting "the tone for the entire communication process between the librarian and the patron" (RASD, 1996, 1.0). In setting the tone, librarians should be welcoming and help the patron feel comfortable in a situation which may be perceived as intimidating, risky, confusing, and overwhelming" (RASD, 1996, 1.0). In order to listen effectively, the librarian should set up her or his interview space in such a hospitable way that the patron will feel comfortable—as I did with Beth, and with other people who enter my office.

Another facet of the Guidelines (RASD, 1996) articulates the fact that "demonstrating a high degree of interest in the reference transaction" will result in a successful interaction (2.0). The Guidelines recommend librarians should face "the patron when speaking and listening" (RASD, 1996, 2.1). Practicing this indicates that the librarian is focusing "his or her attention on the patron" (RASD, 1996, 2.1). Additionally, the librarian should signal "an understanding of the patron's needs through verbal or non-verbal confirmation, such as nodding of the head or brief comments or questions" (RASD, 1996, 2.4). Again, all of these actions have been important in my interactions with Beth and other students.

The third facet, Listening/Inquiring, is a key aspect of the Guidelines. "The reference interview is the heart of the reference transaction and is crucial to the success of the process.... Strong listening and questioning skills are necessary for a positive interaction" (RASD, 1996, 3.0). Besides asking questions to clarify a patron's information need, librarians are encouraged to communicate "in a receptive, cordial, and encouraging manner" (RASD, 1996, 3.2). Open-ended questioning techniques should be used to guide the patron in expanding the description of their need (RASD, 1996, 3.5).

As the above brief review of academic and professional literature demonstrates, listening is an essential part of effective reference. By adopting the concepts of communication, interpersonal skills in conversation, helping relationships, and counseling skills for librarianship, library scholars designed a stronger model for reference work. The focus of the literature, however, is only on the skill development of the librarian, for the sake of providing a successful reference interaction. The reference interview is described in a transactional and utilitarian way. Even Klipfel (2015), who talks about engaging with students in an authentic way and recognizing them as unique beings, is still suggesting a utilitarian transaction. The ultimate goal posed by the library literature is a successful reference interview, not a relationship.

Beyond Transaction to Relationship

The tenets of my Christian faith and calling push me to go beyond a transactional encounter. Scripture provides models and injunctions in which we see people as unique beings created by God who are deserving of careful listening to their needs. In addition to scripture, many religious writers provide insight on why we should cultivate more in-depth personal interactions. The work of Martin Buber, an influential Austrian-born religious philosopher, is one such writer. His *I–Thou* philosophy, described in his book *I and Thou*, offers a starting place for developing a pathway to move from a transactional interaction to a relationship. Buber (1958) describes an *I–Thou* interaction that points to a non-utilitarian relationship. In our work as Christian librarians, we should see interpersonal relationships with patrons as an "I and Thou" encounter where "the spheres in which the world of relation arises" includes "our life with men" (Buber, 1958, p. 6). "If I face a human being as my *Thou*, and say the primary word *I–Thou* to him, he is not a thing among things" (p. 8). "I do not experience the man to whom I say *Thou*. But I take my stand in relation to him" (p. 9). Buber (1958) is saying that encounters among people can move from being objectified transactions to becoming subjective relationships. In this way, the connection between individuals can become truly authentic.

Even more profoundly, *I–Thou* relationships between human beings point us to the ultimate *I–Thou* relationship that exists between human beings and God. In a Christian context, such an understanding reminds us of the words of Jesus, who stated: "Truly I tell you, just as you did it to one of the least of these who are members of my family, you did it to me" (Matthew 25:40, NRSV).

According to Neil Pembroke (2002), a lecturer in pastoral care, Buber felt that the objectification of people "produces a soul-destroying sense of alienation" (Pembroke, 2002, p. 32). Instead, we should strive for a dialogical relation which engenders a "humanizing presence." Pembroke (2002) writes that Buber's purpose in describing this dialogical philosophy was to show that "in the meeting between persons there is also a meeting with God" (Pembroke, 2002, p. 36). Pembroke (2002) takes Buber's idea of *I–Thou*, in his book *The Art of Listening: Dialogue, Shame, and Pastoral Care,* and applies it to the work of pastoral care. He writes that Buber felt "a genuinely loving presence is one which aims at assisting the other in growing into her potential" (Pembroke, 2002, p. 3). Pembroke (2002) proposes that to be genuinely present we need to adopt Buber's dialogical philosophy when interacting with one another. Therefore, as we "enter into dialogue with the other, I accept her uniqueness and particularity and struggle with her in the release of her potential as a person" (Pembroke, 2002, p. 31).

To enter into an *I–Thou* relationship with our patrons, we must practice the art of listening. By listening in a more profound way, we establish an environment in which genuine dialogue takes place. By resisting a merely instrumental interaction with our patrons, we establish a setting in which we are fully present and listening. In this posture, we are able to listen for the claims our patrons are making and attempt to respond faithfully (Pembroke, 2002). When we listen and respond to our patrons in this way, we confirm them as persons (Pembroke, 2002).

While Buber's *I–Thou* is a helpful place to start to build a fuller model for our reference work as librarians who are Christians, recognizing the presence of the Holy Spirit in our interactions with patrons should also be addressed. With that in mind, I find it useful to turn to literature from the disciplines of Spiritual Direction and Pastoral Care to inform a distinctly Christian model for librarianship.

Spiritual Direction

The practice of listening is discussed in the literature of many of the Christian helping professions. In reading through writings on spiritual direction for example, listening is frequently mentioned (Frykholm, 2011; Fryling, 2009; Guenther, 1992; Hart, 1980; McHugh, 2015; Wolsterstorff, 1994). Spiritual directors consider listening an essential skill or practice for their work. Claire Wolsterstorff (1994) says: "Simply put, spiritual direction is more helpfully called a ministry of listening or accompaniment.... The director listens always, encourages often" (p. 19).

Thomas Hart (1980), writing in his book on the art of Christian listening, recommended: "To listen with an attentive and receptive heart until that person is finished is to bestow a gift of great value" (p. 1). He maintained that "there is probably no service we can render other persons quite as great or important as to be listener and receiver to them in those moments when they need to open their hearts and tell someone their story" (Hart, 1980, p. 1). His book on spiritual direction was written to offer guidance in listening to people who work in myriad positions involving a helping relationship. For example, he wrote: "there are more structured helping relationships, such as students coming to teachers with other than academic concerns, clients going to professional therapists, men and women approaching a priest in the sacrament of reconciliation" (Hart, 1980, p. 2). Unfortunately, librarians are not specifically mentioned. The stated purpose of Hart's (1980) book was to "make people more comfortable with the idea of ministering to others in this way" (p. 2).

Hart's (1980) model of the "helper as sacrament" is particularly apropos in our work as Christian librarians (p. 8). "If the church is sacramental, if human beings, in the Spirit of Jesus, are the sacrament of God's presence and action in the world" then "the encounter is sacramental" (p. 9). "Any helping relationship in the context of Christian faith is a mysterious encounter and God is present and at work in it" (p. 9). According to Hart

(1980), listening and helping are key aspects of spiritual direction. These aspects can readily be applied to Christian librarianship. In fact, some of the same language on librarianship as a helping relationship is used in the library literature (Bunge, 1999; Lukenbill, 1977; Penland, 1970).

Margaret Guenther's (1992) writing, in her book entitled *Holy Listening: The Art of Spiritual Direction*, expands the sacramental encounter. Guenther (1992), an Episcopal priest, describes the interaction between director and directee as a "covenanted relationship" in which "the director has agreed to put himself aside so that his total attention can be focused on the person sitting in the other chair" (p. 3).

These examples, borrowed from spiritual direction, provide the basis for a model of reference work that involves listening in a more personal, sacramental, and holier way than what the standard library literature employs. Guenther (1992), for example, describes spiritual direction as "listening to the story ... as a dialogue and sometimes the listener-director must become active in helping shape the story" (pp. 22–23). It is in this vein that I listened to Beth's vocational story—and helped to shape it—when she shared her situation with me in my office.

Indeed, when performing reference work, it is my role to listen to the stories of those who seek me out for help. As I listen, I am also open and attentive to the presence of the Holy Spirit, who is the mediator who "stands in the centre between my neighbor and myself" (Bonhoeffer, 1948, p. 84). The Holy Spirit is present, prompting me regarding the questions I might ask, in order to help the patron understand their needs, both in reference and in life.

Carmelita

While staffing the reference desk, Carmelita, an undergraduate business major, stopped by to ask for help understanding a passage of a text written by St. Augustine of Hippo. She was reading the text in order to write a paper assigned by a professor who taught a class on "Christian Formation" that all Seattle Pacific University students must take. Since I am not an expert on interpreting Augustine, I suggested that we read through the passage together. After twenty minutes pouring over the passage, Carmelita expressed her thanks and went back to working on her paper. About an hour later, she returned to the desk and inquired whether she could pose another question. With great earnestness and curiosity, she asked me why God forgives people over and over again for the same sin. Carmelita shared her bewilderment as to why God would be so forgiving. A precious conversation ensued about grace, a concept with which she did not seem to be familiar. Listening to Carmelita's profound questions eventually resulted in an ongoing friendship. During her senior year, she visited me a number of times to update me on her job searches. She often shared her fears about her future. In an *I–Thou* posture, I offered her the gift of listening to her story to the end. Carmelita appreciated the time I took to be present with her and to encourage her questions about spiritual and vocational matters.

Pastoral Care

Similar to the literature on spiritual direction, many books and articles have been written on the essential nature of listening when offering pastoral care (Baab, 2014; Hedahl, 2001; Moschella, 2011; Pembroke, 2002; Riain, 2011). Lynne Baab (2014), a Presbyterian clergywoman who writes about the power of listening in ministry, offers a rich model which is applicable to the work of Christian librarians. Much of the language on listening that Baab (2014) uses can be applied to the work that I do as a Christian librarian. For example, she writes that "listening to someone patiently and carefully is a great gift, and compassionate listening communicates love and acceptance" (Baab, 2014, p. 7). She says that Christians "are called to be in the world as Jesus was in the world, so it is worth noting that Jesus was a champion listener" (p. 8). For Baab (2014), the gift of a "listening ear communicates love and grace ... which are qualities found abundantly in Jesus" (p. 9). I especially appreciate the phrase Baab mentions as a guide for her ministry: "holy listening" (p. 9). Baab (2014) borrowed the term "holy listening" from Craig Satterlee, a bishop in the Evangelical Lutheran Church of America. He described holy listening as an endeavor in which one discerns "the presence and activity of God in the joys, struggles, and hopes of ordinary activities" (as cited in Baab, 2014, p.9). Satterlee writes, "From a Christian perspective, holy listening ... takes the incarnation seriously; it dares to believe that, as God was enfleshed in Jesus of Nazareth, so God is embodied in other people and in the things around us" (as cited in Baab, 2014, p.10). For Baab (2014), when we listen, the "Holy Spirit enables us to perceive the presence of Jesus in wildly diverse people and places, and our listening becomes holy" (p. 10).

Amy

Sometimes, faculty colleagues are also my patrons. Amy, a faculty person, is one who reaches out to me often, seeking help with her research. During a recent visit from Amy, we had a holy encounter. As she entered my office, she looked exhausted. I removed my backpack from my worn, comfy patron chair, so she could sit down. I closed the office door, pulled up my chair, and grabbed my pad and pen, ready to take notes as she detailed her research interests. She shared that she had spent several days trying to find research on school counselors working with neuro-diverse students, but to no avail. Part way into Amy's explanation, she started to share about her son, who is on the autistic spectrum, and thus neuro-diverse. She teared up as she expressed her concern that someday, school officials might misinterpret her son's behavior. In light of recent school shootings, she worried that staff at her son's school would misread his behaviors, which could result in him being categorized as a danger to those around him. Amy was concerned about her son's inability to express his frustration and anger in appropriate ways. She feared that his behavior would be perceived as intending something threatening. She sought me out, looking for assistance in finding school counseling literature that suggested productive ways to work with neuro-diverse students in order to help them communicate effectively. What began as an information seeking transaction resulted in a holy encounter as I prayed with her regarding her worries.

Combining Buber's work with the practices of spiritual direction and pastoral care, which help us to see the essential role of the Holy Spirit's prompting, we can now move forward in proposing a new model of reference work for Christian librarians.

Holy Listening/Conclusion

If I see my work as the living out of a calling and ministry, then practicing holy listening with patrons as they share their stories, their struggles, and their hopes for their academic and personal lives, should be paramount. What would it look like to apply the concept of holy listening to the reference work I do as a Christian librarian? What would it look like if I were to listen to my patrons in such a way that I expect both the patron and me to encounter God in the interview?

As I sit with patrons in an *I–Thou* posture, I seek to perceive the presence of the Holy Spirit in each one. I listen for how God is working in their lives, which is evident when they describe their research in passionate ways. Holy listening as a librarian who is a Christian goes beyond the utilitarian goal of merely providing information or a successful reference transaction. Rather, the purpose is to practice listening to the patron in a reference interview because I care for them. The ministry, or call, in my work as a reference librarian who is a Christian is to listen because Jesus, through the mediation of the Holy Spirit, calls us to listen. In the act of listening, I see each patron as a unique creation of God. I listen to them as Jesus would.

Regarding specific practices, engaging in holy listening includes establishing eye contact, smiling, and focusing my full attention on the patron. Doing so expresses genuine concern for them, so that they know that they are loved by God and me (RASD, 1996; Hart, 1980). Holy listening means hearing our patron's story all the way to the end before engaging in a back-and-forth dialogue (Guenther, 1992; Hutchins, 1944; Pembroke, 2002; RASD, 1996, 3.3). Holy listening requires one to ask questions that "cut to the heart of the matter" (Guenther, 1992, p. 24; Taylor, 1967). Holy listening requires one to be prayerfully open to the presence of the Spirit throughout the interaction. Holy listening happens when the librarian uses questioning techniques to encourage the patron and point them to God (Hart, 1980; RASD, 1996; Taylor, 1967). Holy listening is bestowing a gift on my patrons when they share their research stories with me (Hart, 1980).

As I listen to patrons, might I be listening for how God is working in them through their studies? By practicing the art of question negotiation, might they begin to understand the grace that is apparent in the work they are doing? As I engage in holy listening, rather than only focusing on a successful interview, I also can prayerfully discern God's activity in their lives and, if appropriate, invite them to discover where God is with them in their studies (Fryling, 2009).

It is important, however, to be sensitive to where a patron is spiritually. For example, it is not appropriate to engage in a spiritual discussion with a patron who is not open to such a discussion. While sometimes the reference encounter involves explicit discussions of one's faith, at other times, when meeting with patrons, the care and listening I practice offers a more implicit *I–Thou* interaction. For instance, the time I spent with numerous Saudi Arabian students is typically an example of an implicit *I–Thou* relationship. When I meet with Saudi students, I do not usually inquire about their religious beliefs. However, in seeing them as unique creations of God, I still offer holy listening and am attentive to the presence of the Holy Spirit in the meeting. Consequently, I feel that they understand that I care for them—so much so that some of them asked me to be the faculty advisor for the Saudi club on campus.

Another example of reference work where the *I–Thou* relationship was implicit was the help I provided to Josiah, a PhD student from Tanzania. During his five years of doctoral work at SPU, Josiah spent a lot of time talking with me about his research, which addressed the use of traditional tribal music to enculturate Tanzanian children in the norms of their indigenous society. In the course of his reference appointments, Josiah asked me if I would go and visit his village and organize a library in the secondary school.

Initially, I did not agree to go. But over the next year, he persistently and patiently asked me when I was "going to start the library." I kept putting him off with various lame excuses. Mostly, my fear was that, just because I was a trained as a librarian, it did not mean I actually knew how to *set up* a library in a majority world nation. Eventually, I ran out of evasions and was no longer able to say "no" to the prompting of the Holy Spirit. After that, Josiah and I spent much time together, as I listened to his dreams for the secondary school library. It was important for me to listen carefully to his story and his wishes so that I would do what was culturally appropriate and not what I imagined was correct. When I eventually did travel to Tanzania in order to organize the library, I had the chance to spend time with Josiah and his family. This led to an ongoing relationship that is having an impact on many students in Josiah's village—and at my university. This friendship involved an implicit *I–Thou* relationship. I believe that the work we have done together in Josiah's village points to God.

By combining ideas from library literature and RASD Guidelines with theological insights and the practical aspects discussed by spiritual directors and pastoral care scholars, we can begin to describe the idea of holy listening in reference work. Holy listening is engaging with our patrons, not in a transactional way, but in an *I–Thou* way, that recognizes the presence of God in the space and in the person with whom we meet. Holy listening recognizes the sacramental nature of the interaction with our patrons (Hart, 1980, p.9). Holy listening requires showing interest in our patron, not simply for instrumental reasons, but for the purpose of being present to our patrons and recognizing the Holy Spirit's presence in the encounter (Hart, 1980, p. 9; Guenther, 1992; Pembroke, 2002; RASD, 1996). This sort of practice means providing a reference interview where listening is a holy encounter between the patron, the librarian, and God.

Notes

1. All names have been changed.
2. For a more substantive literature review, see Marie L. Radford's (1999) chapter titled "Literature on the Reference Interaction." In M. L. Radford (Ed.), *Literature on the reference transaction: Interpersonal communication in the academic library.*

References

American Library Association. (2017). *Strategic directions*. Chicago. Retrieved from http://www.ala.org/about ala/sites/ala.org.aboutala/ files/content/governance/StrategicPlan/Strategic%20Directions%202017_Update.pdf.
Baab, L. M. (2014). *The power of listening: Building skills for mission and ministry*. Lanham, MD: Rowman & Littlefield.
Bonhoeffer, D. (1948). *The cost of discipleship*. (R. H. Fuller, Trans.). London: SCM Press.
Bonhoeffer, D. (1954). *Life together.* (John W. Doberstein, Trans.). New York: Harper & Brothers.
Brill, N. I. (1973). *Working with people: The helping process*. Philadelphia: Lippincott.
Buber, M. (1958). *I and Thou* (2d ed.). (R. G. Smith, Trans.). New York: Charles Scribner's Sons. (Original work published 1923.)
Bunge, C. A. (1999). Beliefs, attitudes, and values of the reference librarian. *Reference Librarian, 31*(66), 13–24. http://dx.doi.org/10.1300/J120v31n66_05.
Frykholm, A. J. (2011). Holy listening. *Christian Century, 128*(26), 26–29.
Fryling, A. (2009). *Seeking God together: An introduction to group spiritual direction*. Downers Grove, IL: IVP Books.
Green. S. S. (1876). Personal relations between librarians and readers. Retrieved from http://pacificreference.pbworks.com/f/Personal+Relations+Between+Librarians+and+Readers.pdf.
Guenther, M. (1992). *Holy listening: The art of spiritual direction*. Cambridge, MA: Cowley.
Hart, T. N. (1980). *The Art of Christian listening*. Ramsey, NJ: Paulist Press.
Hedahl, S. K. (2001). *Listening ministry: Rethinking pastoral leadership*. Minneapolis: Fortress Press.
Hutchins, M. (1944). *Introduction to reference work*. Chicago: American Library Association.
Jennerich, E. Z. (1980). Before the answer: Evaluating the reference process. *RQ, 19,* 360–366.

Jennerich, E. J., & Jennerich, E. Z. (1976). Teaching the reference interview. *Journal of Education for Librarianship, 17*, 106–111.

Klipfel, K. M. (2015). Authenticity and learning: Implications for reference librarianship and information literacy instruction. *College & Research Libraries, 76*(1), 19–30. http://dx.doi.org/10.5860/crl.76.1.19.

Koskela, D. (2015). *Calling and clarity: Discovering what God wants for your life.* Grand Rapids: William B. Eerdmans.

Lukenbill, W. B. (1977). Teaching helping relationship concepts in the reference process. *Journal of Education for Librarianship, 18, 110–120.*

Maxfield, D. K. (1954). *Counselor librarianship: A new departure.* Retrieved from https://www.ideals.illinois.edu/bitstream/handle/2142/3984/gslisoccasionalpv00000i00038_ocr.txt.

Maxwell, N. K. (2005). *Sacred stacks: The higher purpose of libraries and librarianship.* Washington, D.C.: American Library Association.

McHugh, A. S. (2015). *The listening life: Embracing attentiveness in a world of distraction.* Downers Grove, IL: IVP Books.

Moshella, M. C. (2011, July 26). Deep listening. *Christian Century, 128*(15), 28–30.

Peck, T. P. (1975). Counseling skills applied to reference services. *Reference Quarter, 14*, 233–235.

Pembroke, N. (2002). *The art of listening: Dialogue, shame, and pastoral care.* Grand Rapids: William B. Eerdmans.

Penland, P. B. (1970). *Interviewing for counselor and reference librarians.* Retrieved from ERIC database. (ED049802).

Penland, P. B. (1976). *Librarian as learning consultant.* Pittsburg: University of Pittsburgh. Retrieved from ERIC database. (ED129247).

Radford, M. L. (1999). Literature on the reference interaction. In M. L. Radford (Ed.), *The reference encounter: Interpersonal communication in the academic library* (pp. 8–24). Chicago: Association of College and Research Libraries.

Reference and Adult Services Division (RASD) Ad Hoc Committee on Behavioral Guidelines for Reference and Information Services. (1996). *Guidelines for behavioral performance of reference and information services professionals. RQ, 36*(2), 200–203.

Riain, N. N. (2011). *Theosony: Towards a theology of listening.* New York: Columbia Press.

Satterlee, C. A. (2006). *Holy and active listening.* Retrieved from https://alban.org/archive/holy-and-active-listening/.

Taylor, R. S. (1967). Question-negotiation and information-seeking in libraries: Studies in the man-system interface in libraries (AF-AFOSR-724-66, Report No. 3). Retrieved from http://www.dtic.mil/dtic/tr/fulltext/u2/659468.pdf.

Tibbets, P. (1974). Sensitivity training: A possible application for librarianship. *Special Libraries, 65*, 493–498.

Wolterstorff, C. K. (1994, January). Listening to another, listening with another. *Perspectives, 9*, 19–20.

About the Contributors

Dana M. **Caudle** is a cataloging and metadata librarian at Auburn University Libraries. She received her master's degree in library and information science from the University of Texas at Austin. She is keenly interested in integrating faith into every aspect of her life, including work, and takes to heart Jesus' command to love our neighbors as ourselves.

Nadine P. **Ellero** serves as head of technical services at Auburn University Libraries. Previously she was the intellectual access/metadata services librarian at the Claude Moore Health Sciences Library at the University of Virginia and a library associate at the National Library of Medicine. She is active in the ALA as an ALCTS mentor and in the NASIG as a member of the mentoring committee.

Nancy **Falciani-White** is the director of the McGraw-Page Library and an associate professor at Randolph-Macon College. She received her doctorate in instructional technology from Northern Illinois University and her master's degree in library and information science from the University of Illinois at Urbana–Champaign.

Jeff **Gates** (MA, biblical studies, Faith Baptist Theological Seminary; MLS, Kent State University) is the information services librarian at Cedarville University, where he enjoys helping students with research. Jeff formerly served as the head librarian at Faith Baptist Bible College & Theological Seminary in Ankeny, Iowa, and as an assistant pastor at Immanuel Baptist Church in Kearney, Nebraska.

Esther **Gillie** is the dean of Regent University Library. She received her doctorate in spiritual formation from Northeastern Seminary. She previously served as the director of the B. Thomas Golisano Library at Roberts Wesleyan College and Northeastern Seminary in Rochester, New York, and she has held library positions at the University of Connecticut, the University of Illinois in Urbana–Champaign, and Sibley Music Library.

Jacob W. **Gucker**, M. Div., MLS, is the director of Kellar Library at the Baptist Missionary Association Theological Seminary. He lives with his wife Rachel and daughter Pearl at Preacher's End Farm. They are members at Grace Covenant Presbyterian Church in Nacogdoches, Texas.

Patricia R. **Harris** is the fifth president of Kuyper College. She served as provost of the college from 2013 to 2017. Prior to that, she served for 15 years as a faculty member and administrator at Asian Theological Seminary in Manila. She received her bachelor's degree from Calvin College, her master's degree from Calvin Theological Seminary, and her doctoral degree from George Fox University.

Robin R. **Hartman**, MA, MLIS, is the director of library services for the Hugh and Hazel Darling Library of Hope International University. She has written for the library's blog as well as various library publications and often presents at conferences. Her professional interests include the organization and communication of information and how it shapes society, integration of faith and learning, the Restoration Movement, and instructional technology.

Paul A. **Hartog** is the director of library services and a professor of theology at Faith Baptist Bible College and Theological Seminary. He earned his master's degree in library and information science from the University of Wisconsin–Milwaukee (where he received a Chancellor's Graduate Student Award) and his PhD from Loyola University–Chicago (where he was a university teaching fellow). He has authored or edited four books.

McGarvey **Ice** is the director of special collections and archives at Abilene Christian University. He previously served as the director of research services at Disciples of Christ Historical Society in Nashville. He maintains an active research program in Stone-Campbell studies. He frequently presents at scholarly conferences and has contributed articles and reviews a number of publications.

Rebecca **Klemme Eliceiri**, founder of BiblioMinistry and Think! Pray! Act!, will never stop encouraging the worlds of the church, the library, and activism to spin in the same orbit. She is a St. Louis, Missouri-area ordained minister in the Christian Church (Disciples of Christ), a faith-based community organizing leader at Metropolitan Congregations United, and a librarian at the St. Charles Community College Library.

Denise D. **Nelson**, Ph.D., is a faculty librarian and the interim director of Ryan Library at Point Loma Nazarene University. She also serves as president of the board of directors for the Association of Christian Librarians, of which she has been a member since 2004. Her research interests include information literacy instruction and student satisfaction with college.

Michelle **Norquist** serves as the director of library services at the Kuyper College Zondervan Library. She has a bachelor's degree in social work from Calvin College and master's degree in library and information science from Wayne State University. Her research interests include user experience, applied research methods (ALEA) in academic settings, and applying Christianity, social work and library leadership in academic library settings.

Steve **Silver** (MLS, Emporia State University; M.Mus., University of Oregon) has been the director of the Edward P. Kellenberger Library at Northwest Christian University since 2006. He is a member of the Oregon Library Association's Intellectual Freedom Committee and has presented on intellectual freedom issues at multiple OLA annual conferences and elsewhere. He also lectures on the history of the English Bible.

Cynthia **Strong** is the librarian for the School of Education at Seattle Pacific University. She received her bachelor's degree from American University and her master's degree in library and information science from the University of Maryland. Prior to her current position, she was a media specialist and teacher librarian in public secondary schools in Maryland and Washington State.

Garrett B. **Trott** is the university librarian at Corban University. He received his bachelor's degree in theology from Multnomah University, his master's degree in theology from Trinity Western University and his master's degree in library and information science from Emporia State University, and he is pursuing a doctorate of ministry with a focal point of leadership from Corban.

Dianne **Zandbergen** served as the director of library services at the Kuyper College Zondervan Library until her retirement from this position in June 2018. Dianne has a bachelor's degree in philosophy from Grand Valley State University, a certificate of Biblical Studies from Kuyper College, and a master's degree in library science from the University of Michigan.

Andrew **Zwart** began his career teaching high school English courses in the Boston public school system. He is the director of Interdisciplinary Studies as well as the director of academic support at Kuyper College. He also teaches a course focused on writing and rhetoric at Kuyper as well as at the Handlon Correctional Facility for the Calvin Prison Initiative.

Index

1 Corinthians: (3:19–20) 112; (4:2) 157; (6:12) 128; (8:9–13) 219; (9:21) 82; (10:17) 139; (12) 185; (12:25–27) 139, 167; (12:27) 139; (13:12) 127; (13:2–3) 81; (13:4–7) 183; (13:8–13) 83; (15:3–8) 107; (16:14) 168; (16:5–6) 71
1 John: (1:1–3) 106; (3:18) 184; (3:20) 106; (4) 186; (4:21) 82; (4:7–31) 181
1 Kings: (3:9) 110; (10:24) 163; (19:11–12) 141; (20:10) 58
1 Peter: (1:10–11) 107; (4:9–10) 66; (5:5) 81; (5:7) 81
1 Thessalonians: (5:18) 82
1 Timothy: (3:1–3) 72; (5:21) 185; (6:6) 82
2 Corinthians: (4:18) 84; (10:5) 83
2 Peter: (1:3) 88; (1:5–7) 81; (1:16) 106; (1:20–21) 107; (3:9) 126
2 Thessalonians: (3:10–11) 180–181
2 Timothy: (3:16) 107; (3:16–17) 87
3 John: (5–6) 72

access 48
ACRL Framework for Information 91, 93, 95, 98, 100, 113, 114, 198, 211
Literacy for Higher Education
ACRL Information Literacy 89, 91, 103, 113, 114
Competency Standards
Acts: (2:44–47) 139; (18:18–28) 219; (22:6–11) 85; (26:24) 81
Adam 56
Adam and Eve 104–105, 110, 112
Alinsky, Saul 13
America Reads 13
American Library Association (ALA) 68, 124, 180, 209, 224, 226
AmeriCorps 13
Anastasius Bibliothecarius 59–60
anger 161–162
assessment 89
Association of American Colleges 29
atonement 57
Auburn University 170–178
Saint Augustine of Hippo 50
authenticity 192

Babel 56, 58, 59
Baby Boomers 165–166
Babylon 62
Badke, William B. 15, 19, 90, 116, 208
baptism 55–56
Bawden, David 77, 78, 81, 82
Berryhill, Cassie 69, 71–72
Bible 11
BiblioMinistry 15, 16, 19
Bonhoeffer, Dietrich 138, 139, 140, 142, 143, 224
Boyer, Ernest 143
Break the Pipeline Campaign 17
Brotherton, Bob 67
Buber, Martin 227–228, 229, 230, 231, 232

calling *see* vocation
Calvinism 52
Campbell, Alexander 11–12
Cane Ridge Revival 11
Canton, Missouri 28
Canton Public Library 27, 31, 37
Carr, Nicholas 88
Cathy, Truett 157
censorship 127
Chick-fil-A 157
Children's Internet Protection Act 135
Christian Church (Disciples of Christ) 10–12, 27–44
Christian Churches 27–44
Christian Education 15, 16, 19, 50
The Christian-Evangelist 35, 37
The Christian Standard 30, 37
church 12, 15, 16–17, 21, 49
church governance 12
Churches of Christ 27–44
Claerbaut, David 3–4
Clifton Strengthfinder 163
collaboration 144, 217
collection development 38, 46, 130–132
Collins, Jim 156
Colossians 73; (1:10) 180; (1:16) 110; (1:17) 111; (2:3) 90; (3:8–9) 183; (3:11) 185; (3:12–25) 183; (3:17) 180
communion 50, 59, 60, 61

The Communist Manifesto 131
community 17–18, 21, 45, 60, 66, 124, 125–126, 129, 138–153, 159, 160, 180, 181–182, 183–184, 184–185, 189–190, 191–192, 210, 227–228
conflict 161, 164–165
constructivism 19, 21
covenant 51–52, 57
creation 104; new 48, 55, 60
critical librarianship 209
culture 59
Culver-Stockton College 28, 29, 30, 31, 32

Dallas, Texas 49
Daniel: (12:4) 83; (12:13) 83
David, King 52
Davis, Donald G., Jr. 126, 129, 180, 181, 182, 183, 184, 185, 186
Dean, Kendra Casey 11
DeGroot, Alfred Thomas 30, 32, 35, 36
democracy 209
Deuteronomy: (17:9) 112; (30:19) 126
DeVries, Mark 11
Diaspora 57, 58
dignity *see* human dignity
discernment 108–111
Disciples' Identity Statement 12
Disciples of Christ Historical Society 32, 33, 34, 37, 38, 39, 40
diversity 38
Dowling, Enos E. 30, 35

Ecclesiastes 139; (3:1) 81–82; (3:6) 82; (3:11) 110; (12:12) 81
Eden Theological Seminary 13
education 14, 15
end times 83
Ephesians: (2:8–9) 93; (4) 159; (4:15) 164; (4:18) 105; (4:25) 164; (4:26–27) 161; (5:23) 191
epicureanism 53
eschatology *see* end times
ethics 112
evangelism 60
Eve 56
exodus 55–56
Exodus: (34:6) 126

237

Index

expertise 111, 115–118
Ezekiel 58

faculty 115
Faith-based Community Organizing 16–18
fake news 209, 211
Farley, Edward 13–14
fear 17
feedback 161
fellowship *see* community
Fifty Shades of Grey 131, 132
financial stewardship 156–157
First Amendment of U. S. Constitution 125, 209; *see also* freedom of speech
Fister, Barbara 90
flipped church 10, 14, 20–22, 23
flipped learning 21, 22
Fortune, Alonzo Willard 31, 32
Foster, Richard 88, 140, 158
free will 126–127
freedom 128–129
freedom of speech 123–124; *see also* First Amendment of U. S. Constitution

Galatians: (3:28) 139, 185; (5:14) 82; (5:20–21) 183; (5:22–23) 82; (5:22–26) 159; (5:26–27) 183; (6:1) 127; (6:2) 82; (6:7–8) 108; (6:9–10) 142
Garden of Eden 58, 59, 210
Garrison, Winfred Ernest 30
Genesis 57; (1) 110; (1:26–28) 104; (1:26–31) 104; (1:27) 126, 156; (2) 110; (2:7) 104; (2:15) 104; (2:17) 104; (2:18) 104, 119; (2:18–19) 104; (2:19–20) 104; (2:24) 191; (3:2–3) 104; (3:6) 112; (3:8) 104; (3:16–19) 104; (4:2) 105; (4:20–22) 105; (29:34) 56
globalization 76
God 115
Green, Samuel 224–225
Greenleaf, Robert 160, 171, 172–176
Greg, Walter Wilson 36
growth, spiritual 88–89

Hartog, Paul 79
Hebrews: (4:16) 161; (5:12–14) 84; (6:10) 73
helping profession 207, 224
higher education 105, 107, 110–111, 112–113
Holmes, Arthur 219–220
hospitality 60, 67, 66–75
human dignity 158
human resources 154–169
humility 192
Hutchins, Margaret 225

image of God 58, 83, 112, 126–127
information 105–106; anxiety 76–86, 77–78, 79, 207–212, 212–213, 216; discernment 20; ethics 79–80; evangelism 20; literacy 13, 14, 15, 18, 19, 48, 49, 87–102, 103–122, 198–199, 208; overload 49, 76–86, 77–78, 80; search process 207, 212, 213–214; stewardship 19–20
insight 108–111
instruction 87–102
intellectual freedom 123–137
Internet filters 132
intervention 199–203
Isaiah: (5:21) 112; (6:1–5) 83; (44:24) 110; (45:18) 104
Israel 55

Jacobsen, Douglas 4, 5, 189
Jacobsen, Rhonda Hustedt 4, 5, 189
James: (1:5) 111, 115, 163; (1:19) 184, 223; (2:1) 185; (2:8) 82; (2:9) 185; (2:15–17) 71; (2:26) 184; (3:15–17) 112; (4:6) 81
Jeremiah: (10:12) 112; (33:3) 162
Job: (4:8) 106; (12:13) 112; (37:16) 106
Joel 2:13 126
John: (1:18) 89; (1:46) 106; (6:25–70) 210; (6:67) 126; (7:25–31) 210; (10:35) 107; (13) 157; (13:35) 181; (18:6) 84; (18:37–38) 210
Johnson, Dru 106, 107, 110
Joshua: (1:8) 84
journalism 209
justice 17, 18

Kahoka, Missouri 28
knowledge 104–105, 105–107, 108, 113–118
Kuhlthau, Carol 196–203, 213–220
Kuyper, Abraham 82

Last Supper 157
laypeople 12
leadership 15, 170–178
Levi 56
Leviticus: (26:3–4) 108
lifelong learning 19, 88–89, 218
listen 162, 223–233
liturgy 48, 49, 50, 52, 59
love your neighbor 95, 131, 156–157, 179–180, 181–182
Luke: (2:52) 91; (6:27) 185; (6:37–42) 187; (10:25–28) 181; (13:20) 132
Luther, Martin 198–199

Malachi: (2:6–7) 56
management 154–169
Mark: (9:33–35) 157; (10:8) 191; (11:25) 187; (12:28–34) 181; (12:29) 181
Martin, Jim 16, 17, 18
The Matrix 52, 53
Matthew: (4:4) 110; (5:13) 70; (5:15) 70; (5:19) 110; (6:14–15) 187; (6:25–34) 81; (7:1–5) 161; (7:12) 158, 184, 185; (14:22–23) 141; (18:15–17) 127, 161; (18:20) 139; (18:21–25) 187; (22:34–40) 124, 181; (22:35–40) 158; (22:37) 82; (22:37–40) 199; (22:39) 82; (25:14–30) 158; (25:40) 72, 227; (28:19) 181
Maxfield, David 225
Maxwell, Nancy Kalikow 45–46, 226
meaning 109
mediation 46–48, 60, 199–203, 215
Mein Kampf 131, 132
mentoring 163
metaliteracy 15, 16, 19, 20, 23–24
Metropolitan Congregations United 16–17
Meyer-Briggs Type Indicator 163
mission 21, 22, 73
missional faith learning 10, 19–20, 21, 22, 23
Missouri College Union 29
Missouri Historical Society 33
Missouri Library Association 29
Monser, John Waterhaus 30
Moseley, J. Edward 32
Moses 55–56, 57
Myers, Chad 18

Nashville, Tennessee 39
Nehemiah 9:6 110
Noll, Mark 146
North Central Association of Colleges 29
Nouwen, Henri 141, 142, 146
Numbers: (23:19) 106

Oden, Amy 66, 67, 72
Ostercamp, Matthew 51

Passover 55
pastors 12
paterfamilias 53–54
patrons 52
Paul, Apostle 57, 71, 72
perception 108–111
Philippians: (1:9) 81, 84; (2:3) 184; (2:3–4) 142, 181; (4:6) 81; (4:8) 89
place, library as *see* space
Pohl, Christine 67, 68, 69, 70, 71
post-truth 87–88
Postman, Neil 94
prayer 141, 145–146
preaching 22
Prickett, John 27
priesthood 46–47, 56, 60
Proverbs: (1:7) 115; (2:1–8) 112; (2:2–5) 110; (2:2–11) 115; (2:6) 108; (3:5) 108; (3:7) 111, 112; (3:11–12) 161; (4:7) 81; (9:10) 84; (11:14) 112; (15:22) 112; (24:6) 112; (25:11) 163; (26:12) 112; (27:17) 126; (30:2–6) 81
Psalm: (1:2) 84; (8:3–8) 92; (13:20) 112; (19:7) 111; (23) 55; (23:5) 159; (24:1) 125; (42:1) 110; (104:24) 112; (111:10) 162; (119) 84; (119:34) 110; (119:66) 115; (119:73) 110; (119:99) 110; (119:104) 110; (119:125) 110; (119:130) 110; (119:144) 110; (119:169) 110; (121:2) 110; (127:1) 69; (133:1–3) 139; (136) 192; (143:5) 84; (147:5) 108
Puritanism 52

Index

Qumran 57

Reference and Adult Services Division (RASD) 224, 226–227, 231, 232
Reference and User Services Association (RUSA) 68, 70, 71
reference interview 61, 128, 189–205, 206–222, 223–233
relational intelligence 190
relationships *see* community
renewing 54
research process 93–100
research question 61, 147
resources 110, 147
respect 185–186
resurrection 21
Revelation: (1:12–20) 86; (4:6) 110; (21:9–11) 58; (21:22) 58
Riley, Edgar C. 31, 33, 35
Robinson, Henry Barton 31, 32, 33
Robinson, Lyn 77, 78, 81, 82
Romans: (1:17) 198–199; (1:18–19) 109; (1:20) 106, 110; (2:14–15) 109; (3:11–12) 105; (3:23) 127; (8:1–17) 186; (8:20–23) 104; (8:38–39) 192; (11:33) 112; (12) 185; (12:1) 54; (12:2) 82, 84; (12:5) 139; (12:10) 183; (12:13) 72; (12:16) 112, 185; (12:19–21) 187; (13:1–6) 186; (13:8) 82; (15:24) 71

Saccone, Steve 192–196, 201, 202
sacrament 54, 61–62
sacrifice 54–55, 56
satisficing 81, 212, 217
scholarship 18, 143–145

Scriptures, Hebrew 55
Secular Franciscan 170
seminary 15, 18
Sermon on the Mount 70
servant-leader 172–176
service 54, 68
Seymour, Jack 19
Shechem 56
sin 47, 83, 127–128
Sinai 56, 58
Smith, Gregory A. 4, 6, 154, 180, 181, 186, 189
Smith, James K. A. 5, 48, 50–51
social media 95, 207–208
solitude 140–143, 144–145, 145–146
Solomon 56
space 58, 68, 69–71, 73–74, 138–153, 223–224
Spencer, Claude Elbert 27–44
spiritual growth *see* growth, spiritual
Sports Illustrated 132
stacks, closed 47
Stewart, Kenneth J. 48
Stone, Barton 11
Stone-Campbell Movement 27–44
students 114
supervision 154–169

tabernacle 47, 55, 56, 57–58
teachers *see* faculty
template 96, 98
temple *see* tabernacle
therapy 206
They Say/I Say 94–95
Titus: (1:7–8) 72; (2:7–9) 181; (2:7–10) 186; (3:13) 71

Toffler, Alvin 77, 207
Torah 52, 57
transformation 54
trinity 138, 190–191
Trott, Garrett B. 180, 185
truth 125–126, 131, 210–212
Tucker, John Mark 180, 181, 182, 183, 184, 185, 186

uncertainty 197, 210
understanding 104–105, 108–111, 113–118
University of Illinois 28, 29
University of Missouri 28

values 18, 68, 73
The Village Church 49
vocation 14–15, 18, 45, 59, 139, 170–178, 179–181

Walton, John H. 48, 57, 59
Ware, Charles Crossfield 31, 32, 35
water 55–56
Weaver, John B. 68–69
Willard, Dallas 140, 158
wisdom 20, 104–105, 111–113, 113–118, 128
witness 183
Workplace Prayer 182, 188
worship 5, 14, 22, 48, 49–53, 54–59, 66, 139
Wrather, Eva Jean 32, 33
Wright, N.T. 48, 53–54, 57, 58, 59
Wurman, Richard 77, 78

Zechariah 56